RADICAL PLURALISM AND TRUTH

To David Tracy
Friend, Teacher, Scholar, Priest, Theologian

RADICAL PLURALISM AND TRUTH

DAVID TRACY AND THE HERMENEUTICS OF RELIGION

Edited by Werner G. Jeanrond
and Jennifer L. Rike

Crossroad • New York

1991
The Crossroad Publishing Company
370 Lexington Avenue, New York, NY 10017

Copyright © by Werner G. Jeanrond and Jennifer L. Rike

All rights reserved. No part of this book may be reproduced, stored in a retrieval system, or transmitted, in any form or by any means, electronic, mechanical, photocopying, recording or otherwise, without the written permission of The Crossroad Publishing Company.

Printed in the United States of America

Library of Congress Cataloging-in-Publication Data

Radical pluralism and truth : David Tracy and the hermeneutics of
  religion / edited by Werner G. Jeanrond and Jennifer L. Rike.
     p.   cm.
  Includes bibliographical references.
  ISBN 0-8245-1118-2
  1. Religious pluralism. 2. Hermeneutics—Religious aspects.
3. Tracy, David. I. Jeanrond, Werner G., 1955– . II. Rike,
Jennifer L., 1950– .
BL87.R24   1991
291.1'72–dc20   91-34236
                                                              CIP

Acknowledgment is gratefully made to New Directions Publishing Corp. for permission to quote the poem Helen from H.D., *Collected Poems 1912–1944.* Copyright © 1928 The Estate of Hilda Doolittle.

CONTENTS

Preface		vii
Introduction: Radical Pluralism and Truth in the Thought of David Tracy *Jennifer L. Rike*		ix
Part I:	**Pluralism in the Thought of David Tracy**	
1.	Radical Pluralism and Liberation Theology *Gregory Baum*	1
2.	David Tracy and the Debate about Praxis *Dermot A. Lane*	18
3.	Biblical Criticism and Theology: Toward a New Biblical Theology *Werner G. Jeanrond*	38
Part II:	**Pluralism and the Hermeneutics of Religion**	
4.	Conversation in Gethsemane *Nicholas Lash*	51
5.	Rhetoric and Religion: Are They Essentially Wedded? *Wayne C. Booth*	62
6.	Hermeneutics and the Question of the Self *Nathan A. Scott, Jr.*	81
7.	Feminist Hermeneutics, Scriptural Authority, and Religious Experience: The Case of the *Imago Dei* and Gender Equality *Rosemary Radford Ruether*	95

8. Reading the Gospels in the Light of
the *Window of the Evangelists* at Chartres Cathedral
Seán Freyne 107

9. Another Troy for Her to Burn:
The True Story of Euripedes' Helen
Mary Gerhart 121

10. Hesiod: Religion and Poetry in
the *Works and Days*
David Grene 142

Part III: Pluralism and the History of Religions

11. Another Path to Truth: From Ritual
to Theology in Judaism
Jacob Neusner 161

12. Pluralism in Christology
John Macquarrie 176

13. Love and Justice
Paul Ricoeur 187

14. The "One World":
A Challenge to Western Christianity
Johann Baptist Metz 203

15. Pluralism and Intolerance in Hinduism
Wendy Doniger 215

Part IV: Interreligious Dialogue

16. Dialogability and Steadfastness:
On Two Complementary Virtues
Hans Küng 237

17. Toward a Hermeneutics of Interreligious Dialogue
Claude Geffré 250

18. Problems in the Case for
a Pluralistic Theology of Religions
Schubert M. Ogden 270

Bibliography of David Tracy
Stephen H. Webb 286

Contributors 294

PREFACE

THE RADICAL PLURALISM of our times raises profound and far-reaching issues for those of us seeking to live with intellectual, moral, and spiritual integrity. These issues have engaged the spirit and work of David Tracy throughout the past twenty-odd years. We could think of no more fitting tribute to him on the occasion of his fiftieth birthday than to devote a volume of essays, written by his friends and colleagues, to precisely the issues raised by pluralism in the search for truth. It is but one small way to thank David for encouraging and guiding us with his work, his life, his spirit in our personal attempts to embrace pluralism.

David Tracy was born on 6 January 1939, in Yonkers, New York. He received his Licentiate (1964) and Doctorate in Theology (1969) at Gregorian University in Rome. He taught from 1967 to 1969 at the Catholic University of America, and from 1969 to the present at the University of Chicago Divinity School where he was named Distinguished Service Professor in 1985, and Andrew Thomas Greeley and Grace McNichols Greeley Distinguished Service Professor of Roman Catholic Studies in 1987. He also was appointed to the Committee on the Analysis of Ideas and Methods in 1981. David Tracy was one of the founding editors of *Religious Studies Review* and served as coeditor of the *Journal of Religion* and *Concilium*, as well as a member of the editorial boards of several other journals. He was elected to the American Academy of Arts and Sciences in 1982 and received honorary doctorates from the University of the South in Sewanee, Tennessee, Fairfield University in Connecticut, and the Catholic Theological Union and Rosary College in Chicago.

Through his classes, lectures in the United States and abroad, and writings, he has exerted a profound influence on the study of religion and theology internationally—and more. As Van Harvey has written:

> When it comes to this kind of knowledge, to the question of who I am, what I have learned is indissolubly connected with my teachers. . . . We are what we are, and our interpretations are what they are, because certain truths are

indissolubly and powerfully wedded to certain persons in our historical pasts. (*The Historian and the Believer*, p. 287)

David's gentle, generous, and humble spirit, his quick and incisive intelligence, and his total devotion to the theological task and the Christian faith (in him, inextricably tied to one another) have deeply touched countless numbers of his students, friends, colleagues, and coreligionists.

In the spirit of David Tracy's own life and work, Werner Jeanrond and I encouraged submissions written with the intention of furthering Tracy's own project of constructing fully public theology imbued with an authentic and responsible approach to pluralism. Our plan was to give to him as he has given to us, by engendering many more conversations on the meaning and truth of religious—especially Christian—faith. Our contributors have responded warmly with insightful and provocative essays covering the broad range of his interests and thought. As a result, this collection of articles not only introduces major aspects of Tracy's work but also represents a wide spectrum of religious and theological studies today—from the plurality of pluralisms of what David calls our unnameable present, to interpretation theory, conversations with religious classics, pluralisms within different religious traditions, and interreligious dialogue.

This volume also manifests noteworthy cooperation. Werner and I especially wish to thank the contributors for their patience during the complex process of revising drafts of articles. We also thank Stephen Kepnes for approaching us with the initial idea of a *Festschrift* for David; Frank Oveis, our editor at Crossroad Publishing Company, for his support and guidance along the way; and Dean Robert C. Neville and Associate Dean John Berthrong of the Boston University School of Theology for their support.

I personally wish to thank my colleague Harold Oliver for his unflagging encouragement, Mary Gerhart for her wise counsel and editorial advice on a number of matters, Herb Golder for his assistance with classical texts, and June Goudey for her extensive bibliographical help. I also want to add a note of appreciation in loving memory of my mother, Sophy Antkowiak Rike, who so embraced pluralism in her own life that she ensured I did also.

We thank J. C. B. Mohr (Paul Siebeck) Publishers, Tübingen, for permission to reprint in English "Love and Justice" by Paul Ricoeur, and the *Journal of Religion* for permission to reprint "Problems in the Case for a Pluralistic Theology of Religions" by Schubert Ogden.

Jennifer L. Rike

INTRODUCTION: RADICAL PLURALISM AND TRUTH IN THE THOUGHT OF DAVID TRACY

Jennifer L. Rike

"MAY YOU LIVE in interesting times" runs a Chinese curse often cited by David Tracy. Those who have wrestled with the profound ambiguities of our times grasp well the proverb's status as curse not blessing: interesting times can be not just "thought provoking" but "perilous." Now surely it is better to live in thought-provoking than in boring times, but these times provoke *so* much thought that, as David Tracy has eloquently argued, we are at a loss to find a name for them.[1] These times confront us with a crisis of meaning, as a plethora of conflicting interpretations of our lives and faiths vie for our attention and embrace.

One thing is certain: the age of modernity and its Western, monistic Eurocentrism are over. But what comes after modernity? What should we call these times and how can we understand them? They are, without doubt, *radically pluralistic*, and the pluralism of the contemporary milieu perplexes us and confronts us with starkly unique challenges. The need to respond to these challenges is especially acute for those of us who profess faith in the loving and just God of the Judeo-Christian traditions, for this faith calls us to respond with the integrity made possible by genuinely self-transcendent knowing and loving. It calls us to use our reflective and critical capacities, not just in daily life but in adjudicating the claims to truth of the religious traditions which

---

1. David Tracy, "On Naming the Present," *On the Threshold of the Third Millennium* (London: SCM Press; Philadelphia: Trinity Press International [= *Concilium* 1990 (1)]) 66–77.

have nurtured us or which we have subsequently encountered. It calls us to recognize and come to know not just those "others" in immediate proximity to our own centers with whom we normally converse but those "others" whom immediacy tends to shut out, to shove away from the center to the periphery. Only then does our faith express our own inherent drive toward unity as it is grounded in the one Creator-Redeemer God of this world and its peoples.

At the heart of the challenges of our unnameable present lies the question of truth. What *is* truth? How do we attain it? How do we choose among conflicting claims to it? While the answers to the last two questions can be specified easily enough in certain disciplines—such as mathematics, formal logic, or the "hard" sciences—by delineating the methods appropriate to determining the kind of truth at issue, they become much more complex when we move into the areas of the "softer" sciences, such as sociology, psychology, historiography, and religious studies. For there is no single technique or method that guarantees success in these—what is a hard as opposed to a soft science, anyway? What can we mean by hard and soft data, when clearly the data themselves are not literally but only analogically either? What is literally as opposed to symbolically true when we try to understand, say, the lives and untimely deaths of John Fitzgerald Kennedy and Robert Kennedy, or Watergate? The truths of these lives and events far exceed the bare data about the Kennedys' political careers and assassinations, or the specific details of the actual break-in at the Watergate. How do we adjudicate the conflicting claims to truth of, say, the Gospel of John as opposed to the Gospel of Mark, the *Bhagavad Gītā* or the *Tao te Ching*? These issues are particularly acute for Christianity, which historically has claimed that its truth applies universally to all.

Too often in the history of Western civilization, truth has been spoken of as a kind of entity, a monolith, which different traditions—both within Christianity and outside it—possess in different ways and to varying degrees. The legacy of the Enlightenment was forever to shatter the illusion that attaining unconditional truth was a possibility (except perhaps as Hegel's "mad and secret dream"), much less one realized by certain ecclesiastical authorities and theological traditions; for Enlightenment philosophy—British empiricism and the critical philosophy of Immanuel Kant—argued conclusively that all knowledge is finite, structured, and empirically conditioned by its origins in human subjectivity.

But disillusionment with the claims of traditional authorities to absolute knowledge brought with it empowerment for the autonomous knower, for the Enlightenment also disclosed the capacity of critical and practical reason to achieve genuine knowledge in all realms of existence—perhaps not the absolute knowledge that encapsulates the whole, but finite, relative, increasingly adequate perspectives on the whole. It freed individuals to take full possession of their cognitive powers by following through with their innate impulse to question everything freely, ignoring the constraints of tradition. It bequeathed to modernity a new morality of knowledge: as Kant enjoined, *sapere aude*, dare to know and dare to know *for oneself.* One should not passively rely on the dicta of traditional authorities for what one believes or what one should be and do, but rather one should assume responsibility for determining the nature, meaning, and value of different realities for oneself, and act on those determinations. To the scientist it charged that all past deposits of scientific and technological knowledge and their methodologies be subjected to continuous scrutiny in light of the evidence emerging from new data and scientific-technological advances.

For the believer and the theologian, the challenge has become yet more complex, especially since the rise of historical consciousness in the nineteenth century. Charged to question the very traditions and authorities that had imbued them with the *felt, lived* confirmation of the truth of the Christian faith, they were forced to recognize that many of its claims crumbled before the critical eye of historical and scientific modes of investigation and scholarship, while others defied all of the usual modes of explanation and validation. They were then confronted with a conflict of commitments, between loyalty to the witness of their faith traditions and communities, on the one hand, and fidelity to the impetus of inquiry to follow the logic of the arguments and the emerging evidence to whatever conclusions they might suggest, on the other.[2] The resolution of this apparent conflict precipitated revolutions in the development of new disciplines of inquiry relevant to determining the meaning and truth of the various modes of divine revelation—scriptural texts, historical events and persons, doctrines, and rituals. These disciplines include historical-critical modes of research into the Bible, literary and rhetorical criticism, linguistic analysis, hermeneutics, and anthropology, to name but a few. These, in turn, required a reevaluation of the nature of religious and theological truth. No longer was the Bible understood to be simply the literal Word of God, a historical narrative with little remainder, but a complex interweaving of oral and written

---

2. Van A. Harvey did groundbreaking work on this issue in *The Historian and the Believer: The Morality of Historical Knowledge and Christian Belief* (New York: Macmillan, 1966). This issue motivates much of David Tracy's work; see especially *Blessed Rage for Order: The New Pluralism in Theology* (New York: Seabury, 1975) 1–14.

traditions of various literary genres expressing the distinctive theological perspectives of the Jewish and Christian peoples of God.

Setting the believer and theologian free to question openly established perspectives on the sacred has opened a Pandora's box of diverse if not contesting viewpoints. David Tracy has suggested that there are fundamentally two types of conflict of interpretations. First, there has arisen a conflict of interpretations of the very phenomena of religion, which were inevitably suggested by the different disciplines investigating them and demanded by the complexity and ambiguity of the phenomena themselves. Second, freedom to consider other ways of being religious presented by the other great religious traditions (most notably Confucianism, Buddhism, Hinduism, Taoism, and Islam) has precipitated a conflict of interpretations of the way to understand and relate to the sacred.[3] This confusing array of interpretations leaves most of us wondering how to choose among them. Historical and scientific consciousness has wrested from us the luxury of sitting smugly serene and secure, convinced that a single formulation of the truth of the Christian faith or some depository of its tradition has all of the answers for all time. The blessings of our expanding horizons bring with them the curse of knowing only one thing with absolute certainty— that there is none.

What, then, is the nature of religious and theological truth? How can we adjudicate conflicting claims to it in this radically pluralistic situation? Shall Christians reject all pluralism as contrary to true faith in the transcendent God of Jesus Christ, or resign themselves to the dull tolerance that would "let a thousand flowers bloom"? Is there a proper response to this pluralism, one that neither lapses into a repressive monism nor scatters itself in an anarchic eclecticism?

These questions have dominated the thought of David Tracy for over two decades. Throughout (to date) eight books and well over one hundred articles, reviews, and responses to his work (see Stephen Webb's comprehensive bibliography concluding this volume), Tracy has wrestled with the problems raised for theology today by the secular morality of knowledge initiated by the Enlightenment and the pluralism of this unnameable present after modernity. His own approach to the pluralism of the contemporary religious and theological context is to enjoin an authentic, responsible, and, in the final analysis, hermeneutical pluralism. This pluralism is *authentic* because it respects both the subjectivity of the human knower and the distinctive variety of the objective phenomena to be known. It is *responsible* because it proposes open

---

3. See, for instance, Tracy, "Creativity in the Interpretation of Religion: The Question of Radical Pluralism," *New Literary History* 15 (1983–84) 290–93.

and serious consideration of the potentially infinite number of perspectives demanding attention, while refusing to forgo critically evaluating them by assuming that they are all equally valid.

Thus, to be truly responsible in approaching pluralism, Tracy argues, is to be *hermeneutical*, for basically two reasons. First, this approach recognizes that the plurality of interpretations of different religious phenomena is rendered necessary by the cognitive and moral ambiguity of the phenomena themselves and the varying perspectives and modes of appropriation assumed by historical subjects. The ambiguity is *cognitive* insofar as the richness and complexity of the phenomena support diverse interpretations, as, for instance, the long conflict of interpretations over Paul's Epistle to the Romans climaxing in the Reformation schism testifies. It is *moral* insofar as religious beliefs and authorities have served to oppress and destroy as much as to fulfill and heal. Can we forget that the same church gave birth to St. Francis of Assisi and the Crusades? Second, it demands evaluating the different proposals in light of criteria of adequacy appropriate to the phenomena under scrutiny, and this calls for developments in hermeneutical theory. This authentic, responsible, and hermeneutical pluralism is the authentic response of faith: it responds to the complexity of the pluralistic present with the *fascinans et tremendum* marking an encounter with the sacred.[4]

Tracy's understanding of authentic, responsible pluralism is informed by his early work with Bernard Lonergan. Lonergan, known as a transcendental Thomist for his retrieval of the epistemology of Thomas Aquinas in light of the issues raised by Immanuel Kant, argued for the pivotal role of judgment in attaining the real. He analyzed human consciousness into four invariant and recurrent modes of operation— experience, understanding, reflection or judgment, and decision. The self-transcending dynamism of human inquiry leads us to seek out the data of experience, to ask all of the questions relevant to achieving insight and rendering the data intelligible, and, through further reflection on the data and accumulated insight, to determine through specific judgments what is, in fact, the case. Thus, the determination of reality in judgments of truth then becomes the basis for further reflection to determine its value and import for decision and action.

This dynamic structure of human cognition places a burden on the individual knower to exercise it properly, in accordance with its true

---

4. See especially "The Question of Pluralism in Contemporary Theology," *Chicago Theological Seminary Register* 71(2) (Spring 1981) 29–32; *Plurality and Ambiguity: Hermeneutics, Religion and Hope* (San Francisco: Harper and Row, 1987). The latter is Tracy's main text on the issues of pluralism and interpretation in religion.

nature. As Lonergan and Tracy enjoin: Be attentive, be intelligent, be reflective, be responsible, and, if necessary, change! Tracy developed this Enlightenment "turn to the subject," which was taken by Lonergan and the other transcendental Thomists, into a hermeneutical one. His work lives out of the creative tension between German idealism and Anglo-American empiricism, between an acknowledgment of the limits put on human understanding—especially theological understanding—by the structure of human cognition, and a respect for the intellect's ability to know the real through reflection and inference grounded in concrete, historical experience. All knowledge of the real—all "truth"—is constructed through the cognitional activity of the skilled knower and so is relative to the personal and historical perspective of that knower. Yet truth is not totally relative: since the real exists independently of the subject, and since the nature of the data, the insights used to organize it, and the judgments made to determine it can be tested repeatedly (both independently by the knower and intersubjectively through dialogue with others), truth can be said to be both objective and shared, and the relative adequacy of various formulations of the truth can be adjudicated. From this perspective, no absolute viewpoint upon the whole is possible, only a moving viewpoint, always in the process of reevaluating its past judgments in light of new evidence, always alert to possible inadequacies in its determinations and evaluations of the real.

The innately conditioned and historical character of all knowing has far-reaching and profound implications for theology. The first implication was pushed to the fore by Kant: how do we avoid being trapped by the clutch of our immediate context and extend our knowledge beyond the range of sensible experience to the ultimate in meaning, value, and truth? Or, in light of the nineteenth-century development of historical consciousness, since we are so deeply embedded in concrete historical contexts that all of our knowledge is grounded in particular experiences, how do we reach beyond the specific to the universal and transcendent? The second implication was recognized by Friedrich Schleiermacher, but its impact has been fully appreciated only in the twentieth century: to understand, to make sense out of the given, is a creative and reconstructive act which is profoundly indebted both to past attempts and to present ingenuity. Or, alternatively, insofar as we understand our experience first in terms of specific kinds of language and since this language does not simply *name* entities that exist totally independent of the knower but always *inteprets* the given in light of prior understanding, we can never fully escape the influence of the past interpretations embedded in language upon present understanding. Indeed, there are no "brute" facts, no uninterpreted experience. To understand *is* to interpret.

Introduction

David Tracy's genius has been his deep insight into this basic fact, for which he has argued with deceptively simple eloquence:

> Interpretation seems a minor matter, but it is not. Every time we act, deliberate, judge, understand, or even experience, we are interpreting. To understand at all is to interpret. To act well is to interpret a situation demanding some action and to interpret a correct strategy for that action. To experience in other than a purely passive sense (a sense less than human) is to interpret; and to be "experienced" is to have become a good interpreter. . . . Whether we know it or not, to be human is to be a skilled interpreter.[5]

His most original and lasting contributions to theological reflection and method have stemmed from his exploration and development of the implications of the hermeneutical character of all understanding and the resulting pluralism of our time. In this he has moved beyond the critical realism of his neo-Thomist forebears to a far more hermeneutically nuanced position that draws from a variety of sources, including transcendental philosophy, phenomenology, Anglo-American empiricism, and various philosophies of language to develop a genuinely public theology that responds to the legitimate demands of the Enlightenment morality of knowledge without falling prey to its own limitations. Properly theological reflection, he argues, is the mutually critical correlation of an interpretation of some dimension of the Christian fact with an interpretation of some dimension of human experience or the human situation. To be genuinely public in its claims to truth, theology must develop criteria of adequacy to adjudicate the relative adequacy of different interpretations of each source of theological reflection so that any genuinely attentive, intelligent, reflective, and responsible person can understand them. In *Blessed Rage for Order*, he developed such criteria for fundamental theology, and in *The Analogical Imagination* he did so for systematic theology.[6] (A volume on practical theology is projected.)

Tracy's appreciation of the hermeneutical character of understanding is key to his evaluation of the contemporary scene and the proper response to it. The Enlightenment's emphasis on the role of autonomous reason had powerful, transformative effects on later historical developments. Still, Tracy argues, it ultimately became destructive, because it obscured the positive effects of the creative, interpretive capacities of human consciousness and of the enlightening, guiding roles of cultural and religious traditions, which are themselves end

---

5. *Plurality*, 9.
6. *Blessed Rage*, 64–87 and throughout; *The Analogical Imagination: Christian Theology and the Culture of Pluralism* (New York: Crossroad, 1981) 99–178. For briefer accounts of the call to public theology, see numerous articles listed in the bibliography.

products of those capacities. Reacting against the negative, oppressive forces of ecclesiastical authorities, Enlightenment thought promoted the ideal of free and autonomous reason, shorn of any shackling and obfuscating prejudices, emancipated from the false prejudgments of the past to follow formal modes of argument to (purportedly) purely objective truth. But this ideal ignored the inevitable and often positive function of tradition in offering insight into the human condition and destiny, as well as genuinely humanistic and communal values in culture, morality, and spirituality. As a result, it distorted the true nature of rationality and human selfhood, and these distortions bore bad fruit in modernity.[7]

Modernity's overly optimistic predictions for the future were based in its conviction that once unburdened by tradition (understood to be anachronistic and self-defeating by definition) humanity could achieve pure self-consciousness and freedom and create abundance and equal opportunity for all. Understanding the proper exercise of reason to be the development of formal arguments, attentive only to the most factual of data and not to the deeper, more varied experiences and values of the entire human community, encouraged the purely instrumental use of reason to pursue wealth and power through industrial and technological development. The promise of a richer, more egalitarian society devolved into a consumer's paradise for some, a harsh and dehumanizing wasteland for millions of others whose voices have been drowned out by the inexorable forces of modern "progress." The fuller life of humanity promised by autonomous existence collapsed into a possessive individualism, desperate to fill up the emptiness of solitary life with material goods. In other words, while initially encouraging pluralism, the Enlightenment views of rationality and selfhood ultimately discouraged it.[8]

But, Tracy argues, modern faith in the value of human autonomy and reason, and in the "fact" of progressive growth toward greater self-consciousness, freedom, and justice, has been radically undermined in this century by interruptions so massive that they mock any attempt to account for them—the two World Wars and the Holocaust. The nuclear arms race (only recently partially defused) and escalating ecological disasters threaten us with new and potentially even more devastating modes of annihilation. Since traditional values and communities were themselves, in various and sundry ways, responsible for these atrocities, most prior sources of guidance and reassurance are now rife with doubt.

---

7. Tracy, "God, Dialogue and Solidarity: A Theologian's Refrain," *Christian Century* 107/28 (October 10, 1990) 902–5; "Creativity in the Interpretation of Religion," 294–96.

8. "On Naming the Present," 69–73.

Introduction   xvii

Largely as a result of the obvious failures of the modern experiment, the voices of those "others" on the periphery of the white, Western centers of power and privilege are now receiving more attention. Those groups which have been marginalized, neglected, and oppressed now challenge those who suppose that their good is everyone's good, those who would annihilate all difference for (in Foucault's inimitable phrase) "more of the same."[9]

Tracy's own roots in transcendental Thomism (not to mention his own generosity of spirit) open him to accepting the validity of the many contesting voices claiming our attention and respect now. We can no longer delude ourselves into thinking that the world has one center, he insists; it has many. Dealing with the polycentrism of our unnameable present demands that we allow the others to become more than projections of our worst fears or best desires but genuine others commanding our attention and response. Responding to them requires first and foremost that we attend to ourselves, to discern the distinctiveness of our own perspectives and their differences from others'. Indeed, how could we do otherwise? Since it is impossible, in principle, to transcend totally our own perspectives, we can best avoid thrusting them upon others by examining ourselves: the more we understand what prejudgments inform our own positions, the better prepared we are to grasp the real differences at issue in any interpretation at all.[10] Secondly, and as an intrinsic dimension of the first, given the cognitive and moral ambiguity of our own cherished traditions, pluralism requires that we develop and execute hermeneutics of suspicion and of retrieval to come to understand our favored traditions anew. The feminist and liberationist appropriations of the work of those masters of suspicion Marx, Nietzsche, and Freud serve to alert us to the ways in which these traditions have not just led us into error but have systematically distorted our perceptions and representations of reality and its manifestation of the divine. Too often these distortions have served to legitimate the status quo—usually the power and authority of Western, white institutions.[11]

Tracy sharply distinguishes his own approach to pluralism from two typical, antimodernist positions—fundamentalism and neoconservatism. Fundamentalism recognizes the distinctively human need for personal and historical meaning rooted in communal values and traditions, but denies the historical relativity of its favored traditions and the need for the continual, critical, and constructive reappropriation of

---

9. Ibid., 66–72; see also *Plurality*, 67.
10. "On Naming the Present," 67–68.
11. *Plurality*, 87, 112–14.

those traditions to ensure their relevance and validity. For this reason, it can never be a serious option for those who feel called to be personally reflective and responsible in their faith. Neoconservatism recognizes historical relativity and the necessity for retrieval, but fails to appreciate the distortions manifest in its own insufficiently consistent and self-critical reappropriations of these traditions. There is no experience without interpretation, and these interpretations are all too subject to distortions so comprehensive as to elude detection from strictly within themselves. For this reason, Tracy insists that not only contemporary experience of the dreadful effects of human waywardness but also the mystical and prophetic traditions within Christianity itself positively demand that we be vigilant to identify and correct all possible distortions in understanding. This vigilance requires, first, that we listen to the voices of those oppressed and marginalized by mainstream traditions and, second, that we develop criteria of adequacy drawn from hermeneutics of suspicion gauged to expose such distortions. The Christian faith itself makes this imperative:

> For the memory of the Christian is, above all, the memory of the passion and resurrection of Jesus Christ. It is that dangerous memory which is most dangerous for all those who presume to make his memory their own. And *that memory releases the theological knowledge that there is no innocent tradition, no innocent classic, no innocent reading.* That memory releases the moral insistence that the memory of the suffering of the oppressed—oppressed often by the church which now claims them as its own—is the great Christian counter-memory to all tales of triumph....[12]

While antimodernism retreats from the bad news of modernity, postmodernism runs headlong into it. The decentering of selfhood begun by the recognition of pluralism finds its logical conclusion in the loss of subjectivity in postmodern deconstructionism. Postmodernism, alerted by the castastrophes of modernity, has exposed the falsity of modernity's view of time and of its subject's capacity to achieve total self-possession in knowledge and freedom. The bourgeois subject with its attachment to "more of the same" has been abandoned in the pursuit of otherness and difference. As Nathan A. Scott, Jr., argues in "Hermeneutics and the Question of the Self" later in this volume, all is a-sea in the total indeterminacy of texts and selves deconstructing themselves as the encounter with difference exposes contradictions in themselves and in others.[13]

While we should not mourn the passing of the self-deluded modern subject, Tracy argues, deconstructionism cannot, on its own terms,

12. "On Naming the Present," 76–77 (emphasis added).
13. Ibid., 77–80.

account for the ethics of resistance to modernity which it seems to encourage. "How can resistance be secured without some agent—not, to be sure, the false self-grounding subject of modernity, but rather the responsible self of the great prophets?"[14] Postmodern thought should not be totally dismissed, however, for it serves as a powerful corrective to modernity by reminding us that the subject is always changing and always under trial, awakened from its false complacency by the cries of the "other," the marginalized, the poor, and the oppressed. Thus Tracy revisions selfhood in terms of the "subject-in-process-under-trial": the subject awakened from its cozy slumber by the cacophony of voices of concrete others, and transformed into a historical subject of mystical-prophetic resistance and genuinely postmodern hope waiting expectantly for the arrival of divine judgment and promise. This subject allows its projects, its possessions, its very being to be touched and transformed by the calls of the other to conversation, liberation, and solidarity, for this is the call of the living God made concrete.[15] Precisely this dual focus marks Tracy's later theological reflections: first, on a hermeneutics centered in the other and not the self; second, on the prophetic-mystical envisionment of the divine and the action to which it calls us to save us from the more deadly dynamics of this unnameable present.[16]

From the perspective of Tracy's hermeneutical account of intra-Christian pluralism, then, the moral and cognitive ambiguity of the multidimensional Christian tradition makes multiple interpretations both inevitable and desirable. This pluralism is intensified, Tracy repeatedly notes, when Christianity encounters other world religions. A more detailed review of his entire body of work would demonstrate that he distinguishes a number of pluralisms, and this plurality of pluralisms is the topic of the first section of this volume. In "Radical Pluralism and Liberation Theology," Gregory Baum analyzes and reconstructs Tracy's views of and responses to pluralism to suggest that, by distinguishing among pluralisms, we are in a better position to direct developing liberationist perspectives toward the eschatological future of postmodern hope. If we are genuinely to feel the influence of alternative perspectives, however, we must be prepared for more radical reformulations of not just the content but the *ways* of doing theology. In this spirit, Dermot Lane explores Tracy's ongoing development of a practical theology in "David Tracy and the Debate about Praxis." Taking his cues from liberation theology, Lane discusses the relationship between theory and praxis in the theological task. Along a similar vein, in

14. Ibid., 78; see also *Plurality*, 83, 105–7.
15. Ibid., 83–84.
16. "God, Dialogue and Solidarity," 902.

"Biblical Criticism and Theology: Toward a New Biblical Theology," Werner Jeanrond argues that Tracy's hermeneutical perspective on theological reflection requires a thorough revamping of the ways in which the various theological disciplines mutually inform one another, especially through greater attention to the role of praxis in informing biblical criticism.

To understand a tradition is to interpret it, and the interpretation process requires a relevant and illuminating example—a paradigm—for a given tradition. An integral part of Tracy's project to defend the public character of religious and theological truth is his understanding of the classic as paradigm. Religious truth is not the private province of those who remain within a confessing faith community, but is, in principle, accessible to any intelligent and responsible person open to grappling with the task of interpreting a religious tradition, especially its classics.

Classics are those realities—persons, events, symbols, rituals, or texts (Tracy's favorite)—whose ongoing interpretation has created and recreated meaning for a particular culture or religion. In his words, classics are entities that bear an "excess" and "permanence" of meaning. Their excess is such that they cannot be definitively interpreted for all time. (Ones that can be are mere period pieces.) Their permanence is such that they continually command our attention, although during any given period one classic may be eclipsed by others only to reemerge as historical developments occasion it. They endure through time and acquire their own history of reception and interpretation: they are "an example of both radical stability become permanence and radical instability become excess of meaning through ever-changing receptions."[17] Paradoxically, they are very specific in their historical origins and modes of expression and yet somehow attain universal significance by presenting alternative possibilities for human understanding and existence. The classics are perhaps the most compelling way in which we are confronted with difference, for they command our attention even when we are loathe to give it by presenting us with intriguing new possibilities. Good interpreters will allow themselves to be challenged by those possibilities to reexamine their past understandings and standards and will put their very selves at risk in their responses.[18]

Tracy characterizes the process of interpretation in terms of conversation. To interpret a text is to converse with it, and such conversation is itself understood as a kind of game. The interaction between classic text, for example, and interpreter, as between persons in conversation, has its own rules by which each player must abide for the game to

---

17. *Plurality*, 24.
18. Ibid., 12.

continue. The dynamic of the conversation is created by the questions raised by the text and those subjects inquiring into its meaning and truth. The conversational game, like all games, requires that the players let go of their usual self-consciousness and allow the dynamic of the inquiry into the text to take over. This requires that they follow certain rules of the game, the hermeneutical equivalents of the transcendental imperatives Be attentive, be intelligent, and so on, such as: Speak carefully to convey as accurately as possible what you mean; be prepared to defend your position, offering warrants and backings for it; consider all relevant evidence; listen carefully and respectfully to your conversation partners and take their views seriously (provided they too are serious and neither joking nor mad); be prepared to correct and, if necessary, to confront your partner and to change yourself.[19]

Still, it must be admitted that it is exceedingly rare that all of these rules are followed and genuine dialogue between interpreter and text actually occurs. Completely authentic conversation may, in fact, never happen. Interruptions, ignorance, and prejudgments become massive blind spots; fear and downright perversity obstruct the flow of conversation and the dynamic of question and answer pursued by the interpreters in relation to the text and to one another. Appropriating Habermas's notion of an "ideal speech situation," Tracy considers the ideal conversation/interpretation to be a counterfactual regulative ideal.[20] In "Conversation in Gethsemane," Nicholas Lash argues for a different use of Habermas to illuminate the difference that a focus on the dynamic tension between "the counterfactual and the possible, between tragedy and hope" can make.

Interpretation, like conversation, is both a discipline and an art. As both it employs techniques, methods, and argumentation, Tracy argues, but the process of mutual illumination that occurs in the dynamic of question and response cannot be reduced to any or all of these. Formal arguments, transcendental arguments, topical, dialectical, and rhetorical arguments are all useful and at times necessary, but these should be marshaled to disclose further the possibilities suggested by the classic under interpretation, and that is done best by dialogical investigation into the meanings presented by it. Wayne Booth explores further the precise relationship between rhetoric and religious truth in discourse in "Rhetoric and Religion: Are They Essentially Wedded?" to undermine the common prejudicial understanding of rhetoric as mere tropes and flourishes somehow tangential to religious truth itself: reflection on good rhetoric leads to the recognition of religious truth.

---

19. Ibid., 19.
20. Ibid., 26.

So what is truth? Especially, what is religious truth, and what do classics have to do with conveying the truth of a religious tradition? Truth is of various sorts, and, as a result, the judgments necessary to establish it require the sorts of arguments, warrants, and backings specific to the kind of truth at issue. If all understanding is interpretation, Tracy writes, then surely so is judgment of the truth.

> Reality is what we name our best interpretation. Truth is the reality we know through our best interpretations. Reality is constituted, not created or simply found, through the interpretations that have earned the right to be called relatively adequate or true.[21]

Religion concerns ultimate things—ultimate meaning, value, and reality or the "sacred"; as a result, religious truth bears upon the Ultimate, especially from the perspective of how persons relate (or should relate) to It. Theology is secondary reflection on the faith witness of individuals and communities to their experiences of the Ultimate and their perceptions of how their relationship to It transforms their lives and the history of the cosmos (or will or should transform it). Ideally, in the process of understanding/interpreting such witness, theology demonstrates the relative adequacy of its various formulations of the sacred and of humanity's relationship to it. Clearly, a correspondence theory of truth in the sphere of religion is adequate only in some positivists' pipe dreams: there are no entities or specific events or configurations of events that correlate in any finally convincing fashion with the Ultimate Reality mediated by but never simply identified with those entities or specific events. Reflection on what happens in attempting to understand the faith witness of a religious classic suggests another theory of the truth of religion.

For Tracy, to interpret a classic is to surrender oneself to a process in which both the validity of a tradition and of one's own identity is at stake. To allow ourselves to be taken up into dynamic conversation with a classic in pursuit of its meaning and truth is to open ourselves to the possibilities it presents. Such possibilities are not strictly identical with our preunderstanding of the meaning and truth of the classic under consideration or with our personal horizons of its subject matter. To converse with the classic is to recognize and appreciate its difference and its *difference as possibility* for the self and its understanding. This difference is never total; we encounter a similarity in difference in which sometimes the similarity, sometimes the difference predominates. To imagine the other as other and yet, somehow, also as possible is to exercise our analogical imagination in pursuit and recognition of

---

21. Ibid., 48.

truth. The classic discloses even as it conceals possibilities which the skilled interpreter then recognizes in the sense of *re-cognizes*—identifies and reconceives—by imaginatively reconstruing the horizon of possibilities of the classic. The objective event of the disclosure/concealment of possibilities in the classic finds its correlate in the event of recognition of those possibilities as genuine and their frequently transformative effects upon the subject.[22]

In religious classics, the perception of difference is intensified by their attempt to portray the Ultimate in meaning, value, and reality (however It is named), and the proper mode of relating to It. From this vantage point their disclosures/concealments of the Ultimate Ground of all become occasions to interrupt our complacent attempts to construct ordered wholes out of our lives. They call us to resist more of the same—be it mediocrity, evil, or anything else that blocks our self-transcending openness to difference. They call us to eschatological hope—to seek a future genuinely transformed by that Ultimate Reality and our self-transcending response to It.

Religious classics, then, deal with the most fundamental questions of human existence, those questions that arise when we attempt to realize the most fundamental dimensions of our humanity liberated from all distortion. In *Blessed Rage for Order,* Tracy understands these fundamental questions as limit questions: the self-transcending dynamism of inquiry leads to the formulation of questions that ask about the ultimate goal of the operative type of inquiry or about extreme but common human experiences, that is, the *limits-to* human inquiry and experience. Such questions then give rise to others concerning the fundamental structures of human understanding and existence, questions about the *limits-of* understanding and existence, which include how they are disclosive of the ultimate grounding condition of their possibility. When we seek to render reality intelligible through various sorts of scientific inquiry, we are eventually forced by the dynamism of the inquiry itself to ask about the existence of a ground to all such intelligibility at the limit of human understanding. When we feel compelled to inquire about the relative value of various courses of action, we are, in effect, led to ask whether moral behavior might have any value at all, especially in light of the evidence to the contrary, and we are eventually led to ask about an ultimate ground of the ordering of values that emerges. When we experience life at-its-limit, so to speak, in the boundary situations of guilt, anxiety, and suffering, and in the ecstatic experiences of joy, love, reassurance, and creativity, these depth

---

22. Ibid., 20–22, 28.

dimensions of human existence themselves disclose even as they conceal humanity's relationship to the Ultimate Ground of all.[23]

Religious classics disclose the answers that their traditions give to those questions about our most basic presuppositions, their Ultimate Ground of reality and the proper relationship to It. They themselves are concrete, historical expressions of the searches other persons have undertaken to find meaning—even ultimate meaning—in their predicaments, and of the revelations that they have received in response. They present us all too often with alien and wonderful vistas which cast our own settled horizons askew but, because of the strange echoes they provoke in the depths of our own beings, resist easy dismissal. But to know these echoes to be more than private illusion and to become convinced that the meaningfulness of proferred possibilities has, in fact, some claim to validity require the development of criteria of adequacy—first, to determine whether the interpretation of a particular classic is relatively adequate to the kind of entity it is and, second, to determine whether those possibilities are adequate to human experience. This is the task of a truly public theology. This is the project which Tracy sets all who would attempt to take theology seriously in this radically pluralistic world.

Perhaps the best—or even the *only*—way to determine the validity of this theory of religious and theological meaning and truth is to attempt to think through one's own public and pluralistic theology by entering into conversation with one's own favorite religious classics or with those who are doing it for themselves. The intent of this volume is to continue the conversation begun with David Tracy's work in theological hermeneutics. The order of the remaining contributions opens up a path of reflection and conversation that he would encourage all of us to follow.

First, in the articles remaining in Part II, "Pluralism and the Hermeneutics of Religion," we invite you, the reader, to join our contributors in conversation with four religious classics—two from Christianity and two from ancient Greek religion. We invite you to take them as more than examples of a theory of the classic and to enter imaginatively into their worlds of possibility.

In "Feminist Hermeneutics, Scriptural Authority, and Religious Truth: The Case of the *Imago Dei* and Gender Equality," Rosemary Radford Ruether wields a feminist hermeneutic of suspicion and its correlative criteria of adequacy on the classic creation narrative, which describes God creating Adam "in the image of God, male and female" (Genesis 1:27). Since this text, in spite of its apparent egalitarianism,

---

23. *Blessed Rage*, 92–109.

served historically as an instrument of oppression, it confronts us with the issue of the nature of its relevance and validity—its authority—for those Christians concerned to promote the well-being of women as much as of men. In another contribution with a feminist motive, Mary Gerhart employs Julia Kristeva's work on the language of mythology to unravel the multiple, frequently conflicting representations of the woman/goddess Helen found in the plays of Euripides: in the androcentric symbolic order of Greek mythical consciousness Helen functioned to legitimate it, but in her semiotic role she became a bearer of resistance to it from within. The tension between the two roles, Gerhart argues, suggests new possibilities for retrieving the meaning and truth of this goddess for today. Seán Freyne takes the *Window of the Evangelists* at Chartres as a key to understanding the distinctive theological horizons of each of the Gospels by calling attention to the complex interweaving of traditions which connects a different Israelite prophet with each evangelist's interpretation of Jesus. Finally, in "Hesiod: Religion and Poetry in the *Works and Days*," David Grene explores Hesiod's understanding of man's servitude to the gods in the labor of farming to inquire about the value of hard work, success, and failure at the plow and, with it, the ultimate validity of moral behavior in a cosmos ruled by such inscrutable gods.

In Part III, "Pluralism and the History of Religions," we invite you to consider the ambiguity and plurality of different religious traditions and the issues they raise for an authentic, responsible, and hermeneutical pluralism. In "Another Path to Truth," Jacob Neusner analyzes the history of the frequently ambiguous and conflicting interpretations of Jewish ritual for making a person ritually clean after contact with a corpse to demonstrate how ritual can function like myth to structure a world and to render life away from the Jerusalem Temple meaningful for the diaspora Jew.

The outsider's monolithic perspective on Christianity is forever undermined by our next three contributors. From the perspective of the history of Christian doctrine, John Macquarrie explores the long and varied history of interpretations of the meaning of Jesus Christ in "Pluralism in Christology." In "Love and Justice," Paul Ricoeur builds a bridge between the poetics of love and the prose of justice, between the logic of superabundance and the logic of equivalence, to confirm their irreducible plurality in unity in the Christian faith. In "The 'One World': A Challenge to Western Christianity," Johann Baptist Metz reflects on the complex problematics of the ongoing globalization of Christianity in light of two facts: (1) the meaning of the Christian faith cannot be extracted from its own Western cultural mantle, and (2) that mantle is intensely morally ambiguous. How then can Christianity be extended throughout the globe and genuinely rooted in many diverse cultures so that it neither loses its identity nor subjects the receiving cultures to the potentially devastating effects of Western technological and industrial society?

In "Pluralism and Intolerance in Hinduism," Wendy Doniger grapples with issues in Hinduism that are implicit in the essays on Christianity as well: What resources or tactics does any given religious tradition have for ordering and unifying the admittedly irreducible plurality of perspectives within it? Do the presence of such resources necessarily entail a tolerance of pluralism on a sociological level? In other words, in what ways can each specific religious faith support the tolerance of differences found in genuinely authentic and responsible pluralism? Her astute analysis of the pluralistic Vedic and Vedantic traditions of Hinduism and their various offshoots offers invaluable insight into the roots of violence in India today, even as it suggests that there are no easy rules of inference between intellectual and sociological pluralism, nor easily discernible ways to mollify rabid intolerance.

In our fourth and final section, we invite you to consider the problematics of interreligious dialogue raised for Christian theologians by increased awareness of alternative ways of being religious found in other world religions. Like David Tracy, our contributors seriously question whether it is truly possible, from an epistemologically and hermeneutically self-critical perspective, to develop a theology of religions that is not decisively influenced by one's own confessional history and perspective. Like him, all three express their concern to maintain their confessional commitment to faith in Jesus Christ while remaining open in a genuinely pluralistic spirit to being informed by the meaning and truth of other religious traditions. Hans Küng characterizes the nature, necessity, and promise of two virtues, dialogability and steadfastness, for engaging in the rigorous and self-disciplining process of interreligious dialogue and specifies the criteria essential to carrying out such dialogue while maintaining the uniqueness of Christianity's claim to truth. The task of maintaining both the openness to other religious traditions required by a pluralistic attitude and the fidelity to one's own religious heritage required by authentic, responsible, and hermeneutical pluralism is the subject of Claude Geffré's "Toward a Hermeneutics of Interreligious Dialogue." In the process, he presents a history of recent ecumenical efforts that set up the current context for such dialogue, and he develops criteria of adequacy for it. Finally, Schubert Ogden discloses some problems in the case for a pluralistic theology of religions by critiquing three recent attempts to do so presented by Gordon Kaufman, Rosemary Radford Ruether, and John Hick. While not pretending to prove conclusively that any pluralistic theology of religions which assumes that some common content exists among all of the great religious traditions is impossible, Ogden demonstrates that the arguments presented by these three theologians fail to support their cases.

Our invitation to explore the issues raised by an authentic, responsible, and hermeneutical pluralism concludes here with a complete bibliography of David Tracy's work compiled collaboratively with him by Stephen Webb. Just as we know that this bibliography catches David Tracy midstream, we hope that this volume offers added impetus to the growing chorus of conversations joining him in his life task—to defend and develop a fully public theology and an authentic, responsible, and hermeneutical approach to pluralism.

PART ONE

PLURALISM IN THE THOUGHT OF DAVID TRACY

1
RADICAL PLURALISM AND LIBERATION THEOLOGY

Gregory Baum

DAVID TRACY'S THEORY of pluralism enables him, in *The Analogical Imagination*, to make a brilliant defense for liberation and political theologies, persuasive even to those reluctant to agree.[1] While he himself followed a different trajectory in his own original theological proposal, he understands liberation theology to be an important corrective for ecclesiastical traditions and their theological teachings which through uncritical practice have become too closely identified with the interests of the dominant class. The category of "corrective" is, as we shall see, the key to his general theological approach. It enables him to offer positive interpretations of theological and philosophical trends with which he otherwise disagrees. Through it he makes room for theologies that follow approaches different from his own, understanding them to be correctives for reductionistic theological or philosophical ideas that exercise power in church or society. In developing his own critical theology, reaching toward depth and wholeness, Tracy reveals his intellectual humility by remaining ever open to correctives uttered by persons with different historical experiences or groups caught in different historical situations.

But what does Tracy mean by pluralism? First, we shall examine his theory of "the pluralism of traditions." Tracy appeciates and defends the pluralism of theologies within the Roman Catholic Church, the pluralism of the wider Christian traditions and their theologies, and the pluralism of the great world religions. He also offers a positive

---

1. David Tracy, *The Analogical Imagination: Christian Theology and the Culture of Pluralism* (New York: Crossroad, 1981) 390–98.

interpretation of the plurality of philosophical schools. Since behind the pluralism of traditions stands a faith in a transcendent reconciling power, Tracy's theory implies a theology of history and an ethical summons to dialogue and cooperation.

Second, we shall examine Tracy's idea of "radical pluralism," which in my opinion is only indirectly related to his pluralism of traditions. More than most theological authors Tracy is perplexed by the plurality of interpretations that contemporary thinkers give of the present cultural crisis. For a number of reasons, among them the Holocaust, all of the inherited certainties have dissolved. The resulting confusion and uncertainty, according to Tracy, constitute "the uncanniness" of the present moment.

Finally, we shall examine these two ideas of pluralism from the perspective of liberation theology.

The Pluralism of Traditions

The rich concept of the pluralism of traditions is contained in *The Analogical Imagination*. Great traditions, grounded and supported by classical events and classical texts, Tracy argues, are living, creative, self-correcting spiritual movements. Because classics transcend their historical period, have surplus meaning, and exercise universal appeal, great religious and philosophical traditions are open to new historical experiences and are capable of responding to them creatively. Because the classics have a certain breakthrough power, they are able to generate new perspectives and spark revisionist trends within the great traditions. For Tracy, then, religious and intellectual traditions are plural, dynamic, autoregenerative historical phenomena.

Tracy applies this concept to the internally diversified Christian tradition—to the plurality of Catholic theologies and to the plural Christian confessions, including their various theologies. They all merit respect; they all deserve a hearing; and they all make a contribution to the creative conversation out of which Christians encounter their classical texts and through which they constitute their living tradition.

Introducing the notion of "corrective," Tracy is able to interpret in a positive way even passionate, one-sided theological points of view. If interpreted as expressions reaching out for the whole, these viewpoints appear defective. But if they are seen as correctives, as warnings shouted at a community that has dangerously narrowed its perception of the whole, then one-sided emphases play a positive role. Even when examining the plurality in the New Testament itself, Tracy regards the "eschatological" and the "doctrinal" as important correctives serving the church's primary mission of proclamation, correctives that have retained their importance throughout history.[2] The eschatological pronounces God's judgment on a community comfortably reconciled with the powerful, and the doctrinal offers conceptual clarity to a community confused and divided over the words in which to proclaim Jesus Christ. These one-sided elements can make their positive contribution only in the back and forth of the plural churches' ongoing conversation reaching out for the whole.

These manifold forces become a danger to the Christian tradition when no one is listening, when the conversation stops, when a narrow perception of wholeness is endorsed as the final norm, or when correctives become the full message. But Christians, like all human beings, are summoned to wholeness and depth. The pluralism of which Tracy speaks calls for openness, willingness to be addressed, humility, eagerness to learn, and readiness to redefine one's tradition in fidelity to past and present.

This pluralism, Tracy believes, should also inform the interaction of Christianity with the other world religions. The self-affirmation of colonized peoples and the subsequent collapse of political colonialism have taught Christians an important lesson. Having come to acknowledge with repentance that the Christian claim to absoluteness has been used to legitimate colonial domination, Christians are now ready to respect the great world religions, enter into conversation with them, and discover the spiritual treasures contained within them. Addressed by the wisdom in these religions, Christians are compelled to reread their own classics and reinterpret their own religious traditions. Here, too, the ongoing conversation involving many partners enters into the self-constituting, historical dynamics of Christianity and the other religious traditions.

We note that this pluralism of traditions, from one point of view new and daring, is from another conservative in the best sense of the word. It is not a relativistic pluralism that considers all religions equally true and all Christian confessions equally reliable witnesses of God's revealed word. Tracy's call for openness, humility, and ongoing conversation does not necessarily invalidate the self-understanding of a church that regards itself as an orthodox and unique witness to divine revelation. All that is asked of such a church is the commitment to depth and wholeness: the church must be willing to enter into dialogue, permit itself to be seriously challenged, and then be ready to be addressed again by its own classics and in response to them move

2. Ibid., 265–68.

forward to a more adequate self-understanding. What Tracy demands from such a church—his own, in particular—is to recognize its own tradition as a vital, dynamic, self-constituting process, not free of ambiguity, in which the conversation with others must play an essential part.

As a Catholic, Tracy gladly listens to Luther, Calvin, and Thomas Muenzer. Yet what he learns from them he wants to introduce to the intra-Catholic theological conversation and thus make fruitful for the dynamic process of Catholic renewal. And, I suppose, he expects the heirs of the Reformation to let themselves be challenged by the Catholic tradition and to react creatively by renewing their own Protestant traditions. Such a conservative proposal does not merit the title of "radical pluralism." What Tracy has in mind is actually a worldwide ecumenism of religious traditions and their theologies.

What follows from the preceding is that for Tracy the pluralism of traditions is not a given, does not express a state of affairs, but rather refers to something to be done, a universal human task. Tracy's pluralism outlines a historical project. It proposes procedures for inter-religious and ecumenical dialogue and for developing confessional theologies, and it looks forward to the revivifying transformations these procedures will generate in the various religious traditions. The engagement in these procedures, Tracy believes, is inspired and carried by a transcendent reconciling power. Tracy's proposal of the pluralism of traditions implies a believing commitment to a divinely grounded, worldwide historical process.

David Tracy's understanding of the pluralism of traditions is very different from the prevailing pluralism, widely endorsed in contemporary society, that confines itself to praising the right of individuals to follow their own truth and choose their own values. This is the pluralism of the shopping mall. If people do not hear the call to depth and wholeness, they are likely to be content with personal opinions. That this individualism-cum-relativism has become the dominant trend in present-day American culture has been brilliantly documented in Robert Bellah's *Habits of the Heart*. With Bellah, Tracy laments the pluralism produced by arbitrary options and lazy thinking, unwilling to be challenged intellectually. Tracy recognizes the ideological use made of this pluralism in contemporary society, where significant conflicts are drowned in a sea of personal opinions. For Tracy, as for Tocqueville and many other thinkers, an unrooted person, a person not identified with a religious or secular wisdom tradition, is a prisoner of public opinion and hence unfree.

Tracy recognizes the hostility of modern culture to his own proposal of the pluralism of traditions. What he fails to do, however, is to inquire fully into the historical forces that have produced this modern culture.

But even in the churches and the world religions, the theory and practice of this pluralism have their enemies. Even in the sphere of religion, pluralism is vulnerable and in need of defense and vindication. Tracy proposes that there are four "sins" that damage the pluralism of traditions: the sin against openness (the refusal to listen to the other), the sin against depth (the acceptance of reductionist explanations), the sin against justice (the unwillingness to recognize the ideological role played by religion), and the sin against compassion (the indifference to the suffering caused by religious conflicts). Tracy mentions these threats to pluralism throughout *The Analogical Imagination*, but he does not explore them in any detail. Nor does he ask what historical forces promote these sins. He prefers not to dwell on evil.

In my judgment, Tracy's pluralism of traditions is a magnificent proposal that deserves fullest support, but the dynamics operative in the self-constitution of the religious traditions need to be looked at more critically. I shall return to this point below.

In his early *Blessed Rage for Order*, Tracy appears to affirm a similar pluralism of philosophical traditions. What he argues concretely is that Christian fundamental theology, charged with examining the openness of contemporary thought to the divine, must engage in conversation with several distinct philosophical traditions, including transcendental Thomism, process thought, linguistic analysis, phenomenology, and the philosophy of praxis. These philosophical traditions, committed to depth and wholeness, constitute themselves through an ongoing, critical, self-reflective intellectual conversation. Tracy's own brilliant analysis shows that these philosophies, in reliance on their classical texts, have reviewed their inherited ideas and judgments, deepened their insights into the human condition, and in some instances recognized limit situations in secular experience that call for religious interpretation. He concludes therefore that God-talk is not a foreign language but has decipherable meaning for the modern philosophies in which contemporary society achieves its deepest self-understanding.

In his own Catholic context, this is an exciting conclusion. In the past, Catholic theologians relied almost exclusively on the Aristotelian-Thomistic tradition and believed—or were told—that modern philosophies were not appropriate partners for dialogue. Tracy's work urges Catholic theologians to appreciate the pluralism of philosophical traditions, each one alive with an inner dynamism that allows it to transcend the secularity of its origin and be open to the God question.

But do the philosophical traditions examined by Tracy really represent the intellectual life of contemporary society? Do they really provide the ideas and values that shape the decisions made by the important political, economic, and cultural institutions? It seems to me that in modern capitalist society, especially in the Anglo-American world, there exists a venerable, empiricist intellectual tradition—eminently influential to this day—with classical authors such as Hobbes, Locke, and Hume, turning more utilitarian with Bentham and Mills and more scientific with contemporary philosophers, an intellectual tradition that has consistently entertained an atomistic and mechanistic understanding of human beings—humans without soul and without solidarity—and acted as the theoretical ally of capitalism with its implicit view of humanity as utility maximizer. It seems to me that this scientific empiricism is the prevailing philosophy guiding the major institutions of our society, the great bureaucracies of government and industry and certain sectors of the university.

David Tracy would probably argue that the classical authors of this tradition offered important correctives in their day and vindicated human rights against arbitrary aristocratic rule, but that the lesser representatives of this tradition were not seriously committed to depth and wholeness. Tracy does not deny that positivism and utilitarianism are powerful ideas dominating contemporary society. But if these are the prevailing ideas, then his pluralism of philosophical traditions seems to paint an excessively hopeful picture of contemporary thinking.

Radical Pluralism

We now turn to another pluralism that plays an important role in Tracy's theology. In *The Analogical Imagination* Tracy speaks of "radical pluralism" and the "radically pluralistic present."[3] For him there is something altogether unique about the contemporary situation: it is radically plural, confused, riddled, and incomprehensible, and at the same time it demands attention, makes us uncover the hidden, and opens us to otherness. Radical pluralism has negative and positive connotations. Tracy calls it "the uncanniness" of the present age. The uncanny is a translation of "das Unheimliche," a German word referring to something that produces uncertainty and fear and yet suggests the possibility that behind the puzzling, threatening circumstance a gracious surprise lies in waiting.

Tracy develops the uniqueness of the present situation along several lines. He repeatedly refers to the horrifying, death-dealing events of the twentieth century, for which there are no parallels in the past. The Holocaust has destroyed the Enlightenment hope in progress and the

3. Ibid., 339–64.

older, Renaissance faith in humanity. Mass destruction of human beings has come to belong to the order of the day. Even if the atomic bomb has been used so far in only one war, the continuing production of nuclear arms and the ongoing perfection of conventional weapons reveal that mass destruction of human beings has become an element of the rational planning that governments undertake in preparation for the future. What is new in the present is that we now possesss the technology to destroy the whole of humanity.

There is, moreover, the disturbing discovery of the limits of nature and the frightening recognition that the pollution and destruction of the environment by modern, industrial development have damaged the earth to such an extent that the survival of human beings is by no means assured. What is new in the present situation is that we can survive only if we so choose, only if we turn to sustainable development and create an ecologically responsible society.

A third death-dealing power of the present is the increasing spread of hunger in the poor countries of the southern hemisphere. The famines, often of genocidal proportions, are related to the global economic system that reaches from the industrialized center of the northern hemisphere to the outlying regions to the south, creating hinterlands that serve the center with labor and natural resources and in doing so undergo involuntary urbanization, suffer cultural disintegration, and lose the ability to produce food for their own needs.

These death-dealing powers make us, the privileged, question our own age, but we cannot agree among ourselves about what is going on in society. What is new in the present, according to Tracy, is that we are unable to name our own age.[4] Is society still a rational project on the way to Enlightenment progress? Or was the Enlightenment a misguided historical interlude after which society is now trying to return to a more communal, value-committed culture? Or are we entering an altogether new phase where the certainties of the past, whether they were rational and scientific or mediated by the inherited values, have become meaningless, and where all we can do in the circle of our friends is to explore our own experiences?

Of course, every age is a riddle to itself. In every age, people have been deeply divided in their interpretations of what was happening and where they were going. This was startlingly true in Western society of the nineteenth century when people wrestled with one another over conservative, liberal, socialist, or anarchist interpretations of the

---

4. See David Tracy, "On Naming the Present," in *On the Threshold of the Third Millennium* (special issue of *Concilium*, February 1990; London: SCM; Philadelphia: Trinity Press International) 66–85.

historical moment. We are also well aware that conflicts of this kind characterized the culture of Palestine that we encounter in the New Testament, when Pharisees, Sadducees, Zealots, Herodians, and the disciples of Jesus offered quite different interpretations of their historical situation.

The ambiguity of the present moment, Tracy argues, is quite different. He develops especially two themes. There exist, first of all, the critiques of culture produced by the masters of suspicion—Marx, Nietzsche, and Freud, to name the most famous—which question our thoughts, feelings, and actions and reveal the ambiguity of all cultural self-expressions. Because people struggle to protect and promote their vulnerable, constricted self-identities and in doing so introduce distortions in their consciousness, the culture they produce, whatever it may be, is incapable of understanding itself. More than that, the same critiques of culture render problematic the classical traditions, be they religious or secular. The growing recognition that all traditions are flawed moves Tracy to speak of our new homelessness.

This homelessness strongly affects Christian thinkers. Tracy argues that a distinguishing mark of the contemporary situation is the present conflictual pluralism on what are "the worthwhile fundamental questions" that should now be asked. When Tracy proposed his theory of theological pluralism, he recognized that what distinguished the various theologies from one another were not simply different sets of concepts but also and especially different worthwhile fundamental questions, emerging from the historical context, to which these theologies sought to reply. Tracy clearly affirms the contextual character of theology. Theology wrestles with the central salvational issues as they are perceived by people in their historical situations. But what is the worthwhile fundamental question addressing us in the present crisis? "Radical pluralism," as Tracy defines it, makes it impossible to give an answer to this question.

But there is more. Radical pluralism also means that we have learned to listen to groups and peoples who in the past were excluded from the conversation of the educated elite. We have discovered that even the sciences, despite their emphasis on objectivity, carried the bias of the scientists who invented and produced them, males of a certain class and culture. Society cannot come to self-knowledge unless it is willing to listen to the voices of its low-status members and its subjugated groups. Society must listen to women. Those engaged in this conversation affirm radical pluralism as a positive moment: they consequently resist the temptation to create a rational synthesis of the many voices, as if reason had the power to reconcile so many diverse perspectives. Reason itself has lost its innocence.

Radical pluralism also means that we have to listen to non-Western cultures, societies, and religions. This aspect of radical pluralism is related to Tracy's pluralism of traditions. While in the past comparative studies in religion and culture often tended to look upon the others from the standpoint of the Western religious or intellectual traditions, the pluralism advocated by Tracy recognizes the pluri-centric character of the world. There is no center. As among the galaxies, there are many centers. Tracy only hints what this insight might mean for Christian theology. Again, it would be a betrayal of radical pluralism if one wished to produce a new theory that would integrate the different traditions and their various perspectives. We have to learn to respect the "otherness" of the world religions and of non-Western cultures.

Radical pluralism, this "uncanniness" of the present, is frightening because it undermines our certainties and questions our assumption of a common humanity; but this uncanniness also suggests—and this is the element of hope in it—that behind the confusion and lack of coherence stands an as yet unnameable newness, destined to reveal itself as gracious reconciling power.

Pluralism and Liberation Theology

Let us now consider Tracy's notion of pluralism from the viewpoint of liberation theology. "Liberation theology" names a field of theologies based on what in ecclesiastical language is called "the preferential option for the poor." The preferential option includes two commitments: the first is to read society and its texts from the perspective of the poor and powerless; the second, to give public witness of one's solidarity with their historical struggle for emancipation. The option for the poor has therefore two dimensions, one hermeneutical and the other practical.

This twofoldness constitutes liberation theology as a "praxis," which is here defined as the interaction between knowledge and action oriented toward human emancipation. While all forms of theology recognize the impact of knowledge on practice, liberation theology is keenly aware that there is also an impact of practice on human consciousness and hence on the reading of social reality and its texts. In matters dealing with ethics and religion, the entry into truth demands an antecedent alternative practice.

From the perspective of liberation theology, Tracy's original theological project outlined in his early *Blessed Rage for Order* was somewhat puzzling. The distinction he then made between the conversations of theology with three different communities—the university, the church, and the social order—created the impression that he regarded the university and the church as outside or above the social order, unaffected by society's social, economic, and political conflicts. In his later writings, this impression disappears. Tracy has come to recognize with increasing clarity that it is impossible to understand the debates in the university and the church without taking into account the historical condition of society. While Tracy strongly opposes reductionist interpretations of intellectual and religious conflicts, he clearly acknowledges a political dimension in all arguments dealing with important ideas, be they secular or religious.

Liberation theology looks upon Tracy's pluralism of traditions as well as his radical pluralism with great sympathy. It sides with Tracy's idea against the notion of pluralism advocated by certain American theologians, most outspokenly perhaps Dennis McCann,[5] who try to devise a universally acceptable form of public discourse for the United States in its present, pluralistic condition. Since American society is made up of a plurality of groups and communities, each with its special values and traditions, it would be unjust if the public good of the republic were defined by a single group, the heir of power and privilege. The public good should be determined, these authors propose, by an ongoing public conversation, following the rules of democracy, in which each party argues in defense of its own interests and is in principle open to accepting rational compromise that offers proportional satisfaction to all parties, without special privilege to any one of them. What rules the pluralistic society here is commonly accepted rational discourse.

By contrast, David Tracy is highly suspicious of the commonly accepted rational discourse. He recognizes ideological distortions in the public discourse of any society, created as it is by an elite that has access to power, privilege, and formal education. That is why "interruption" is an important concept in his theology. (An issue of *Concilium* co-edited by him is called *The Holocaust as Interruption*.[6]) The normative discourse that a society, be it secular or sacred, creates for its own use excludes from the conversation the sectors suffering oppression, and for this reason such discourse remains essentially ambiguous. That is why moments of interruption must be taken with utmost seriousness. They have a message to which society must listen.

Looked upon from Tracy's perspective, McCann's proposal of pluralism appears to be a political ideology that seeks to silence the cries of

5. Dennis McCann and Charles Strain, *Polity and Praxis* (Minneapolis: Winston, 1985); McCann, *New Experiments in Democracy* (Kansas City, MO: Sheed and Ward, 1987).
6. *The Holocaust as Interruption*, ed. Elisabeth Schüssler Fiorenza and David Tracy (*Concilium* 175; Edinburgh: T. & T. Clark, 1984).

the poor and the marginalized who are unable or unwilling to use the commonly recognized discourse. The very attempt to designate the oppressed sectors of society—be they women, the poor, or the racially despised—as "special interest groups" is an effort to disguise the injustice inflicted upon them. In contrast, Tracy insists that the victims must be heard, even if this should explode the inherited rationality.

Still, the perspective of liberation theology also raises some critical questions. As I suggested above, Tracy's pluralism of traditions puts the main emphasis on the trusting conversation between these traditions, on listening, learning, gaining new insights, self-correction, and imaginatively expanding one's spiritual and intellectual inheritance. In a paragraph on the enemies of this pluralism, Tracy does mention the sin against justice, which for him means above all the refusal to recognize the ideological role played by religion in society. He is aware that the dynamics that widen the distance between various religious traditions and create hostility between them has to do with their entanglement in the structures of political and economic power.

Liberation theology would insist more than does Tracy that it is the task of the trusting conversation between the traditions to analyze the historical conditions that feed their respective ideological deformations. More than that, liberation theology would have to add that conversation, while precious and important, is not enough. Representatives of the plural traditions will have to stand together against the historical causes of injustice, especially those from which they have inherited their falsifying biases. What is demanded, from the viewpoint of liberation theology, is an alternative practice, that is, gestures and acts of solidarity with the movements that wrestle against these unjust structures. Such a practice would modify the consciousness of the participants and affect the reading of their own religious tradition. While Tracy's thought is sympathetic to emancipatory political engagement, he has not gone out of his way, except possibly quite recently, to demand a new practice as an indispensable dimension of the quest for theological truth.

The reason for this absence, it seems to me, is related to Tracy's notion of "radical pluralism." This notion, as we saw above, is a collective category that brings together different troubling experiences that undermine the confidence of our contemporaries in the various sources of science, wisdom, and religious truth we have inherited. We are overwhelmed by the Holocaust and its continuing presence in other massacres; we are deeply disturbed by the ideological distortions present in the Christian and secular traditions of the West; we are confused by the lack of agreement among contemporary intellectuals regarding the present cultural crisis; and we are excited by the possibility of discovering the "other" religion and the "other" culture we have ignored in the past. But is it useful to unite these different factors under the common label of radical pluralism? I do not think so.

In my opinion, to speak in terms of the common label tends to undermine our trust in the critical concepts derived from the Enlightenment which do help us to make sense of the society in which we live. Constructing a single category allows the massive crimes committed by our civilization and legitimated or even encouraged by our intellectual traditions to weaken the confidence of our contemporaries in the critical methodology our civilization has also developed. Tracy's radical pluralism is, in my opinion, an echo of the postmodern idea that Holocaust and Gulag are arguments demonstrating that every affirmation of a context-transcending normative vision has a built-in orientation toward totalitarianism.

Despite the occasional postmodern rhetoric, Tracy actually defends modern critical theory. Here are two sentences of a long paragraph dealing with the impact of the economic infrastructure on culture and the realm of ideas.

> Only when we understand history as process, humanity as social, as always a result of its own labor, can we understand the profoundly alienating reifications of the socioeconomic base hidden and awaiting unmasking in all "culture." Only then can we uncover—beyond the fetishism of facts endorsing the status quo and the idealism of philosophers and humanist critics—the actual conflicts of society reflected in all cultural expressions.[7]

The entire paragraph is closer to the Frankfurt school than to the postmodern repudiation of critical theory.

It seems to me, therefore, that one might usefully deconstruct the notion of radical pluralism. I wish to distinguish between (a) the shaking of the foundation caused by reflection on the evils of Western society and the relativizing of the Western religious and philosophical traditions caused by the recognition of "other" religions and "other" cultures, and (b) the confusion caused by the multiple interpretations given of the present cultural crisis. The self-questioning of Western society here designated as (a) is indeed "unheimlich" or "uncanny," generating remorse, fear, and helplessness while at the same time suggesting the possibility of release and new discovery. But the confusion caused by the disagreement of intellectuals, here designated as (b), is not a unique phenomenon. It is frustrating, but not uncanny. On a previous page, I recalled the irreconcilable interpretations present in nineteenth-century Europe and first-century Palestine. What follows from this is that the chorus of discordant voices cannot be used to invalidate the

---

7. Tracy, *The Analogical Imagination*, 347.

critical theories derived from the Enlightenment and to discount them as principles of explanation.

While liberation theology laments the dominance of instrumental reason in contemporary society, it does not reject the entire Enlightenment tradition: it still trusts the critical methods capable of uncovering the extent to which economic and other forms of domination are reflected in the realms of ideas, culture, and religion. Liberation theology resists the postmodern proposal that these theories must be rejected because they make universal claims. The above quotation suggests that Tracy also resists the postmodern idea, even if his discourse occasionally reflects postmodern sensibilities. His definition of radical pluralism, I have suggested, is a concession to postmodern thought.

After reading his recent essay "On Naming the Present,"[8] I am inclined to believe that Tracy has moved into the field of liberation theology. I offer two reasons for thinking so, one related to the evolution of his thought and the other to a change in the self-understanding of liberation theology. Tracy's essay emphasizes the mystical and political dimensions of contemporary Christian existence defined in terms of resistance and hope. Looking back, Tracy points to the ninety-sixth issue of *Concilium* (1974), entitled *The Mystical and Political Dimension of Christian Faith*, as a groundbreaking work that prompted the theologians connected with this international review to explore the emancipatory dimension of Christian spirituality. By concentrating on the "mystical-political" or, as he prefers to call it, the "mystical-prophetic," Tracy has moved very close to liberation theology. For he now calls for an alternative practice, resistance and hope, as the prerequisite for the attainment of religious truth.

At the same time liberation theology has also moved into a new phase. Since the sixties, vast numbers of people on several continents believed that in their society profound social change toward greater justice was a historical possibility. I need only recall the liberal optimism of the Kennedy years, the challenging civil rights movement, the opposition to the war in Vietnam and to American imperialism, the women's movement, the struggle of black people and other marginalized groups for recognition, and among intellectuals the creation of a new political imagination. At the same time there were anticolonial struggles in Africa, liberation movements in Latin America, and socialist experiments on several continents. It was during this time that Christian communities in struggle, aided by their intellectuals, first developed liberation theology. The alternative practice that grounded liberation theology at that time was support for concrete political

---

8. Cf. n. 4 above.

movements. Paul Tillich, speaking of the twenties in Germany, designated as a *kairos* a period of time in which structural social change toward greater justice was a historical possibility and a realistic hope. The period beginning with the sixties was such a *kairos*, but this period has come to an end.

In the eighties the government-supported shift to liberal or monetarist capitalism, the reorganization of capital around the giant transnationals, and the subsequent globalization of the economy have profoundly affected societies in the southern hemisphere and in the northern hemisphere. Structural adjustment policies imposed by the international financial institutions on the southern nations, unable to pay their debt, forces the respective governments to neglect their own population and promote economic activities that serve the interests of the developed north. The result has been growing misery and hunger. Liberation movements have been weakened not only by strong-arm policies of governments but even more by the hopelessness of the situation.

Even in the northern hemisphere, governments are introducing structural adjustment policies designed to enable their nations to be competitive on the global market. This means privatization, deregulation, tax breaks and other advantages for transnational corporations, cutting social programs, lowering the salaries of public sector employees, raising the price of public services, humiliating organized labor, and so forth. Even socialist or social democratic governments (France, for instance, or Australia) were forced by the capital market to adopt neo-liberal or monetarist policies. And the result has been the same everywhere: massive unemployment; job insecurity right into the middle class; the shift of the job market to unskilled, temporary, or part-time work; the decline of neighborhoods; and misery in the streets.

For me the recent Gulf War was the publicly approved massacre that sealed in blood the new political-economic order, begun over a decade ago, devised to enhance the material well-being of a privileged minority and abandon to the margin the rest of the globe's population. Those who refuse to play by the rules will be penalized. In the present period there is no historical possibility for structural social change toward greater justice, neither in the southern hemisphere nor the north. The *kairos* has come to an end. The period we have entered—and who knows how long it will last!—I name, using another biblical image, "wilderness."

In the wilderness, liberation theology joins David Tracy in defining Christian existence in terms of resistance and hope. The dark night of the soul, often thought to be meaningful only for the few, is becoming a way of life for the multitude. When Christians pray during a *kairos*, "Thy kingdom come, thy will be done on earth," they hope to see with their own eyes an example of God's justice. But when they utter the same prayer in the wilderness, they hope that God's work among them will be one of preparation. Hope here pushes them more deeply into their spiritual resources. They become more aware of their roots at the point where these touch the underground river.

2

DAVID TRACY AND THE DEBATE ABOUT PRAXIS

Dermot A. Lane

THERE IS AT PRESENT an important debate taking place in theological circles between what may be loosely called liberal theology and liberation theology, between contemporary theology and practical theology, between so-called academic theology and pastoral theology. Simplistic accounts of this debate tend to polarize the issues, suggesting that one side is concerned exclusively with the intellectual credibility of theology in a way that maintains the existing social order and that the other side is focused primarily on practical issues of justice with a view to transforming the surrounding social order. Is theology about the content of Christian faith or is it about the praxis of faith? Is such a distinction viable in the light of the global crises facing humanity?

One very particular expression of this debate concerns the relationship between hermeneutics and praxis in theology. The issues here are even more complex because hermeneutical theology does claim to embrace a form of praxis and praxis theologies do in fact involve the exercise of a particular hermeneutics. Of course part of the problem at this level concerns the meaning we attach to the word praxis. The term "praxis," like its predecessor "experience," is extremely slippery and can be made to mean just about anything. One theologian who has been quite deliberate and circumspect in the use of this word praxis is David Tracy. Throughout his writings, from *Blessed Rage for Order* (1975) up to *Plurality and Ambiguity* (1987), Tracy has given careful and constructive consideration to the importance of praxis in theology. In 1983 he wrote:

Indeed, I believe it can be plausibly argued that the greatest shift in the modern period is not the shift from classical theory to either positivist or critical theory, nor the shift from classical *techne* (or craft) to modern theory-laden technology, but the shift (directly related to the earlier shifts of both theory and *techne*) of *praxis* itself.[1]

The purpose of this paper is to explore David Tracy's theology of praxis and to relate this to discussions about praxis in liberation theology. In one sense it may seem premature, even unfair, to review Tracy's theology of praxis, since he has promised a book on practical theology which he tells us will deal more explicitly with the whole question of praxis.[2] However, it could be argued that what Tracy has already said about praxis is sufficient to justify some initial tentative probings on the place of praxis in his theology. Further, he has already written at least two significant articles on practical theology which give us a preview of the direction that his promised book on this subject will take.[3]

Praxis in *Blessed Rage for Order*

In *Blessed Rage for Order* (1975) Tracy sets out to tackle the crisis facing modern theology. This crisis is ultimately a "crisis of the cognitive claims"[4] concerning revelation, God, and Christ brought about by disenchantment with mystification by the theologian and by disenchantment with disenchantment by the secular mind. To resolve this cognitive crisis Tracy proposes a revisionist model of theology. Within this model there are two sources of theology, namely, "common human experience and language" and the "Christian tradition" as expressed in its classical texts. These two sources are brought together through a revision of Paul Tillich's famous method of correlation.

For Tracy there are three areas in theology—fundamental, systematic, and practical theology—which seek to address the three publics of the

---

1. D. Tracy, "The Foundations of Practical Theology" in *Practical Theology: The Emerging Field in Theology, Church and World*, ed. D. F. Browning (New York: Harper & Row, 1983) 74.
2. D. Tracy, *The Analogical Imagination: Christian Theology and the Culture of Pluralism* (New York: Crossroad, 1981) 96 n. 104, 98 n. 117.
3. See Tracy, "Foundations"; idem, "Practical Theology in the Situation of Global Pluralism," in *Formalism and Reflection: The Promise of Practical Theology*, ed. L. S. Mudge and J. N. Poling (Philadelphia: Fortress, 1987).
4. D. Tracy, *Blessed Rage for Order: The New Pluralism in Theology* (New York: Seabury, 1975) 5.

academy, the church, and society respectively. The primary concern of *Blessed Rage for Order* is fundamental theology.

He describes fundamental theology as a philosophical reflection on both the meanings disclosed in our common human experience and the meanings disclosed in the primary texts of the Christian tradition. Systematic theology seeks to retrieve the meanings contained in the classical Christian texts through the methods of hermeneutics. Together, fundamental theology and systematic theology provide an appropriately reconstructed *theoria* and this becomes the basis for the practical theologian to work out new possibilities of praxis.[5]

In the final chapter of *Blessed Rage for Order*, significantly entitled "History, Theory and Praxis," Tracy outlines what possible light a revisionist fundamental theology might throw on the pressing questions of a theology of praxis. He notes that it was neither a liberal theology of praxis nor a neo-orthodox theology of praxis that inspired the present concern for praxis. Instead, what has really brought about the emerging political and liberation theologies of praxis is a rereading of the Bible and Marx. On the one hand, there is the biblical retrieval of the eschatological symbols of hope within Judaism and Christianity. On the other hand, there is at the same time a rediscovery of and a theological reinterpretation of the classical Hegelian-Marxist notion of praxis. In particular there is a reappropriation of Marx's observation that the task of philosophy, and now of theology, is not simply to interpret the world but to change it. Within this context, Tracy is careful to point out that praxis should not be identified with practice; instead, praxis properly understood is about "the critical relationship between theory and practice whereby each is dialectically influenced and transformed by the other."[6]

In spite of these real gains Tracy holds that the revisionist theologian must retain a "critical hesitation" about going down the road with the emerging theologies of praxis.[7] For one thing, they are still too heavily influenced by the neo-orthodox model of theology. More specifically, Tracy suggests that these theologies of praxis "are not faithful to the full demands of praxis."[8] By this he means that the turn to praxis has not sufficiently transformed the theories informing these theologies, and he notes by way of example how G. Gutierrez does allow praxis to transform the idea of development but fails to do this in regard to the major Christian doctrines within his own important book

5. Ibid., 240.
6. Ibid., 243.
7. Ibid., 244.
8. Ibid.

entitled *Theology of Liberation*.9 In effect, Tracy's reservation about these theologies of praxis concerns "their lack of critical-theoretical rigour"10 and the absence of a worked out critical social theory.

In conclusion, Tracy calls for a practical theology informed by sociologists, economists, and critical theorists that would ground its praxis in the *theoria* derived from revisionist fundamental and systematic theologies. In making this plea Tracy insists that this proposal is a task for the future which at the moment he can only point toward in a manner that is "merely anticipatory."11

The Analogical Imagination and Liberation Theology

In *The Analogical Imagination: Christian Theology and the Culture of Pluralism* (1981) Tracy continues his threefold theological project, now paying particular attention to systematic theology. *The Analogical Imagination* is by far Tracy's most important theological work to date: it is more than just a book about the method of systematic theology; it is systematic theology in motion. Driven by Tracy's admirable passion for public accountability in terms of the criteria and discourse that systematic theology employs, it is a model of consistency concerning the hermeneutics of classical and religious texts with particular reference to the event of Jesus Christ as witnessed to in the scriptures. Throughout *The Analogical Imagination*, Tracy seeks to be inclusive in his interpretation of the pluralistic and conflicting readings of the Christ-event. The key that keeps the theological conversation open in the midst of so much pluralism is the analogical imagination, a doctrine that affirms difference within unity.

A thread running through *The Analogical Imagination* is the publicness and interrelatedness of fundamental, systematic, and practical theology. It is within this context that he touches on a practical theology of praxis. As elsewhere in this book, Tracy is inclusive in his treatment of the different theologies of praxis, almost to the disadvantage of his own gently but firmly stated preferences. All theologies of praxis are united in the demand for some form of personal involvement

---

9. Ibid., 255 n. 35. Though this criticism may have been valid in 1975, it is no longer sustainable given Gutierrez's subsequent transformation of theological theory on God in *On Job: God-Talk and the Suffering of the Innocent* (New York: Orbis, 1987), on poverty in *The Power of the Poor in History* (London: SCM, 1983), and on spirituality in *We Drink from our own Wells: The Spiritual Journey of the People* (London: SCM, 1984).
10. Tracy, *Blessed Rage*, 246.
11. Ibid., 240.

at the human and social level of structures in the world. Further, most theologies of praxis emphasize that praxis must be related to theory not simply as theory's application or practice but as theory's own originating and self-correcting foundation. To this extent praxis sublates theory but not vice versa.[12] More specifically, the praxis of liberation theologies demands personal involvement in the liberating transformation of some particular social evil such as economic exploitation, dependency, elitism, racism, or sexism. Further, according to liberation theologies of praxis, the only way of resolving the problem of the truth status of the cognitive claims of Christianity and modernity is not by better or more theories but by the involvement of human beings in liberating the particular social situations of injustice.

Thereafter, Tracy distinguishes between two schools of thought concerning praxis, one being the classical Aristotelian understanding of praxis and the other being some form of Hegelian-Marxist vision of praxis. The Aristotelian school of praxis, taken up in a particular way by Bernard Lonergan in this century, emphasizes the need for intellectual, moral, and religious conversion in the life of the theologian as a result of his/her self-transcending subjectivity. This change is effected ultimately by the gift of the love of God flooding our hearts. This approach to praxis insists that "doing the truth" involves "saying the truth" so that orthopraxis grounds orthodoxy.[13] This does not mean that the role of the practical theologian is to apply theological theories worked out elsewhere. Instead, a foundational unity exists between the intellectual, moral, and religious conversion of the theologian and the theologian's praxis. The foundation of praxis, in this view, lies in the transformed subjectivity of the theologian.

The other approach to praxis, the one found in European political theology and Latin American liberation theology, is influenced by one form or other of the Hegelian-Marxist analysis of the dialectical relationship of theory and praxis. These theologies of praxis require an ideology critique of church, academy, and social situation insofar as these are the causes of injustice in the lives of people. Further, the model of truth operative in these praxis theologies is transformative rather than disclosive.

The difference between the classical theology of praxis and the political/liberation theologies of praxis is mirrored in the debate between the hermeneutical approach of Hans-Georg Gadamer and the praxis orientation of Jürgen Habermas. According to Gadamer, the disclosive power of the classical Greek tradition is sufficient in the public

---

12. Tracy, *Analogical Imagination*, 69.
13. Ibid., 70–71.

forum to effect societal praxis. For Habermas a purely hermeneutical approach all too often simply serves the status quo. The world we live in today is controlled by systematically distorted structures of communication. We can no longer assume that such distortions can be transformed by hermeneutical reflection and rhetorical persuasiveness alone. Like Gadamer, some theologians believe that the persuasive power of good hermeneutical work is sufficient to transform contemporary praxis. These theologians, in the words of Tracy, "seem too content with a relatively unexamined trust that the rhetorical persuasiveness of those retrieved meanings will prove sufficient to transform individual and societal practice."[14] On the other hand, political theologians, following Habermas, emphasize the relative powerlessness of rhetorical persuasion in a situation of systematically distorted communication. What is required instead is some form of a Christian critique of the reigning ideologies.

The issues at stake in this debate between hermeneutical theology and liberation theology, between classical theories of praxis and post-Marxist theories of praxis, are substantive and important in relation to the whole of theology as fundamental, systematic, and practical. Tracy summarizes these issues under five headings.

The first issue concerns the meaning of truth within theology. Is it some form of correspondence, or empirical verification, or falsification, or coherence, or adequacy to proper language use, or relation to common human experience, or consensus, or disclosure, or transformation? Here Tracy is insistent that it is a mistake to separate the disclosure and the transformation models of theological truth. After all, real knowledge is in some sense participatory, and all good theory is grounded in the praxis of intellectual integrity. Authentic disclosures of truth bring with them some form of transformation, and the experience of transformative truth in praxis effects at the same time a disclosure of what is now recognized to be the case.

The second issue concerns the need in theology for more empirically based social analysis and critique of ideology as a check against all theological theories and praxis. At the same time these empirically based analyses are themselves in need of critical theory and praxis if we are to move beyond the status quo. The third issue highlights the centrality of conversion to Christian faith and thought within the biblical and Christian tradition. "Is it not the case that Christian faith, hope and love are first praxis related realities for a transformed agent . . . before they are expressed in cognitive claims or right beliefs?"[15] If this is the

14. Ibid., 74.
15. Ibid., 76.

case, then there does seem to be solid grounds for a transformation model of theological truth and the praxis desired by both Aristotelian and Hegelian-Marxist formulations. The fourth issue concerns the biblical grounds for a social-political dimension to Christianity as found in the prophetic and apocalyptic traditions of the Bible. These traditions in turn assume the presence of God's activity in history, especially in the history of the oppressed. The fifth issue is about recognizing the way political and liberation theologies have recovered forgotten aspects of the Christian tradition: eschatology, prophetic and apocalyptic elements, the subversive memory of suffering, and the cross.

There can be no doubt, Tracy admits, that theology since the time of the Enlightenment has been concerned too exclusively with "the crisis of cognitive claims" and that this concern has at times involved theology in distorted notions of reason as instrumental and practice as technique. To this extent the shift to praxis is surely to be welcomed. Equally, the shift to praxis can help theology realize "that the major question in our situation is not the crisis of cognitive claims, but the social-ethical crisis of massive suffering and widespread oppression and alienation in an emerging global culture."[16] This crisis of cognitive claims does not simply disappear with the shift to praxis, however. The need for argument, criteria, warrants, and evidence continues to exist. Likewise, the need for certain necessary abstractions from the concrete and the existence of the ideal of conversation as found in most forms of fundamental and systematic theology remain in force. Above all, what the shift to praxis in political and liberation theologies calls for is greater "collaboration" and more "conversation" among the different parts of theology.[17] In this way the differences between fundamental, systematic, and practical theology are differences not of conflict but of complementarity because in the end each is concerned with speaking a truth about God that can, in principle, be heard by all.[18]

One further difference noted by Tracy between systematic theology and practical theologies of praxis concerns their relationship to the Christ-event. Systematic theology, by and large, is grounded in the manifestation and proclamation of the Christ-event. On the other hand, for practical theologies of praxis, what is important is that individuals become doers of the Word in history and not simply hearers of the Word, going beyond the individualism of existential-transcendental theologies and affirming the primacy of social praxis. At the same time, however, Tracy notes that these political and liberation theologies of praxis are

16. Ibid., 78.
17. Ibid., 79.
18. Ibid., 81.

in fact operating out of a proclamation or manifestation model of theology of one kind or another.19 According to the theology of praxis, we must move from a theology that safeguards the harmony of the world at the expense of the actual and real conflicts in society made manifest by the Christ-event. This means that theology today must retrieve the prophetic heritage of Judaism and Christianity, the preaching of the reign of God by Jesus to the poor, the liberating but dangerous memory of Jesus, the contradictions and conflicts exposed by the cross of the crucified One, and the proleptic vindication of history disclosed by the resurrection of Jesus Christ. This will require an unmasking of the existence of present oppressive economic, political, and social structures of both church and world. Above all, it will involve realizing that the promise of God's eschatological future, anticipated in Christ, is something that commands and empowers the disciples of Christ today to different forms of liberating praxis in the here and now.

Further Developments

After these two major books Tracy wrote two significant articles outlining the broad direction that a practical theology of praxis might take. The first of these articles is "The Foundations of Practical Theology" published in 1983 and originally delivered in 1981 as a lecture to a conference on practical theology at the Divinity School of the University of Chicago. This article provides a basic heuristic schema for practical theology as a public theology. In it Tracy suggests that the first task for any practical theology is "to clarify the theories with which practical theologians enter the realm of praxis."[20] He rejects two common models of practical theology. The first model simply applies theological theories worked out elsewhere and ends up leaving theological theory unaffected by praxis. The second model merely negates theory and affirms the primacy of praxis forgetting that "all praxis, like experience, is in fact theory-laden."[21]

By way of introduction to practical theology, Tracy suggests that all theology including practical theology is about articulating mutually critical correlations of the meaning of the Christian fact and the meaning of the contemporary situation. The way we interpret the contemporary situation will in fact shape the kind of questions we ask and these "in turn will influence and be influenced by the symbols from

---

19. Ibid., 390.
20. Tracy, "Foundations"; see n. 1 above.
21. Ibid., 62.

Christianity selected to interpret the Christian vision relative to the question."[22] For example, one can choose the crisis of cognitive claims or the existence of alienation or the presence of massive suffering in the world as one's point of departure. Whatever starting point is adopted, however, recognition must be given to the pluralistic realities of the global situation.

Against this background Tracy addresses explicitly the issue of practical theology. He overviews the Aristotelian distinction between *theoria, praxis,* and *techne,* to conclude that while the Aristotelian tradition is important it cannot be fully retrieved today without taking account of the Hegelian and Marxist tradition on praxis. In the light of this he gives a programmatic description of practical theology as "the mutually critical correlation of the interpreted theory and praxis of the Christian fact and the interpreted theory and praxis of the contemporary situation."[23] Ultimately, the working out of practical theology must become a collaborative exercise involving at least four steps: (1) the development of models of human transformation informed by the human sciences including theology; (2) the analysis of public claims to human transformation; (3) the employment of a critical hermeneutics in working out steps 1 and 2; and finally (4) the mutually critical correlation of the secular model of praxis with faith models of praxis. This latter step should be informed by a faith working through justice and love, and guided by an eschatological hope.[24]

A second article entitled "Practical Theology in the Situation of Global Pluralism" was published in 1987.[25] In this second article Tracy acknowledges that practical theology grows more important and more difficult year by year, and he reflects upon three different possibilities concerning the nature of the correlation between the Christian fact and the contemporary situation. Sometimes a practical identity can be seen to obtain between the two interpretations; at other times the correlation is one of similarity in difference (i.e., analogical); and at still other times the correlation may be one of nonidentity between the interpretations, as, for example, in political, liberation, and feminist theologies.

In the normal course of events practical theology will direct itself to local needs and local communities. At the same time, however, practical theology must take account also of the global situation because of the relationship that obtains between the local and the global. "Some dialectic of the local and the global, therefore, presses upon all practical

22. Ibid., 65.
23. Ibid., 76.
24. Ibid., 76–78.
25. See n. 3 above.

theology."26 Tracy proposes three global issues that should be taken on board by practical theology, namely, interreligious dialogue, the ecological crisis, and the nuclear threat. In addition to these three critical issues, practical theology should also include a more comprehensive understanding of nature and the cosmos as part of its interpretation of the contemporary situation. Shifts in the interpretation of the world situation have occurred which work to relativize the issue of cognitive claims.27 These shifts focus on the crisis of Western modernity itself and the emerging global pluralism. Therefore, the move to include other religions as part of the conversation that might take place in practical theology must embrace the praxis concerns which impinge on all religions in all situations, the "ethical-political-religious concerns (especially for justice) and also the religious *praxis* traditions of spirituality and piety."28 One example of such a praxis concern is the existence of massive global suffering, which in fact interrupts every conversation among religions; another is the ecological crisis facing humanity. The impending ecological destruction is so clear that no serious concern with historical justice can ignore it. The third praxis concern is the nuclear threat.

If these praxis concerns are going to influence the conversation in practical theology, then more attention needs to be given to cosmological questions, which concern not only the origin and nature of the world but also the destiny of individuals and of history as inextricably bound up with the destiny of the cosmos. Such a turn to cosmology has been made possible in recent times as a result of the changes that have taken place concerning the method and content of both science and theology. The old warfare between science and theology has come to an end, and a new era of dialogue—indeed of mutually critical correlations—between science and theology has commenced. Further, there is growing unease with the exclusively anthropocentric emphasis of much contemporary theology. It is becoming increasingly clear that we cannot fully understand the meaning of redemption without reference to creation and that a theology of history must include some relationship to nature. Equally, the categories of "God" and "self" cannot be adequately grasped without some reference to the cosmos. If political and liberation theologies are to be faithful to their own demands of theory and praxis, they must take more account of these cosmological issues. This means, in effect, rediscovering the place of nature in

---

26. Tracy, "Practical Theology," 140.
27. Ibid., 145.
28. Ibid., 153 n. 14.

history, relocating redemption in the context of creation, and recovering the meaning of God and self in relation to the cosmos.²⁹

Ongoing Dialogue concerning Praxis in *Plurality and Ambiguity*

In a book entitled *Plurality and Ambiguity: Hermeneutics, Religion and Hope* (1987), Tracy takes up the question of hermeneutics once again and elaborates an understanding of interpretation on the model of a conversation. The human act of interpretation involves three realities: a "phenomenon to be interpreted, someone interpreting that phenomenon and some interaction between these first two realities."³⁰ The interaction between the phenomenon to be interpreted—be it law, action, ritual, symbol, text, or events—and the person interpreting is best understood along the lines of a conversation. The model of interpretation as a conversation enables Tracy to deal effectively with the ever-increasing problems of pluralism and ambiguity, difference and otherness.

The basic strategy for coping with these issues is in continuity with his book *The Analogical Imagination*. He sees conversation as "that unnerving place where one is willing to risk all one's present self-understanding by facing the claims to attention of the other."³¹ A fundamental characteristic of good conversation is the ability to take seriously the existence of different interruptions. These interruptions include things like the radical plurality disclosed in postmodern studies of language and the "terror of history"³² which is so pervasive in the late twentieth century. Other interruptions come from voices protesting against the systemic "isms" surrounding this century: "sexism, racism, classism, elitism, cultural parochialism." Within these multiple conversations it is religion that provides the ground for resistance and hope, resistance "to more of the same," and hope in the future. Ultimately, it is belief in God that makes "all the difference for a life of resistance, hope, and action."³³

In the midst of this fast-moving book, Tracy's concern with praxis emerges as a kind of subplot running through the discussions of hermeneutics. Indeed, the tension between hermeneutics and praxis surfaces

---

29. Ibid., 146–52.
30. D. Tracy, *Plurality and Ambiguity: Hermeneutics, Religion, Hope* (San Francisco: Harper & Row, 1987) 10.
31. Ibid., 93.
32. Ibid., IX.
33. Ibid., 68, 84, 110.

from time to time, and in a few strikingly honest conversations we find Tracy critiquing Tracy, as it were.

Tracy again insists that every act of interpretation involves a moment of practical application: "without some *applicatio,* there is no real hermeneutical *intelligentia* or *explicatio.* In this sense the contemporary hermeneutical concern with praxis is entirely correct."[34] At the same time he cautions that this concern with praxis must not become an excuse for abandoning the intellectual demands of theory or the fuller complexities of interpretation.[35] Within the context of this emerging tension between hermeneutics and praxis he acknowledges his own preference for a theology of the interpretation of the religious classic. He admits that "our seeming inability to respond to other than classic examples is clearly an ambiguous phenomenon"[36] that needs to be checked against everyday examples of living a religious life. The theologian must be open to other forms of hermeneutics that can illuminate his task of interpretation, especially the hermeneutics of retrieval and suspicion, of explanation and critical theory. In particular he instances those theologies which seek to unify the mystical and the political as well as the liberation theologies of the basic communities of the Third World as important correctives to academic theology. These theologies, with their practical hermeneutics, have important lessons for academic theology. They help to overcome the claim that only a scholarly elite can interpret religious classics. They remind us that the ultimate reality revealed in the Judeo-Christian classics has a preference for the poor, the oppressed, and the marginalized. In the light of this Tracy argues that "the readings of the oppressed—however different and even uncivil by some tired standards of what can count as civil discourse—must be heard and heard first."[37] These are readings that "the rest of us need most to hear."[38]

However, the imperative to learn to listen to the conflictual readings of the oppressed is only a first lesson, and as such it must be followed by some form of "active solidarity."[39] Only in this way will we be able to hear the voices of the Third World and to understand their demands for transformation that go beyond what those of us in the First World have ever imagined.[40] Tracy concludes by emphasizing that what is

34. Ibid., 101.
35. Ibid., 101, 10, 107.
36. Ibid., 96.
37. Ibid., 104.
38. Ibid.
39. Ibid., 106.
40. Ibid., 107.

really needed in theology today is the coming together of the mystical and the political, of hermeneutical theology and liberation theology into a new conversation and solidarity. "What conversation is to the life of understanding, solidarity is to the life of action."[41]

This summary of the development of Tracy's thought on praxis indicates something of its range, depth, and subtlety, its openness to and appreciation of liberation theology, and its increasing concern to insert the emerging theologies of praxis into the wider concerns of theology. At times, Tracy raises questions about the agenda of liberal, modern, and academic theology in terms that are often more impressive than the objections raised by liberation theology itself. At all times he shows a deep awareness of the contribution of liberation theology to the rest of theology. To this extent it seems unreasonable and ungenerous to polarize Tracy's theology against that of liberation theology or to suggest that Tracy's method and that of liberation theology are somehow mutually exclusive.[42] Such a reading of Tracy fails to take account of his emphasis on the importance of listening to interruptions in the conversation of theology, the call to hear the voices of the poor and to hear them first, the demand for active solidarity, the need to recognize both transformative and disclosure models of truth, his critique of the "unconscious elitism" of the academy in its readings of texts and situations,[43] his relativizing of the importance of the crisis of cognitive claims, his admission of the singular importance of ethical-political-religious questions relating to global suffering, and finally his questioning of the unexamined assumption of the power of rhetorical persuasion.

Nevertheless there are questions that must be raised which go beyond Tracy's clear appreciation of the fruits of liberation theology with regard to the specific area of praxis and method. Is Tracy's talk about praxis the same as the praxis talk of liberation theology? Do Tracy and liberation theology share the same point of departure? Are Tracy and liberation theology operating out of the same set of assumptions and presuppositions concerning our interpretation of the contemporary situation? An initial discussion of these questions requires a brief account of liberation theology's understanding of praxis.

---

41. Ibid., 113.
42. Traces of this negative evaluation can be found in R. Chopp's otherwise challenging and important article "Practical Theology and Liberation" in *Formation and Reflection: The Promise of Practical Theology*, ed. L. S. Mudge and J. N. Poling (Philadelphia: Fortress, 1987), and in the important book by A. Hennelly, *Theology for a Liberating Church: The New Praxis of Freedom* (Washington, DC: Georgetown University Press, 1989) chap. 3.
43. Tracy, *Plurality*, 104–5.

The Praxis of Liberation Theology according to Gustavo Gutierrez

In seeking to understand the role and meaning of praxis in liberation theology we will confine ourselves to the tried and tested writings of Gustavo Gutierrez, paying particular attention to the question of theological method since that is one of the primary issues in the debate concerning hermeneutics and praxis. In his now classical work *A Theology of Liberation*, Gutierrez describes theology "as a critical reflection on praxis in the light of the Word."[44] Theology therefore assumes the existence of a prior commitment to praxis and comes only after praxis. The type of praxis in question is a liberating praxis of solidarity with the poor. The source of this praxis is the prereflective, self-involving activity of faith. A number of points need to be made more clear about these deceptively simple statements of Gutierrez.

Theology, within this perspective, "comes only after involvement"[45] and as such is a "second step" coming "at sundown."[46] Theology is a critical reflection that takes place "from within, and upon historical praxis."[47] The process of critical reflection draws on the resources of scripture and tradition as well as social analysis in addressing the economic, social, and political praxis of the church and society. What is distinctive here, perhaps even controversial, about liberation theology is its point of departure. Liberation theology claims that the prior commitment to praxis comes from faith and that this faith is ultimately something which is existentially self-involving and practical. The faith in question, therefore, is not primarily belief in a set of theoretical statements that seek verification in practice; instead, the faith in question is a prereflective practical commitment to those who are exploited. Thus, the praxis of personal involvement is an internal demand of faith, and theology gives objective expression to this praxis of faith by way of critical reflection. It is this particular point of departure that enables Gutierrez to say that liberation theology "is not so much a new theme for reflection as a new way to do theology."[48] Instead of starting from a universal theoretical position, liberation theology grows out of a critical reflection from within and upon a particular praxis of liberation

---

44. G. Gutierrez, *A Theology of Liberation* (Maryknoll, NY: Orbis Books, 1973) 13.
45. G. Gutierrez, "Faith as Freedom: Solidarity with the Alienated and Confidence in the Future," in *Living with Change, Experience, Faith*, ed. F. A. Eigo (Villanova, PA: Villanova University Press, 1976) 42.
46. Gutierrez, *Theology of Liberation*, 11.
47. G. Gutierrez, "Liberation *Praxis* and Christian Faith," in *The Power of the Poor in History* (Maryknoll, NY: Orbis Books, 1983) 60.
48. Gutierrez, *Theology of Liberation*, 11–16.

internal to faith itself. In this way, liberation theology seeks to make the particular praxis of faith "more self-critical, and hence more comprehensive and radical."[49] Its starting point, therefore, is the particularity of the praxis of faith in a concrete historical situation. From this perspective, theology must give up its claim to having at its disposal timeless, disembodied, universal truths available for application to particular questions and historical situations. Instead it must move from the particularity of historical and liberating praxis to the expression of the universal significance of that particular praxis of liberation. We cannot bypass the mediating function of the particular praxis of faith into some realm of pure theory.

For Gutierrez, the turn to praxis in theology requires "breaking with . . . old ways of thinking and knowing."[50] The praxis of liberation "is . . . the matrix of all authentic knowledge."[51] In effect, "knowledge is bound up with transformation. We come to know history . . . in the process of transforming it and ourselves."[52] This new way of knowing in liberation theology is often referred to as "the epistemological break."[53] Our rough sketch of the place and role of praxis in liberation theology hardly does justice to the rich writings of Gustavo Gutierrez or indeed to the ever-expanding output of theological material from the Third World. It does, however, provide a context for some initial dialogue between Tracy's theological enterprise and the project of liberation theology, more specifically for a conversation between hermeneutical theology and praxis theology.

Tracy and the Praxis of Liberation Theology in Conversation

It is within the more particular conversation about praxis that differences do begin to emerge between Tracy and liberation theology. These differences include questions about the meaning of the word praxis, the point of departure in theology for today, the epistemological break, and the interpretation of the contemporary situation.

---

49. G. Gutierrez, "Liberation Praxis and Christian Faith," in *Frontiers of Theology in Latin America*, ed. R. Gibellini (Maryknoll, NY: Orbis Books, 1979) 23; see also Gutierrez, *Theology of Liberation*, 13.
50. Gutierrez, "Liberation," in *Frontiers*, ed. Gibellini, 20.
51. Ibid., 19.
52. Ibid., 18–19.
53. Though this term is used more frequently by J. Sobrino, for example, in *The True Church and the Poor* (London: SCM, 1985) chap. 1, nevertheless it is also present philosophically in the writings of Gutierrez.

Concerning the elusive meaning of the word praxis, there do appear to be real differences between Tracy and liberation theology. These differences become particularly evident when Tracy talks about "the praxis of conversation," the "praxis of hermeneutics," and the "praxis of authentic intellectual development." In these instances, he is talking about praxis in at least two different senses. In some instances Tracy is referring to the intellectual activity that takes place in the interpreter as he/she converses with the text. In other instances he is talking about human activity as the outcome of a theory, that is, an activity that results from understanding and interpretation.[54] These two modes of praxis are quite different from the praxis of liberation theology; these two modes of praxis seem to be informed by and large by the classical praxis-tradition of Aristotle. On the other hand, when liberation theology talks about praxis, it is talking about the activity of individuals who are committed from within a basic Christian community to the alleviation of a particular injustice through a process of transformation. This praxis is reactive to the existence of distortions and exploitations supported by the status quo. This understanding of praxis in liberation theology is informed mainly by some version of the Marxist critical theory tradition. Clearly we are dealing here with two different meanings for the word praxis and two different traditions informing these meanings. Furthermore, the praxis that Tracy talks about is the outcome of second-order reflection, whereas the praxis of liberation theology is, initially at least, bound up intrinsically with a first-order prereflective commitment of solidarity in faith with the poor. This first point of difference between Tracy and liberation theology leads us directly to the second, namely, the point of departure for theology.

For Tracy the point of departure for practical theology is principally the *theoria* derived both from fundamental theology through philosophical reflection on the religious dimension of common human experience and from systematic theology through the hermeneutics of classical religious texts. For liberation theology the point of departure is the personal commitment of people on the ground to social and political efforts to transform the status quo of suffering, injustice, and poverty. But what is the source of this commitment to the praxis of solidarity for liberation? Is it not as Tracy would ask, like all praxis, theory-laden and therefore the outcome of some form of reflective interpretation? Liberation theology would reply that the source of this praxis of solidarity is the prereflective, intuitive commitment of faith to liberation. It is perhaps here more than anywhere else that the difference between Tracy and liberation theology emerges.

54. See Tracy, *Plurality*, 101.

According to liberation theology there are, broadly speaking, two ways of doing theology. On the one hand, theology can, in the spirit of the Greek tradition, arise out of a sense of wonder and awe about the world as it is. This approach acknowledges the given order of the world and the organic harmony of society as part of the object for reflection in theology. On the other hand, theology can, in the spirit of liberation theology, arise out of a deep awareness that there is something intrinsically wrong with the way the world is and the way society is structured: there is a strong sense that things could be otherwise, and this generates an unease and a dissatisfaction with the way things are in the world and the way they are structured in society. Liberation theology is driven by a deep empathy and solidarity with the suffering of others which it knows prereflectively to be wrong and open to change. It is this response of a praxis of solidarity that involves liberation theology in a reflective process of analysis, interpretation, and transformation, with praxis sublating theory. This particular approach and point of departure need to be further elaborated because of their importance to liberation theology.

One such elaboration can be found in Edward Schillebeeckx, who captures the spirit of this different point of departure for liberation theology. Schillebeeckx frequently discusses what he calls the "negative experiences of contrast."[55] Our experience of the world is one that is full of contrast and contradictions. There are experiences of evil, suffering, and misfortune all around us, and equally there are experiences of goodness, joy, and meaningfulness. For Schillebeeckx "this experience [of contrast] is clearer and more evident than any 'knowledge' that philosophy and science can give us."[56] Further, "for most people this is not a thought at all, but an experience which they cannot escape."[57] As a result of this experience of contrast there is for many an "invincible human indignation at injustice and innocent suffering" in the world, and this in turn creates an openness to the possibility of another situation.[58] There is a reaction within the human spirit against evil, suffering, and exploitation which provokes commitment to a praxis of liberation.

In other words, this prereflective commitment to the praxis of liberation is something that precedes theological reflection, becomes the

---

55. E. Schillebeeckx, *For the Sake of the Gospel* (London: SCM, 1989) 46; see also idem, *God the Future of Man* (London: Sheed & Ward, 1969) 136, 154–55; idem, *Jesus: An Experiment in Christology* (London: Collins, 1979) 621–22.
56. Schillebeeckx, *For the Sake of the Gospel*, 46.
57. Ibid.
58. Ibid., 47.

object of theological reflection, and judges theological reflection. The stimulus to reflection in liberation theology does not come from theological theory but arises rather from a prereflective commitment to the praxis of liberation. This praxis of liberation both as the point of departure and as an ongoing reality becomes foundational for the whole of liberation theology. Liberation theology accords this importance to the praxis of liberation because of the historical, existential, and soteriological significance of this particular praxis.

The third point of difference between Tracy and liberation theology relating to praxis concerns their respective approaches to reality. Here it must be noted of course that there are no neutral approaches to or interpretations of the human situation. Tracy's interpretation of the human situation seems to be based primarily on a hermeneutics of goodwill vis-à-vis the social and political structure of the world as given. To be sure, he acknowledges the mounting need for interruption, suspicion, and critique within this understanding of society. Further, he clearly has a predilection for the extraordinary expressions of religion as found in the classical texts, and insists on the need to retrieve these through the model of interpretation as conversation in getting theology started. On the other hand, liberation theology, in virtue of its prereflective commitment to the praxis of liberation, sees society in terms of conflict. Its aim is the transformation of the given social and political structures, which it perceives to be unjust and sinful. In the end, liberation theology argues that conversation is not enough—even the conversation that includes the voices of the poor among its participants is not enough—because it is a conversation among those who are ultimately unequal and is therefore fraught with mistrust and suspicion. The removal of this mistrust and suspicion will only be gained by a liberating praxis of solidarity with those who are suffering and exploited. It is this praxis of liberation addressed to the poor in the first instance that will open the way to a genuine conversation.

A final difference between Tracy and liberation theology relating to praxis concerns the complex area of epistemology. For Tracy the primary source of knowledge and understanding is to be found in disclosures through conversation with the classical texts. For liberation theology, the actual experience of liberating praxis is the central source of knowledge and understanding. The experience of transforming unjust situations is regarded as a significant moment providing new knowledge and understanding for the shaping of theological theory. As we have seen, Tracy argues in favor of disclosure *and* transformative models of truth. Liberation theology opts, at least, for the reversal of this order, highlighting the primacy of "knowing by doing" over "knowing by reflecting."[59]

Conclusion

It remains to be seen whether these differences between Tracy and liberation theology are, to use an expression of Tracy, differences of conflict or differences of complementarity. Real openings exist in Tracy's theology to date for the critical adoption of the perspectives of liberation theology into his promised work on practical theology. These openings include his recognition that the theological landscape has been changed irretrievably by liberation theology,[60] his affirmation that the readings of the oppressed must be heard in the conversation of interpretation and "preferably heard first,"[61] and his discernment "that the major question in our situation is not the crisis of cognitive claims, but the social-ethical crisis of massive suffering and widespread oppression and alienation in an emerging global culture."[62] The incorporation of these principles into Tracy's proposed third volume on practical theology would have significant implications for the public profile of theology in the academy, church, and society. It would mean rearranging the relationships and primacies that presently obtain between fundamental, systematic, and practical theology. This should not be understood as a pitch for a new kind of imperialism in theology but rather a recognition of the apocalyptic signs of the times in which we live. Liberation theology itself is the first to admit that its task is "interim" and "transitional,"[63] and that the primary concerns of theology will shift with the human, political, and religious needs of individuals within history. However, given the massive existence of needless suffering and poverty in the world today, given the nuclear threat and what it symbolizes, and most of all given the emerging ecological crisis, it must be said that a theology which does not address these particular questions in terms of a liberating praxis as a point of

---

59. The suggestion that *praxis* is a primary source of knowledge and understanding is developed at greater length by D. Lane in *Foundations for a Social Theology: Praxis, Process and Salvation* (Dublin: Gill & Macmillan, 1984) 72–82 and in "Praxis" *New Catholic Encyclopedia*, vol. 23, Supplement 1978–88 (Washington, DC: Catholic University of America, 1989) 390–94.
60. D. Tracy, "Introduction," in *The Challenge of Liberation Theology: A First World Response*, ed. B. Mahan and L. Dale Richesin (Maryknoll, NY: Orbis Books, 1981) 1.
61. Tracy, *Plurality*, 104.
62. Tracy, *Analogical Imagination*, 78.
63. G. Gutierrez, *The Power of the Poor in History*, 20.

departure is in danger of simply protracting the existence of much theory without praxis and so much practice without theory within the academy, church, and society.

In the meantime, if liberation theology is to succeed, it too must take due account of David Tracy's outstanding contribution to the self-understanding of theology today. This will mean incorporating Tracy's sophisticated theory of hermeneutics in reference to the different forms of praxis, liberating and otherwise, operative within society and church. After all, it has been the relative neglect of hermeneutical attention by theology to the praxis of politics, economics, and modern science that is responsible in part for the global threats facing humanity today. It will also mean developing with greater theological rigor, as Tracy himself suggests, the epistemological implications of liberating praxis for the whole of theology, and giving more attention to the ecological crisis and its cosmological implications in the quest for justice, peace and the preservation of the earth in our world today. Attention by Tracy to the praxis method of liberation theology and consideration by liberation theology of the hermeneutical theology of Tracy are prospects that will yield fruit to both in the future.

3

BIBLICAL CRITICISM AND THEOLOGY: TOWARD A NEW BIBLICAL THEOLOGY

Werner G. Jeanrond

THE RECENT CONTRIBUTION of David Tracy to theological hermeneutics has helped countless theologians worldwide to rediscover the significance of hermeneutical thinking for their theological tasks and the benefit of participating in the global conversation on adequate methods of human understanding. Since Friedrich Schleiermacher reconnected theology and hermeneutics in a programmatic way nearly two centuries ago, no other theologian has advanced the understanding of the role of hermeneutics in theology as much as David Tracy.

In this article I propose to reconsider the relationship between biblical criticism and Christian theology and, with it, to show Tracy's decisive contribution to theological hermeneutics and the next step called for by his contribution. Recognizing the imperative under which his work places us is essential, for we are now at a juncture in history when once again both subdisciplines of Christian reflection—biblical criticism and Christian theology—may go their separate ways. It appears that hermeneutics, which originally emerged with the promise of bringing and keeping the two subdisciplines more closely together, may now promote a new divorce between both partners. How could that happen, and what can we do in order to avoid such a divorce?

I wish to examine these questions and make some suggestions toward a reconsideration of the function of hermeneutical thinking in Christian theology. I shall begin by discussing briefly some features of the development of modern hermeneutics. In the second section I shall review the importance of biblical criticism for the praxis of Christian faith. In the third and final section I shall examine the significance of David Tracy's and Friedrich Schleiermacher's contributions to our discussion of future options for the relationship between biblical and theological studies.

What Has Hermeneutics Done to Theology?

Early in the 1970s when I began my theological studies in Germany, my fellow students and I were very unhappy about the rigid division of labor in our theological faculties. In the biblical courses we learned how to master the texts of the scriptures philologically and historically, and in our theological courses we were taught how to understand the development of Christian theology and its current state. There was really no official connection between these disciplines, and professors who dared to cross the lines between them were considered traitors by some of their colleagues. Two centuries of hermeneutical thinking did not seem to have yet made a lasting impression on the organization of theological thinking and theological education—at least in some of the Roman Catholic faculties of theology. Thus, when we then came into contact with literary criticism, philosophical hermeneutics, and Friedrich Schleiermacher's theological method, we students felt that we had found the keys that would open the doors to a renewal of theological labor and to a more unified approach to the understanding of our particular religious tradition and its changing context. However, two decades later I must conclude that the hermeneutical discussion in theology has also yielded new problems and divisions.

The Hermeneutical Imperative

There can be no doubt that we theologians have been enormously enriched by participating in the debate on adequate methods of text interpretation. The recognition of the dialectical relationship between reader and text, the examination of textual genres of communication and their specific claims to attention, the rediscovery of Schleiermacher's grammatical and psychological modes of interpretation, the commitment to ideology critique, the awareness of a host of distorting factors in the process of reading, and the insights into our logocentric approach to texts and readers have challenged all interpreters to become more careful about their claims and to be more self-critical altogether. It would seem that the conditions of adequate reading of biblical, doctrinal, and other texts have now been so thoroughly examined that Christian theologians could return to their other tasks, which include interpreting the Christian tradition anew for the faith praxis of new generations. Methodologically, theologians are now more realistic about and sufficiently aware of their interpretative possibilities and limitations. Theologians such as Bultmann, Ebeling, and Ogden have celebrated this triumph of hermeneutics, and more recently Schillebeeckx, Geffré, Metz, Tracy, and Küng have begun to explore the features of a new community of theological interpreters, who in turn would want to participate in the worldwide attempt at understanding one's own and anybody else's religious tradition.[1] Finally, the vision of a global understanding has emerged as the new hermeneutical paradise at the horizon of our methodological reflection. Not only can biblical scholars and theologians now work together; in fact, all well-meaning thinkers in the entire world have been encouraged to join the mutually critical effort of understanding one another and everybody's traditions.

Surely, hermeneutics has made the world better by preparing the ground for this worldwide conversation on the nature, the past and the future of our universe. To be sure, structuralist and poststructuralist thinking has not lastingly disturbed this picture. Rather, the discovery that the assumed center of the universe — understood either in terms of God or the interpreter himself or herself — was an illusion cherished uncritically by former generations of interpreters has enforced our conviction today that only a mutual and a mutually critical understanding of the many different and possibly even radically different centers can bring us more closely together. Radical pluralism thus not only is not an argument against hermeneutics but leads to an even stronger demand for more hermeneutics. The world, it seems, has turned hermeneutical. Its new moral maxim reads: Understand yourself and the other in such a way that the method of your understanding could be adopted by everybody as the universal method of understanding everything and everybody.

This hermeneutical imperative has certainly many attractive features: It promises a more successful interfaith dialogue;[2] it invites all interpretative efforts to join forces; it represents a maturer version of existentialist thinking insofar as it demands the transcendence of a purely individualist approach both to particular texts and traditions and to the universe as a whole; and, generally speaking, it incorporates the lasting concerns of all kinds of critical movements. Therefore, no one could seriously question the fine achievements of the hermeneutical tradition. Undoubtedly many theologians today know better what it means to understand, and they have made major advances in terms of actually

---

1. See my discussion of hermeneutics in *Theological Hermeneutics: Development and Significance* (New York: Crossroad, 1991).
2. See David Tracy's most recent book *Dialogue with the Other: The Inter-Religious Dialogue* (Louvain: Peeters, 1990).

"understanding" their respective traditions and even aspects of other traditions.

But is there not also a darker side to the present concern with hermeneutics in theology? Does not the concentrated effort at *understanding* everything lead to an oversubscription to certain reflective activities at the expense of others? Could it not be that the shift toward hermeneutics has led a number of theologians anew into the narrow confines of German idealism? By this charge I do not mean that Germans necessarily exercise a bad influence on theology, nor do I wish to suggest that the German idealist tradition is a bad development *in toto*. All I wish to say is that the overemphasis in that tradition on *understanding* may lead theologians away from some of their other important tasks.

Theology aims not only at understanding. As a speculative discipline—to use Schleiermacher's term—it also includes a reflection on the principles and strategies of Christian action in this world. Thus, what seems to be required most urgently is a sharper discussion of how these two tasks are related. In other words, how do the theory and praxis of reading the texts of our tradition and the theory and praxis of political action in this universe relate to each other in Christian theology? And how do biblical criticism and constructive theology relate to each other in terms of promoting such a theory of adequate Christian praxis?[3] That these are urgent questions for contemporary theology will be clear when we consider for a moment what has happened in some of the less hermeneutically minded areas of the present theological geography.

The Call for Praxis and the Rise of Fundamentalism

Latin American liberation theologians are not the only ones to call for a new approach both to the Bible and to theology in general. In view of the massive social and economic problems that people in the southern hemisphere have been facing for a long time, the traditional strands and methods of European and North American Christian theology have come under attack. The gap between a theology that understands all but does not promote concrete liberating action, on the one hand, and the more or less spontaneous awareness of Christians that the God of Israel

---

3. Of course, the biblical texts are and can be studied outside the framework of a theological approach. But Christian theology cannot fulfill its tasks without studying the scriptures.

and of Jesus Christ is a God who is involved in their daily struggles against poverty, exploitation, oppression, and the various misuses of power, on the other, has grown so great that traditional European and North American theologies have lost most of their credibility in these parts of the world. A powerful exception is Dietrich Bonhoeffer's political action and the surviving fragments of his theological reflection on political action in the world, which have contributed to the emergence of political theologies in the first and the third worlds. The arrival of hermeneutics in our theological faculties has, of course, further encouraged the discovery of systematic distortions in communication, the often hidden interests in the process of understanding, and the particular ideologies operative in our Christian discourse (biblical and postbiblical). But by stressing the need for proper methods of understanding, the hermeneutical concern has at times overshadowed the practical concern and has, as a result, mostly unconsciously led to the widespread illusion that once a phenomenon of the biblical tradition or any other literary tradition is understood, the intellectual goal has been achieved. Thus, one other aspect of speculative theology, namely, the reflection on possible responses to the reconstructed meanings of the biblical texts or any other literary text, has been pushed into the background, and the constructive or political task of theology has been neglected or left to those forces which so far have not undergone any form of hermeneutical purification.

While reader-response criticism in the northern hemisphere has been concerned with the theoretical intricacies of reading texts, quite a different kind of reader-response praxis has emerged with regard to the biblical texts in all parts of the world, a phenomenon described in a rather wholesale fashion by the term "fundamentalism." While we biblical hermeneuts strive to know all about understanding, our fundamentalist neighbors have responded already to the biblical texts in their own pragmatic, though uncritical, way. This split between the critical insights of hermeneutically sophisticated theologians into their literary tradition and the uncritical application of biblical texts by a rapidly increasing number of Christian readers of the scriptures shows striking similarities to the split between academic theology and popular piety in high and late medieval Europe. Then, too, large sections of the Christian population cultivated their own popular versions of supernatural piety while theologians established more and more refined methods of theological thinking in and for the academy. However, then, unlike today, most of those Christians were illiterate and therefore did not have the means of making constructive and critical use of the biblical texts themselves for their spiritual challenge and journey. Today, although mostly literate, the vast majority of Christians are left with their uncritical views of biblical and other texts while we theologians concentrate on the foundations of critical thinking and further discuss the opportunities and limitations of human understanding and their implications for biblical criticism. What we have been neglecting more and more is the creative task of constructing theological programs in which our best critical insights into the meaning of the scriptures are put to use for the faith praxis of contemporary Christians and their church communities.

Biblical Criticism, Theology, and Christian Praxis

It seems that what we need urgently in theology today is a more integrated method of theological reflection in which our insights both into the biblical texts and into the process of reading are mediated by our search for principles and strategies of political action. Of course, these interests of a political theology are not the only legitimate interests for a reading of the scriptures, but they are essential for a Christian theology that approaches the scriptures as one of its sources for the development of programs for the transformation of the world. And the great global conversation advocated by hermeneutically minded theologians does present a suitable context for the genuinely pluralistic discussion of such political programs. In fact, such a material discussion of theological programs for political action will further enhance the dignity of the Christian contribution to the global conversation insofar as now not only epistemological and methodological issues but also political issues are debated.

Let us turn now more concretely to the relationship between biblical criticism and theology. How can the insights of recent biblical criticism inform theological thinking, and how can the reflection on theological methods influence biblical criticism? I wish to approach this twofold question by examining briefly a number of related proposals.

In response to the later work of Martin Heidegger and to Rudolf Bultmann's use of the earlier Heidegger's hermeneutical considerations, a number of theologians such as Gerhard Ebeling and the late Ernst Fuchs have undertaken hermeneutical reflection in theology. However, their interest in hermeneutics consisted in the hope that it would help contemporary theology to return critically to the Reformers' theology of the Word. According to Ebeling, interpretation is called for whenever the normal function of the Word is disturbed, but he hastens to qualify this claim: "The aim of such interpretation cannot, however, be anything other than the removal of the obstacle which prevents the word from mediating understanding by itself."4 Thus, for him the task of hermeneutical theology is to make human beings more aware of the self-manifestation of the Word of God in the scriptures. The goal is, as Ernst Fuchs put it, a hermeneutics of agreement (*eine Hermeneutik des Einverständnisses*).5 Hence, hermeneutics functions here as the tool to renew the older Protestant tradition. Seen in the context of the German idealist notion of *Bildung*, what this kind of theological hermeneutics achieves is education for a discovery of the Word in the Bible (and only there) and a reflection on the means of corresponding to this Word.

One of the problems with this kind of understanding of hermeneutics is that it threatens to automatize the process of understanding. It reduces it to an almost technical process of discovering that which has always been assumed to be there in the first place. Hans-Georg Gadamer's philosophical hermeneutics of tradition suffers from a similar reductionism. Both he and Ebeling know very well what they want to find: Gadamer wishes to rediscover the Greek tradition of truth reflection and to reestablish its authority, and Ebeling wishes to approach the Bible in such a way that the Reformers' Word-of-God theology receives a renewed authority. Both want us to enter their respective tradition and to fuse with its authoritative horizon.

Over against such automatized versions of hermeneutical application, it would be of great benefit for contemporary theology to subscribe to a more open-ended search for the meaning of the biblical texts. Both the host of approaches to the Bible developed over the last two centuries and the great number of general theories of reading offer, of course, a very confusing picture, but they also promise a more original discovery of the meaning of biblical and other texts than the one promoted by either Gadamer or Ebeling.

What the literary study of the biblical texts, for instance, has achieved is the treatment of each individual book of the Bible as a *text*, that is, as an interpreted composition and not just as a sum of quotes from which one might select verses. The newly rediscovered text may be studied in terms of how it refers back to its particular and never interest-free history of formation, a method developed from the older approach to the Bible by historical-critical exegetes. The text can also be examined in terms of what imaginative possibilities of living it entails. Paul Ricoeur has advocated such a perspective. It is a welcome result of the literary reading of the Bible that it has freed us *from* an overemphasis on historiography and *for* an appreciation of whether the text and its

---

4. Gerhard Ebeling, "God and Word," in *Hermeneutical Inquiry*, vol. 1, *The Interpretation of Texts*, ed. David Klemm (Atlanta: Scholars Press, 1986) 219.
5. Ernst Fuchs, *Hermeneutik* (2nd ed.; Bad Cannstadt: Müllerschön, 1958) 136.

particular history have actually something to say to us today. Thus, we may ask anew how we could make good and critical use of these existential impulses which the text may have to offer to us today. In other words, what the literary reading of the biblical texts has made possible again is the enterprise of a biblical theology, not one that knows what it seeks, as in the case of Ebeling, but one that genuinely seeks for new and possibly better ways of understanding God and for new and possibly better ways of living in God's presence and shaping our lives accordingly.

In the preface to the second edition of his commentary on Paul's Epistle to the Romans, Karl Barth complained that the historical-critical exegetes were not critical enough, because they did not see what was actually at stake in the biblical texts.[6] While I agree with this statement, I disagree with Barth's own subsequent method of developing a biblical theology. Although he named his dogmatics "Church Dogmatics" and thus pointed to the social context of his theological reflection, he never advanced to theological reflection on the biblical text which was open to a mutually critical relationship with any other tradition or movement. Barth knew what he thought of the world and of all intellectual exercises that were concerned with the world— namely, not much. Therefore, he was also unable to provide theological insights into the possibility of a theology of resistance when the Nazi machinery took charge of Germany. While he personally opposed the Nazis very strongly, his theology was unable to offer theological criteria for political action in general and resistance to the Nazis in particular because it had not examined the biblical texts and the texts of the church tradition or indeed the current methods of reading these texts either in terms of how they might have fostered fascist thinking themselves or in terms of how they offered critical and constructive possibilities for contributing to a transformation of the world. In conclusion, then, Barth offered yet another variety of biblical criticism where the boundaries of biblical reading were fixed before the act of reading could begin.

David Tracy, my final example, is committed to the open-ended process of reading the biblical texts and of conversing about adequate methods of reading. He has taken account of all of the different approaches to hermeneutics in general and to biblical criticism in particular and attempted to overcome the dogmatisms lurking in all of these approaches to the text. He does not want to avoid the conflict of interpretations, and he encourages us to tackle the problems of the plurality and ambiguity in all texts and in all of our interpretative efforts. But his reflections remain at times within the confines of

---

6. Karl Barth, *Der Römerbrief* (Zurich: Theologischer Verlag, 1978) xii.

understanding with the occasional reference to liberating action or political programs. He does admit that it "is true that the point is not to interpret the world but to change it. But we will change too little, and that probably too late, if we do not at the same time change our understanding of what we mean when we so easily claim to interpret the world."[7] Although I agree with this statement, I think that we should press on and link in a dialectical fashion the interpretation of both our classical texts and our views of the universe with our reflection on principles and strategies of action.

Toward a New Biblical Theology

I hope to have shown in this article that the future course of Christian theology depends on the particular level of integration between biblical criticism and constructive theological projects. The options available to us so far seem to be the following: (1) We could continue to develop theories of biblical interpretation without linking them to the need for programs of responsible action in the world and thus remain within the confines of the German idealist notion of *Bildung* by mere understanding. (2) We could ignore hermeneutics in the future in favor of following the call for praxis and just use the biblical texts as proof texts in a pragmatic way. (3) We could follow Barth and the representatives of the so-called New Hermeneutic such as Fuchs and Ebeling to a narrowly defined hermeneutics of agreement with the Word of God as mediated by a Reformation-style reading of the scriptures. Or (4) we could agree with the pluralistic project of interpretation as advocated by David Tracy, but link it now dialectically to the development of principles and strategies of Christian action in this world.

Tracy has, of course, addressed the relationship between theory and praxis, but for him praxis means historical action itself, for instance, "the event of a liberating praxis."[8] What we are looking for here is a mode of thinking that allows for a dialectical relationship between theories of biblical interpretation and theories of Christian action, that is, a speculative framework in which the different theoretical tasks of theology are united once again.

Friedrich Schleiermacher, the father of modern hermeneutics, does offer such a paradigm for a genuinely dialectical theology. Having

---

7. David Tracy, *Plurality and Ambiguity: Hermeneutics, Religion, Hope* (San Francisco: Harper & Row, 1987) 114.
8. David Tracy, *The Analogical Imagination: Christian Theology and the Culture of Pluralism* (New York: Crossroad, 1981) 398.

insisted in his *Speeches* that religion constitutes a dimension of human nature in its own right alongside metaphysics and morality, he nevertheless went on to stress their inseparable relationship. Religion, speculation, and praxis form the triadic foundation on which human projects can be adequately shaped.9 He thus contradicted both Kant's and Hegel's philosophical foundations of human action. Moreover, by defining dialectic as the reflection on the art of conversation,10 by establishing the social character of language,11 and by limiting understanding to nothing more than approximation,12 Schleiermacher (long before Lévinas and Ricoeur) had pointed to the other human being as the co-constitutive partner in all existential projects. Unfortunately, the way in which he overcame some of the legacy of German idealism had not been fully appreciated for a long time. Only recently have Schleiermacher's proposals received closer attention.13 For him education for understanding is not a goal in itself. Rather hermeneutics only makes sense as the other side of rhetoric, and both as subdisciplines of dialectic.14 Speaking and understanding are the two means of proper conversation about the projects of life. In his works on ethical questions Schleiermacher developed such concrete principles and strategies of political action, and both in his theological encyclopedia and in his *Glaubenslehre* he never lost sight of the ecclesial context of theology.15 In fact, he stressed that no doctrine of Christian faith makes sense outside the social context of the church, and that the definition of church is itself an ethical action.16

I am not arguing that we all ought to become Schleiermacherians in

---

9. Friedrich Schleiermacher, *On Religion: Speeches to Its Cultured Despisers*, trans. Richard Crouter (Cambridge: Cambridge University Press, 1988) 103: "Praxis is an art, speculation is a science, religion is sensibility and taste for the infinite."

10. Friedrich Schleiermacher, *Einleitung zur Dialektik (1833)*: "Dialektik ist Darlegung der Grundsätze für die kunstmäßige Gesprächführung im Gebiet des reinen Denkens." In F. D. E. Schleiermacher, *Dialektik (1814/15)—Einleitung zur Dialektik (1833)*, ed. Andreas Arndt (Philosophische Bibliothek 387; Hamburg: Felix Meiner, 1988) 117.

11. F. D. E. Schleiermacher, *Hermeneutik*, ed. Heinz Kimmerle (2nd ed.; Heidelberg: Winter, 1974) 34.

12. Ibid., 62–64.

13. See, e.g., Gunter Scholz, *Die Philosophie Schleiermachers* (Erträge der Forschung 217; Darmstadt: Wissenschaftliche Buchgesellschaft, 1984); and Wolfgang H. Pleger, *Schleiermachers Philosophie* (Berlin and New York: de Gruyter, 1988).

14. Schleiermacher, *Hermeneutik*, 76.

15. Friedrich Schleiermacher, *Kurze Darstellung des theologischen Studiums zum Behuf einleitender Vorlesungen*, ed. Heinrich Scholz (4th ed.; Darmstadt: Wissenschaftliche Buchgesellschaft, 1977) esp. §§ 3–7; and Friedrich Schleiermacher, *Der Christliche Glaube*, vol. 1, ed. Martin Redeker (7th ed.; Berlin: de Gruyter, 1960) §2.

16. Ibid., 12 (§2).

our theological pursuits, only that here we have one speculative approach to theology that links the theological task essentially to ethical concerns. Here "understanding" is appreciated as one, and only one, among the necessary tasks of Christian theology. Schleiermacher attempted to develop a theology in this framework. What is important for us here is not so much his particular theory of text interpretation, nor his own particular attempt at interpreting the biblical texts, but his insistence that all of these critical tasks constitute only parts of the larger theological exercise.

Although I agree in principle with Schleiermacher's approach, I would like to argue that biblical criticism ought to be seen as one essential task of theology that may be distinguished but never separated from the overall ethical (or political) concern of Christian theology. If we can say that the biblical texts offer narratives of human experiences with God and human reflection on the relationship between God and the world, and if our aim is to interpret these texts with a view to developing modes of communal existence in this world, then we are on our way toward a "new biblical theology." I insist on the adjective "new" in order to highlight that this form of biblical theology wants not only to understand the theology of the biblical texts but also to develop a practical theology in the light of what these texts have to say in terms of how humans could live more responsibly.

PART TWO

PLURALISM AND THE HERMENEUTICS OF RELIGION

4 CONVERSATION IN GETHSEMANE

Nicholas Lash

The Difficulty of Conversation

NO CONVERSATION is reported in the garden of Gethsemane—not, that is, until Judas arrives with the forces of law and order. God's Word, of course, continues to be uttered: Jesus acts, and suffers, and speaks. Jesus speaks but is not spoken to, even if, in Luke's version as it has come down to us, he is mysteriously "strengthened." Jesus addresses in agony the silence of his Father and in sadness the silence of his sleeping friends, who, even when awakened, "did not know what to answer him" (Luke 22:43; Mark 14:10).

David Tracy, whose discussion of "conversation" is among the best things in an excellent book, allows that "conversation is a rare phenomenon." He is at pains to keep in mind the horror of our times, that "strange mixture of great good and frightening evil ... of startling beauty and revolting cruelty, of partial emancipation and ever-subtler forms of entrapment," which, as he half admits, makes "ambiguity ... too mild a word" to characterize our circumstance. And the dialectic of enlightenment is admirably evoked in his insistence that "suffering, however repressed, eventually erupts to subvert our most basic modern belief: the belief that somehow we can think our way through once more."[1]

Yet, for all the elegance and sensitivity of his account, it risks too softly stating the paradox of our predicament. He knows, of course, that there can be no question of simply settling for, or juxtaposing, the fact, on the one hand, that conversation—real conversation, conducted in accordance with the "hard rules" he lays down for it—is so rare a

---

1. David Tracy, *Plurality and Ambiguity: Hermeneutics, Religion, Hope* (San Francisco: Harper & Row, 1987) 18, 70, 77. On the last point, see Nicholas Lash, *Easter in Ordinary: Reflections on Human Experience and the Knowledge of God* (London: SCM, 1988) 85–86, 280–85.

phenomenon as never, or hardly ever, actually to occur and, on the other, the *requirement* that such conversation be taken as the paradigm of noncoercive, nondominating, nondestructive social relationships.[2] It follows that, if we are neither to alleviate the bleakness in our description of the facts nor slacken the requirement, we must give some account of how these two positions may coherently be simultaneously affirmed.

In order to deal with this difficulty, Tracy construes Jürgen Habermas's "ideal speech situation" as counterfactual regulative ideal. Although "we never find ourselves in the ideal speech situation," the "regulative model is useful for sorting out the ambiguities of all actual communication."[3] Such language would suggest that in place of conversation we have some kind of muddle, confusion, or misunderstanding. We have these things, of course, in abundance, but what really renders conversation so rare and fragile an occurrence is the far darker and more deadly fact of sin. What we have, in place of conversation, are the deafness of self-interest and terror, the lies of "official spokesmen," the distorted apocalyptic of the new right, and, around and underneath all other voices, almost inaudible, the whimpering of dying children.

In this note, offered in gratitude for David Tracy's work (and in celebration of many excellent conversations that we have, in fact, enjoyed), I want to argue for a rather different reading of Habermas's intentions: a reading that concentrates on keeping in play the *tension* between the counterfactual and the possible, between tragedy and hope. Whether the resultant fine tuning is worth the candle is a question I shall consider at the end. For now, I willingly admit that I may be doing little more than issuing a warning against one possible *mis*reading of Tracy's text. He would, after all, agree with me that, where the relationships between ethics and eschatology are concerned, we neither simply live "as if" nor wait around until our dreams come true. In the light of Easter, we are given the possibility and hence have the duty, even in Gethsemane, of keeping conversation alive.

To "acknowledge that language is discourse" is, among other things, to acknowledge that understanding what someone says requires consideration of the circumstances in which that person says it.[4] This paper is being written during Holy Week 1989. The content of its

---

2. Some of these "hard rules" are specified in Tracy, *Plurality*, 19. In a note to this passage he admirably argues, against Jürgen Habermas, that "the model of conversation [is] more helpful for understanding human communication than the model of explicit argument" (p. 118).
3. See Tracy, *Plurality*, 26.
4. Ibid., 61.

production, therefore, is not merely that of sharply focused annual concentration on Gethsemane, Calvary, and the empty tomb, but also that of the *fatwa* pronounced from Teheran against Salman Rushdie on 14 February, of the latest attempt—by means of a "new oath" unilaterally and uncollegially imposed upon the universal church taking effect on 1 March—to pervert the criteria of Catholic orthodoxy into agreement with the officials of the Holy Office, and of the tenth anniversary of the accession of a government whose ruthless concentration of power and wealth has, by systematic manipulation of figures and descriptions, rendered the increasingly impoverished poor of Great Britain ever more invisible and inaudible. It is in *this* world, in which discourse is darkened by hegemonic monologues such as those of Khomeini and Ratzinger and Thatcher, that I read "When no question other than our own is allowed, then conversation is impossible."5 It is against *this* background that I offer the following observations on the status of that apparently impossible requirement, the "ideal speech situation" whose discourse would be true conversation.

The Ideal Speech Situation

The best place to begin is with Habermas's own characterization of the "ideal speech situation." Already in 1965, he claimed that all human speech necessarily presupposes a situation or state of affairs in which agreement is arrived at freely and without constraint, determined only by the force of the better argument. "Our first sentence," he said, "expresses unequivocally the intention of universal and unconstrained consensus." However, this state of affairs nowhere, in fact, obtains. "Only in an emancipated society," he went on, "would communication have developed into the non-authoritarian and universally practiced dialogue from which . . . our idea of true consensus [is] always implicitly derived. To this extent the truth of statements is based on anticipating the realization of the good life."6 Habermas described the ideal speech situation thus:

> neither an empirical phenomenon nor a mere construct, but rather an unavoidable supposition reciprocally made in discourse. This supposition can, but need not be, counter-factual; but even if it is made counterfactually, it is a fiction that is operatively effective in the process of communication. Therefore I prefer to speak of an anticipation of an ideal speech situation. . . .

5. Ibid., 18.
6. Jürgen Habermas, "Knowledge and Human Interests: A General Perspective," in *Knowledge and Human Interests* (London: Heinemann, 1972) 314.

[It is] not merely a regulative principle in Kant's sense; with the first step towards agreement in language we must always in fact make this supposition.... The anticipation of an ideal speech situation has ... the significance of a constitutive illusion which is at the same time the appearance of a form of life. Of course, we cannot know a priori whether that appearance is a mere delusion—however unavoidable the suppositions from which it springs—or whether the empirical conditions for the realization (even if only approximate) of the supposed form of life can practically be brought about.[7]

This notion of "a situation of absolutely uncoerced and unlimited discussion between completely free and equal human agents" became so central to Habermas's thought as to serve, according to Raymond Geuss, "as a transcendental criterion of truth, freedom and rationality."[8] It is therefore hardly surprising that it has received a great deal of attention from the commentators. However, before considering the most important and most puzzling feature of the account (the feature which Tracy's reading risks oversimplifying), there are three general criticisms of Habermas's thought that I wish simply to recall.

The first concerns his tendency to become "more Kantian than Marxian." "In some of his earliest essays," says Geuss, "Habermas follows Adorno and holds a contextualist view of reflection; then, some time in the mid 1960s, he seems to have been frightened by the spectre of relativism, and retreated into a kind of transcendentalism." A more benign explanation of the shift would be that, like several other thinkers in the Marxist tradition, he found it increasingly difficult (especially after 1968) to identify any social group that could plausibly be expected to act as the agent of revolutionary social change. "Critical theory," says McCarthy, "finds itself in a familiar embarrassment; there is no organized social movement whose interests it might seek to articulate."[9]

Whatever the reasons for the shift, it has served to heighten the rationalism implicit in his position, and this is the focus of a second cluster of criticisms. "Habermasian man," says Agnes Heller, has "no body, no feelings ... one gets the impression that the good life consists solely of rational communication." Similarly, Rüdiger Bubner accuses

---

7. J. Habermas, "Wahrheitstheorien," in *Wirklichkeit und Reflexion: Walter Schulz zum 60. Geburtstag*, ed. H. Fahrenback (Pfüllingen: Neske, 1973) 258–59. Translation quoted from Thomas McCarthy, *The Critical Theory of Jürgen Habermas* (London: Hutchinson, 1978) 310.

8. Raymond Geuss, *The Idea of a Critical Theory: Habermas and the Frankfurt School* (Cambridge: Cambridge University Press, 1981) 65, 66; cf. McCarthy, *Critical Theory*, 307–10.

9. McCarthy, *Critical Theory*, 380, 385; Geuss, *Idea of Critical Theory*, 64.

him of "compressing the entire spectrum of practical communication in society into the model of the seminar discussion." Again, Henning Ottmann: "The repression-free communication, some readers might be tempted to conclude, is only an ideal of communication for intellectuals."[10] Tracy's preference for "conversation" rather than "argument" makes much the same point.

The general form of Habermas's reply to such criticisms is that the notion of "communication free of domination" is purely *formal*: "it does not extend to the concrete shape of an exemplary life-form"; it "can count as a necessary condition for the 'good life,'" but no more. It is neither a description nor a prediction of what he calls "the historical articulation of a felicitous form of life."[11]

Marx has been criticized on the grounds that, although his account of the "prehistory" of humanity (that is to say, of human history before the definitive or final revolution) can be construed in tragic terms, the prospects that he entertained for *post*-revolutionary existence were infected with an unwarranted optimism which entailed an illegitimate overriding of the tragic dimension.[12] The third criticism of Habermas is that, in respect of the past as well as of the future, his account of human evolution, of human progress, comes dangerously near to similarly overriding the tragic. "No future," says Agnes Keller, "will give back the lives destroyed in their youth, no future can make us forget the horrors, the miseries, the bloodshed and the tears of the past and the present."[13]

Habermas agrees:

There remains a stain on the idea of a justice that is bought with the irrevocable injustice perpetrated on earlier generations. This stain cannot be

---

10. Agnes Heller, "Habermas and Marxism" in *Habermas: Critical Debates*, ed. John B. Thompson and David Held (London: Macmillan, 1982) 22; Rüdiger Bubner, "Habermas's Concept of Critical Theory," in *Habermas*, 52; Henning Ottmann, "Cognitive Interests and Self-Reflection," in *Habermas*, 96. A similar criticism is voiced by John Thompson: "it is difficult to see why subjects can be said genuinely to agree about something only when their agreement is induced by the force of better argument, as opposed, for example, to the feeling of compassion or the commitment to a common goal. . . . What Habermas's assumption of symmetry seems to neglect . . . is that the constraints which affect social life may operate in modes other than the restriction of access to speech-acts, for example by restricting access to weapons, wealth or esteem" ("Universal Pragmatics," in *Habermas*, 129). Anthony Giddens criticizes "the model of society which results" from the theory of communicative action on the grounds that it "seems to embody no account of *contradiction*, and to underplay the significance of *power* and *struggle* in social development" ("Labour and Interaction," in *Habermas*, 160).
11. Habermas, "A Reply to my Critics," in *Habermas*, ed. Thompson and Held, 228.
12. See, e.g., the closing chapters of my *A Matter of Hope: A Theologian's Reflections on the Thought of Karl Marx* (London: Darton, Longman & Todd, 1981).
13. Keller, "Habermas and Marxism," 40.

washed away; it can at most be forgotten. But this forgetting would have to leave behind traces of the repressed. The contradiction that is inherent in the idea of complete justice, owing to its in principle irredeemable universalism, cannot be dissolved.[14]

Nevertheless, he admits that "the concept of communicative rationality" (a concept in which, as we have seen, the notion of the ideal speech situation serves as criterion of truth, freedom, and rationality) "does contain a utopian perspective." We are, at last, getting close to the ambiguity at the heart of Habermas's position when we hear him go on to say: "Nothing makes me more nervous than the imputation . . . that the theory of communicative action . . . proposes, or at least suggests, a rationalistic utopian society. I do not regard the fully transparent society as an ideal, nor do I wish to suggest *any* other ideal—Marx was not the only one frightened by vestiges of utopian socialism."[15] If we bear in mind that "critical theory" claims, on account of its political (and hence practical) character, to possess emancipatory power, then the juxtaposition of this "nervousness" with the acknowledgment that the concept of communicative rationality contains "a utopian perspective" points to a dilemma that recurs in all forms of the Marxist tradition (and, as we shall see, elsewhere).

Utopian Prospect or Regulative Ideal?

One way of approaching this central paradox or ambiguity in Habermas's position is by noticing the idiosyncratic character of his use of the concept of "anticipation." We have already seen that the claim that the ideal speech situation is "anticipated" in all human speech is intended to remind us that it is neither, on the one hand, a described or predicted actual state of affairs nor, on the other, *merely* a "regulative principle."

Habermas seems to want it to be more than a regulative principle because the contention is that, in all of our conversation, we necessarily (if acting rationally) *strive* for the perhaps unattainable state of affairs which "appears" in our discourse and which our discourse presupposes. And he wants it to be less than an empirical phenomenon because, first, as he once put it (in a formulation he later modified): "no historical society coincides with the *form of life* that we anticipate in the *concept*

---

14. Habermas, "Reply to my Critics," 246–47.
15. Ibid., 227–28, 235. It is, I think, a pity that Habermas does not more clearly differentiate the senses of "utopian" which he (like Marx) employs: on Marx, see Lash, *A Matter of Hope*, 234–39.

of the ideal speech situation"¹⁶ and, second, because we are not in a position to predict the long-term future of the human race.

To "anticipate" the ideal speech situation, then, is at least implicitly to recognize such a situation to be a necessary condition of rational discourse and to act upon this recognition, while neither predicting that any such situation will, in fact, be realized, nor speculating as to the form that such realization could take.¹⁷ But (to be blunt) does it make sense to speak of "anticipating," of looking forward to, that which we have no good reason to expect? Is it not at best quixotic and at worst irresponsible to take as criterion of truth, freedom, and rationality the perhaps quite delusory "appearances" of an unrealizable "form of life"?

Habermas's critics and not uncritical admirers usually adopt one of three strategies for dealing with the difficulty. Thus, in the first place, the most straightforward solution is to suggest that, in this crucial matter of the *status* of the "ideal speech situation," Habermas is, unfortunately, confused. Bubner, for example, sees Habermas's position as marking simply the latest stage in the history of Marxist fusion (or confusion) of two meanings of the term *Kritik* in "classical German philosophy" (roughly: a Kantian and a left-Hegelian meaning). He therefore accuses Habermas of being "unwittingly affected by that very confusion of [*Wissenschaft*] and revolution which he sharp-sightedly criticizes in Marx."¹⁸

The other two strategies acquit Habermas of charges of confusion or incoherence by supposing him to be referring, in the last analysis, *either* to an expected outcome of existing states of affairs *or* to a merely regulative ideal. Thus, for example, according to Steven Lukes, Habermas "postulates the possibility of society reaching a stage of transparent self-reflection, among parties who are 'free and equal,'"¹⁹ while (on the

---

16. Jürgen Habermas and Niklas Luhmann, *Theorie der Gesellschaft oder Sozialtechnologie—Was leistet die Systemforschung?* (Frankfurt: Suhrkamp, 1971) 140–41. Quoting the passage a decade later, Habermas accepted the criticism that this formulation risks "short-circuiting ... the mediations between the ethics of discourse and the practice of life," as if we could "directly take from this ethic the standards for something like an ideal form of life" ("Reply to my Critics," 261–62).

17. "'Anticipate' does not mean 'predict' for Habermas.... A critical theory ... does not predict *that* the agents in the society will adopt and use the theory to understand themselves and transform their society, rather it ... asserts that these agents 'ought' to adopt and act on the critical theory where the 'ought' is the 'ought' of rationality" (Geuss, *Idea of a Critical Theory,* 57, cf. p. 66).

18. Bubner, "Habermas's Concept," 42, 56. Ottmann echoes both aspects of this criticism but speaks, more ironically, of "the convergence of the problems of a 'critique' which is supposed to be both a theory of knowledge in general and a critical liberation within a historical situation" ("Cognitive Interests," 84; cf. p. 79).

19. Steven Lukes, "Of Gods and Demons: Habermas and Practical Reason," in *Habermas,* ed. Thompson and Held, 134.

other side) the jumping-off point for the present paper was David Tracy's description of the ideal speech situation as a useful regulative model.

It is quite clear, however, from Habermas's texts, that he refuses to be helped off the horns of his dilemma. But, this being so, how is he to be acquitted of the charge of incoherence or confusion? The answer (in outline, echoing widely renewed interest in the primacy of practical reason) is to be sought in the recognition that the criteria of coherence are not reducible to that which can be rendered wholly perspicuous or transparent to "pure" reason. In order to put some flesh on that exceedingly skeletal remark, I next wish to appeal, more explicitly than I have done so far, to theological considerations.

The Character of Christian Hope

There is no better place to start than with consideration of the celebration of the Eucharist. Such celebration, properly performed, is not merely the distillate of Christian memory, experience, and hope,[20] but also the paradigm of extra-eucharistic or "secular" discourse and behavior. As parable of God's kingdom, and hence as paradigm of our duty, the Eucharist does indeed fulfill a regulative function, exhibiting criteria by which all *un*relationship, *un*brotherhood, all domination and division, may be judged.

The function of the Eucharist, in relation to God's promised kingdom, is not, however, *merely* regulative. As parable or "pledge" of "future glory," each celebration (in which, even now, something of gracefulness is given: "mens impletur gratia") "anticipates" the glory it proclaims. The "anticipation" of God's kingdom in each celebration, then, constitutes "the appearance of a form of life." But it is at just this point, apparently, that the analogies break down because most Christians would resist suggestions that the anticipation of God's kingdom in the celebration of the Eucharist—and in all that striving and struggle for relationship and redeemed community which is, in the Eucharist, paradigmatically dramatized—is merely fictional, that it has simply "the significance of a constitutive illusion."[21]

Suppose we said, however, that in the celebration of the Eucharist our true future in God finds fictional appearance. The point of this

---

20. The classic expression of this conviction remains that of the Latin liturgy's vesper antiphon for the feast of Corpus Christi: "O sacrum convivium, in quo Christus sumitur; recolitur memoria passionis ejus; mens impletur gratia; et futurae gloriae nobis pignus datur."

21. See the passage from Habermas quoted above, p. 54.

formulation would be twofold. On the one hand, it reaffirms the "more than merely regulative" function of the parables of the kingdom. Christian eschatology is not reducible to ethics. It declares, announces, celebrates the fact that, in God's time and way, "all shall be well and all shall be well and all manner of thing shall be well." On the other hand, it serves as a reminder that, in spite of all appearance to the contrary, eschatology is not at all a matter of speculation about, or attempted imaginative depiction of, our unknown future in God. Eschatology, as Karl Rahner tirelessly insisted, is not a preview of future events.[22]

Where Habermas's version of critical theory is concerned, we have noted his insistence that the notion of an ideal speech situation is purely formal and "does not extend to the concrete shape of an exemplary life-form."[23] Such purely formal discourse does, undoubtedly, also have its place in Christian theology's more philosophical districts. For the most part, however, the language of theology, like the language of liturgy and preaching and poetry, is rich with "material" texture in parable, narrative, and metaphor. We *do* paint pictures and tell stories of the kingdom, and it is important that we should. My suggestion that our true future in God finds, in such parables, *fictional* appearance is intended to remind us that not even the best and truest and most appropriate of the stories that we tell lifts so much as the smallest corner of what Newman called the curtain hung over our futurity.[24] We may, in the Spirit of the risen Christ, be given strength to stay awake, to remain attentive, but the darkness of Gethsemane remains the place of Christian hope, the context of all attempts at conversation, all "anticipations" in history of God's still future kingdom.

Coherence and Credibility

It is now time to return to the charge of incoherence or confusion. One form of this charge is to the effect that, in order for the "ideal speech situation" to serve as criterion of truth, freedom, and rationality

---

22. See Karl Rahner, "The Hermeneutics of Eschatological Assertions," in *Theological Investigations*, vol. 4, trans. Kevin Smyth (London: Darton, Longman & Todd, 1966) 334; "The Question of the Future," in *Theological Investigations*, vol. 12, trans. David Burke (London: Darton, Longman & Todd, 1974) 181–201. For some remarks of mine on how Julian of Norwich's announcement is and is not to be construed, see Nicholas Lash, "All Shall be Well: Christian and Marxist Hope," in *Theology on the Way to Emmaus* (London: SCM, 1986) 202–15.

23. Habermas, "A Reply to my Critics," 228.

24. See John Henry Newman, *Apologia Pro Vita Sua*, ed. and introduction by Martin J. Svaglic (Oxford: Clarendon Press, 1967) 217.

Habermas must suppose this nonexistent and perhaps unrealizable ideal to be, nevertheless, in some way directly accessible to our minds and imaginations. The price he pays for admitting this (so runs the charge) is to be guilty of ignoring "the mediations between the ethic of discourse and the practice of life," illusorily supposing that "one can directly take from this ethic the standards for something like an ideal form of life."25

Habermas has little difficulty in disposing of this version of the charge by pointing out that "the model of sickness and health" shows that it is perfectly possible to appeal to "standards for judging a form of life to be more or less misguided, distorted, unfortunate or alienated" without thereby supposing the operation of such standards to be a matter of "approximation to ideal limit values."26 There is no such thing as "perfect health," and all utopian dreaming to the contrary (a dreaming fostered by the fact that there is much money to be made from its advertisement) merely distracts us from attending effectively to the particular sicknesses of particular people and places and times. And, thus distracted, we do nothing for the healing of the world, but merely contribute to its deepening disease.

Christianity is, and has ever seen itself to be, in the business of healing. Jesus healed the sick, and the gospel proclaims the healing, whole-making, or "salvation" of the world. The gospel, however, does what no philosophy or social theory could have warrant to do: it proclaims the *absolute* healing of the world. Therefore, in times and places when the *Weltanschauung* is shaped by fantasies of "progress," of humanity's ever upward march toward some sunlit and utopian future, some unending day, Christians are especially vulnerable to the temptation of supposing that the work of our redemption is indeed a matter of "approximation to ideal limit values."

But this *is* a temptation, and it is to be resisted for just the reasons that Habermas resists its philosophical versions. The healing of humanity remains a permanent task, a task that requires, in each set of circumstances, *fresh diagnosis*. What we are given for this task is not some blueprint from which, bypassing the labor of diagnosis, we could "directly take . . . the standards for something like an ideal form of life." What we are given, in Christ, is, on the one hand, a *criterion* to be continually recovered through the labor of interpretation and, on the other, in that "sacrum convivium," the sustenance of hope.27

25. Habermas, "A Reply to my Critics," 261.
26. Ibid., 262.
27. On Jesus Christ as "criterion," see Karl Rahner, *Foundations of Christian Faith: An Introduction to the Idea of Christianity*, trans. William V. Dych (London: Darton, Longman & Todd, 1978) 157–58.

Habermas's holding of the *tension* between ethic and expectation is not, as I read it, either incoherent or confused. It is, however, bounded or determined by its status as philosophy, as reasoned proposal, as a serious and sensible attempt to indicate how we might make sense of things. Christianity's task, in relation to such proposals, is not to claim that we know extra facts about the future of the world of which philosophy is ignorant. It is, rather, our responsibility to *show*—by quality of life in dedication to the work of healing—and, as an aspect of that showing, to *say* (though, in our culture, finding the proper words for this and an appropriate register of discourse is far from easy) that hope-ful labor is worthwhile, permissible, sustainable, that what may *seem* mere travail, treadmill-fruitless, is in fact pregnant with Easter joy.

In the end, God heals absolutely. But we work in the meantime. The end is in God's hands, not ours. But *what* God absolutely heals is *everything*. Does this mean, then, that the "stain" of past irrevocable injustice can, after all, be "washed away"? It most certainly may *not* be "forgotten." Repression brings no true healing. Washing away the stain is not a matter of forgetfulness, but of baptism, of transformation, transfiguration—of making the scars even of the crucified in glory shine. We do not understand this, though we know it to be true. In that sense, being unable to render perspicuous to our imagination the "complete justice" that is our hope, we can agree with Habermas that the inherent contradiction cannot be resolved.

One expression of the contradiction is the acknowledgment that conversation is at once impossible and required of us. Better to sustain the paradox than slide either into despairing of the possibility of healing human speech or into the illusory supposition that healed speech, true conversation, is ever easy or lies within our grasp. If I read Habermas right, he stands closer to the general drift of Tracy's admirable reflections on the "ambiguity" of all our circumstances than the latter's brief and misleading remarks on "ideal speech conditions" would suggest.

We may be spoken to (as the disciples were). We may even be enabled to reply. "The rest," as Tracy says, "is prayer, observance, discipline. . . . Or the rest is silence."[28] And yet, in Gethsemane and on Calvary, the silence answering our cry utters, in fact, God's last transforming Word.

28. Tracy, *Plurality*, 114.

5
RHETORIC AND RELIGION: ARE THEY ESSENTIALLY WEDDED?

Wayne C. Booth

THAT RHETORIC AND RELIGION are somehow related has been obvious to everyone who has thought about it. In modern times, however, the most usual way of relating them has been as handmaiden to master: serious study of religion or theology or plain faith yields the truths that rhetoric then must propagate. Most divinity schools have courses in preaching in which students study and practice the techniques that are often called "rhetoric." Some even have full programs leading to degrees, but students in such programs are usually only those who plan to become ministers. Almost no programs include the serious and prolonged study of rhetoric, for all students, as an essential intellectual companion to the study of religion.

This divorce is curious, especially when viewed in the light of how opponents of religion have tended to lump the two so closely together as almost to make them identical: as if to say, "religion is nothing *but* empty rhetoric, *mere* rhetoric: the art of manipulating people to believe what the rhetor wants them to believe." Aggressive prophets of a scientistic world view have spent about equal energy attacking what they have seen as two equally shoddy manifestations of irrationality—religion and rhetoric, twin dark burdens of ignorance inherited from the pre-scientific past. Indeed, for such "scientismists,"[1] religious belief depended for its unfortunately prolonged survival precisely on the survival of fake forms of demonstration and proof, unscientific lines of

---

1. For fuller definitions of various notions of "scientism" and of alternative rhetorics, see my *Modern Dogma and the Rhetoric of Assent* (Chicago and London: University of Chicago Press, 1974), esp. chap. 1; and "The Idea of a *University*, as Seen by a Rhetorician," in *The Vocation of a Teacher* (Chicago: University of Chicago Press, 1978), chap. 19.

argument; now that we have scientific thought, they have argued, we can see that religion depended for its very life on mere rhetoric: wedded partners indeed.

Neither of these ways of tying rhetoric to religion—as handmaiden or as happily wedded offenders—can tempt anyone to inquire seriously into their deeper relations: *rhetoric,* seen not as a mere way of winning arguments but as an indispensable and universal human practice, the "art of discovering warrantable beliefs and improving those beliefs in shared discourse";[2] *religion,* seen not as a benighted inheritance from the dark ages but as a universal human need and practice. Discussions of how these two relate to each other, or perhaps even depend on each other, have thus been rare indeed. In my university library's card catalogue and computer memory, I find the expected thousands of entries under religion and thousands under rhetoric, ancient and modern; I find hundreds—a whole drawer full—under "Religion and Science," and overlapping hundreds under "Science and Religion." There are a fair number of works about the rhetoric of this or that religious thinker or the religion of this or that rhetorician. But when I look under "Religion *and* Rhetoric," looking for theories about how they relate to each other causally or interdependently, I find one title, and when I look under "Rhetoric *and* Religion" I find one other, Kenneth Burke's *Rhetoric of Religion.*[3]

Of course library catalogues can tell us only what labels have been thought general enough to serve as titles. If we pursue our topic— Kenneth Burke's topic—behind the deceptive labels, we find thousands of discussions, from ancient times to yesterday, of how rhetoric, under *somebody's* definition, either serves or leads to *somebody's* definition of religion. Still, I think it is safe to say that most thinkers today, including rhetoricians and theologians, would consider my question quite peculiar: Are rhetoric—the whole art of appraising the reasons we offer each other for our beliefs—and religion—however we define it— *essentially, constitutively* wedded, or are they, like so many young couples these days, merely inclined to share a pad from time to time until more attractive mates come along?

The assertive version of that question is this: Why will the student of rhetoric be led, inescapably led—provided that he or she pushes the inquiry with full rigor—to religion? I shall not claim, as Cardinal Newman did, that honest rhetorical thought will lead to some one particular religion.[4] I claim only that it will lead to a recognition that

2. Booth, *Modern Dogma,* p. xiii.
3. Kenneth Burke, *The Rhetoric of Religion: Studies in Logology* (Boston: Beacon Press, 1961).
4. John Henry Newman, *An Essay in Aid of a Grammar of Assent* (London, 1870).

some religious questions, and even *some* religious answers, can be cognitively meaningful. Rhetoric, when viewed not as mere manipulation but as our entire range of resources for discoursing together when we disagree, will lead not only to a serious *study* of religion and of religious language, as Burke's wonderful book demonstrates, but to *religion*, to religious belief itself. My claim is not only that these two subjects, as interesting "fields," or "areas," reveal interesting relations. I want to argue that whenever any inquirer pursues rhetoric vigorously into its true habitat, whenever anyone thinks hard not only about how to persuade to belief but about the grounds of human persuasion, whenever anyone asks honestly how it is that minds can ever meet at all through symbol systems, sooner or later that inquirer will discover that the entire enterprise depends on belief in . . . well, I ask my readers to choose their preferred God-term to complete that sentence. My own obvious temptation, as a student of how words get themselves validated when we view them with the greatest possible rigor, is this: belief in a God conceived of as the Word which was God and was with God "in the beginning."

But to use such language at this point would wrongly suggest that this whole project must have a Christian bias. I hope instead that before I am done the God I am talking about will be sufficiently de-denominationalized, *pluralized*, to suit anyone's spirit of ecumenicalism—the spirit that in fact always presides over any serious discussion of rhetoric and that has so wonderfully penetrated the work of David Tracy.

Those who know Kenneth Burke's highly original book will see how my project parallels yet still differs from his. Burke asks, "What must we say about our language, and particularly about our God-talk, whether or not there *is* a God?" And he finds, tracing a path roughly similar to the steps of the traditional ontological proof for the existence of God, that in the very nature of our human language there is an irresistible, hierarchical drive toward God-terms, terms that "perfect" the scale of values implicit in all language. In other words, a serious study of rhetoric, of the whole range of uses to which we put language, cannot for him be undertaken without doing a "logology," a study of the hierarchies that lead to linguistic capstones for those hierarchies: God-terms for the "perfect," though humanly unattainable, realization of the qualities embodied in those hierarchies.

My suggestion here is that Burke's serious study of rhetoric should have led him one step further, to a recognition that his logology (similar to what I have lately been calling "rhetorology," about which more later) finally requires a *theology* for its validation: the study of rhetoric does not lead only to a study of God-*talk*; it leads to a serious embrace of some conception, however loose-joined or "pluralized," of the divine.

That suggestion will on the current scene hardly be recognized as self-evident. Indeed, many might think that the opposite claim is self-evident: that there has been and always will be a conflict here. On the one hand, we have rhetoric and rhetorology, which is the study of how various particular rhetorics or discourse communities interrelate, undercut, or support one another. These together constitute the practice and study of symbolic conflict among fallen creatures as they pursue their always multiple, limited, and conflicting ends in history. On the other hand, we have religion and theology, which are the worship and study of a perfect Being who is beyond conflict, the Author of *our* being, who is not dependent on our contingencies and not—except in rather peculiar ways—dependent on history. He/She/It may teach us certain rhetorical forms—the rhetoric of prayer, for example, or of the homily—and they may teach us how *not* to talk ("Thou shalt not bear false witness"). But in what sense can the study of how we *do* talk lead us to divinity?

Certainly I cannot point to any sustained historical tradition in which a majority of those who have studied rhetoric, under the usual definition, have in fact been driven by it to religious faith. On the contrary, it would be easier to point to traditions in which rhetoric was thought to be the enemy of truth, and perhaps especially of religious truth—the great misleader of humankind, the master resource of Beelzebub. Just as Plato saw most forms of rhetoric as dangerous sophistry, the very opposite of philosophical inquiry into stable truths, so Augustine felt that his career as a rhetorician had in fact led him to forms of egocentric practice that postponed his conversion. Though he later decided that rhetoric need not be utterly banned from his life, since he needed it as a tool in combatting evil and falsehood (*De doctrina christiana*, book 4), Augustine never suggested that what he called rhetoric had by itself led him to religious conversion—except, of course, in the very special sense in which for Augustine all events in his life proved to have been blessedly useful in leading to his conversion. I suspect that most people in most periods who have known anything about these vast domains, rhetoric and religion, would have felt a stronger sense of conflict between them than of a deep conceptual and practical interdependence.

Obviously if we think of religion as based on revelation of fixed truths, unmediated by human discourse or efforts to understand discourse, we are likely to think of rhetoric as religion's enemy, or at least as presenting obstacles to faith. All revelations that are not simply kept private are expressed in symbolic forms that are subject to critical study by the student of comparative rhetoric, what I think of as the rhetorologist. Once that study has begun, the unique claims of any one revelation are soon placed under question. Rhetorologists (including those more traditionally called hermeneuticists) cannot even decide on a single version of what a simple divine proclamation *means*, let alone on how it relates to other claims to divine proclamation. Was it not rhetorology of a special kind—the kind that looks closely at the divergent rhetoric of different scriptural texts—that produced the "higher criticism," which in turn dissolved the classic scriptures into collections of mutually incompatible utterances?

This seeming quarrel between religion and rhetoric changes its appearance, however, if we look not at whether people have explicitly talked about the two slippery words in the same context but rather at the parallel decline of reputation of the two domains, from the sixteenth century to the early nineteenth.[5] I speak of a parallel decline of two domains, but in fact the domains overlap so intricately that it is often difficult to distinguish them in a given moment of decline, just as it is impossible to distinguish them in any one serious effort to resist the decline. When Cardinal Newman wrote his *Grammar of Assent*, was he resisting the decline of rhetoric or the decline of religion? Both, simultaneously. Though he called his rhetorical study a grammar, his whole project was, as one of David Tracy's students, Walter Jost, has shown, essentially a rhetorical inquiry.[6] Almost every serious thinker up to and including Bacon and Descartes believed that serious discussion about religious topics—that is, shared rhetoric about them—made sense, or at least *could* make sense. Beneath all of the controversies about religion there was general agreement that religious propositions could be argued about intelligibly, even though of course not apodeictically. This was thought to be so because beneath or beyond or above or within all disagreements lay a religious truth to be pursued, discovered—however elusively—and worshiped. Though some of the disputants sought to establish a single, monistic path to that truth and seemed by their dogmatic behavior to justify the skeptic's claim that

---

5. The decline of religion has been traced far too many times to need citation. The decline of a serious encounter with a serious rhetoric, a decline effectively resisted only in recent decades, is not quite so well known. See, e.g., Gérard Genette, "Rhetoric Restrained," in *Figures of Literary Discourse*, trans. by Alan Sheridan (New York: Columbia University Press, 1982), originally in *Figures III* (Paris, 1972); Chaim Perelman and L. Olbrechts-Tyteca, *The New Rhetoric: A Treatise on Argumentation*, trans. John Wilkinson and Purcell Weaver (Notre Dame: University of Notre Dame Press, 1969). For a careful tracing of the fate of rhetoric through the centuries, see *The Present State of Scholarship in Historical and Contemporary Rhetoric*, ed. Winifred Bryan Horner (Columbia, MO: University of Missouri Press, 1983).

6. See Walter Jost, *Rhetorical Thought in John Henry Newman* (Columbia, SC: University of South Carolina Press, 1989).

rival religions simply cancel each other out, many others illustrated Jesus' assertion that "in my Father's house are many mansions": though strait may be the way and narrow the gate toward the end of the journey, there are indeed many ways, and on each of those ways a genuine spiritual progress is possible. Our talk about better and worse ways, and about better and worse forms of travel, though necessarily diverse and often even seemingly contradictory, could still be at its best as rational as the most obviously scientific talk.

By the late nineteenth century, however, only a small and increasingly embattled group still embraced the notion that the religious enterprise is rationally defensible and debatable. There were, of course, many powerful resistance movements in every period—perhaps the three most important in English being Butler's *Analogy*,[7] Coleridge's amorphous, diffuse, but enormously important importation and development of German thought, and Newman's later grammar. But despite these and many other holding actions like Kant's *Religion within the Limits of Reason Alone*[8] and Hegel's monumental work, most would-be intellectuals by the time, say, of Leslie Stephen and Samuel Butler could more easily understand their professed agnosticism—tough, honest, brave, dictated by the limits of "reason"—than they could understand the seeming irrationality of a Newman that a properly clarified reason, a reason essentially rhetorical, would lead the thinker to God.

By the twentieth century, the best-known defenders of religion had come increasingly to talk about it as a matter of pure, ungrounded faith alone, a faith thought of as maintained *against* reason. The many accounts of the warfare of science and religion tended to reinforce the notion that religion, the very stuff most threatened by science, is on the side of irrationality, while science, whatever else it was, seemed to be the ultimate product of genuine rationality. So the world of thought came to be sharply divided for most thinkers between faith and reason, between values—always to some degree merely asserted, not known—and facts, about which reason alone could reason.

Now the conventional way to explain this first decline—the loss of faith among those who honored reason—is to point to scientific advances, first Newton's, then the geologist's and chemist's, then Darwin's, and perhaps then Freud's. I would suggest a different emphasis. Without questioning the importance for individual thinkers of the shocks

---

7. Joseph Butler, *The Analogy of Religion, Natural and Revealed, to the Constitution and Course of Nature* (1736). A good introduction to the decline of religious rhetoric can be found simply by tracing the fate of Butler's *Analogy* in university curricula from the mid-eighteenth century through the nineteenth.

8. Immanuel Kant, *Religion within the Limits of Reason Alone*, trans. Theodore M. Greene and Hoyt H. Hudson (1793; New York: Open Court Publishing Co., 1960).

administered by these giants' progressive removal of the masks from the "natural," I suggest that the deeper shock was administered by a second loss, subtler and less visible: the loss of faith in rhetorical modes of inquiry in all subjects, not just religion. The scientific revolution was only in part a matter of shocking specific discoveries; the true shocker for them was the rising belief that there were only two proper paths to knowledge, the path of empirical investigation and the path of strict logical deduction. All else was mere illusion—useful, perhaps even necessary, for making our way through daily life, but illusion nonetheless. Traditional rhetorical modes of telling truth—the reliance on such topical resources as testimony and tradition, the dependence on analogy and metaphor, on shared emotions and commitments and other rhetorical resources—*all that* had been responsible for millennia of scientific error, and now we were ready, by giving up *all that*, to enter a new era of genuine purgation and discovery.

Thus over the centuries rhetoric suffered what in the perspective of current revivals of interest in it seems an astonishing decline. That decline took two main forms—a progressive narrowing of the domain of rhetoric, for those who still did study it at all, and a progressive lowering of its status, for those who studied other things. Rhetoricians increasingly defined their subject as the mere art of winning in controversy, and within that art they increasingly worked only with the devices of surface eloquence—the ways we have of making our positions attractive, *after* we have arrived at those positions by routes other than rhetoric.[9] The heart of rhetorical inquiry, the art of discovering *good* reasons, had already been seriously weakened in the Renaissance. But by the time of George Campbell in the eighteenth century, students of rhetoric increasingly defined it as what is left over *after* the hard thinking has been done. Notice how Campbell limits rhetoric, in his influential *Philosophy of Rhetoric*, as he leads up to what he calls "qualities *strictly* rhetorical":

> Purity [of style] . . . may justly be denominated *grammatical* truth. It consisteth in the conformity of the expression to the sentiment; . . . as *moral* truth consisteth in the conformity of the sentiment intended . . . to the sentiment actually entertained by the speaker . . . ; and *logical* truth . . . in the conformity of the sentiment to the nature of things. The opposite to *logical truth* is properly error; to *moral truth*, a lie; to *grammatical truth*, a blunder. . . . But it is with the expression as with the sentiment, it is not enough to the orator that both be true [as determined by grammar, morality,

---

9. See Tom Conley, "Booth's *Company* and the Rhetoric We Keep" (review of my *The Company We Keep*), *Rhetorica* 8:2 (Spring, 1990), and *Rhetoric in the European Tradition* (New York: Longman Publishing Co., 1990).

or logic]. A sentence may be a just exhibition, according to the rules of the language, of the thought intended to be conveyed by it, and may therefore, to a mere grammarian, be unexceptionable; which to an orator may appear extremely faulty. It may, nevertheless, be obscure, it may be languid, it may be inelegant, it may be flat, it may be unmusical.[10]

The qualities of style that are *strictly rhetorical* are thus for him vitality, elegance, musicality—not sources of truth at all.

Once theorists of rhetoric had reduced it in this way to the devices for heightening or sweetening a truth discovered by other means, it is no wonder that everyone else inferred that rhetoric is the relatively trivial stuff that is left over after reality has been addressed, the icing on the cake. A lamentable necessity, it betrays our weak human need for sugar-coating our truths. Truth is discovered by procedures dictated by what came to be called objectivity; it may or may not then be sweetened by rhetoric, depending on whether weak minds find the pill otherwise unpalatable.

By the twentieth century, "rhetoric" became not just the necessary sweetening—it was poisonous sweetening that should be banned by some FDA of scholarship. You will look a long time in our media—all of which of course have their very being in rhetoric—before you will find any questioning of the sharp distinction between reality, truth, and responsible action, on the one hand, and sleazy dubious rhetoric, on the other. In the *Los Angeles Times* a while ago, I saw a typical headline: "RHETORIC, A LEGACY OF STRIFE, MARK ULSTER'S BIBLE BELT." The article makes quite clear that whenever "rhetoric" is the legacy, something was wrong with the ancestor.

In the various recent tracings of the double decline—of faith in a religion conceived as inherently rational and of belief in rhetoric as a form of rational inquiry—various villains have been blamed: Erasmus, Ramus, Descartes, Locke, the French *philosophes*, the whole of the Enlightenment, the philosophers of rhetoric of the eighteenth century like Campbell. Diverse causal chains have been suggested. Fortunately we do not have to decide precisely who killed cock robin to detect a curious interdependence of the two domains in their decline. One way to dramatize their symbiosis might run as follows.

Let us imagine, in a little mental experiment, a world consisting entirely of intelligent, well-informed thinkers, fully aware of and respectful toward modern scientific developments—thinkers who believe that when faced with any intellectual problem, our resources for

---

10. George Campbell, *The Philosophy of Rhetoric*, ed. Lloyd F. Bitzer (1776; Carbondale, IL: Southern Illinois University Press, 1963) 214–15 (italics added).

solving it are only two. The first resource is *observation* with our senses, extended (as we now quite marvelously can extend them) with scientific tools like electron microscopes, particle accelerators, and telescopes in space. The second resource is *thought* about such observations, that thought consisting either of inductions, adding up particular observations into generalizations, or of deductions, conducted according to strict rules of logic that ultimately can be expressed in mathematical formulas.

Some of our thinkers will develop more subtle versions of the so-called hypothetico-deductive model, in which we think out possibilities based on hypotheses that are to some degree plausible in the light of previous knowledge, and then conduct experiments that reveal hard proof as to whether the hypotheses are justified. But every cognitive proposition, everything really known, can be either empirically or analytically validated. Whenever we want to be really rigorous in our thinking, we will subject each suspected truth to a systematic effort to "falsify" it, to doubt it with every conceivable means of doubt. Only those beliefs that can be tested by the test of falsifiability are in fact worthy to endure as truth.

Now let us set that world of imaginary, fair-minded, and objective inquirers, purged, you see, of confidence in rhetoric, to work on the domain of religion, religion conceived in whatever way is for you its most fully articulated, most defensible form. What will they discover?

Will they not quickly discover, using that kind of scientific theory of rhetoric, that not a single proposition that *any* religion cares about can survive those tests? The criterion that requires us to doubt whatever can in theory be doubted will wipe out with one stroke every religious category, every religious tradition, and every moral or ethical corollary of every particular religion. Our imaginary community must conclude, in all honesty, that in fact nothing can be known about any of *that*, for or against, except for the one rather important matter that it simply cannot be said to have any establishable truth at all. Deprived of the rhetorical resources of shared emotion and commitment, the resources of metaphor and analogy, and of all other forms of eloquence, deprived of a notion of rhetoric as inquiry, rhetoric as an art of invention through exploration of shared commonplaces, this imaginary community would easily wipe out every issue of our journals and every book or essay about religion except for those that pursue archaeological, philological, or historical reports on who said or did what in the past.

It is not my point here to attempt any kind of refutation of those scientistic partisans or of the paradigm of reasoning with which they have worked.[11] That paradigm has been collapsing rapidly for decades,

---

11. To me the most penetrating recent critique of what I have called scientism is

on its own. Indeed, it falls apart as soon as we ask those eager inquirers to subject the grounds of their enterprises to their own test of falsifiability. Can you prove, we ask, with *your* methods of disproof, that one should seek scientific truth? That one should honor data-as-found rather than fudging the evidence? Can you show that to pursue truth is any more noble than running an efficient gas chamber in Nazi Germany? No, we cannot, they must reply, echoing Bertrand Russell's forlorn confession whenever he placed such questions to himself.[12]

"But can you doubt," we go on, "that any of this matters, one way or another?" "Of course we can," their reply must run. "Since we are committed to doubting whatever we cannot prove, we must doubt every proposition that can *in theory* be doubted. So we must finally merely assert, on faith alone, the validity of our own enterprise." Of course, nobody in practice follows that path out to such conclusions. Even Karl Popper, the prophet of the test of falsifiability, makes clear that he does not depend on the criterion of falsifiability for testing many of the values entailed in his enterprise. He relies on rhetorical proofs.[13] But consistency would require answers like those I have just given.

Perhaps this mental experiment will serve as a brief suggestion that religion and rhetoric somehow work in the same direction, or at least that they fall victim to the same intellectual strokes. But to show this much is by no means to show that they are integrally connected, that indeed they exhibit a form of symbiosis. Can I seriously argue that any genuine revival of serious rhetorical study, and especially of the kind of comparative rhetorical study I am calling rhetorology, must have a favorable effect not only on religious study but on religious faith as well?

Obviously, any proof for such a highly dubitable notion—dubitable and not by any means easily falsifiable—must be of the essentially contestable kind that rhetoric always depends on. We look only for rhetorical probabilities here. But are there in fact *good reasons* for expecting that the secular academic world, once it decides to revive rhetorical study, will be led to repudiate the secular vision of a godless, impersonal universe and to begin inquiry instead into the nature of the Word, that symbol-laden center that must, in the beginning, now and always, enable all this talk: The great I Am who makes us in His/Her

---

Charles Taylor's *Sources of the Self: The Making of the Modern Identity* (Cambridge, MA: Harvard University Press, 1989).

12. See W. Booth, "Bertrand Russell's Rhetoric and the Dogmas of Doubt," in *Modern Dogma*, chap. 1.

13. Karl Popper, *The Logic of Scientific Discovery* (London: Hutchinson, 1959). Popper in later editions modifies his views considerably, to take into better account nonfalsifiable truths.

image as rhetorical creatures, ever attempting to increase our chances of critical understanding through symbolic exchange? Can we say that rhetoric, leading inevitably to rhetorology, ends in theology?

A relatively easy way to answer would be to follow Plato in casting off the lower forms of rhetoric, as low, cheap, or "mere," and then to pursue the higher kind—what he generally calls not rhetoric but philosophy or dialectic. We could then show that the higher kinds are in fact a logology that is indistinguishable from theology. But I will not pursue here that somewhat easier, though still perilous, path. Rather, I propose that we expand our thinking of rhetoric to include all of its guises, from the sleaziest attempt to deceive to the noblest philosophical argument. Rhetoric for now will be the whole art that attempts to provide reasons for changing our minds, reasons no matter how "unreasonable," reasons impure, disguised, tricky, reasons offered to ourselves as well as reasons offered to others. What could there be about the very nature of such an all-embracing art that would entail belief in a creative force that by *its* nature requires us to try hard to improve our use of the art? It seems obvious that if there is such an entailment, it will not be stateable in any single formulation: if religion and rhetoric are indeed inextricably connected, it will be by multiple threads discoverable in a plurality of languages. The entailment(s) we are pursuing will never be finally and fully pinned down in any one version of religious language.

Let us take an extreme but common case of what most of us would agree to call "bad" or "mere" rhetoric. A politician promises in a public speech that if elected he will not raise taxes, while knowing full well that taxes must be raised. In short, he lies, and knows that he lies, for the sake of getting elected. That is to say, he hopes to change the voters' minds, using reasons that he knows are false. What does his act imply about what we call the world? His lie makes no sense, to him or to us, unless he himself believes at least the following:

First, he must believe that people are not machines to be programmed mechanically or animals to be conditioned, but symbol-makers-and-users to be appealed to through symbols—his lie. If we are *not* rhetorical creatures, he should surely seek power some other way than by lying to us—bribery, torture, killing. To tell a lie presupposes that one has given up, at least for the nonce, all other means of getting one's way, and it is thus to acknowledge that the person addressed is the same kind of creature as the liar: "Unlike any other creature we know or can conceive of, you, the lie-ee, are my kind of person, susceptible to symbolic exchange." Nobody lies to a machine—what could it mean to lie to a computer? No killer bothers to persuade with lies when persuasion is not needed: a pistol shot will take care of you precisely as a rifle shot will take care of the deer or elk that I hunt. Shooting you I deny your personhood; lying to you I acknowledge it. As soon as I find that I must talk with you and try to persuade you, I accept you as my own kind.

This forces the liar, secondly, to acknowledge in his act (and to believe, if he once thinks about it) that the universe has somehow tossed up from its depths this strange kind of possibility: the exchange of symbols as reasons for belief and action. Scientific modernism somehow lost the sense of wonder about this radical difference between a possible universe in which only *signals* are exchanged among its parts—weak and strong gravitational forces, pheramones, pointings, growls, and grunts—and a universe in which the parts exchange *symbols*. The liar acknowledges that the world is really this second kind of world, and though in the moment of lying he no doubt does not share the wonder at the process, he exemplifies it, willy-nilly. His reliance on rhetoric proclaims a most amazing grace, the gift of symbolic worlds that we all inherit.

Third, he thus imports value into that world: he in a sense declares that to live in such a world is a *better* way to live than to live in a world of brute sign-exchange. The lying politician has *chosen* rhetoric as a preferred way of life: though he may in his heart lust after the day when he can establish himself as an absolute dictator and kill off all his enemies, he has at least for the moment acceded to this *other* world.

The next step will to some of you seem even shakier than those I have taken already. But remember, we begin here with one of the assumptions that we hope to have underlined as we come out—namely, that in all talk about religion our proofs must be at best less rigorous than we have been taught to expect when the word "proof" is used. We cannot demonstrate to anyone determined to doubt that any of our steps makes sense. The next step depends even more obviously on that famous precondition explicitly discussed by many theologians and exemplified by all: we must believe in order to understand. We must assent to *something* in order to believe *anything*. We must first agree to assent to what we already cannot in good faith seriously doubt—cannot doubt, in other words, except in the artificial modes of doubt that result when we play the doubting game. Here we will doubt only those propositions for which we have good specific reasons for doubt, not just those theoretical programs that undertake to doubt everything we cannot demonstrate scientifically or logically. Thinkers in the positivist tradition were eager to show that all such believing in something that cannot be proved, within a given total system of belief, was false, since obviously circular. But—to repeat—by now it is generally recognized that all thinking, including that of the positivists in their attacks, depends on initial acts of credence, of assent, that are not provable within the given system of thought.

Let us suppose that our lying politician really wants our vote and is therefore willing to talk with us about his lie, once we have caught him. The conversation might begin like this:

Q. Now tell me, Mr. Vice President, when you said you would not vote for raising taxes, did you *know* that you were lying?

A. No, I did not know that I was lying. I sort of knew that taxes might have to be raised and that I might finally vote to raise them, but I didn't *know* that I was lying.

At this point the conversation may stop. The questioner is nonplussed. But he might then turn in a new direction, one that we could explore on another occasion: the rhetorical and religious implications of self-deception. In what kind of universe does the very notion of being self-deceived make sense?

But here we resist that direction and return instead to imagine that our liar replies, "Oh yes, I knew that I was lying," and we continue as follows:

Q. Then you also knew, at the moment of lying, what would not be lying?

A. Of course.

Q. So you knew what would be true?

A. Of course.

Q. Then you knew, at that moment, the difference between truth and falsehood?

A. Of course.

Q. But please tell me, Mr. Vice President, is there really a difference between truth and falsehood?

At this point he might conceivably say, "No, there is no real difference and it doesn't matter how one talks: everything is equally lies and truth"—an answer that would not lead us to religion at all but to one or another of the genuine irreligions—or, as Aristotle suggests when discussing the denial of the law of noncontradiction, to silence (*Metaphysics* 3.2.2; 4.6.12). But who could ever give that answer honestly? In rejecting the distinction, our liar has simultaneously given up his rhetorical effort with us, because we will just have to stop listening to anyone who denies that some answers to questions (perhaps his own) are better than others.

So he will more probably answer something like this: "Yes, there is a real difference between a lie and the truth, a difference that I can usually recognize, even though my higher goals require me sometimes to violate it." With that answer, he is, of course, caught in our toils, provided he will talk with us long enough to discover that old Platonic truth: If there is a *real* difference between a lie and truth, and if some goals are really "higher" than others, then there must be a real difference between knowledge and opinion, a difference that in a sense oversees and controls our efforts to determine what is knowledge and what is faulty opinion.

And suddenly our politician will have leapt out of his domain of shoddy rhetoric and entered another rhetorical domain entirely—that of inquiry into which of our statements affirming a truth is *really closer* to the truth, which of our goals is really higher. This domain is often called philosophy or theology, but we can now see that it can also be called rhetorical inquiry, because it is simply another manifestation of symbolic exchange, the effort to understand one another and to *improve* that understanding. Little did the politician know that he would end up here when he told his everyday lie.

What marks the halls in which rhetoric is queen as distinct from the halls in which a scientific philosophy tries to rule is that rhetoric requires us at every stage of any argument to listen to one another, to attend to the other party's arguments *as if* they might make better sense than our own. A lukewarm version of this requirement is the kind of training that most rhetorical schools insist on: the student must learn to defend both sides of any given case. To do that you must of course study the opponent's case as well as your own. The corrupt schools teach you to do that in order to refute all opponents. But if you do it well, if you do it genuinely, what is likely to happen? You may very well discover that the opponent's case in fact makes as much sense as yours, maybe more. You enter your opponent's mind; your opponent's mind enters yours, and, before you know it, your mind has been forced either to reject your former precious truth or, now that you see a bit deeper, you must embrace both your old truth and your opponent's new one.

Corrupt versions of what is called rhetoric of course depend on skepticism about the very possibility of that happening; there is for them no real difference between any two positions, only a difference in skill of presentation. The good rhetorician in that view is the one who can make any cause, including the worst one, look like the better one. But the genuine spirit of rhetorical inquiry says something quite different: your opponent's views almost certainly have more to be said for them than you have yet discovered. You may even end up caught in that other mind. Your own views certainly—not *almost* certainly but certainly—have more to be said against them, more to be said of their limitations, than you have yet realized. The best truth you can hope for out of this encounter will thus be a dialectical truth emerging from the encounter, a truth different from what either of you began with. And that truth in turn, you can be certain, will be fragmentary, partial, limited, in need of further dialogue, further dialectical modifications, and so on *ad infinitum*. ("Certain?" I'm caught in a paradox? Perhaps.)

By this point, obviously, religion has long since entered the picture. What do we mean if we say that the dialectical inquiry must continue without limit? Do we mean that it simply goes in a circle, with nobody really getting anywhere, only suffering the illusion that improvement is occurring? Or do we mean that genuine progress is made, even though the final, full truth remains forever elusive? If we mean that no progress is made, we are again joining the irreligious, but we are also violating the whole inherent, natural, inexpungeable rhetorical spirit of humankind. How many people in human history have ever in fact believed for long that no real progress is ever made in discussion with others, no steps *ever* taken toward better understanding? Anyone who believed that and lived in accordance with the belief would surely soon go mad or perish.

We all know from experience that some arguments, even about "nonscientific" matters, do get somewhere, that some views *are* superior to some other views, that some beliefs we earlier held have been corrected or improved by our encounters with reasons provided by other people or by our own further thinking. But that knowledge must be rejected as finally unreal *unless* there is in some sense or other a truth that is superior to any one of our formulations of particular truths—superior both in the sense that it is the goal of our efforts and in the sense that it somehow contains, or is the sum of, all of the particular truths we may hit upon along the way.

Of course, it is theoretically possible, once we have been led by rhetorology to postulate the necessity of such a supreme truth, validating our rhetorical encounters and judgments about better or worse, to doubt its "actual existence"—*if* we are committed to systematic doubt. It is possible to believe that though we *need* a notion of truth or validity to validate our rhetorical exchanges it just isn't *there*. But can anyone doubt the existence of genuine differences in *degree of adequacy* of statements, once the postulate has been *thought about* as experienced in daily rhetorical exchange? Our lying politician certainly could not doubt it. Would any part of our lives make sense if we in fact gave up this postulate? And if it would not, which step is more reasonable, to embrace the postulate or to reject it, on the grounds that it has not yet been fully tested by abstract epistemologies?[14]

As many a reader will have recognized, what I have just traced is a rather loose-jointed version of one traditional proof for the existence of

---

14. See Taylor's notion of the Best Account Principle, as an alternative to the falsifiability principle (*Sources of the Self*, esp. pp. 71–74).

one traditional conception of God, God as the truth of truths. It is a symbol-user's version of the ontological proof.[15] To think of the grounds of arguing together is to be persuaded of the very existence of those grounds. Of course, the great God "symbol-exchanger-and-validator," as dimly discerned here, is by no means all that traditional theologians meant by "God." Our inquiry does not, so far, say much about God's power and personality. But it may get us started in thinking about why serious thought about rhetoric must lead the thinker to take religion seriously.

The weak proof would of course work more forcefully if we began not with a lying politician but with more respectable kinds of rhetoric, especially one of the best kinds, the kind that we attempt, or should attempt, to practice whenever we take part in an academic discussion or write an article or a book. At our best we practice a rhetoric of inquiry that assumes the relative inadequacy of every particular view and yet at the same time the existence of some sort of center of standards of what would make a more *nearly* adequate view. Those of us who, like David Tracy, pursue the significance of a plurality of catholicisms, or a plurality of world religions, know that there is a pitfall threatening on either side of our path: the belief that all world views are equally valid, provided they are held to sincerely and passionately, and the belief that our present way of holding to the one right world view needs no improvement and should ideally serve all people in all circumstances. It is precisely in this respect, when we discuss honestly, that we start a long way further up the spiral of logology or rhetorology than does my lying politician. The curious thing, however—curious when we think of hundreds of previous efforts, including my own, to distinguish *good* rhetoric from *mere* rhetoric[16]—is that we find ourselves moving along the same path that the liar unwittingly suggests.

Even this leaves us with a host of troublesome questions. Perhaps the most threatening one is this: once we assent to rhetorical proofs, will they not bring back into respectability many of the wild beliefs that we have learned to see as dangerous nonsense—taught as we were by the very kind of empirical and logical thinking that we must go beyond? The scientistic modes of critical testing here questioned, joining a large list of thinkers in the past few decades, had one thing to be said for them: they provided cheap and easy ways to refute reprehensible rivals

15. Anselm, *Dialogue on Truth*, translated and with an introduction by Richard McKeon, in *Selections from Medieval Philosophers* (New York: Columbia University Press, 1929) 1:142–84.
16. See, e.g., W. Booth, "Mere Rhetoric, Rhetorology, and the Search for a Common Learning," in *The Vocation of a Teacher*.

to our endeavors—stuff like alchemy, astrology, astro-projection, literal reincarnation, and so on, semi-respectable intellectual programs that can in fact, when investigated carefully and without the protective shield of "falsifiability," provide threateningly plausible accounts of themselves. Once rhetorical paradigms are admitted for all thinking, we raise difficulties for ourselves about how to show the world the difference between "normal science" and "pseudo-science," defensible religions and satanic destructive cults like that of Charles Manson. After all, does not every fraud, every charlatan, every fake medium, every Sunday morning evangelist, every Reverend Jones, offer us plausible reasons for belief, reasons that in a rhetorical perspective look a lot stronger than they do in a good hard old-fashioned scientific perspective?

I cannot really meet this problem here, except to say that I think we would all be better off if we had to figure out just what is really wrong with any public offering—be it magical, scientific, religious—instead of relying on the simple formula, "It's not scientific," or "It's been scientifically disproved." Some of my colleagues are deeply troubled by the conviction that our world is being drowned in irrationalism—they mention deconstruction in philosophy, literary criticism and history; critical legal studies; and so on. But I don't think it's bad for anyone to have to state just why this or that challenge to our beliefs seems irrational. To increasing numbers of thinkers, the scientific disproof of all religion, on the grounds that *some* historical claims of *some* religions violate "natural law," seems now highly dubious, supported not by good reasons but by shaky and unexamined general principles. Is it bad for those of us who join this trend to be forced to think again about our first principles and our methods of demonstration? My claim is that it is in the very effort to explain why one set of scientifically dubious beliefs or customs is defensible while another one superficially like it should be repudiated that our most profound intellectual schooling occurs. When religions clash, as they always will, they clash in their rhetorics— that is, in the total range of the "reasons" they offer for belief. When rhetorics clash, they lead us to see how inescapable our diverse religious commitments really are.

I wish I could end on a clearer, cleaner, more decisive note. Every rhetorician longs for resounding perorations, just as every scientific inquirer longs for clear, decisive proofs. But this subject, like all genuine religious inquiry, must always lead to conclusions that are at best probable, tentative, "reasonable," but not settled beyond all possibility of doubt.[17]

17. For a variety of subtle demonstrations of why all serious religious inquiry must end in some degree of irresolution, and why such inquiry is nonetheless not doomed to be

The main conclusion should be obvious: religious studies and rhetorical studies depend on each other for their future vitality. On the one hand, serious rhetorical study, including the study of the most important classical rhetorical texts, must escape the bounds of rhetoric departments, classics departments, English departments: it must permeate every discipline, just as serious philosophical inquiry did in olden times and only rarely does now. A student of any subject who has not thought about the rhetoric employed in front-line inquiry in that subject, and about how a "rhetorologist" might relate that rhetoric to other inquiries, is—well, let us say that student is dwelling in the devil's workshop.18 On the other hand, serious reconsideration of traditional religious arguments must escape the present restriction to tiny enclaves within divinity schools, a restriction that leaves religious belief vulnerable to what seems like easy refutations by positivists in one generation and deconstructionists in the next. Students of rhetoric or religion who have not thought rhetorically about the traditional theological topics that "died" when their support from rhetoric was removed have dealt with only fragments of each subject.

And so—as is often the case with me lately—I conclude with a plea for a kind of universal spread of rhetorology, but this time with the claim that it should finally be indistinguishable from a revived and deepened theology. Let rhetorical studies flourish, everywhere, in and out of the academy, in and out of the churches. My hope is for more scholars willing to undertake studies of how we might improve our ways of talking together—not just studies limited to how we do it, as too many rhetorical studies by postmodernists are limited, but of how we might *improve* it: not just how we might do it better, technically, but how we might improve it, *really*. Such scholars would be marked by their radical critique of the divorce of rhetoric and reality—of the notion that we get in touch with reality with some method that is untainted by rhetoric and then sell our results *with* rhetoric; here they would join the best of the deconstructionists. Such scholars would see rhetoric not only as inquiry, rhetoric not only as epistemic (to use one newly fashionable phrase), but rhetoric as the co-creator of reality itself, rhetoric as the Word that was God and that was with God.

But if my pluralistic assumptions are correct, any such peroration

---

*irr*eligious, see Leszek Kolakowski, *Modernity on Endless Trial* (Chicago: University of Chicago Press, 1990), esp. section II: "On the Dilemmas of the Christian Legacy."

18. For a model of how such rhetorical inquiry might be best conducted within a classically isolated discipline, see Don McCloskey, *The Rhetoric of Economics* (Madison, WI: University of Wisconsin Press, 1985); idem, *If You're So Smart: The Narrative of Economic Expertise* (Chicago: University of Chicago Press, 1990).

employing words from some one tradition must be inherently misleading. The wedding I've been celebrating here, the wedding that was consummated the moment the two first human creatures went beyond blows and gestures and *talked,* must by its nature be celebrated in many different encodings. And none of us can know, in advance of living within one or more of the codes, just which of them should be labeled "true" or "false."

6

HERMENEUTICS AND THE QUESTION OF THE SELF

Nathan A. Scott, Jr.

"PLURALITY," SAID HANNAH ARENDT in her Gifford Lectures, "is the law of the earth."[1] It may not always have been the case, but it is surely so in our own late time, and it is precisely the heed that David Tracy has given to this primary fact of our culture that has propelled him in the direction taken in much of his recent work. Plurality, indeed, we seem to be facing on every side—plurality among the living traditions that shape the major intellectual forums of our period, plurality therefore of languages and forms of life, plurality in methods of argument and styles of inquiry, plurality in the universe of religious discourse (where we face enormous diversity not only among the great religious systems but also, and often most arrestingly, within each of the multifaceted traditions stemming from these systems, so that in relation, say, to the Christian tradition Harnack's old question concerning the "essence of Christianity" seems virtually unanswerable). Wherever we turn we encounter plurality—even, as Freud and his various heirs have taught us to recognize, within the life of the self. And thus it is not surprising that David Tracy's pilgrimage as a theologian has brought him now to a juncture at which he finds it necessary to accord centrality to the hermeneutical question, the question as to how one may best understand and interpret an environing otherness which at every point confronts us with multifariousness and diversity.

In part, of course, the special charm which his theological work has had for us is consequent upon his refusal of any sort of self-

---

1. Hannah Arendt, *The Life of the Mind: Thinking* (New York and London: Harcourt Brace Jovanovich, 1978) 1:19.

protectiveness that might exempt him from (as he speaks of it) "that morality of scientific knowledge which ... [the theologian *qua* theologian] shares with his colleagues, the philosophers, historians, and social scientists. No more than they, can ... [the theologian]," as he says, "allow his own—or his tradition's—beliefs to serve as warrants for his arguments." Which is for him to say that the venture of the theologian "should be characterized by those same ethical stances of autonomous judgment, critical reflection, and properly sceptical hardmindedness that characterize analysis in other fields."[2] Moreover, he makes it a matter of assumption that the theological project may not licitly have recourse to any arcane or occult region of data, since, like one of his masters, Paul Tillich, he conceives theological enterprise to be an affair of *correlation* between "Christian texts and common human experience."[3] And he insists that in that aspect of theological work that involves phenomenological reflection on the *Lebenswelt* integrity will be guaranteed only by the strictest attention being paid to the human sciences. So, given his conviction that the theologian must dwell in a public arena, one considers it to be for him altogether in character that, in canvassing the present scene in hermeneutics (as he does in his book of 1987, *Plurality and Ambiguity*), he should in no way seek to evade what is challenging in the most radical forms of contemporary skepticism.

Since in our phase of civility it is undoubtedly Jacques Derrida who presents the key case of this skepticism, it would be well, as we measure Tracy's response, for us to have immediately before us the substance of Derrida's position, as it is set forth in such books as *Speech and Phenomena, Of Grammatology, Writing and Difference,* and *Margins of Philosophy*. Though his thought has many sources—in Hegel, Nietzsche, Husserl, Heidegger, Lévi-Strauss, to mention but a few—it is perhaps Ferdinand de Saussure whom we need first of all to have in view, since Derrida's whole program seems to want most essentially to collapse the distinction so central to Saussure's epoch-making book of 1911, *Cours de linguistique générale*—the distinction, that is, between *le signifiant* and *le signifié*, the signifier and the signified. True, Derrida, like Saussure, thinks of a text as constituted of signs: indeed, he likes to regard it as simply an affair of *"noir sur blanc,"* as nothing more than so many black marks on white paper. And, again in the manner of Saussure, he takes the meaning of these signs to consist in what they are *not*, in their "difference" from other signs within a given linguistic

---

2. David Tracy, *Blessed Rage for Order: The New Pluralism in Theology* (New York: Seabury, 1975) 7.
3. Ibid., 43–48, 64–71.

system. So, since their meaning resides in what they are not, the meaning of a particular sign is absent from the sign itself and is therefore something evanescent, fugitive, occult. Moreover, what can the signifier be said to be a "sign of," since to consult a dictionary is only to be confronted with alternative signifiers? And, when the meanings of these are in turn checked, we find ourselves again confronted with still other signifiers, and so on *ad infinitum*. All our signifiers, in other words, merely bear upon themselves the traces of other signifiers—and thus the very distinction between *le signifiant* and *le signifié* proves in the end to be an utter delusion. For what we dwell amidst is the unending play (*jeu*) of significations whose meanings are always deferred into an ever more distant future: meaning, it appears, is forever "not yet."

Nowhere, in short, is it possible within the terms of Derrida's scheme of thought to locate any kind of "presence," any kind of being or reality which is outside the play of signification and on which our thought and language might be taken to be grounded. And it is precisely the large hospitality it has given to a "metaphysics of presence" that accounts for his wanting to jettison very nearly the whole of the Western philosophical tradition, since this is a tradition, from Plato to Heidegger, whose last recourse has been to some ultimate referent (the "transcendental signified")—whether it be God or the Idea or the Self or substance—which has been conceived to be prior to all discourse and the foundation of all experience and thought. But Derrida lays it down that, however comforting such "logocentric" projections may be, they are in the final analysis nothing more than systemic functions of the linguistic process—and, as such, deserving to be relegated to the discard as merely "metaphysical."

In this version of things, then, there is nothing at all that can be counted on to "center" language, to limit the "free-play" of the significatory process, and to establish stable referents outside language for spoken and written utterance, since, even were it analytically possible to isolate *le signifié* as an object of inquiry, it would be found, inevitably and in the nature of the case, to be simply another sign-system, its accessibility to the mind being necessarily a consequence of its having been constituted by some *signifiant*. Outside language, in other words, there is only *le néant*—which, as Derrida would warn, is not itself to be taken as presenting any sort of alternative ontological principle, since nothing is, quite simply, nothing. So, since *"il n'y a riens hors du texte,"* texts open out into the abyss of that infinite and ungrounded process of signification initiated by the signs within the text itself, that abyss wherein all signifieds are collapsed within signifiers.

And what, then, is the task of the interpreter? It is, as Derrida suggests, to do nothing other than to plunge into the significatory process initiated by a given text, joyously affirming a world in which a superabundance of signifiers makes both error and the achievement of truth impossible. And, given the well-nigh infinite chain of indeterminate significations initiated by the text, the *work* of the interpreter will involve not so much a dismantling of the text as a demonstration of how it dismantles itself with respect to all such views of it as would posit for the text anything resembling a stable and definable meaning. When we begin to tackle a text, in other words, we are committing ourselves to what Frederic Jameson calls a "prison-house of language,"[4] and the job of the hermeneut is to make it clear that within this labyrinth there is no kind of *archē* or *telos*, no guiding thread—nothing but the interminable chain of signification into which the constituent words of the text have been locked by their myriad usages in various languages across the entire span of historical time. Which means, of course, as the hermeneut undertakes to expose how dizzyingly vast is the number of all those irreconcilable meanings forming the sediment with which any key term of a text is endowed, that his or her discourse inevitably takes on the character of a kind of free association infinitely surpassing anything that could have been dreamt of in that long-ago time when we sometimes suspected that the Empson of *Seven Types of Ambiguity* found the main grist for his mill in the O.E.D.

It is such ideas as these that have become the commonplaces of the new hermeneutics that derives from Jacques Derrida, as well as from such relatively recent decedents as Roland Barthes and Michel Foucault and Paul de Man, all of whom are "occupied," as Edward Said remarks of Foucault, "with the vacant space between things, words, [and] ideas."[5] The notion of any sort of primal covenant between word and world is declared to be but a dream, and those who want now to be our principal overseers are eager to persuade us of the essential emptiness or weightlessness of texts, this weightlessness being consequent upon the absence of any transitive relation borne by texts to things extrinsic to the world of textuality itself. Language, indeed, says Foucault, is marked by a "radical intransitivity," since it "has no other law than that of affirming . . . its own precipitous existence; and so," as he tells us, "there is nothing for it to do but to curve back in a perpetual return upon itself."[6] In short, to use George Steiner's figure, "the deed of semantic trust"[7] between Saying and Being is broken.

4. See Frederic Jameson, *The Prison-House of Language: A Critical Account of Structuralism and Russian Formalism* (Princeton: Princeton University Press, 1972).
5. Edward Said, *Beginnings: Intention and Method* (New York: Basic Books, 1975) 285.
6. Michel Foucault, *The Order of Things: An Archaeology of the Human Sciences*, an anonymous translation of *Les Mots et les choses* (New York: Vintage Books, 1973) 300.
7. George Steiner, *Real Presences—Is There Anything In What We Say* (London: Faber & Faber, 1989) 91.

But what needs also to be noticed is that so ghostly is the universe to which we are committed by deconstructionist ideology that, within the terms of its protocols, even the human image itself must be found to be strangely insubstantial and vaporous. For if the meanings of signs are always scattered and deferred, if they are never a part of the signs themselves, how can I make "present" to another my thoughts and feelings and intentions, my own inwardness, my own reality as a person— and not only to another but to myself as well? If *le signifiant* never manages to reach the absolute presence of what Derrida calls "the transcendental signified" and if, as a consequence, the domain of signification is without any bound or terminus, then not only is language "decentered," but so, too, is the self as well, since it becomes, inevitably, "little more than . . . a speaking pronoun, fixed indecisively in the eternal, ongoing rush of discourse."[8] We may still find it convenient to use first-person verbs in reference to the human individual as an agent of certain vocal and bodily acts, but the new clerks would have us understand that in point of fact what they with a great hauteur speak of as "the transcendental subject of traditional humanism" is merely an invented fiction without any true ontological status. At best, the "I" is nothing more than a linguistically encoded stereotype emanating from the particular cultural matrix by which it was formed: which is to say (in the manner of Saussure) that *parole* is but an epiphenomenon of *langue,* and thus, far from being the impresario of language, the human agent is in truth its slave. As it turns out, that center of creative intelligence posited by Descartes' *Cogito, ergo sum* is only a vulgar illusion bereft of any Archimedean point with reference to which it might be certified as having even a provisional authority. It is along such lines as these that the testimony of the new *avant-garde* moves.

Now it is not surprising that, having faced this testimony with steady and unwavering forthrightness, David Tracy should wryly recall Vladimir Nabokov's adage to the effect that "'Reality' is the one word that should always appear within quotation marks."[9] But one is somewhat surprised at his finding it possible to steel himself even to the point of being prepared indeed to *celebrate* our being "all de-centered egos now,"[10] for this appears to represent a betrayal of the hermeneutical norms with which he would keep faith.[11]

---

8. Edward Said, *Beginnings,* 287.
9. David Tracy, *Plurality and Ambiguity: Hermeneutics, Religion, Hope* (San Francisco: Harper & Row, 1987) 47.
10. Ibid., 50.
11. When, under the influence of the new *mystique* of deconstruction, confidence in the very idea of selfhood begins to be shaken, we need to remember that any strict phenomenology of the *Lebenswelt* will surely indicate that persons do regularly undertake certain projects and carry forward actions that so manifestly guarantee certain

Expectably, given his great natural courtesy of spirit, he takes his stand in the line of such theorists of interpretation as Martin Buber and Emmanuel Levinas and Hans-Georg Gadamer, who have in various ways conceived interpretation to be itself at bottom a mode of conversation. And he follows Paul Ricoeur in taking textual exegesis to be the principal business of hermeneutics.[12] "Interpretation seems a minor matter," he says, "but it is not. Every time we act, deliberate, judge, understand, or even experience, we are interpreting.... To experience in other than a purely passive sense (a sense less than human) is to interpret.... Whether we know it or not, to be human is to be a skilled interpreter."[13] The interpretative situation, as he reckons, involves, first, the interpreter facing some phenomenon or text awaiting interpretation and then the interaction between the two. And this interaction he conceives to be an affair of conversation. The phenomenon or text which is to be interpreted must be allowed to speak, and it must be "listened" to with the most scrupulous attentiveness, for, as Tracy warns, unless it is allowed really to say what it wants to say, unless its otherness is permitted to exert its full claim upon us, the great likelihood is that the interpreter will simply "domesticate" it within the system of his "pre-understandings" or her already established expectations.[14]

A right and proper *politesse* must, in other words, control the hermeneutical transaction: we must not witlessly impose our own categories and perspectives and values upon the text at hand: with its own inner rhythm and dynamic, it must be allowed to address us and interrogate us, to bid for a kind of dialogue. Whereas the interpreter, on the other hand, must enter unreservedly into the exchange, being prepared not merely to reduce what is being encountered to "more of the same"[15]

---

outcomes that we may reasonably conclude the outcomes to have been intended. And not only does intentional action inevitably posit *agency*, but we also find ourselves to be *agents* who are committed to the pursuit of certain goods (such as social justice and the alleviation of suffering and fidelity to family and friends). Moreover, it does appear that our sense of our own inwardness, our certainty that we are indeed creatures with inner depths and spaces, is consequent upon our knowledge of our having elected such commitments to numerous projects and to numerous values of fundamental import. And it would seem that to disavow the *idea* of selfhood which has emerged out of this whole order of experience would be for us then to become strangers to ourselves and to risk even an essential mutilation of our common *humanitas*. See, for example, Charles Taylor, *Sources of the Self: The Making of the Modern Identity* (Cambridge, MA: Harvard University Press, 1989).

12. See Paul Ricoeur, *Freud and Philosophy: An Essay on Interpretation* (New Haven: Yale University Press, 1970) 20–36.
13. Tracy, *Plurality*, 9.
14. Ibid., 17–19.
15. Ibid., 15.

but to submit to such a cross-questioning as will initiate some new conceptualization of his or her horizons. The kind of game that true conversation entails—and Tracy is emphatically insistent on the figure of game[16]—requires beyond all else *answerability:* the text addresses and interrogates, and the interpreter in turn *answers,* and out of this dialectical interplay between interpreter and text the result of the hermeneutical event gradually evolves—namely, that appropriation of the text that leaves both text and interpreter somewhat different from what they were before each began to bear upon itself the pressure of the other. The game has, of course, "some hard rules: [you] say only what you mean; [you] say it as accurately as you can; [you] listen to and respect what the other says, however different or other; [you are] . . . willing to correct or defend your opinions if challenged by the conversation partner; [you are] . . . willing to argue if necessary, to confront if demanded, to endure necessary conflict, to change your mind if the evidence suggests it."[17] *These are the rules of the game:* "no purely autonomous text, . . . no purely passive reader. There is only that interaction named conversation."[18] As Hillis Miller said in a period antedating his conversion to deconstruction,

> . . . the proper model for the relation of [the interpreter] . . . to the work he studies is not that of scientist to physical objects but that of one man to another in charity. I may love another person and know him as only love can know without in the least abnegating my own beliefs. Love wants the other person to be as he is, in all his recalcitrant particularity. As St. Augustine puts it, the lover says to the loved one, "Volo ut sis!"—"I wish you to be." If the [interpreter] . . . approaches the [work] . . . with this kind of reverence for its integrity, it will respond to his questioning and take its part in that dialogue between reader and work which is the life of . . . [interpretation].[19]

Now all this is well and good, and Tracy's fidelity to a dialogical norm in theory of interpretation is admirable, particularly in the degree to which it prepares him as a theologian to reckon with the radically pluralistic ethos of the age. But, then, his equally admirable irenicism in relation to new insurgencies in hermeneutical theory prompts him toward a somewhat questionable position. He wants not to be convictable of having neglected to heed "the linguistic turn" that has so deeply shaped the course taken by hermeneutics since Wittgenstein and

16. Ibid., 17–18.
17. Ibid., 19.
18. Ibid.
19. J. Hillis Miller, "Literature and Religion," in *Relations of Literary Study: Essays on Interdisciplinary Contributions,* ed. James Thorpe (New York: Modern Language Association, 1967) 126.

Heidegger, and the deftness with which he appraises the work of thinkers like Barthes, Foucault, Derrida, Lacan, Habermas, Karl-Otto Apel, and Richard Rorty suggests that he has paid a closer kind of attention to such material than perhaps any other theologian on the American scene. Indeed, so determined is he not to shut himself off from this whole movement, particularly in its deconstructionist mode, and so eager is he to elect a conciliatory stance that, with a surprising alacrity, he makes some very crucial concessions—that meaning is dispersed along the interminable chain of signifiers and that the ego is, therefore, without any center, that the autonomous self is, to be sure, an illusion. True, the force of his acceding to Derrida's dicta about the dispersion of meaning is very considerably mitigated by his adherence to an important lesson laid down by Paul Ricoeur, who has reminded us that the hermeneutical endeavor is devoted not to the study of signs but to the study of discourse. And this is a consideration that puts us in view of a most crucial proviso. For, even if it be granted that Derridean doctrine about the "free-play" of signification has some relevance to what holds *within* the system of a given *langue* (where, to be sure, signs only refer to other signs and these to still others), when, as in all concrete utterance, sentential forms are used, language, as Ricoeur bids us to remember, "is directed beyond itself" to the circumambient world, for the reason that sentential utterance aims at predication.[20] Semantics (which is the science of syntax) cannot, in other words, be collapsed into semiotics (which is the science of signs), as contemporary deconstructionists undertake to do. So, as he keeps this lesson in mind, Tracy's argument takes a happy turn when he insists that

> the analysis of language move past words to sentences and eventually to texts ... [since] language is neither system alone nor use alone ... but discourse. ... To discover discourse is to explore language as a reality beyond individual words in the dictionary, beyond both synchronic codes (*langue*) and individual use of words (*parole*). ... .[21]

In short, as it turns out, meaning is really not something ultimately scattered and dispersed along the whole chain of signifiers.

But he is perhaps less circumspect regarding the status of the self in these poststructuralist days of our misery, for, in this connection, he fails, as it would seem, to take the necessary step out of—dare one use so exigent a word in relation to so gifted and elegantly perceptive a

---

20. See Paul Ricoeur, *Interpretation Theory: Discourse and the Surplus of Meaning* (Fort Worth: Texas Christian University Press, 1976) chap. 1.
21. Tracy, *Plurality*, 61.

theologian?—nihilism. He appears to assume that what the deconstructionists contemptuously speak of as "traditional humanism" posited a "purely autonomous ego"[22] untouched by any sort of contingency, wholly present to itself and taking itself to be the measure of all things. And thus, in relation to such an overweening monarchism, he welcomes the therapy administered by poststructuralist terrorism through its "de-centering" of personhood. But surely it is impermissible to attribute such a conception of selfhood to figures so diverse as Augustine, Shakespeare, Milton, Pascal, Coleridge, Kierkegaard, Dostoievski, and the later Wittgenstein—as impermissible indeed as would be the attribution of such a doctrine of the self to some other group of major strategists of thought in the Western tradition representing an equal diversity and selected equally at random. One finds it difficult to understand how it might be possible to sustain the thesis that any doctrine of the unity of selfhood implicitly posits the self as wholly present to itself and as "purely autonomous." Reinhold Niebuhr, for example, a Christian thinker whom David Tracy greatly admires, would have been astonished and scandalized by the proposition that at the heart of consciousness there is only vacancy, only fissures and cavities and breaks. But, then, he would have been equally astonished by any proposition to the effect that the self is wholly present to itself, for not only did he have a lively awareness of how much the psychoanalytic encounter reveals the patient's self-alienation, but (in his Gifford Lectures, *The Nature and Destiny of Man*, or in such a book as *The Self and the Dramas of History*) he probed with a shrewdness unsurpassed even by Pascal our boundless capacities for self-evasion and self-deception. And the profundity with which he analyzed the embarrassments and confusions attendant upon our finitude makes his allegiance to any conception of the self as "purely autonomous" inconceivable. Which is to say that it may be too large an assumption to suppose that any and every vision of selfhood as unified or "centered" stands in need of the special kind of therapy that deconstructionist ideology wants to proffer.

But what one finds most puzzling is Tracy's failure to see the contradiction between the kind of hospitality he is prepared to offer deconstructionist doctrine and the wonderfully humane kind of hermeneutical program to which he gives his suffrage. It is to be borne in mind, for example, that the "de-centering" of the self is of a piece with the assassination of the author in poststructuralist theory which holds that the truly decisive cultural fact is not the creativity of the authorial imagination but the impersonal system of language-structures which shapes and authenticates all human utterance: our gestures in the

22. Ibid., 82.

direction of *parole*, in other words, figure forth nothing more than that system of norms and rules constituting the *langue* off which they ricochet. Though innocence may take Gustave Flaubert to be the creator of *Madame Bovary*, the novel is really nothing other than the "utterance" of certain preexistent genres of narrative and certain established procedures of storytelling, so that, far from Flaubert being the author of the text, the real author is in point of fact Language itself. And thus, given the assassination of "the transcendental subject" and the destabilization of meaning that results from its dispersion along the chain of signifiers, are we not bound to conclude that any such "conversation" as the hermeneutical transaction will entail must be an affair of "nothingness" encountering "nothingness"? Is it not the case that the deconstruction of the "I" and the erosion of the text make any sort of genuine dialogue between the two quite impossible? Does not, in other words, George Steiner have the matter in hand when he suggests that the relation between reader and text, as conceived in poststructuralist theory, involves simply one kind of autism confronting another?[23]

These hard questions take on a particular poignancy at the point where Tracy begins to consider the kind of school for the interpreter that offers itself when he or she undertakes disciplined conversation with "the religions." Here, of course, pluralities are mounted on pluralities—many different visions of Ultimate Reality, many different understandings of the paths leading to liberation, many different models of religious enlightenment, and these being differences not only *between* Judaism, Hinduism, Islam, Buddhism, and Christianity but also *within* each of these great traditions. The scene, in other words, is one that is calculated to remind "the postmodern subject" that "any route to reality must pass through the radical plurality of our differential languages and the ambiguity of all our histories."[24] "The purely autonomous ego was mortally wounded when it was found that, if language was not its instrument, then the subject was no longer in control." Yet, as Tracy says, "the subject, however chastened and transformed, has not been erased."[25] But, if the subject has evaporated into the free-play of signification, if the self has been thoroughly and irreclaimably de-centered, what could "the postmodern subject" possibly be? If the deconstruction of the self is, as we are assured, an accomplished fact, precisely *who* is it, then, on whom we are to count for such a conversation with "the religions" as will strengthen the various types of resistance that they promote with respect to all monistic and "totalizing" schemes (whether

---

23. George Steiner, *Real Presences*, 82.
24. Tracy, *Plurality*, 82.
25. Ibid.

they be social-political or intellectual)? This troublesome issue is nowhere addressed in his recent book on hermeneutics, *Plurality and Ambiguity*.

But, beyond all these issues, perhaps the most fundamental question needing further clarification is that which concerns the ground on which the notion of interpretation-as-conversation is to be validated. I find Tracy's way of describing such a hermeneutic to be enormously attractive, but it does seem odd that at no point does he venture any response to the powerful critique of the conversational model that E. D. Hirsch set forth in the 1960s.

Hirsch's polemic was largely elicited by the extreme skepticism expressed by Gadamer in *Truth and Method* regarding the possibility of establishing any determinate meaning for a given text. From Gadamer's standpoint, of course, the hermeneutical situation is a dialogical situation: that is to say, the text, though it has its own otherness and presents a distinctive "world" marked by a particular structure and dynamic, is yet not unimplicated in the historical reality of the interpreter, for it wants to *speak* to him or her, and it bids for a response. True, the interpreter lives within his or her own horizon: he has his own established ways of construing experience, and these will not be merely suspended if he brings some real integrity of personal vision to his reading. But the text may challenge the interpreter's established perspectives, and, indeed, in the degree to which it proves itself to have the kind of power we call cogency, the interpreter will find his own conception of how the world is ordered being submitted to a sort of interrogation. Whereas the interpreter who wants seriously to go out to meet that which is before him will gladly consent to be thus addressed, though all the while confronting the text with his own *Lebenswelt*, his own self-understanding, his own sense of the human reality. And it is this free interchange between the interpreter and the text that constitutes for Gadamer the essence of the hermeneutical situation. The text wants to be "re-actualized" in the living dialogue between itself and the interpreter: it wants to be rescued from the alienation in which it finds itself as merely a piece of writing. And it will not even begin to "thematize" the concrete, historical reality of the interpreter's life until he or she consents to meet it as a real partner in the dialogue for which it yearns. Which means that the text does not begin to have any real life until its *speaking* begins to be *listened to*, until it is caught up into a dialogue with an interpreter, and its fullest life is realized in the moment of the "fusion of horizons" (*Horizontverschmelzung*), the fusion of its own horizon with that of the interpreter. But, of course, since each interpreter will bring to any given text his or her *own* horizon, Gadamer quite candidly (and even insistently) declares, "There cannot . . . be any one interpretation that is correct 'in itself.'"[26]

Now, given its complexity, E. D. Hirsch's critique does not lend itself to swift rehearsal, but suffice it to say that he is prompted to conclude that Gadamer's general position—and, by extension, he may be taken also to have in view any similar theory of interpretation as conversation—does, in the degree to which it posits indeterminateness of textual meaning, line itself up behind a kind of hermeneutical nihilism, or, as he likes to speak of it, "cognitive atheism."[27] Gadamer, as he would claim, supposes "that we can only understand a text in *our* own terms, but this is a contradictory statement since verbal meaning has to be construed in *its* own terms if it is to be construed at all. . . . If we do not construe a text in what we rightly or wrongly assume to be its own terms then we do not construe it at all."[28] Hirsch's own attempt to ground an objectivist hermeneutic in Husserl's intentional theory of human consciousness has, to be sure, been vigorously contested by David Hoy[29] and Frank Lentricchia,[30] and various others, and his critique of Gadamer is by no means unanswerable. But to ignore the kind of question he raises is surely a tactical miscalculation, since a frank reckoning with his animadversions would have the effect of forestalling any charge that an exposition of a dialogical hermeneutic is by way of making it appear to be something less problematic than it may well be.

But, now, after all such questions as I have raised have been thoroughly ventilated and even after one or another of his readers has found his formulations at this or that point to be debatable, there are few who would gainsay the brilliance of the kind of inquiry David Tracy has been conducting since the early 1970s in such books as *Blessed Rage for Order* and *The Analogical Imagination* and *Plurality and Ambiguity.* Though *Plurality and Ambiguity* is more emphatically focused on the hermeneutical problem than his earlier writings are, this theme is a major

---

26. Hans-Georg Gadamer, *Truth and Method* (New York: Seabury, 1975) 358. (It is said on the copyright page that "the translation was edited by Garrett Barden and John Cumming from the second [1965] edition," and it *may* be that Messrs. Barden and Cumming did, indeed, produce the English translation. But, given the strange language employed by the publisher, this must be a matter of conjecture.)

27. See E. D. Hirsch, *Validity in Interpretation* (New Haven: Yale University Press, 1967) 245–64. See also Hirsch's *The Aims of Interpretation* (Chicago: University of Chicago Press, 1976) 1–92.

28. Hirsch, *Validity in Interpretation,* 135.

29. See David Couzens Hoy, *The Critical Circle: Literature, History, and Philosophical Hermeneutics* (Berkeley and Los Angeles: University of California Press, 1978) 11–40.

30. See Frank Lentricchia, *After the New Criticism* (Chicago: University of Chicago Press, 1980) 257–80.

motif of his entire work. For he is constantly to be found attempting in as serious a way as possible to reckon with (to use a favorite term of his) all the "interruptions" that are occasioned by the necessity of the theologian's search for ways of understanding and interpreting the "global crisis of meaning"[31] that stems from the radically pluralistic culture we face in these late days of the twentieth century. He remains a loyal son of the Roman Church (locating himself, to be sure, in the ranks of the Church's "loyal opposition"), but he takes it for granted that "the [mere] announcement of his own tradition's beliefs does not and cannot constitute . . . evidence for his fellow community of historical or philosophical inquirers—*or even for himself* as one committed to the morality of autonomous critical inquiry. . . ."[32] He wants, in other words, to keep "a fidelity to open-ended inquiry, a loyalty to defended methodological canons, a willingness to follow the evidence wherever it may lead."[33] So, as one confronts the pluralism of the age, there must be "interruptions" of the Christian theologian's systematic and constructive work. But Tracy's theological conscience tells him that one must summon up something more than mere openness to plurality and (as Ricoeur phrases it) "the conflict of interpretations," that a lazy kind of "consumer-tolerance"[34] is not good enough. And what is perhaps his most original and profound contribution to hermeneutical theory is his retrieval of the whole concept of the analogical imagination.

Attractive as is the general tenor of his argument in *The Analogical Imagination*, the details of it are not so consistently clear as one would like them to be, but I hope I am not wrong in taking him to be saying in effect that the hermeneutical situation to which Christian theology is committed is one that perforce involves a reckoning at every point with discontinuities. The theologian, for example, in handling a "second-order" kind of reflective language stands at a great distance from the originating religious experience and its classical expression. Moreover, there is the primary disproportion to be faced between the world and God. And, in assessing the relation of Christian texts to "common human experience," the theologian in our period must come to terms with the inordinate multiplicity of interpretations regarding what that experience most truly entails, to say nothing of "the conflict of interpretations" embraced by the theological community itself. Indeed, on every side, as it seems, the hermeneutical encounter thrusts the theologian into attempts at the decipherment of otherness, and Tracy wants

---

31. Tracy, *Blessed Rage for Order*, 4.
32. Ibid., 6.
33. Ibid., 7.
34. Ibid., 3.

to suggest that this undertaking will be most fruitfully facilitated by disciplined efforts at discerning "real similarities-in-real difference": the necessary route, in other words, is that of the analogical imagination which, in Aristotle's familiar formula, seeks "to spot the similar in the dissimilar."

Analogical procedures, of course, never yield the logical tidiness of univocal patterns which overpower all contrariety and make it submissive to some unity of sameness. But, as that wonderfully acute Jesuit critic, the late Fr. William Lynch, reminded us a generation ago in his remarkable book *Christ and Apollo*, "A truly analogical idea crackles with light and makes other things crackle with the same and yet with their own light."[35] And it is a similar perception that prompts David Tracy to feel that it is the stratagems of the analogical imagination that offer the best chance at the kind of horizon that will beckon us toward "the genuine conversation open to all in our pluralistic present."[36] Happily, he is (at the time of my writing—1989) but a mere sprig of fifty years of age: so it may be assumed that his hermeneutical program will be more fully fleshed out in the books he will be producing in the coming years, and I have no doubt but that such questions as I have raised he will resolve in the work that lies ahead.

35. William F. Lynch, S.J., *Christ and Apollo: The Dimensions of the Literary Imagination* (New York: Sheed & Ward, 1960) 156.
36. David Tracy, *The Analogical Imagination: Christian Theology and the Culture of Pluralism* (New York: Crossroad, 1981) xii.

7

FEMINIST HERMENEUTICS, SCRIPTURAL AUTHORITY, AND RELIGIOUS EXPERIENCE: THE CASE OF THE IMAGO DEI AND GENDER EQUALITY

Rosemary Radford Ruether

FEMINIST HERMENEUTICS works out of the dialectical tension between truthful accountability to past tradition and new creativity in response to the ethical and theoretical challenges of present times. It is a tension to which David Tracy has been singularly attentive in all of his own work, both in his reflections on hermeneutics and theological method, and in his own astute exercises in interpretation. He is, indeed, a model of a theologian who combines critical fidelity to church tradition with responsible concern for the life of the church today in relation to the many human religious quests for meaning. This essay on the relation between scripture, tradition, and experience in Christian feminist hermeneutics attempts to express a similar fidelity by exploring the meaning of the *imago Dei* for gender equality.

Genesis 1:27, which describes God as creating Adam in the "image of God, male and female," has traditionally been, and continues today to be, a key scriptural reference point for Christian discussion of anthropology and gender. Most contemporary Christian theologians take the original intent of this text to be egalitarian. Both men and women were made by God in the divine image. Both share in the divine image equally, and this establishes the full and equal humanity of both genders.

Feminist theologians have shared this assumption that the original meaning of this text was egalitarian. Postscriptural Christian theological traditions that have denied women's full humanity are thus proved to be unscriptural by reference to this text. Christian feminists, Catholics as well as Protestants, have followed the Reformation way of using scripture to invalidate later Christian tradition by proving that the tradition contradicts the original meaning of scripture.[1]

In this essay I wish to raise basic questions about Christian feminist appeal to scriptural authority, given the fact that such feminists do not regard the whole of the canonical scriptures as authoritative and indeed see much in these scriptures as sexist, that is, ethically and theologically false. More specifically I wish to suggest that the original meaning of the text of Genesis 1:27 was closer to the Christian tradition that denied women's full humanity than it is to modern egalitarian interpretations of this text. If this is the case, on what basis can Christian feminism claim this as an egalitarian proof text against the tradition?

I will begin by discussing the way this text is used in contemporary Roman Catholic documents. Although these documents overtly claim that the text is egalitarian, they prove unable to carry through this claim consistently. This is because they maintain the view that women cannot be ordained because they cannot "image Christ."

I will then discuss the asymmetrical reading of this text in classical Christian tradition and its consistency with the original scriptural intent as that has been suggested in contemporary scriptural scholarship as distinct from modern theology. I will finally discuss the dilemma of feminist hermeneutics in its use of scripture to critique tradition and suggest an alternative way of relating experience and tradition, including scripture.

The American Catholic bishops in their pastoral letter "Partners in the Mystery of Redemption" take Genesis 1:27 as their theological starting point.[2] They take for granted that this text means, and has always meant, the full equality of women and men in the image of God. They see this text as establishing both an equal relation with God and also a relation of egalitarian mutuality or partnership between women and men, personally and socially. They organize their letter around the theme of partnership, seeking both to reflect on and to promote this

---

1. See, e.g., Anne Carr, *Transforming Grace: Christian Tradition and Women's Experience* (San Francisco: Harper & Row, 1988) 31.
2. "Partners in the Mystery of Redemption: A Pastoral Response to Women's Concerns for Church and Society," The U.S. National Conference of Catholic Bishops, Washington, DC, April 1988.

partnership relation of men and women in the three spheres of home, paid work, and the church.

Despite this bold beginning, the bishops are unable to carry through this partnership model in any of these three spheres. Their presuppositions remain those of patriarchal clericalism. They still assume that women's essential vocation is motherhood and men's essential vocation is outside the family in society. The asymmetrical gender model of family and work has been softened but not fundamentally changed in their thinking.

But this failure to carry through the egalitarian partnership model becomes most obvious when they turn to the question of ministry in the church. Here all they are able to offer is an auxiliary and subordinate relation of women as lay ministers to an all-male ordained clergy. The root of this failure is the bishops' endorsement of the 1976 Vatican Declaration against women's ordination, which said that women cannot be ordained because they are ontologically incapable of "imaging Christ."[3] This brings the bishops' christology into contradiction with their purported theological anthropology. What does it mean to say that women are in the image of God equally with men but that they cannot "image Christ"? Is not the fundamental role of Christ to be the "image of God" (e.g., Col 1:15; 2 Cor 4:4)?

The same contradictions, although in even more convoluted form, are found in the papal statement of September 30, 1988, "The Dignity and Vocation of Woman."[4] The Pope also begins by affirming the full equality of men and women in the image of God. Both sexes are said to possess rationality and to share in the dominion over the rest of creation. God's original intention for humanity was one of egalitarian mutuality between the sexes. The Pope also sees maleness and femaleness as mirrored in the Trinity: there God is said to have both male and female qualities. The equality and mutual love between the persons of the Trinity mirror what is to be the relation between men and women. Sin distorted this intended relation between the sexes and created wrongful domination of men over women. But redemption in Christ is said to overcome this domination and to restore women to their full dignity. Christ in his ministry displayed a full acceptance of women, contrary to his culture. Women are included in the prophetic gifts poured out through the Holy Spirit at Pentecost and in the general

---

3. "Declaration on the Question of the Admission of Women to the Ministerial Priesthood," The Vatican, October 15, 1976.

4. Pope John Paul II, "The Dignity and Vocation of Women," The Vatican, September 30, 1988.

priesthood by which the whole church proclaims the redemptive mystery of loving service to one another.

Yet when the Pope treats Jesus' presumed establishment of the Eucharist and the ordained priesthood at the Last Supper, we are told that women were intentionally excluded by Christ.[5] This is because Christ represents the "bridegroom" in relation to the church as his "bride." This relationship is assumed to be essentially one of the superiority and headship of the "masculine" over the "feminine." Women cannot represent the "masculine" and hence cannot represent Christ in the ordained ministry. Thus the Pope too claims that, although women image God, they cannot image Christ.

This contradiction between anthropology and Christology in contemporary Catholic official documents reflects an effort to hold on to a subordinationist view of women's status in relation to the redemptive work of God while accommodating to the contemporary social reality of women's new status as an autonomous person in civil society. The result is a new version of the split between nature and grace, creation and redemption. Women are said to be equal in the created order and hence in secular society but subordinate in the redemptive "mystery" that connects Christ with the eucharistic priesthood.

The roots of this Catholic view that women cannot image Christ and so cannot be ordained lie in the patriarchal anthropology of Augustine and Aquinas. However, in this classical tradition, anthropology and Christology were consistent. Women were said to lack the image of God in themselves. The male was seen as the collective image of God, both for himself and for the female. The woman was included in the divine image only by being included "under" the male as her "head."

This Augustinian view was further developed in Thomas Aquinas, who adopted the Aristotelian anthropology that defined woman as a defective member of the human species, lacking the fullness of human nature mentally, morally, and physically. Only the male possesses "perfect" or complete human nature, and hence only the male can represent the human as such. The maleness of Christ is not simply a historical fact but an ontological necessity. In order to possess the fullness of human nature, Christ must be male.[6]

This classical Catholic view, denying that women possess the image of God in themselves and including them in it only under the male as their head, is not inconsistent with the Genesis 1:27 text itself. Phyllis Bird, in her careful exegesis of this text, has shown that the expression "male and female" is not intended to modify the phrase "image of God."

---

5. Ibid., section 26.
6. Thomas Aquinas, *Summa Theologica*, Q. 85, arts. 1–6.

Division into male and female is for the purpose of reproduction and is a characteristic that humans share with animals, but not with God, who is not gendered.7

The quality of being God's image is possessed by humanity collectively, but not in relation to their bisexuality. The term "image of God" suggests the ancient Near Eastern theme that sees humanity as servant of God in relation to God as Lord. Humanity is seen collectively as God's royal servant, exercising divine dominion over God's creation as God's representative.8 However, the religious sociology of the priestly author of this text makes it certain that he took for granted that this sovereignty over creation was exercised in practice by the male head of family. The term "Adam" was thought of as including women in an androcentric collective sense, just as the male head of family was thought of as including under himself and corporately representing all the dependent members of the family—women, children, and servants.

This scriptural text appears to us today to make male and female equal as images of God only because this patriarchal social and legal assumption is not spelled out. But to read the text this way is to read into the text individualistic presuppositions of modern democratic societies that were foreign to the social context of the author. The author of the text belonged to a society where only the male head of family was assumed to be able to exercise public autonomous personhood. He did so not only in his own name, but as the corporate representative of those "under him." Since sons could grow up and slaves be emancipated and become householders, it was women who were assumed in this system to be incapable "by nature" of becoming autonomous persons in their own right. Since they could never exercise domination as autonomous persons, they were not in themselves "images of God" or persons able to represent divine domination and sovereignty over creation.

The New Testament theological development, particularly in the writings of Paul, continues to reflect this patriarchal assumption that women were subordinate and under male headship in the order of creation. But this assumption was modified by the development of an eschatological Christology in which gender was nullified and women were

---

7. Phyllis Bird, "Male and Female, He Created Them: Gen. 1:27b in the Context of the Priestly Account of Creation," *Harvard Theological Review* 74 (1981) 129–59. An expanded version of this article will be published in *Image of God and Gender Models*, ed. Kari Borresen (Oslo: Solem Forlag, forthcoming).

8. Contemporary Hebrew scripture scholars have come to a general consensus that the essential meaning of the term "image of God" in this text is that of dominion over creation as God's representative. See Gunnlaugur Jansson, *The Image of God: Gen. 1:26–28 in a Century of Old Testament Research* (Stockholm: Almquist & Wiksell, 1988).

included as spiritual equals of men. One way of understanding this contradiction between women's inclusion in redemption in Christ, in whom there is neither male nor female, and her subordination as women in creation, is to presuppose a prelapsarian androgenous Adam prior to the fall into bisexuality.

Christ is then seen as restoring this prelapsarian androgenous Adam by annulling sexual activity and reproduction in the eschatological redemptive state. The celibate woman anticipates this eschatological state of spiritual equality, but only by renouncing those roles which make her woman. It is typical in patristic literature to speak of the celibate woman as having overcome her specific female nature and as having been raised to the moral and spiritual status of maleness. Thus woman is included in spiritual potency in Christianity, but only by rejecting her femaleness and being included in an a-sexual androcentric view of spiritual humanness.[9]

The seeming contradiction in Paul's writings between Galatians 3:28, in which the new humanity in Christ overcomes the division into male and female, and 1 Corinthians 11:3, in which woman is subordinate to man as man to Christ and Christ to God, is explicable when put in the context of these anthropological assumptions. As head of the eschatological humanity, Christ is seen as restoring "man" to "his" prelapsarian state. This is assumed to be an androcentric androgynous state prior to gender differentiation, or rather prior to the separation of the female from its original inclusion in the male androgene.

In Christ the baptized are taken up into this male-identified a-sexual state. Women, as nonsexual persons, can be included in this male-androgynous Christ-likeness (Gal 3:26–28). But, considered as woman in relation to man in sexual divison of labor in the family, women are not included in the image of God. They stand under male dominion, just as men stand under the dominion of Christ and Christ under God (1 Cor 11:3).[10]

Later Catholic tradition attempted to work out this relation between women's inclusion in an asexual redemptive humanness, restored in Christ, and their subordination as sexual persons. Both Augustine and Thomas Aquinas take for granted that women are redeemed in Christ. Woman shares equally the spiritual personhood of redeemed humanity,

---

9. See Guila Sfameni Gasparro, "Image of God and Sexual Differentiation in the Tradition of the *Enkrateia*," and Kari Vogt, "Becoming Male: A Gnostic and Early Christian Metaphor," in *Image of God and Gender Models*.

10. I follow here the exegetical work of Lone Fatum, "Image of God and Glory of Man: On the Condition of Women in the Pauline Congregations," in *Image of God and Gender Models*.

but only though an asexual humanness, not as woman. As woman she represents the creaturely and the nondivine. As woman she cannot image God or represent Christ, but represents the somatic and carnal realm, that which is ruled over by God and by God's representative, man.[11]

This inclusion of woman in asexual generic humanness laid the basis for the further development in liberal democratic societies of recognition of woman's civil personhood in society. But this development could take place only through the dissolution of the ancient patriarchal and feudal belief in corporate personhood. Modern democratic societies are based on an individualistic concept of the personhood of, at least, all legal adults (excluding children and mentally incompetent persons). Only in the context of this individualism can woman be accepted as an autonomous person and hence as one who exercises dominion over herself (and so is in the image of God).

However liberalism was originally inconsistent in its view that "all men" were "created equal." It originally excluded women and other dependent persons in the family from this civil equality. Only by breaking up the corporate and feudal concept of the family could woman be granted civil personhood. But this was assumed only to define her legal and political personhood in public society. In the family or in the sexual division of labor, she remains subordinate. Thus, liberalism and also socialism remain unable to overcome the new version of the division between woman's asexual equality in the public order and her subordination in the sexual division of labor.

How does feminism relate to these patriarchal traditions, religious and secular? I suggest that feminism starts not with scripture or tradition but with the feminist experience of women affirming themselves as autonomous persons, not only in legal and political relations, but also in sexual relations. It is often said that feminist hermeneutics starts with "experience," but what is left unsaid in this formula is that the experience that is assumed here is feminist experience. By feminist experience is meant a consciousness-raising experience in which women shake off their indoctrination into feeling themselves dependent and inferior and claim themselves as fully capable of self-determination.[12]

---

11. See Kari Borresen, *Subordination and Equivalence: The Nature and Role of Women in Augustine and Aquinas* (Washington, DC: University Press of America, 1981; French original 1968).

12. See Rosemary Ruether, "Feminist Hermeneutics: A Method of Correlation," in *Feminist Interpretation of the Bible*, ed. L. M. Russell (Philadelphia: Westminster Press, 1985) 111–16.

The key feminist anthropological question is not how gender relates to the image of God, but rather how gender relates to humanness. Is there one essential human nature, and women and men both equally possess a generic humanness? Or does gender differentiation mean that each gender possesses a distinct and different kind of human nature? Feminists are divided between dualist and monist views of human nature.[13]

Feminist dualists see women as possessing a distinct and different humanity from men. This humanity is typically seen as superior, fuller, more sensitive, and more moral than that of men. Thus dualistic feminism tends to reverse classical patriarchal androcentrism. Men are seen as defective and partially human. Men can become fully human only to the extent that they can develop the more fully human qualities represented by women.

Feminist monists, by contrast, believe that there is a fullness of humanness of which both men and women are equally capable. But this humanity has been distorted for both men and women by gender socialization. Liberation from patriarchal socialization will allow both men and women to develop their full and essentially the equivalent humanness.

Feminist theology starts with its experience of female autonomous "humanness" and, from this context, attempts to situate itself in relation to men, to society, and to God. This is, in reality, not unlike what male theology has done. The difference is that feminist theology must be more explicit about this partiality, while male theology has concealed the way its claims to start with God and God's revelation is, in actuality, a projection of male patriarchal experience.

Feminist theology assumes that the definition of God as a ruling class male in classical theology is, in fact, a projection upon God by patriarchal males of their own social experience, thereby relating God to women and "nature" accordingly. The theology that teaches that only the male is fully made in God's image is, in actuality, a theology in which the male makes God in his image. This ideological critique of the androcentric bias in the image of God theme in scripture and tradition changes fundamentally the nature of the discussion.

A feminist construction of theology starts with the feminist question of a just and truthful anthropology. It asks how can women situate their experience of their full and autonomous personhood in relation to men, society, and God in a way that does justice to this experience. The God question for women, as for all oppressed people, is a question of theodicy. Does God support the realization of our full humanity or not? If the

---

13. See Carr, *Transforming Grace*, 117-33.

God of the Christian tradition does not support it, then this God is not our God.

Feminist theology assumes that the true divinity who created and sustains the world is indeed on the side of that fullness of human personhood which we experience as our true and redemptive self. Thus a God of scripture and tradition who denies this relation between God and us is a sinful distortion and not the true God. We can affirm a God revealed in scripture only in the sense of a God behind scripture that is glimpsed between the lines as a just God, but whose reality has been distorted by the patriarchal receptors and interpreters of God.

The question that is always raised for those with this starting point in the experience of oppression is: How do you know that your starting point is not subject to equally sinful distortions? What is the norm by which you can have certainty? I believe that there is no such infallible norm by which we can be certain. What we have as finite human beings is not certainty but a certain trust in the coherence of ultimate reality and assurance that our experience is capable of being in touch with this ultimate reality. But our formulations must be constantly tested by the ethical results of the appropriated theories for our experience.

This ethical criterion can be formulated in terms of the classical Jewish version of the golden rule: Do not do to others what you do not wish others to do to you. The ethical criterion is understood here in the broadest sense in the way theories manifest themselves in just and loving relations that promote the fullness of human personhood in mutuality. On the basis of this ethical test, we need to make our way experimentally along the path to a fuller and fuller, but never final or perfect, understanding of how we should relate to one another.

Feminist theology thus bases itself on just relationality. On this basis it seeks authentic relations between men and women, between some women and other women, between men and women of different classes and races, and between humans and nonhumans. It understands God as the creator, sustainer, and renewer of the just relationality that can promote our redemptive fullness of being.

All our images of God are metaphors and projections from our human standpoint of an ultimate ground of being and new being that is beyond all such images. The question is not whether there are some images that are not human projections, but rather what human projections promote just and loving relationality, and which projections promote injustice and diminished humanness. Our images of the God–self relation may be more than, but cannot be less than, that which promotes goodness in human relations.

How does this feminist view, which starts with feminist experience and then constructs morally appropriate understandings of God out of this experience, relate to biblical authority? What is the authority of the Bible and its interpretation in Christian tradition for feminist hermeneutics? I have argued that the Christian feminist claim to find in texts like Genesis 1:28 a proof text for a nonpatriarchal God, by which Christian tradition can be critiqued, is mistaken. If anything, it is the Christian tradition that developed toward a more inclusive view of women's spiritual potency than was assumed in the original Genesis text.

Christian feminism builds on an evolution in Christian tradition that had begun to include women in Christ-likeness. But feminism goes beyond this past by shaking off the asexual and androcentric limits of that tradition. Christian feminism takes a radical new step along this path, but one with roots in a reinterpretation of Jewish scripture begun in the New Testament and continued in the church fathers and in modern Christianity. In this sense Christian feminism is a new step in the development of tradition.

The feminist practice of hermeneutics cannot appropriate the Protestant tradition that assumed an infallible scripture as the certain guide for the critique of tradition, but neither can it make uncritical use of the Catholic view of unbroken development of scripture and tradition.

The Catholic view that one must take into account both what a text meant in scripture and its unfolding in the development of interpretation in tradition better suits the feminist practice, but it is inadequate. *De facto*, Catholic hermeneutics, particularly in official Catholic documents, tends to accept whatever interpretation the contemporary Magisterium sees as suiting its purposes, regardless of historical accuracy to either scripture or past periods of historical tradition. This is the kind of eisegesis that we have seen in the Catholic documents discussed in this essay.

Protestantism arose along with new methods of textual and historical study in the Renaissance. It sought to undercut what it saw as bad traditions of the recent past by returning to what it believed was the "original" meaning of scripture. It assumed that the original meaning of the scripture text was recoverable and infallibly normative, while nonscriptural tradition was fallible.

This theory was contradictory from its beginning. Christian tradition originally developed by putting aside the parts of the Hebrew scripture it saw as unethical and so as no longer normative. On the basis of this critical and selective use of Hebrew scripture, Christians developed the New Testament. Although Christians carry along the Hebrew scriptures in their Bible, there is no way Christians can claim this whole collection of writings as equally normative without falling into unacknowledged contradictions.

The historical-critical method, which was developed by Protestant scholars to discover and vindicate the "original" meaning of the scriptural text as its normative and infallible meaning, in fact has undermined the foundational thesis of the infallibility of this original meaning. It forces us to see the text in its original context, as an expression, in many cases, of assumptions and world views that are more foreign and unacceptable to us than more recent Christian traditions. The result is a largely unacknowledged split between modern theology and historical exegesis.

Feminist hermeneutics cannot be controlled and limited either by a Protestant concept of *sola scriptura* which has proved impossible to carry out in practice or by a Catholic developmentalist idea of scripture and tradition that covers over the breaks and novelties in this development. Rather, we should attempt to gain a clear and nonapologetic understanding of what particular ideas meant in their original scriptural context and in their various contexts in different periods of historical interpretation.

The purpose of this clarification of the past is not to limit ourselves to this past but rather to situate ourselves honestly in relation to it, making clear the points at which we are engaged in moderate novelty, developing ideas that can be seen as implicit in it, and even where we are radically new tradition makers, breaking new ground.

Why bother to situate ourselves in relation to this scriptural and historical tradition at all if we cannot be limited by it or ultimately controlled by it? I believe the reason for this is that no one thinks in a vacuum. We are a part of historical communities of thought, and we also must take responsibility for the future of historical communities and their effects on the world community. It is in order to situate ourselves truthfully in relation to the past of which we are a part, and also to take responsibility for the life of such communities today, that we confront the meaning of scripture and tradition and ask about its truthful use today.

For the sake of the redemptive future of those historical communities for which we take particular responsibility, we must be able to claim the authority to be new tradition makers, related to but transcending past interpretations. This will not make our interpretations certain and ethically infallible. But it will free us from false apologetics toward the past. In our reconstruction of key symbols, we must be rigorously truthful about the ethical defects of past understanding and practice.

But we must also be aware of the partiality of our own context. This means that we must be especially open to critique from those others whose humanity has been most often diminished and denied by groups of people whose privileges we share. Our criteria for what is true is, finally, what is most ethically redemptive for us all, in our interrelations with each other. We too will fail to express and live out this hope fully, as all past incarnations of our Christian community have failed to do so. But we must do for our times what they did for theirs. We must seek to put our best understanding into practice, trusting in that divine Spirit who is as much present today as in any past time.

8
READING THE GOSPELS IN THE LIGHT OF THE WINDOW OF THE EVANGELISTS AT CHARTRES CATHEDRAL

Seán Freyne

RECENT STUDIES of the Gospels have canvassed the aid of both ancient comparative literature and modern literary theories in their efforts to define the gospel genre more precisely. In casting their nets so widely New Testament critics may well be guilty of ignoring the more obvious source of literary and theological inspiration available to the early Christians, namely, the Hebrew scriptures, particularly in view of the task they undertook as eyewitnesses and ministers of the word. Recently, I was reminded of that fact on revisiting Chartres cathedral, where I spent some time reflecting on the *Window of the Evangelists*. Could it be, I asked myself, that the medieval artists who designed and executed the window had a better appreciation of the Gospel writers' intentions than we modern and postmodern critics? The visit certainly prompted me to view again the Gospel stories with a fresh eye under the direction of the Chartres artists.

The window consists of a circular centerpiece in the upper section depicting the risen Christ in glory surrounded by the twelve apostles. Underneath are five panels—a central one of the virgin and child, flanked on either side by two panels, each with a giant-sized figure carrying a dwarf on his shoulders. These figures are identified as prophets and evangelists in the following pairings: Mark is carried by Daniel, Matthew by Isaiah, John by Ezekiel, and Luke by Jeremiah.

Two features of this depiction struck me as particularly interesting in the light of current theological discussions. First, there is the conscious juxtaposition of the Jesus of history (the child and its mother) and the risen Christ at the center of the window, thus acknowledging the common Christian confession to which David Tracy has recently drawn our attention: "We believe in Jesus Christ with the apostles." Even more striking is the portrayal of the evangelists as dwarfs and the prophets as giants. This provocative presentation challenges the canonical triumphalism of much patristic exegesis encapsulated in the dictum "Novum in vetere latet; vetus in novo patet." The depiction was provoked apparently by a saying first attributed to John of Salisbury, and thereafter a commonplace in the medieval schools, as Europe rediscovered its lost heritage after the dark ages: "We today are carried forward on the shoulders of the giants of the past; we can see further because we have been raised higher." Thus, the Christocentrism of the canon gives way here to a humanistic discovery that all of our knowledge is indeed dependent on prior knowledge, and this principle is seen to be as operative at the Christian turn of the ages as at any other period of human history.

Such a provocative rethinking of the relationship of the New to the Old Testament prompts a further exploration of the individual pairings of prophets and evangelists and their possible interdependence. Recent discussions of intertextuality from a structuralist perspective seek to avoid reducing to source criticism under another name the insight that every text is dependent on all previous texts, in that as verbal communication all writing must draw on previously articulated linguistic codes, even when these are lost or forgotten. Yet critics such as Jonathan Culler are prepared to allow for some narrowing of the focus if intertextual reading is to be a meaningful exercise.[1] In the following discussion we shall not seek to establish genetic relationships between the respective prophets and evangelists—though in some instances this cannot be denied—but instead we shall concentrate our attention on aspects of the later works that are provoked by a conscious recollection of the prophetic voices, as suggested by the designers of the window. By following the lead of the medieval artists we hope to experience the different evangelical pictures with a sharpened appreciation of their vision and perspective. From this discussion it will, I believe, emerge that however much the various Gospels can be compared with other Greco-Roman literary productions of their period, their writers shared in the discursive practices of the Israelite prophetic tradition in the first instance, and that means in the literary as well as the theological practices of that tradition.

1. See Jonathan Culler, "Presuppositions and Intertextuality," in *The Pursuit of Signs: Semiotics, Literature, Deconstruction* (Ithaca, NY: Cornell University Press, 1982) 100–18.

Daniel and Mark

Marcan studies have identified the apocalyptic traits of the earliest Gospel and the frequent overt allusions to Daniel, but there has been little exploration of the Marcan story in its various elements against the backdrop of Daniel, the most complete literary prototype of an apocalyptic writing within the Hebrew Bible.[2] At the level of source criticism Daniel, it is generally recognized, has drawn on two quite discrete collections of court tales and visionary accounts.[3] At the narrative level, however, these supplement each other in terms of the total, dramatic effect. In the early chapters Daniel's faithful adherence to his Jewish faith in an alien environment shares the backward-looking dimension of all narrative. Set in the Babylonian/Persian period, the central character, Daniel, shows himself to be truly wise, and his readiness to suffer for his particular beliefs marks him out as the heroic figure who is rewarded both by the gift of mantic wisdom (interpretation of dreams) and a special insight into the divine plan for history—God's secret mystery (*rāz*) (chaps. 2–6). His God is "the God of Gods" and "the revealer of Mysteries." Indeed, there is the suggestion that Daniel should be treated as a god because of his wondrous powers, only for him to be cast subsequently into the lions' den because of his refusal to obey the royal edict prohibiting prayer to his god. Confronted either by adulation or torture, Daniel as the truly wise one (*maśkîl*) remains faithful to his God, deeply conscious as he is that God alone is the source of his powers and that this God will vindicate him in the end for his constancy.

Vindication does come to Daniel within the narrative in terms of the visionary experiences of the second half of the book (chaps. 7–12). Daniel's ascetic life-style in terms of prayer and fasting mark him out as "a man of God," a worthy recipient of special divine communications on behalf of others, who like himself are wise (*maśkîlîm*) and who endure suffering for their beliefs. Thus, his role changes from that of exemplary figure to representative. Already in the opening chapter, Daniel's friends also share the epithet "wise ones" (1:4, 17), and in the latter half of the book their numbers are widened to those whose role it is to instruct the people in wisdom and who through suffering for their beliefs will be rewarded with astral immortality (11:35; 12:2–3). Thus, the wisdom of Daniel, though highlighting his miraculous powers in the court tales, is much more inclusive, embracing God's total

---

2. H. C. Kee, *Community of the New Age: Studies in Mark's Gospel* (Philadelphia: Westminster, 1977) 45–49.

3. J. J. Collins, *The Apocalyptic Vision of the Book of Daniel* (Missoula, MT: Scholars Press, 1977) esp. 1–19.

plan for history, especially in regard to his elect—the people of the saints of the Most High.

When one approaches the Marcan Jesus with the figure of Daniel fresh to the mind's eye, certain aspects of the portrayal claim the reader's attention in a particular way. To begin with, the narrative falls into two distinct sections, rather similar to that of Daniel. Jesus, like Daniel, is a heroic figure, highly successful, not in a politically threatening situation but in one in which evil powers control the lives of people, and his triumphs are attributed to his wisdom (*dynameis* and *sophia*, Mark 6:2). The second half of the work is also revelatory, but in a way different from Daniel. The secret plan of God (*mystērion*, 4:10) is disclosed not through revelations to be written down by the main character but through his actions, which are presupposed in the case of Daniel, though not narrated. True, two apocalyptically colored scenes, both having clear allusions to Daniel—the transfiguration (9:2–9) and the farewell discourse (chap. 13)—bracket the narrative of Jesus' journey to suffering and vindication at Jerusalem. Yet the seeing that the author/narrator wishes to highlight is not in the first instance that of the future victory in visionary form, though that is clearly envisaged in imagery borrowed from Daniel (Mark 13:20; 14:61), but rather that which occurs in the midst of the present distress (Mark 10:46–50; 15:39). There is then a change of perspective to the present as the time of meaningful disclosure in and through the faithfulness of Jesus to God's plan. Yet Mark, like Daniel, views this present as meaningful only in the light of God's total and imminent victory. Indeed, by casting his final scene in an apocalyptic coloring (whiteness, vision, fear, 16:1–8) Mark ends his narrative on a purposely ambiguous note—a triumphant seeing in Galilee within history or at the parousia?

Prayer and fasting were the ascetical practices that Daniel and the others who are called to share his experiences engaged in when confronted with the divine mystery (2:28; 6:11; 9:3, 20; 10:2–4). Jesus, too, fasts and prays in Mark's account, but there would appear to be a subtle change of perspective from the pre-text. Jesus' prayer occurs in Mark not at times of divine disclosure but at moments of failure among the disciples (1:35; 6:46; 14:12), and fasting is a necessary preparation for a successful encounter in the present with the evil one, both for Jesus and for his disciples (1:13; 2:29; 9:29).

The characterization of the Marcan disciples as recipients of special revelatory experiences (4:10f.), but as lacking in comprehension of their true import, is a well known feature of Mark's narrative. The *maśkîlîm* in Daniel nowhere fail to live up to their role as *maśkîlê ʿam*, "instructors of the people." Yet there are certain features of the Marcan characterization of the disciples that do stand out in bolder relief when seen in the light of the Danielic treatment of its chosen group.[4] Foremost among these is the interpreted nature of the wisdom that Daniel and his associates receive, whether mantic (chaps. 2 and 5) or visionary (chaps. 7 and 9). This aspect is further highlighted by the emphasis on writing and written messages (7:1-2; 10:21; 12:9). Written messages call for decoding, and Daniel was given the gift of such interpretation (5:17). Presumably, the same gift was required to interpret correctly the hidden messages of the visions also, and the inference is that Daniel and his associates are suitably endowed and can instruct others accordingly. The Marcan disciple/reader is told: "let the reader understand" (13:14), an injunction that applies to the whole work and not just to the apocalyptic discourse. Throughout the narrative, Jesus functions as the interpretative mediator of the hidden meanings of his deeds and words for the disciples (4:13, 33-34; 7:17). They in turn are to form such an ongoing interpretative community for others in the midst of crisis according to the manifesto dealing with their election (Mark 3:13-19). Like the *maśkîlîm*, they too are to instruct, which means interpret, and for that they need to be empowered, since the struggle is none other than the apocalyptic battle against the evil one who can snatch the word from the heart or even impede their own understanding of the mystery (4:15; 8:34).

There has been considerable discussion about how the designation "apocalyptic" might best be applied to Mark's work. Gospels have a backward orientation as well as a present and future dimension, whereas apocalypses are freed from this "historical" requirement and are totally oriented to the future.[5] Yet Daniel, we have seen, does look backward, however fictitiously, through the court tales, to the Babylonian and Persian periods and is also concerned with present tribulation and future vindication. Thus, the matter of defining genres precisely according to formal criteria calls for a flexible approach. Our reading of both works together suggests that they have much more in common than a mere listing of allusions to Daniel in Mark could reveal. The pairing in the Chartres window has interesting possibilities for our understanding of both texts.

Isaiah and Matthew

Unlike the modern biblical critic, both Matthew and the designer(s) of the Chartres window read Isaiah as a single work. It is remarkable

---

4. S. Freyne, "The Disciples in Mark and the Maskîlîm in Daniel: A Comparison," *Journal for the Study of the New Testament* 16 (1983) 7-23.

5. See William Beardslee, *Literary Criticism of the New Testament* (Philadelphia: Fortress, 1970) 56-57, for some very suggestive comments on this comparison.

how resistant we are to thinking of the book other than in terms of first, second, and third Isaiah, each assigned to its different historical epoch. Undoubtedly, our modern historical awareness has helped enormously to illumine this collection of prophetic oracles. Yet when read as a whole it does disclose a coherent point of view on Israel's relationship with its God—and it is this story line that gives unity to the whole. We move from an intermingling of oracles of messianic blessing and judgment (part 1), to a sense of triumphant restoration through exile and suffering (part 2), to a sober reflection on the current ills that beset the community as it encounters "let down" from the peak experience of restoration while seeking to keep alive the messianic vision for all Israel (part 3). This story is embedded, loosely to be sure, in a plot that has various historical characters (Ahaz and Cyrus) and some that are not clearly identifiable (the servant of Yahweh), but from the point of view of subsequent readers the fact that we are dealing with over two centuries of Israelite history makes no difference to the unity in the message conveyed: Israel's destiny depends on its response to God's saving action, which is mediated through the historical circumstances of Israel's existence among the nations.

Matthew, as a scribe trained for the kingdom, develops a similar line in changed historical circumstances. His plot becomes the cipher through which the same divine purpose is reenacted. The historical rejection of Jesus and the destruction of the temple in Jerusalem together with the subsequent world mission are all read as one story of messianic visitation, leading to purification of a remnant through suffering, but rejection of unfaithful Israel, followed by a call to the restored community to live out the messianic ideal in the present. In bringing together into one story line the experiences of Jesus as remembered by his followers and those of his own community in the wake of the post-70 C.E. Jewish experience, Matthew achieves the same temporal ellipse as does the book of Isaiah in its present form. From the point of view of God's purpose for Israel in history both can justifiably bring together events of different historical periods into one overarching plot to illustrate the divine plan at work.

As is well known, of all the Gospels Matthew's is the one that most self-consciously alludes to the Hebrew scriptures with its repeated (thirteen times) formula of the fulfillment of scripture. Among these texts six are explicit references to the prophet Isaiah (3:3; 4:14; 8:17; 12:17; 13:14; 15:7) in contrast to one mention of Jeremiah (27:9)—the only other Hebrew prophet to be mentioned explicitly. Of the other scriptural allusions, two (Matt 1:23; 21:4) are nonattributed citations from Isaiah 7:14 and 62:11. On purely statistical grounds, therefore, we would have to conclude that Isaiah is Matthew's main point of reference and source of inspiration while acknowledging that, for him, the whole of "the Law and the Prophets" can be read prophetically (see 11:17).

An intertextual reading should, however, be concerned with more than mere statistics. Can we claim that Matthew's retelling of the Jesus story has consciously or unconsciously been shaped in its totality by his use of Isaian codes? Does our understanding of the flow of the Matthean narrative improve through a reading of the Gospel that is prompted by the prophetic text? A number of themes come to mind as controlling the whole Isaian work, and they are closely interrelated and reworked in the prophetic imagination even if they may have been drawn from quite disparate traditional motifs. These are the divine protection of Mount Zion, the emergence of a remnant that would be faithful, and the unique role that was to be attributed to Yahweh's anointed. True, this latter element is suppressed to some extent in the second and third parts of the book, but the roles of Cyrus and of the prophet as the Lord's anointed (Isa 45:1; 61:1) only serve to show how elastic the notion could be in different contexts, thus opening the way imaginatively for its unexpected application in Matthew. The book as a whole opens and closes with poems concerning the nations' pilgrimage to Mount Zion (Isa 2:2-4; 66:22-24, repeated at 49:18-26), there to learn the ways of Yahweh in contrast to the counterimage of their marching on the holy city to destroy it (Isa 17:12-14; 10:27-34). The remnant theme provides the basis for the poet's ongoing trust in Yahweh, despite its further elaboration in the servant songs and in the program for the restored community's witness to come in the latter third of the work.

The profile of the ideal king that is developed in 11:1-9 has a strong ethical dimension "giving his verdict with equity for the poor of the land," and the law that goes forth from Zion is envisaged as having a universal significance, not just for Israel but for the nations as well (2:3). Once again this theme also finds expression in the so-called Book of Consolation through the figure of the servant, who is described as a "light for the nations" (49:6). In the closing scene the gathering of the nations is presented as an eschatological reversal of the tower of Babel with the creation of a new heaven and new earth (Isa 66:18-24) with all peoples gathered around the God of Israel on his holy mountain.

This very sketchy thematic reading of Isaiah from a wholistic point of view has interesting possibilities for the Matthean perspective also in view of the very clear points of contact indicated by the list of individual citations. Matthew, too, has a blending of the eschatological Zion and the royal Davidic traditions, but with the adaptation that now the holy mountain where David's son, Immanuel, can be encountered and whence the law will go forth to all the nations is in Galilee not Jerusalem (Matt 5:1; 28:16). The nations—Israelite and Greek—gather around the mountain of revelation to learn wisdom (4:26–27), but the words of Jesus/Immanuel/Son of David must also go forth from the same mountain to all peoples (28:16)—a two-way traffic of the word which suggests the openness of a genuine conversation of sharing and enquiry.

Matthew repeatedly designates the new way as "righteousness," a term that on the basis of Isaiah (among others) calls for as inclusive an understanding as possible comprising peace, integrity, justice in the strict sense—in a word, all of the values necessary to bring about a restored and renewed cosmic order (Matt 3:15; 5:6, 10, 20; 6:1, 33; see Isa 11:4; 32:1–2, 15; 58:1–12). The "messianic miracle" occurs through the achievement of this new way of righteousness, which is also the way of wisdom vindicated by its works (11:17). The blessing of wisdom can be described as an opening of the eyes to see and of the ears to hear (Matt 13:14–15; 11:5; see Isa 32:3 –4), and the new vineyard of the Lord, unlike the old, will produce abundant fruits of righteousness (Matt 21:43; see Isa 27:2–5).

There are other religious themes, symbolic expressions, and ethical instructions that will strike the individual reader. Such similarities should not obscure the fact that by our modern literary sensibilities we are dealing with two very different works—the one a collection of oracles of salvation and judgment interspersed with some scattered biographical and historical information, and the other a narrative account of the life, death, and resurrection of Jesus of Galilee, told from the perspective of the Matthean community's theological vision, social situation, and historical experiences. Nor should they obscure the fact that in all probability Matthew, or at least his Jewish readership, was familiar with an Aramaic version of Isaiah closer to our present Palestinian targumic version than to the Hebrew Masoretic Text, as well as with the Greek text of his gentile converts. Still there can be little doubt that the designers of the Chartres window have pointed us in a very fruitful direction as we explore the thought world and symbolic vision of Matthew, the scribe trained for the kingdom, for whom the belief in the fulfillment of Isaiah's Immanuel prophecy in the career of Jesus has a controlling theological *and*, we maintain, literary influence.

Jeremiah and Luke

Of the four matching pairs, that of Jeremiah and Luke appears the least obvious at first sight, particularly in view of the fact that Matthew, and not Luke, is the only New Testament writer who makes explicit reference to Jeremiah (2:17; 16:14; 27:9). Nevertheless, an initial reflection that the fall of Jerusalem to the Babylonians in 589 B.C.E. and that to the Romans in 70 C.E. have long been recognized as the historical experiences that have deeply influenced each writer prompted further investigation. Luke's use of the Hebrew scriptures is more oblique than Matthew's, a mosaic of biblical allusions and imitations rather than explicit citations. In fact, direct allusions to Jeremiah's text in Luke are less frequent than those to Isaiah, Ezekiel, or Proverbs. Yet statistics alone can be deceptive, and as an initial exploration we might note the contexts in which the Jeremiah citations occur in Luke: prophetic calls of John and Jesus (1:38; 3:2; 4:6), the judgment on Jerusalem and the temple in particular (19:42, 46), and the making of the new covenant (22:19).

Luke's story of Jesus is that of the prophet who is rejected as he journeys through the land calling for repentance, particularly in terms of social justice. This call reaches its climax in Jerusalem, where Jesus virtually takes over the temple, only to be rejected by the religious leaders of the people who have him removed by the Romans as a political agitator (22:3). For Luke, Jesus is the prophet *par excellence*, who is prefigured by such Old Testament individuals as Elijah and Elisha. Could Jeremiah also be plausibly claimed as a precursor to this Lucan Jesus?

Many scholars have remarked on the significance of prophetic biography for the overall message of the book of Jeremiah.[6] For the first time in Israelite literature the prophet's life and fate enter into the message in an explicit way. It is not just that the narrative of Jeremiah's life provides settings for his varous oracles and symbolic gestures; rather, the account of his repeated rejection helps to highlight the underlying divine plan that is working itself out in and through his life's ordeals as he utters his oracles of woe on Jerusalem. Thus, the so-called deuteronomic influence on Jeremiah finds expression in terms of the punishments that will be inflicted on Jerusalem and its leadership because of its refusal to listen to the prophet's warning call to conversion. The fall of Jerusalem enters the larger divine plan for history, therefore, rather than being viewed as direct punishment for Israel's failure.

Jeremiah's biography is certainly that of the rejected prophet—both by his own people of Anathoth and by the powers in the land (11:18–23; 18:18). A sense of bitterness comes through clearly in many of the oracles which hover between self-doubt and self-pity as the prophet seeks to escape the inexorable will of Yahweh with little hope of relief (4:19; 11:18–20). Thus, we are privy to Jeremiah's own internal drama. At

---

6. G. von Rad, *Old Testament Theology*, vol. 2, *The Theology of Israel's Prophetic Tradition* (London: Oliver & Boyd, 1965) 204–5.

one moment, Job-like, he wallows in self-pity; then he looks for revenge, and yet again he begs to be free of the burden of the prophet's call. Here we encounter the new challenge facing the prophetic vocation in his day which required different resources of mind and heart in order to continue to proclaim the message of God's control of history against all appearances, both internal and external. Some have even spoken of Baruch's account of his trials and tribulations (chaps. 36–42) as the passion of Jeremiah. Yet this term could give the wrong impression, as though the author or Jeremiah saw any positive value either in the sufferings or in the way they were borne. Rather, the underlying sense of rebellion comes through as Jeremiah finds the prophetic role making its very full demands, and he is less than convinced that he is capable of bearing the burdens of the office (20:7, 9; see 1:7–8).

Luke's story of Jesus is that of the rejected prophet also. He is already rejected at Nazareth among his own people at the outset of his journey, and, as with the other rejected prophets of Israel's history—including Jeremiah—this only served to broaden his horizons to include concern for all the nations in his purview (see Jer 1:5–10; 50–51). Yet it is in Jerusalem that the prophet must die since his fate is ultimately bound up with the fate of the holy city (13:33). It is there that Jesus' exodus must occur (9:33), and so when the divine plan finally calls he steadfastly turns his face to go to the holy city (9:51; see 19:28). There he too will discover the full demands of his prophetic calling in his great trial or agony (20:39–46). As with Jeremiah, the focal point of Jesus' Jerusalem ministry is the temple (19:45–48; 21:5–7), and there he is rejected by the chief priests, the scribes, and the elders of the people. Indeed Luke, like the other Gospel writers, echoes Jeremiah's condemnation that the temple is "a den of thieves," thereby underlining the social exploitation of the poor by the rich of Jerusalem in Jeremiah's day, which is a central theme of the Lucan Jesus' teaching also. Yet Luke does not apportion blame for the destruction of Jerusalem or the rejection of Jesus in the way that later Christian apologetic was to do. Rather, he highlights Jesus' lament for the city and its failure to recognize the things that are for its peace.

The sufferings of the prophet Jesus in the Lucan perspective are understood in terms of the traditional fate of God's prophet rather than as an atoning offering for sin following the pattern of Isaiah 53. Luke 24:25–27 explains the suffering of Jesus as being in line with that which the Hebrew prophets had foretold—a necessary part of the divine plan for the Messiah to enter his glory (see also Luke 18:31). If Luke had Jeremiah in mind, he certainly did not single him out for special mention, since for him the whole of the Hebrew scriptures was prophetic. Nevertheless, the explicit linking of the fate of Jerusalem with that of

Jesus the Messiah prompts the consideration that Jeremiah and his story must have played a more prominent role in shaping Luke's account than the number of explicit references to the prophetic text might cause one to infer.

Our attention is focused particularly on the passages dealing with Jerusalem and its destruction, since that played such a central role in Jeremiah's message also. Luke has Jesus weep for the city as he comes in sight of it, while also foretelling its destruction in terms that echo Jeremiah, especially chap. 26 (but see Jer 6:9–15 and 10:15) among other Old Testament texts (Luke 19:41–44). In that particular account, recalling the earlier temple speech of chap. 11, Jeremiah had addressed the whole people in the court of the temple, foretelling the utter destruction of the holy place, "like Shiloh," unless they listened to the prophetic message concerning the law. This led to the sentence of death against Jeremiah from the priests and prophets, which was subsequently endorsed by the leaders of the people, while others pointed to the fact that a similar prophecy of ruin had been uttered by previous prophets without their having to suffer for it. For Luke also, Jesus is not rejected by all the people, but only by its religious and lay leaders.

It is difficult to avoid the impression that this Jeremian setting has in some sense provoked Luke's treatment of Jesus' lament for Jerusalem, since it did not know "the things that were to its peace" (19:42). In an earlier passage, echoed here by Luke, Jeremiah castigated the people of Jerusalem who cried out "peace, peace" when there was no peace; "they will perish at the time of their visitation" (6:9–15). Following his lament for the city the Lucan Jesus goes on to foretell its destruction. The ravages of war (probably that of (66–70 C.E.) are an all-too-clear reminder for Luke and his readers of Jerusalem's failures to achieve the peace that its name had been made to symbolize in certain contemporary renderings.[7] Once again we can detect Jeremian influences in the description of the actual Roman siege (Jer 52:4–5), as the scholarly Luke, steeped in the Septuagint, paints his picture with touches from a number of appropriate pre-texts (Luke 21:20–24; see Jer 21:7; Ezek 30:3; 32:9; Zech 12:9).

Jeremiah was the prophet whose life's call was "to tear up and to knock down, to destroy and to overthrow, to build and to plant" (Jer 1:10). His life was largely concerned with the negative side of that mission, as he found himself cast in the role of prophet of doom to his own people at a time when they were prepared to play a political power game rather than trust in their God's care and protection. Luke chooses a most

---

7. I. de la Potterie, "Les deux noms de Jérusalem dans l'évangile de Luc," *Recherches de Science Religieuse* 69 (1981) 59–70.

fitting if tragic setting in view of its history, namely, the Jerusalem temple, to have the child Jesus designated as the one "destined for the fall and rise of many in Israel—destined for a sign who would be rejected" (2:34). Both Jeremiah and Jesus shared in a similar call to challenge the complacency and self-centeredness of their own people at critical junctures in its history, and both suffered a similar rejection. Convinced as they were that God's plan had reached its climax with Jesus, the early Christians were even more perplexed than were those who compiled the book of Jeremiah with its promises of a new covenant in the future (cf. Luke 22:20). Our reading of Luke against the backdrop of Jeremiah suggests that in the figure of the prophet from Anathoth they found one other model in their efforts to understand the inscrutable plan of God. The fact that the Greek Bible had attributed the book of Lamentations to the prophet only added further poignancy to the comparison, given the distinctively Lucan portrait of Jesus too, weeping for the city and encouraging others to share his sorrows (Luke 19:41–44; 23:26–32).

Ezekiel and John

"In the thirteenth year, on the fifth day of the fourth month, as I was among the exiles . . . heaven opened and I saw visions from God" (Ezek 1:1). "You will see the heavens opened and the angels of God ascending and descending on the Son of Man" (John 1:57). Both Ezekiel and John are visionaries who share a central symbol-system that serves to give a common focus to their visions and the ways in which they articulate their respective points of view. For both, the Jerusalem temple, the seat of God's presence to and with Israel, provides a rich repertoire of images and symbols that each can use in their distinctive manner and for their particular readerships. Both, it would seem, are writing after its destruction and consciously searching for appropriate expressions of hope. For Ezekiel there are many such that can be conjured up from his predecessors in Israel's prophetic tradition, but the climax is his elaborate depiction of the new temple (chaps. 40–48). For John the focus is on the temple's replacement by the person of the Word-made-flesh, a perspective that can then be orchestrated with various episodes of Jesus' public career being presented in the light of the great festivals and their ceremonies—Passover, Tabernacles, and Dedication (chaps. 2; 6; 7–8; 10; 19).

For both writers the notion of God's *kābôd*, or glory, is central. Ezekiel's vision includes the departure and return of this mysterious presence (chaps. 11 and 43). Its departure from the Jerusalem temple is at once a moment of poignant loss and a veiled expression of hope, since its departure is from the east gate on the side nearest to the exiles in Babylonia whom Ezekiel seeks to comfort (10:18-22; 11:22-25). It is through the east gate that the glory of God will return to fill the new temple (43:4-5), whence will flow (again, toward the east) the miraculous stream of water that will give a paradisiac abundance to a desert land.

Ezekiel's message of hope is tempered by his symbolic expressions of judgment. Visionary that he is, he does not hold the detailed mirror up to Israel's failures, but sees its sin rather in general terms: it is a rejection of the God who dwells in Israel's midst, a refusal to see and to recognize, that has marked the whole of its sacred history. In particular the leaders, the false shepherds, are castigated for the failures, without, however, exonerating each individual for a particular role in the tragic rejection. In the future Yahweh himself will shepherd his people, gathering them together into one, restoring life where death once reigned. A new heart and spirit will be given. The graves of the dead will be opened and the old divisons transcended in a new, united Israel that will glorify God's name among the gentiles. Thus, the vision as a whole, while focused firmly on Israel and its restoration, has the whole universe within its purview, despite its esoteric, priestly inspiration.

The Johannine witness is succinctly enunciated already in the prologue: "we saw his glory, the glory of the only-begotten of the Father, full of grace and truth" (1:14). As the narrative develops, this glory or presence of God that has tabernacled in Jesus is manifested in his actions leading to his disciples' belief (2:11; 11:15; 20:22). The glory that has entered history and manifests itself according to the Johannine perspective is distinctly reminiscent of Ezekelian images. In the midst of the temple, the Johannine Jesus declares that he is the one from whom the rivers of living water will flow (see Ezek 47:1-2), an image directly related by the narrator to the gift of the Spirit (John 7:38). As a fulfillment of this prophetic utterance we are told that at his death, even as "he gave the Spirit," water and blood flowed from the side of Christ (19:34). Because of his unity with the Father, the Johannine Jesus could take to himself the image of the shepherd who will gather the dispersed flock that has been neglected by its leaders (John 10:1-21). In another of the internal prophecy/fulfillment scenarios of this work, the promise that the tombs of the dead would be opened (5:19) is stunningly realized in the raising of Lazarus (John 11), thereby bringing to fulfillment Ezekiel's vision of the valley of the dry bones coming to life.

Like Ezekiel, John is less interested in spelling out the specific moral demands and social failures of the Jews, God's erstwhile people. It is their blindness that is their sin, a particularly ironic judgment in view of the fact that Jesus as the light of the world is the giver of sight to the blind (John 8:12; 9:1–41). Both writers have a priestly perspective of the holy community (see John 17), and hence the temple and its imagery provide a very suitable symbolic repertoire for defining the community's identity, tasks, and experiences of God's saving presence.[8] Both interpret events as signs, thereby pointing to the deeper and hidden meaning of their message, which calls for a total response. Ezekiel's signs point to God's judgment on Israel's failure now as a matter of urgency, while at the same time serving to highlight future restoration. John's signs are primarily manifestations of the glory of God in Jesus (2:11; 21:25), but each of them also carries the note of separation and judgment for those who are not open to discovery. Thus, the emphasis within their shared perspective is different, as can be graphically seen in their very different exploitation of the image of the vine. For Ezekiel the withered vine symbolizes Jerusalem's and Israel's rejection (chap. 17), whereas for John it serves as the climactic symbol of the new life that has come through Jesus.

Conclusion

The Chartres window has provided a suggestive model for a fresh reading of the Gospel narratives. In their different ways each pairing has offered a highly creative and stimulating perspective from which to approach both the prophetic and the evangelical texts. Their interaction and its impact on our reading go in both directions, it must be acknowledged. If the new is largely a recasting of images and metaphors from the old in order to express other faith experiences, the old, likewise, takes on a new vitality when read in the refracted light of those subsequent pictures. This reflection is not intended to reaffirm canonical Christocentrism under a literary guise, but rather to suggest that Christian theology, in search of new language and images for its God-talk might well return to the whole of the Hebrew scriptures in order to retrieve its classic but largely ignored heritage. The boldest stroke of all in the Chartres window was surely the implied contrast between giants and dwarfs, prophets and evangelists. Therein lies a challenge for contemporary Christian theologians also, both in terms of renewing their own tradition and of exploring common roots with their Jewish counterparts.

---

8. See S. Freyne, "Vilifying the Other and Defining the Self: Matthew's and John's Anti-Judaism in Focus," in *"To See Ourselves as Others See Us": Jews, Christians, Others in Antiquity*, ed. J. Neusner and E. Frerichs, Brown Studies in the Humanities (Chico, CA: Scholars Press, 1985) 117–44.

9
ANOTHER TROY FOR HER TO BURN: THE TRUE STORY OF EURIPIDES' HELEN

Mary Gerhart

RESEARCH ON GODDESSES of ancient times has been most firmly based on statues of mother goddess figures, inscriptions, hymns, and heroic tales of women gods. Research on women of ancient times proceeds on the basis of artistic iconography, necrology, ethnography, and history. And while we have been cautioned not to take literally the descriptions and prohibitions recorded in either image or language, scholarly studies nevertheless have often made empirical facts out of the evidence (e.g., Eva C. Keuls's *The Reign of the Phallus: Sexual Politics in Ancient Athens* [New York: Harper & Row, 1986]). Others have concentrated on the symbolic significance of the figures for psychological insight and inspiration (e.g., Chris Downing's *The Goddess: Mythological Images of the Feminine* [New York: Crossroad, 1981]). Although the results of these approaches have been productive — they have peopled our past with images of women hitherto obscured, distorted, or ignored in androcentric history — the religious significance of "goddess" for theology in general is still in question.[1]

The myths of Helen are a valuable and challenging resource for understanding the goddess, since no fewer than three major variations on the myth were known in ancient times. Only two of the three versions appear in the extant plays of Euripides. By asking why the fertility

---

Parts of this essay appeared under the same title in the *Annual Review of Women and World Religions*, vol. 1, no. 1.

1. Reformist feminist theologians, such as Rosemary Ruether and Elisabeth Schüssler Fiorenza, in different ways, have brought criticism to bear on goddess religions. Radical feminist theologians, such as Mary Daly, often see goddess religions as substituting a female dominance for a male one. But see also the constructive theology of Carol Christ.

goddess version does not appear in the plays of this author, we may remap an understanding of the goddess for our time. But how shall we proceed in the face of three different versions of the Helen story? What is the true story of Helen?

We have learned from Paul Ricoeur that the first task is to listen again to the myths. Myths have not been made obsolete by the specialization of thought in philosophy and theology. By reflecting on the multiple avowals of experience represented in myths, the philosopher is forestalled from any premature closure on questions that require more than logical answers. For Ricoeur, a good philosophical interpretation of narrative is one that accounts for the greatest number of perceived details in the narrative and that does so at the highest level of persuasion. Regarding what is to be perceived, we have learned from Julia Kristeva to observe in what ways the language of myth is doubly bound: bound to the human body and its desires and bound to the body politic and its structures.[2] Kristeva's work in literary and in psychoanalytic theory is particularly apt for a retrieval of Helen from selective memory.

Finally, it is the work of David Tracy on the significance of the goddess for a contemporary understanding of god[3] that inspires the strenuous task of constructing a meaningful, coherent, and appropriate religious meaning of Helen as goddess. With its rigorous celebration of plurality and ambiguity, his work provides an exemplary response to the problem of understanding and appropriating the thealogical significance of figures such as Helen—figures who would otherwise continue to be lost in selective memory.

Once upon a time there was a beautiful woman, born the daughter of Leda of Sparta and Zeus. While still a young girl, she was abducted to Athens by Theseus and Polydeuces. Because the Athenians were aghast at what Theseus had done, he sent Helen away to his mother for safekeeping. After bearing a daughter, Helen was rescued by her brothers, Castor and Pollux. When she grew up, many heroes and chieftains of all Greece made suit for her in marriage, and her foster father, Tyndareus, was frightened out of his wits by the possibility that the unsuccessful suitors would attack him. He thought up the ingenious solution that each suitor had to promise to defend her husband—that is, the one who finally won Helen's hand—if any harm came to him. With or without her consent (we don't know), Menelaus became her husband and heir to the throne.

Meanwhile Paris awarded Aphrodite the golden apple which Eris had

---

2. See Deborah Cameron, *Feminism and Linguistic Theory* (New York: Macmillan, 1985).
3. In unpublished lectures by David Tracy at the University of Chicago, 1988–89.

tossed among the wedding guests at the marriage of Peleus and Thetis, and in return won Helen, said to be the most beautiful woman in the world.[4] The snag was that she was already married. No matter—in the spirit of ancient times, Paris, with his father Priam's consent, set off for Greece, where he was courteously entertained by Menelaus. When Menelaus went to Crete for his grandfather's funeral, Paris abducted Helen.

Here the story breaks into two versions. In version 1, Paris took Helen and married her in Troy, where she bore several children, all of whom died in infancy. In the first version, the Trojan women are divided up among the Greek victors after the war, and Menelaus grudgingly takes Helen back. In version 2, recorded for the first time by Stesichorus (a sixth-century B.C.E. poet who, according to C. M. Bowra, had to placate those of his contemporaries who regarded Helen as a goddess[5]), Helen never went to Troy, having been spirited away to Egypt for the twenty years of the war and its aftermath. There are variations on each of these two versions as well.

Euripides was not the only classical writer to refer to both of the two major versions of the legend. According to Herodotus, Homer must have known both versions but did not find the Helen-in-Egypt version amenable to the demands of epic narrative.[6] Herodotus further argued for the "truth" of the Helen-in-Egypt version (version 2) on the supposition that, had Helen been in Troy (according to version 1), the Trojans would surely have surrendered her rather than have their city destroyed. Herodotus therefore believed the Trojans were speaking truly when they said that Helen was not there.

An older myth, which we will refer to as version 3, predates both the foregoing epic versions of the myth of Helen and the dramatic versions that we will consider shortly. From the third-century B.C.E. poet Theocritus (18.43ff.) and the first-century C.E. geographer Pausanias (3.19.10; 8.23.6–7), we know that before the Homeric epic Helen was originally a nature goddess of fertility and that she had been worshiped in Sparta, Rhodes, and other cities.[7] Both the fertility goddess legend and Helen's

---

4. Aphrodite, Hera, and Athena all claimed possession of the apple of discord. Paris was chosen to settle the dispute: Hera offered him riches and royal greatness; Athena, success in war, and Aphrodite, the most beautiful woman.

5. C. M. Bowra, "Stesichorus," in *The Oxford Classical Dictionary*, 2nd ed., ed. N. G. L. Hammond and H. H. Scullard (Oxford: Clarendon, 1970) 1012–13.

6. The two forms of the variant Egypt story were as follows: first, as in Herodotus, Paris Alexander was blown off course to Egypt on his way back from Greece to Troy with Helen, and Proteus thwarted Paris's kidnapping of Helen by sending Paris off without Helen; second, as in the version used by Euripides, Apollo rescues Helen and transports her to Egypt.

7. See Martin P. Nilsson, *Geschichte der griechischen Religion* (Munich: Beck, 1955) 1:475. M. L. West's Helen (*Immortal Helen* [London: Bedford College, 1975]) by contrast

lineage as specified in the epic myths certify that she was godly.

Whether Euripides suppressed this oldest version of Helen or whether it was not known to him, we find no trace of it in the extant Euripidean plays, believed to be a third of all he wrote. Version 1 is frequently employed alone; version 2 is always presented over and against version 1.

If Euripides did know about this archaic tradition of Helen as a goddess of fertility, why did he not draw upon this third version of the myth? First, it has been noticed that when Euripides wrote about heroes and stories of the Trojan War, he selected events that either preceded or followed the war as it was narrated in the *Iliad* and the *Odyssey*. *Rhesus* (440), his first play, which takes material directly from the *Iliad*, is the only exception. Since the older myth of Helen is neither in the epics as narrated by Homer nor related explicitly to the war, it is consistent for Euripides not to include a reference to Helen's earliest appearance in Greek culture. Second, gods and goddesses function integrally in the plots of Euripides' plays, often in direct relation to the psychological aspects of human characters. Thus, Dionysus in *The Bacchae* and Aphrodite and Artemis in *Hippolytus* both reflect and affect the action of the plays. Conception and birth in the Euripidean plays, however, are usually attributed to the action—frequently the violent action—of gods. Creusa in *Ion*, for example, comes to the Oracle at Delphi to petition for a child to replace the one she had borne by Zeus and abandoned. On the way into the temple, she wonders where women can find justice when power belongs to the unjust, perhaps alluding to the overbearing androcentrism of Greek religion. And when the chorus in *Helen* connects Helen to Demeter, goddess of fertility, and to Persephone, goddess of death, we may speak of a vicarious identification of Helen with fertility goddess.[8] Yet this analogue is only an oblique reference to

---

is a one-dimensional figure: "To poets throughout the ages she has served as the paragon of beauty. Her delinquency is forgiven." Walter Burkert affirmed her divine lineage: ". . . in Sparta Helen was clearly a goddess" (*Greek Religion* [1985] 205). The *Oxford Classical Dictionary* (2nd ed.) surmised that "[H]er non-Greek name, her association with trees . . . and her connexion with birds . . . all fit an ancient, pre-Hellenic goddess, probably connected with vegetation and fertility, better than a dimly remembered princess, or even a purely imaginary human member of an ancient royal family. It is in no wise impossible that an old deity traditionally worshipped by the pre-Dorian population of Laconia had been taken, long before Homer, for an ancestress of their kings." Helen is also referred to as a daemon (see Burkert, *Greek Religion*, 179–81). Alex Persson did not hesitate to group Helen, along with Pasdiphae, Europa, Diktynna, Eileithyia, Aridela, and Aphaia as "invocations of the same deity" (*The Religion of Greece in Prehistoric Times* [Berkeley: University of California Press, 1942] 135). For an elaboration of Helen's association with the Minoan tree cult, see Martin P. Nilsson, *The Minoan-Mycenaean Religion and Its Survival in Greek Religion* (Lund: Gleerup, 1950) esp. 551–52.

8. Hesiod and Homer both state that Helen was the daughter of Zeus and that her

version 3 of the Helen myth. Must we conclude that Euripides was incapable of dramatizing a fertility goddess who also acted in history?

Helen as Portrayed in Euripides: Receiving the Tradition

Of the twenty extant complete plays[9] of Euripides, Helen is referred to by name in ten of the plays, she is among the cast of characters in two of the plays (*Orestes* and *The Trojan Women*), and in *Helen* she is the main character and subject. These references span the corpus of Euripides, with the first in *Rhesus*, his first play (440 B.C.E.), and the last in *Iphigenia in Aulis* (405 B.C.E.), which, with *The Bacchae*, was produced posthumously. (See Table I, p. 126.)

Chronologically, the plays fall roughly into four groups with respect to Euripides' treatment of Helen. Of the first ten of the extant plays, written or produced between 440 and 420, references to version 1 of Helen appear in only three of the plays (*Rhesus*, *Hecuba*, and *The Cyclops*). Of the next four extant plays, written or produced between 419 and 413, version 1 of Helen is referred to in all four plays (*Andromache*, *The Trojan Women*, *Iphigenia in Tauris*, and *Electra*. In *Electra*, version 2 of the Helen myth is introduced as a playbill in the closing lines). Of the last five extant plays, written or produced between 412 and 405, one play (*Helen*) elaborates version 2 of Helen over and against version 1. Of the last three plays (*Orestes*, *Iphigenia in Aulis*, and *The Bacchae*), two together have more references (version 1 or, in *Orestes*, a modification thereof) to Helen than all of the previous plays, excluding *Helen*.

The plays also document an increasing complexity in the character of Helen, both in terms of her relations to characters speaking of her and in terms of her function in the total action of the plays.

In the following quotations, taken from the three earliest plays in the above list, the references to Helen are uniformly derogatory. In *Rhesus*, the chorus of Trojan guards prays that Dolon, one of their warriors, who plans to crawl by night as a spy in the disguise of a wolf to the Greek ships, will kill one of the Greeks:

---

beauty surpassed the beauty of all mortal women, thus implying some generic distinction between mortals and Helen. I am indebted to Paula Sage for calling my attention to the parallel between Helen and Demeter. See also Froma I. Zeitlin, "Travesties of gender and genre in Aristophanes *Thesmophoriazousae*," in *Reflections of Women in Antiquity*, ed. Helen Foley (London and Paris: Gordon & Breach, 1982) esp. 186ff., 197ff.

9. The editions of David Grene and Richard Lattimore (Chicago: University of Chicago Press, 1955–59) have been used throughout.

Table I: Citations to Helen in Euripedes' Plays

(Citations in the play *Helen*, where she appears as the main character, were not counted. Plays whose dates are confidently set by ancient testimony are marked with an asterisk.)[10]

Title of Play	Year Produced	Number of Citations
Rhesus	440	1
*Alcestis**	438	0
*Medea**	431	0
Heracleidae	429	0
*Hippolytus**	428	0
Cyclops	425	2
Hecuba	425	5
Phoenix	425	0
Heracles	424-420	0
The Suppliant Women	420-415	0
Andromache	419	5
*Trojan Women**	415	7
Iphigenia in Tauris	414-410	5
Electra	413	6
*Helen**	412	multiple
Ion	411	0
*Phoenician Women**	411-409	0
*Orestes**	408	29
*Iphigenia in Aulis**	405	15
The Bacchae	405	0

Chorus of Trojan guards:
Might it be Menelaus!
Or might he kill Agamemnon
and bring the head back
as a gloomy gift for the arms of his evil sister
by marriage, Helen. . . . (*ll.* 259-60)

In *The Cyclops*, a racy exchange is the context for the first reference to Helen:

Coryphaeus: Did you take Helen when you took Troy?
Odysseus: We rooted out the whole race of Priam.

---

10. Grace Harriet Macurdy describes the criteria used in determining the dates of the ten plays which are not dated by ancient testimony (*Chronology of the Extant Plays of Euripedes* [New York: Haskell House, 1966]).

Coryphaeus: When you took that woman, did you all take turns
and bang her? She liked variety in men,
the fickle bitch! Why, the sight of a man
with embroidered pants and a golden chain
so fluttered her, she left Menelaus,
a fine little man. I wish there were
no women in the world—except for me. (177–86)

This bawdry humor, irony that is characteristic of the satyr play, nevertheless raises the gender issue explicitly and alludes to Helen as the cause of the war. The other reference to Helen in *The Cyclops* is simply to "that foul Helen" who was carried off.

In *Hecuba*, the Trojan queen, Hecuba, has ample reason to hate Helen. She has lost her daughter Polyxena (sacrificed for the ghost of Achilles), her other daughter Cassandra (taken as slave to Agamemnon), and her grandson Astyanax (slaughtered by a traitor to their family)—all, she thinks, because of Helen:

Hecuba: Whoever hurt him [Achilles] less
than this poor girl [Polyxena]? If death is what he wants,
let Helen die. He went to Troy for *her*;
for *her* he died. (265–66)

Yet Hecuba acknowledges Helen's beauty as well, and for the first time in Euripides—albeit ironically—something nice is said about Helen. If the ghost of Achilles requires "dying loveliness" to appease his hurt,

Hecuba: Look to Helen,
loveliest of lovely women on this earth
by far—lovely Helen, who did him harm
far more than we. (268-70)

The chorus of Trojan women also curses Helen:

Chorus of Trojan women:
Helen, fury of ruin!
Let the wind blow
and never bring her home!
Let there be no landing
for Helen of Troy! (950–54)

In another passage, however, the chorus pushes the blame back to Paris's action and praises Helen's beauty:

Chorus of Trojan women:
That morning was my fate,
that hour doom was done,

when Paris felled the tree
that grew on Ida's height
and made a ship for sea
and sailed to Helen's bed—
loveliest of women
the golden sun has seen. (629–37)

Helen appears as a character for the first time in *The Trojan Women*. In her own defense, she speaks (albeit unconvincingly) of the strength of the goddess who pressures her to go with Paris.

In this first group of plays, therefore, Euripides does not stray from one-dimensional understandings of Helen. He does not go beyond the broadest strokes of version 1 of the received myths of his time. The only complexity is that portrayed through the figure of Hecuba who nevertheless repeats the conventional understandings of Helen.

The plays of the middle group continue to blame Helen for the Trojan War and praise her beauty as well as introduce more complex attitudes. In *Andromache*, for example, Menelaus uses empathy to defend his rescue of Andromache:

Menelaus: Let's just suppose your daughter
Married some citizen and got such treatment,
You'd sit back mum? I doubt it....
When cheated, wife or husband feels the same.
She doesn't like it. He doesn't either,
... Yet he can mend things with his good right arm;
She has to count on friends' or parents' aid.

Menelaus's sympathy for Helen is colored by his own opportunism as well:

Menelaus: Poor Helen had a time of it, not choosing
But chosen by the gods to exalt her country.
For innocent before of arms and battles
Greece grew to manhood then. Experience, travel—
These are an education in themselves.
If coming in the presence of my wife
I steeled myself and spared her, I was wise. (668–86)

Given the wimpy character of Menelaus in this play, it may be too strong to interpret the foregoing lines as evidence of Euripides' critical reflection on gender issues. Nevertheless, four years later, in *The Trojan Women*, for the first time in Euripidean drama, the Greeks in general, rather than Paris or Helen, are blamed for the war. Cassandra (Hecuba's daughter) makes no mention of a political basis for the Greeks' pursuit of Helen: the object, she says, was "an act of love":

Cassandra: For one woman's sake,
one act of love, these [Achaeans] hunted Helen down and threw thousands of lives away. (367–69)

This criticism of the Greeks is overshadowed in the next line by Helen's being referred to as a "vile woman" and later being blamed by Hecuba for having "brought to ruin all our house" (1215). In this play, nevertheless, Helen appears as a character for the first time and, by anticipating the charges that Menelaus will bring against her, speaks for herself in a three-fold argument: (1) It is more appropriate to blame the mother of Paris (Hecuba) than Helen herself for the Trojan War. (2) Helen's misfortune in winning the beauty contest had the good effect of the Greeks' being freed from Asia's domination. (3) It was a strong goddess who intervened twice on behalf of taking and keeping Helen in Troy. Helen's argument is reasonable even though it is effectively countered by Hecuba, and Helen's being treated as a slave along with the Trojan women generates some sympathy for her as a character, especially in contrast with Hecuba and Menelaus, who become progressively less admirable.

In *Iphigenia in Tauris*, Menelaus and Helen are together blamed by Iphigenia for having caused her to be sacrificed by her father, Agamemnon. Unmitigated hatred of Helen by Iphigenia here and by Electra in the next play (*Electra*) continues with little variation. The one exception occurs as a kind of playbill announcement at the end of *Electra* that introduces version 2, the Helen-in-Egypt story. Menelaus, having just come home from the Trojan War, will bury his sister-in-law, Clytemnestra, freshly murdered by Orestes and Electra. Castor, one of Helen's brothers (the Dioscuri), at the end of the play pronounces:

Castor: Helen will help him. She never went to Troy.
Zeus fashioned and dispatched a Helen-image there
to Ilium so men might die in hate and blood. (1280–83)

Thus we see that when Euripides finally introduced version 2, he did so at privileged points in the dramatic action: at the end of *Electra* and at the beginning of *Helen*. In the prologue to *Helen*, the character Helen states:

Helen: Thus, though I wear the name of guilt in Greece, yet here
I keep my body uncontaminated by disgrace. (66–67)

There are many reasons to read *Helen* as a serious play. Yet the play has usually been read as a farce. One wonders if the discrepancy between version 1 and 2 of the Helen myth, a discrepancy explicit in the play, had anything to do with assigning the play to the genre of farce, an assignment that prevents the play from being taken seriously. A few scholars have read *Helen* as a romantic comedy—an interpretation more able to account for more elements of the plot than is farce. What all commentators have overlooked, however, is that the play is also epistemologically interesting in that it raises questions about what constitutes identity and how we know what we claim to know about others. Version 1 of the myth is alluded to only to be discredited in the unfolding of new events. Interpretation is explicitly called for. Teucer says of Tyndareus's sons (Helen's brothers): "[They are] dead, not dead,/ There are two interpretations here" (138–39). Also unique to this play is the reunion scene between Helen and Menelaus:

> Menelaus: I see it, I see it! All the story that she told
> has come out true. O day of my desires, that gave
> you back into my arms to take and hold again! . . .
> Helen: I am so happy, all my hair is rising
> with shivering pleasure, and the tears burst. Husband
> and love, I have your body here close in my arms,
> happiness, mine again. (623–25, 632–35).

Finally, the play *Helen* elaborates on the futility of the war and raises questions about the mixed motives of the Greeks. *Helen* requires a new reading in an age alert to androcentric distortions. For our purposes, however, the change in the portrayal of Helen can be taken as a key issue in determining more comprehensively who Helen is.

In *Orestes*, written about a year before Euripides voluntarily exiled himself to Macedon, the action begins where *Electra* left off (before the reference to version 2 of the myth): with Helen returning to Argos from Troy with Menelaus to bury Clytemnestra. Orestes and Pylades plot to kill Helen and to kill her daughter, Hermione, ostensibly to hurt Menelaus, who had refused their request for an army to wage war for Orestes' release and their safe passage from the country. Apollo rescues Helen from their deadly attack and announces:

> Apollo: Helen lives,
> for being born of Zeus, she could not die,
> and now, between the Dioscuri in the swathe
> of air, she sits enthroned forever, a star
> for sailors. (1634–37)

In a passage that could be interpreted either as a radically unbelievable solution for a hopeless situation or as a symbolic statement of desire for a new beginning, Apollo decrees:

Apollo: Menelaus must marry again,
since the gods by means of Helen's loveliness
drove Trojans and Greeks together in war
and made them die, that [e]arth might be lightened of her
heavy burden of mortality. (1638–42)

A few lines later, Menelaus is further instructed to take the kingship of Sparta, ostensibly because it was "the dowry of Helen, whose only dowry yet has been your anguish and suffering" (1661–63).

In the last play that mentions Helen (*Iphigenia in Aulis*), performed posthumously, Menelaus is his typical self, arguing with Agamemnon that killing Iphigenia is not worth doing "to gain a Helen" (468). Euripides reverts to version 1 of the myth to portray a psychoanalytically fascinating appropriation of guilt by Iphigenia, who is the prime victim of the affair. Beside the usual appellations of "wicked Helen," there is the despair of Iphigenia as she asks,

Iphigenia: Oh, oh—the marriage
of Paris and Helen—Why must it touch
my life? Why must Paris be my ruin? (1236–38)

More poignant is Iphigenia's willingness to give her life as expiation for the destructive situation:

Iphigenia: . . . Because of me, never more will
Barbarians wrong and ravish Greek women,
Drag them from happiness and their homes
In Hellas. The penalty will be paid
Fully for the shame and seizure of Helen. (1379–82)

Iphigenia appropriates the responsibility formerly attributed completely to Helen, Paris, or the Greeks. With this displacement of responsibility, Euripides has moved from myth as origin to myth as referent to the present and vector for a future.

Interpreting the Variance among the Figures of Helen

Among the different figures of Helen from all three versions of the myth, is there an interpretation that will take all three into account? Julia Kristeva provides some leading threads for our task of putting together a coherent identity for Helen.[11]

---

11. Kristeva's explicit attitudes toward religion vary. Whenever she speaks of religion as an ideology, she would have religion *replaced by* aesthetic discourse. In *Tales of Love*,

In Kristeva's theory, the speaking subject is characterized by two modes in relation to her place in the system of language. These modes correspond to two simultaneous roles, which she thinks are exercised simultaneously: (1) the symbolic role by which the speaking subject advances the prevailing public texts and systems of representation, and (2) the semiotic role by which the speaking subject transgresses, ruptures, and transforms the prevailing systems of meaning and representation. For Kristeva, the symbolic is hierarchically regulated and subordinated to "phallic sexuality." The semiotic refers to manifestations of libido and bodily energies, as well as to certain texts which resist replacement by the symbolic order of speech. Most immediately, the semiotic refers to "pre-Oedipal primary processes" experienced as basic pulsions or forces ("chorae") which flow in ceaseless articulations across the body. Some articulations are dichotomous (e.g., life vs. death, pleasure vs. pain); others are heterogeneous (e.g., guilt, shame, fear). Language, in Kristeva's view, is a dialectic between the symbolic (the totality of conventional meanings at any given time) and the semiotic.

For our purposes, it is helpful to think of the collection of images of Helen as she is represented in Euripides as both semiotic and symbolic: symbolic in the sense that the meanings associated with the three versions of the Helen myth have in fact been understood dichotomously (Helen is by turns evil and beneficent, bringer of bad fate and initiator of rescue, human and goddess) and have been reduced to two characteristics (worthy of praise, worthy of blame) related by the genital principle; semiotic in the sense that the broad range of her portrayed characteristics resists translation into any simple proposition. What is most remembered about Helen, a memory reinforced by the sparse images of Helen in the early plays, is her beauty *and* her blame in

---

trans. Leon S. Roudiez (New York: Columbia University Press, 1987), she is a better reader of particular figures (Bernard) than when she attempts to describe religion in general, e.g., Christianity (really, Paul). On the whole, her treatment of religion parallels her treatment of literary theory, which is both deconstructive and constructively analytic. In her early work, she considers the terms "faith" and "religious" essentialist categories, opposed to feminine discourse, which is individuating, flowing, political. In her later investigations, e.g., "Stabat Mater" (in *Tales of Love*, 234–63), she emphasized the ambiguity of religious figures with respect to psychoanalytic meaning.

I am aware that some of Kristeva's readers criticize her work for not being feminist and, more recently, for not being sufficiently political. Toril Moi responded to these criticisms in *Sexual/Textual Politics* (London: Methuen, 1987). See especially pp. 150–73, where Moi argues that Kristeva's contributions to feminist theory far outweigh the shortcomings of her work. For another insightful explication of Kristeva's thought, see Elizabeth Gross, "Philosophy, subjectivity and the body," in *Feminist Challenges: Social and Political Theory*, ed. Carole Pateman and Elizabeth Gross (Boston: Northeastern University Press, 1986) 125–26, 152.

causing the Trojan War and all the evil visited upon both the Greeks and the Trojans.

That the symbolic realm of the Greeks is dominated by the phallic principle is not news to us. That the androcentrically initiated Trojan War was only one of a series of rape/abductions of noble women and goddesses we know well from Herodotus (*Persian History*, book 1).[12] Kristeva helps us to locate and to understand better the internal resistance to patriarchal domination—resistance such as that experienced in reading Euripides' plays. This resistance surpasses a mere surmise about the author's "attitude," such as crediting Euripides with being either a genius or a misogynist with respect to his portrayal of women. We need not attribute the resistance to patriarchal domination found in the plays to the genius of Euripides alone but can understand that resistance more importantly as a tension operating from within the self-identity of the Greeks—a tension between a semiotic realm of paradox, contradiction, *jouissance,* shifting identities and a symbolic order of unreflective genitality. We have already seen evidence that the story of Helen figured prominently in the self-identity of the Greeks. In *Andromache,* for example, we saw Menelaus crediting Helen with the "exultation" of Greece: in the experience of war, he thought, "Greece grew to manhood

---

12. Herodotus outlined a "domino effect" of causes for the Trojan War. According to the wise men of Persia, the Phoenicians were the first offenders: when the women of Argos, including Io, the king's daughter, came down to the Phoenician ship and bought merchandise, the Phoenicians "cried one to another and rushed upon them. Then most of the women escaped, but Io with others was ravished; and they put them in the ship, and departed and sailed away unto Egypt." Next some Greeks sailed to Tyre in Phoenicia and ravished the king's daughter, Europa. "Thus far, it was like for like, but thereafter the Greeks were the cause of the second wrong: they ravished the king's daughter, Medea, at Aea of the Colchians." By means of an ambassador, the king of the Colchians demanded satisfaction and the restoration of his daughter. But the Greeks replied that the Colchians had not given them satisfaction for the ravishment of Io, so they wouldn't give satisfaction for Medea. In the next generation, Alexander, son of Priam and Hecuba, "having heard these things, conceived the desire to get a wife from Greece by ravishing her, knowing surely that he should not need to give satisfaction, because they also gave none. So he ravished Helen. . . ." The Greeks demanded restoration and satisfaction, but were refused. "Now thus far they did but ravish women one from another. But thereafter they say that the Greeks were greatly at fault, for the Greeks began to make war on Asia before they made war on Europe. The Persians hold that to ravish women is wicked, but to be eager for revenge after they are ravished they hold is foolish" (*Persian History,* bk. 1).

Some feminist classicists see in this history a founding of male civilization on the raped bodies of women. For another theory which accounts for male dominance in archetypal situations like the one described in Herodotus, a theory that is compatible with Kristeva's psychoanalytical approach, see Eli Sagan, *At the Dawn of Tyranny: The Origins of Individualism, Political Oppression, and the State* (New York: Alfred A. Knopf, 1985). See also an application of Sagan's theory in Katherine K. Young, "Introduction," in *Women in World Religions,* ed. Arvind Sharma (Albany: SUNY Press, 1987).

then" (668–72). In this sense, the story of Helen and the Trojan War functions as a second genesis for the Greeks, a frequently interpreted founding story which referred back to time when the present became what it was. Kristeva's theory of how meaning and significance come into being makes it possible to reflect on the complete inventory of references and appearances of Helen in Euripides with an expectation that they are significant not only within the context of each play and not only in summary but also as they jockey for position among themselves and in the reader's world of meanings.

On the one hand, we are prevented from reducing the meaning of Helen to beauty and blame or to any easy way of relating these two major themes, even in Euripides' early work. We must attend to figures other than Helen who are blamed as the cause of the Trojan War, for example, Paris or the gods and goddesses (see *The Trojan Women*, 920–26). Rather than assign any essential meaning to beauty and to blame, we are encouraged by Kristeva's theory to see these two strands of meaning in an uneasy relationship with other strands of meaning which conspire to define who the Greeks were.

As a result of Kristeva's theory, we are also encouraged to look for contradictions and interruptions of meaning as an internal critique of the symbolic order. Many nineteenth- and twentieth-century readers of Euripides have been reductionist in the sense that they read in his work only decline and secularization of belief in the gods and goddesses. But while Euripides' treatment of gods and goddesses is decidedly different from that of Aeschylus or of Sophocles, the ambiguity that characterizes Euripides' treatment of the gods deserves more than a swift dismissal. Indeed, within this dismissal there remains to be explored some critics' odd elevation of "true" (read "simple" and "unquestioning") belief which they say is to be found in Euripides' precursors, against the critics' approbation of what they call Euripides' secularization of religion. With Kristeva's theory, these reductive interpretations (e.g., Euripides no longer believes in gods and goddesses; Euripides challenges the existence of the gods) can be seen to eliminate what is ultimately most valuable in understanding the plays.[13] For with Kristeva's theory, as one explicator of her work wrote, "the acceptance of negativity or the fading of meaning can lead to the emergence of a new positivity of meaning" and "the only positivity presently acceptable involves the multiplication of languages, logics and powers."[14] For Kristeva, this

---

13. A good example of this positivist kind of reading can be found in A. W. Verrall's *Euripides the Rationalist* (Cambridge: Cambridge University Press, 1913).

14. Julia Kristeva, "Talking about *Polylogue*," in *French Feminist Thought: A Reader*, ed. Toril Moi (London: Blackwell, 1987) 110.

multiplicity includes language, rhetoric, and literature as "terrains of an accepted madness."[15] We could add to this list of terrains certain aspects of religion as well.

We are now prepared to retrieve the goddess image of Helen according to a religious logic. We have seen that in one of Euripides' last references to Helen, Helen is restored, albeit miraculously, by Zeus, to goddess status, by which she "sits enthroned forever, a star for sailors" (*Orestes*, 1637–38). Her restoration was foretold in *Helen*, where the action is initiated by a trio of women and both Helen and Menelaus are promised divine status after they return to Greece, where their lives eventually end. Euripides' restoration of Helen as a goddess figure is in clear contrast to the uniform denunciation of her in his early plays. This progression of Helen's characterization in Euripides' plays, together with the scattered references to her as fertility "goddess" in Greek culture over four hundred years, culminates in a striking possibility of meaning for us—something that surpasses the *Oxford Classical Dictionary*'s citation of Helen as "one of the most plausible examples of a 'faded goddess.'"[16]

The waning and waxing attached to the meaning of "Helen" combines in one figure the dichotomies of figures of women in androcentric cultures noticed by other feminist critics. Toril Moi, for example, explicating Kristeva's notion of the marginality of women with respect to the symbolic order, thinks that

> women seen as the limit of the symbolic order will ... share in the disconcerting properties of *all* frontiers: they will be neither inside nor outside, neither known nor unknown. It is this position that has enabled male culture sometimes to vilify women as representing darkness and chaos, to view them as Lilith or the Whore of Babylon, and sometimes to elevate them as the representatives of a higher and purer nature, to venerate them as Virgins and Mothers of God.[17]

The figure of Helen as both vilified and venerated represents an especially rich case study of marginality and can be illuminated by means of Moi's general comment on marginality: "In the first instance the borderline is seen as part of the chaotic wilderness outside, and in the second it is seen as an inherent part of the inside: the part that protects and shields the symbolic order from the imaginary chaos."[18] In version 1

15. Kristeva, *Tales of Love*, 169.
16. The *Oxford Classical Dictionary* refers to Helen as a "faded goddess" without alluding to her restoration, except to observe that "the mere fact of being her husband is Menelaus' passport to Elysium" (*Od*. 4.569).
17. Toril Moi, *Sexual/Textual Politics*, 167.
18. Ibid.

of the myth, Helen's beauty remains a seductive power and a bounty to be won. At the same time, by blaming her for the war's tragedies, Greece did not have to face its own ambiguous motives for waging the war.

But by moving to version 2 of the myth in the later plays, Euripides also represents Helen in terms of what Kristeva calls a new ethic, one based not on "Spinoza's biologically-based exclusion of women from ethical decision-making," but instead in a process which expects and involves otherness, distance, and limitation. Indeed, Euripides' plays can be viewed as making possible what Kristeva calls "a structure, a logical discourse . . . that takes two stages into account, the conscious and the unconscious ones, and two corresponding types of performances."[19] As we have seen, the fact that version 2 is developed over and against version 1 can be read as a struggle between two kinds of ethics in which benevolence overcomes vengeance. Clearly the play *Helen* is a full-blown dramatization of Helen as actively restoring Menelaus and his companions to their homeland and overcoming their mistrust in order to be able to do so. In *Orestes*, Apollo rescues the Helen of version 1 from murder by Orestes and Pylades, after which she takes on the divine status of version 2. In another dramatic instance of a mortal achieving divine status in Euripides' plays, Thetis, at the end of *Andromache*, comes to make Peleus, her husband, a divinity forever after he has just suffered the loss of his two sons. In all these instances, the elevation of a human to god/dess might be said to be based on an ethic of love, that is, a love expressing itself as penultimate justice.

As goddess, Helen also participates in an interesting shift in the concept of power in Euripides. One can see a parallel between *Helen* and *The Bacchae* in the sense that both Helen and Dionysus represent, in their respective plays, new conceptions of the divine. Dionysus understands himself as a god, even though the people of Thebes are divided on the issue of his identity. Helen understands herself as a person acted upon by the gods, even though the chorus refers to her both as the daughter of Zeus and the daughter of Tyndareus. But where divinity is "most terrible, yet most gentle to mankind" in *The Bacchae* (860), so too in *Helen* the gods are "complex . . . hard for us to predict" (712). In both plays, the notion of deity is ambiguous and intrinsically linked with human action. Helen is spoken of as having never "shamed her aged father . . . [or her] divine brothers . . ." (720–21) and in this play is given the favor of the gods. Dionysus is said to have come to Thebes in *The Bacchae* to exact retribution for the slander of his mother's character because she conceived a child by Zeus. Dionysus breaks the sheer force of Pentheus's brute physical power and arrogance and lets loose the force

---

19. Julia Kristeva, *Desire in Language* (New York: Columbia University Press, 1980) ix.

of madness. Helen becomes a guide and savior to the Greeks, even though she professes ignorance of what to do next herself and seemingly chances upon successful courses of action. Helen, too, is the site of a remarkable lament in *Helen*, which includes all those oppressed (both Trojans and Greeks) by the Trojan War: the daughters of Troy, Priam's people, Achaeans killed in the war, their wives, Achaeans drowned. The myths of Helen fortuitously complicate the God/power issue so easily reduced to heteronomy in classical discussions of the gods and goddesses.

These images of godliness are different from the essentialist notion of God, which Kristeva describes as meaning that has been bestowed on an "Other (the absolute signifier, God)."[20] Neither polytheism nor monotheism seems adequate to conceptualize Euripides' treatment of the gods. Perhaps some new concept is needed—one that signifies both the unity of existence and the many ways this unity is represented. And on the issue of destiny, it seems clear that as one response to this question the figure of Helen represents the multifaceted phenomena that are gathered together in this concept: on the one hand, the experience of being acted on, being chosen, being graced and empowered; and, on the other, the experience of seizing the moment, playing things by ear, getting a life, taking decisive action.

Is it possible to claim some mitigating effects of Euripidean texts on the androcentric world? We have seen that Helen herself as the emergence of a new goddess at the end of Euripides' work in some sense is like Dionysus as the emergence of a new god in *The Bacchae* (no longer singly executed interventionist power). We might see in these dramatic actions the strength in the power of the "affect" that Kristeva posits— that welling up of resistance to the reified symbolic order. Kristeva cautions, on the one hand, against the temptation to ignore social/ political structures by emphasizing the "affective" and, on the other, against the temptation to ignore the complex process by which gender differences get positioned into the symbolic order. And while Helen and Dionysus are dissimilar in several ways, they both represent in different ways the freedom of god/dess to be god/dess and to be so as the space and ground of new possibilities.

Applied to goddess research, Kristeva's caution can also assist us in constructing a critical typology for a religious understanding of goddess figures. In the first generation of research, goddess traditions are retrieved for the purpose of maintaining equality between female and male models for human aspirations and behavior. In the second generation of research, aspects traditionally regarded as feminine (and therefore

---

20. Kristeva, "Talking about *Polylogue*," 111.

of negligible or less value than those traditionally regarded as masculine) are transvaluated to gain new worth. Thus far, goddess research has been primarily of the first and second types. What is needed in the third generation of goddess research is a study of the historical fluctuations of god and goddess figures in relation to the possibilities for human existence at any given time and place.

What can be said specifically of fertility goddesses in this threefold typology? In the first two stages, fertility goddesses are too often celebrated only for their ties to nature and new life. Only in the third generation are the limitations of the fertility figure made explicit: First, it is recognized that fertility goddesses are not the only deities that have links to nature. Second, it is discovered that fertility imagery is entangled with other imagery and may even have obscured it.[21] In the case of Helen, however, the reverse seems to be the case—namely, that other imagery has obscured the fertility imagery. When other imagery comes to the fore, two effects occur: first, the obscuration and eventual loss of fertility imagery and the fading of divine status, and, second, the opposition to fertility imagery by historic religion, which sought to free human beings from their dependency on natural forces. The transformation of Helen from a fertility goddess to a marginal figure of beauty and blame thus lends itself to investigation as a third generation goddess research problem.

Appropriating the Tradition

But who is Helen, what is she *for us*, moderns with prodigious memories? We find literary appropriations of Helen in this century by two major poets in whom Helen is a central figure: H.D. (Hilda Doolittle) and William Butler Yeats.

Helen appears in H.D.'s poetry from the early 1920s through the 1960s and, according to one reader's account, served as a correlate to her "self-seeking quest," an "encompassing 'self' of which she was only a part."[22] H.D.'s earliest Helen poems treat of hatred and sexual desire and

---

21. See the remarkable essay by Marymay Downing, "Prehistoric Goddesses: The Cretan Challenge," *Journal of Feminist Studies in Religion* 1 (Spring 1985) 7–22, which shows how the seafaring and technological imagery of Minoan goddesses has been obscured by fertility imagery. Downing also cautions that "faith in a goddess ... may have been conceived among the ancient Cretans in quite simple terms, or in thealogically complex and profound terms, and the full range in between as well, just as religious beliefs vary among individuals, and over an individual's lifetime" (p. 14).

22. See Norman Holmes Pearson's "Foreword" to the 1972 edition of H.D.'s *Hermetic Definition* (New York: New Directions, 1972).

frequently resolve the tension between enchantment and revulsion, sex and death, with Helen's death, as can be seen in the following poem:

Helen (1924)

All Greece hates
the still eyes in the white face,
the lustre as of olives
where she stands,
and the white hands.

All Greece reviles
the wan face when she smiles,
hating it deeper still
when it grows wan and white,
remembering past enchantments
and past ills.

Greece sees unmoved,
God's daughter, born of love,
the beauty of cool feet
and slendrest knees,
could love indeed the maid,
only if she were laid,
white ash amid funereal cypresses.[23]

Thirty-seven years later, in her 315-page *Helen in Egypt*, H.D. adopts the perspective of the poet Stesichorus in giving voice to the version 2 of the Helen story.[24] This tripartite poem, composed as semidramatic narrative lyrics with brief prose interludes, portrays Helen as the "scapegoat" of the Trojan War and suggests that war in general is evidence of the self-destructiveness of a culture dominated by masculine values as traditionally defined.

Doolittle's Helen of "Winter Love," a twenty-one page coda to *Helen in Egypt*, is also drawn from version 2 of the Greek myth.[25] This still later Helen, grown old and alone with her memories, struggles to develop a new, less guilt-ridden sense of herself.

Can Helen be otherwise?

One of Yeats's several short poems foregrounds the effect a woman like Helen has on someone's life:

---

23. "Helen" and several other early poems by H.D. can be found in *The Norton Anthology of Literature by Women*, ed. Sandra M. Gilbert and Susan Gubar (New York and London: W. W. Norton, 1985) 1461–82. See also the introduction to H.D.'s work by Gilbert and Gubar, pp. 1457–61.
24. H.D. (Hilda Doolittle), *Helen in Egypt* (New York: Grove Press, 1961).
25. H.D., "Winter Love," in *Hermetic Definition*.

No Second Troy (1910)

Why should I blame her that she filled my days
With misery, or that she would of late
Have taught to ignorant men most violent ways,
Or hurled the little streets upon the great,
Had they but courage equal to desire?
What could have made her peaceful with a mind
That nobleness made simple as a fire,
With beauty like a tightened bow, a kind
That is not natural in an age like this,
Being high and solitary and most stern?
Why, what could she have done, being what she is?
Was there another Troy for her to burn?

The Yeats poem forces us to recognize that asking the question of appropriation, Who is Helen for us? inscribes the personal object of the poem in a dialectic with historical images of Helen. Yeats's rhetorical question, "Was there another Troy for her to burn?" cannily suggests that he was the only Troy available.

What might interest us especially is that the poem's portrayal of "what she is" reiterates the themes of blame and praise, albeit presented as personal assessments. In this way, the poem continues the best-known version of Helen's story: Helen is blamed in the sense that "she filled my days with misery" and "would of late/ Have taught to ignorant men most violent ways"; and Helen is praised in the sense that she had "a mind/ That nobleness made simple as a fire. . . ." But unlike popular memory, which would either praise or blame Helen, the persona of the poem asks a question: "Why, what could she have done,/ being what she is?" The persona recalls what is most attractive about Helen: ". . . with a mind/ that nobleness made simple as a fire, with beauty like a tightened bow . . ." and reinvents her to be unforgettable. So vivid is her memory for the poet and his audience that in the last line he can metonymize the "her" who set fire to Troy—without having to name Helen. Nor does the self-referent have to be stated: the poet is Troy and it is he who has been set aflame.

Yeats's answer, then, is to ask a question: What else was there for Helen to do? Whether Helen is read as Maude Gonne (Yeats's biographical beloved) or as the mythic figure, the poem asserts that there was no other Troy for Helen than the one which became her entrance into both history and the poet's memory. She for whom Troy was allegedly burned is, in the ambiguous fate of both public and personal history, she who burned Troy. Yeats's allusions to Helen in other short poems echo this essential ambiguity.

It is tempting—but naïve—to take these poems by Doolittle and Yeats as representative of contemporary female and male appropriations of the Helen myth. Nevertheless, the poems do represent two distinct responses to the ancient myths: H.D.'s portrayals of Helen are developmental and analytic in terms of who Helen was to her people, whereas Yeats's treatment of Helen is condensed and expressive of a personal experience of a woman, the kind of woman Helen is assumed to be. Thus, the works of the two poets do represent two versions of who Helen is for many contemporary readers. A third version—Helen as a goddess in a usable tradition—is perhaps yet to be imagined.

10

HESIOD: RELIGION AND POETRY IN THE WORKS AND DAYS

David Grene

THE PERSONAL ELEMENT is the last thing to look for information on—or to expect—in reading the classical Greek authors. We hardly know more than the bare facts of the lives of most of them. But, perhaps more important, we know hardly anything about the ambience of those lives—the form that their profession forced on their work. Was Herodotus a businessman? Or how did he manage to stray over all of the earth's surface? Doing what? What, exactly, was the relation of the tragic dramatists to their plays *after* the performance at the Greater Dionysia or the Lenaea? How like are they to modern dramatists, who must always deal with the apparatus of their productions? To such questions our answer must nearly always be: We do not know. One of the reasons we know little or nothing of these things is the extreme infrequency with which Greek authors mention other writers who are their contemporaries or near contemporaries. As far as I know, Plato never discusses either Herodotus or Thucydides. There are, it is true, echoes of ideas between Herodotus and Sophocles, and Pindar and Aeschylus, but these may come about just as easily through some common source. Except for Homer, very few of their great predecessors are mentioned by Greek writers down to the time of Aristotle. This affects us with a kind of grievance. We have lived so much with a close-knit selection of authors known as the Greek classics (and have forgotten that this is a thoroughly arbitrary and artificial unit) that we expect them to have far more to say to us about one another.

The surprise is Hesiod, who, in the *Works and Days*, goes out of his way to identify himself, his father, and something of the facts of their lifetimes, including his father's move to Ascra in Boeotia and his own participation in a poetic contest, which involved his one journey in a boat. These personal touches in the poem are the tip of the iceberg. For some reason, Hesiod, very remarkably among the Greek authors and most notably in contrast to his one great opposite number, Homer (with whom his own name is always linked), wishes to flavor his poem with the sense of the personal. Most important of all, Hesiod has given us a personal reason from his own life as to *why* he wrote the poem. His brother Perses had managed by bribery to induce the "gift-gobbling kings" to award him an unfair share of the family farm. As a result of his indignation, Hesiod sets about proving to his brother the ultimate folly of such injustice, both in the judges and in Perses himself. This leads the poet to account for ethics in cosmic terms and in the history of the world, dealing with both gods and men,[1] in two separate myths, the myth of Prometheus and the myth of the Ages. Also, somewhat paradoxically, Hesiod has decided that since Perses is going to work the stolen farm anyhow, he will instruct him how to farm it well. One might wonder why Hesiod wants his brother to farm well. It might be more reasonable to wish vindictively that he would farm ill and fail. But the thing is, at some level, consistent with Hesiod's greater thesis. What he is going to do is to tell Perses the "real truth" (*Works and Days*, 8).[2] This means, between Perses and Hesiod, the truth most readily available in its exemplar, farming. Farming is the way of life that to Hesiod most clearly reveals man's relation to the gods—to Zeus's harshness and unpredictability, but also to whatever general directions of his, regarding time and fitness, in cultivation of the earth and dealings with family and others, are available to us. It is here that Hesiod's "very truth" to his brother will be most effective, and the discussion of how to farm leads Hesiod into an elaborate and illuminated version of the farmer's year, from end to end.

Once one is impressed by Hesiod's personal emphasis on the reason for his poem, one discovers other suggestive pieces of evidence of its personal character. The first is negative evidence. There seems to be, in the *Works and Days*, no express evidence of professional predecessors, nor even of fictional treatment of professional counterparts of the poet, nor of how the reader is invited to see his work in the context of other works. All of these aspects occur in Homer. Phemius and Demodocus in the *Odyssey* are unmistakably versions of Homer's own role as the recorder of heroic events. Homer speaks through his characters about

1. Throughout this essay, the use of the term "man," "mankind," and their related pronouns is studied. For Hesiod, "man" meant the whole of humanity in its significant aspects, but those aspects were male. He was misogynistic, but still a remarkable poet.
2. Throughout this essay, unattributed numbers in parentheses refer to the *Works and Days*; the translation is mine; the line numbering is standard.

the general nature of poetry applied to real events—which is the heart of his own concern. There is surely a relevance in Telemachus's rejection of his mother's criticism of the minstrel's choice of the war at Troy:

> My mother, why do you grudge the charming minstrel his giving of delight, however his mind stirs him to do so? It is not the minstrel who is to blame, but rather Zeus who gives to gain-seeking men what he will to each one. Do not blame this man for singing of the evil voyage of the Greeks; for men celebrate more that newest song, whichever it is, that flutters about the ears of mankind. (*Odyssey* 1.346ff.)

Surely this is Homer's plug for his own trade, as he imagines it was before his own day, but essentially the same.

Nothing like this is true of the *Works and Days*. Apparently, at least as he sees himself, Hesiod treads in no one's footsteps as he sketches his personal grievances against his brother, and he sees this act as an example of all of man's relation to the gods, and indeed to a complete cosmology. Nor does Hesiod convey any hint of others who have written didactic poems about farming.

There are, of course, other poems by Hesiod, whether they bear his name justly or not, of which this generalization may not be true. The *Theogony*, the *Shield*, the *Catalogue* may perhaps have lived inside of an artistic tradition, maybe inside of something that could be called a Boeotian epic. One must still take account of the *Works and Days*, this extraordinary poem presenting a unique combination of elements— some sort of epic diction, yet hardly Homeric in its employment— treating religion as a matter of daily life and ethics, but rooted also in cosmological myths, allegedly teaching how to farm and equipped to do so with an apparatus covering the farming year. Moreover, it is not only a personal poem arising from Hesiod's grievance against his brother; it is a personal poem full of the personal touches that color Hesiod's mind as he moves back through the remembered sequence of the farming scene. The poetry springs from the depth of his vision and excitement in doing the work and responding to his joy in it. Perhaps it is indeed that otherwise unexampled thing in Greek literature, an entirely personal account of the relation between the writer himself and God, with a traditional religious feeling and a traditional mythology jostling uneasily a new urgency of personal religious truth, buttressed humanly by the aphoristic wisdom of peasant proverbs.[3]

---

2. It is true that M. L. West, in the latest and most thorough edition we possess of the *Works and Days* (Oxford: Clarendon Press, 1978), sees it very differently. He tries hard to connect this work of Hesiod with wisdom books inside of the Mesopotamian tradition. These combine a seeming, but unreal, personal approach to a how-to-do-it theme. Perhaps the links between the *Theogony* (if that is really by Hesiod) and Mesopotamian texts are

The later Greeks certainly accepted some of the early great poets as didactic writers and saw their didacticism as part of their value. Aristophanes in the *Frogs* cites Musaeus and Hesiod, and Homer himself, as teachers of what we would call technical subjects. Obviously one must take the contribution of a comic poet on this subject within the context of his jest, and I do not suggest that Aristophanes thought seriously that Homer's merit lay in teaching regimental maneuvers. Still, the joke comes out of some accepted way of thinking—that one of the merits of the ancients was that they gave instructions in practical matters.

There *are* many unequivocal references to Homer and Hesiod as the earliest authorities on the relations of gods and men. Herodotus and Plato speak of the two ancient poets frequently in this sense. Many readers, Greek or otherwise, of the centuries subsequent to Homer and Hesiod must have known Hesiod's religious teaching as expressed primarily in the *Theogony*. The *Theogony* is what it says it is—the birth of the gods—and undoubtedly that poem is a source of major religious meaning. But the *Works and Days* is also avowedly a religious poem, since it opens with the author's celebration of the greatness of Zeus and begs him, "hearing and seeing," to guide the renderings of law in justice. "And may I for my part tell Perses the very truth" (9–10). It tells Perses and the gift-gobbling kings who gave their corrupt decision in his favor how wrong they were and how stupid. It then launches into a course of teaching Perses, which covers the ethics that are acceptable to the gods and successful with men *and* the theme of how to farm well.

It seems to me quite likely that Hesiod wrote both poems, though probably the *Theogony* first. Each is a formidable complement to the other. The *Theogony* deals with the divine and daemonic aspect of the world—the assembly of gods and the daemons that are included under aspects of human intelligence and states of emotion such as fear, lust, strife, and, perhaps oddest of all, "manslayings." Apparently, all these *reflect* humanity in some sense but have independent existence on the divine side of things. The *Theogony* describes how the cosmos came about, from the divine side of things, yet always, somehow, including in itself humanity.

Perhaps there was a traditional claim for such narrative in Hesiod's time and place. But it looks as if he may have created entirely on his

---

stronger, particularly in their common theological implications. But the evidence of the connections that West needs for the *Works and Days* seems very fragile, and there is a growing inclination in critics now to discount much of what there is. Above all, there is no indication whatever that Hesiod knew of any such tradition behind his own, such as is abundant in Homer.

own the other half of the story found in *Works and Days*—the ethics of humanity vis-à-vis the gods and the relevance of farming to *that* story, when one comes to tell the "very truth." In the myths he draws on to support his cosmology—the Prometheus story and the myth of the Ages—there is a distinct emphasis on process toward good or ill. Process indeed furnishes the outlines of the narrative, and when he teaches Perses (and ourselves) it is through a guided account of the farmer's year. The agricultural teaching is sustained, though it starts only halfway through the poem; the ethical comment and its supporting cosmological myths occupy the first half. As one studies the farming instructions, especially if one yields to some of its grotesque charm, certain of its aspects look very odd indeed.

It does not seem as if Hesiod was really bent on teaching his brother to farm by rules appropriate to farming in Boeotia in the eighth or seventh century B.C. Of course we know very little accurately about this farming, but here and there over the world there are still elemental systems of farming that make us understand what Hesiod's farming *must* have been like. In fact, it does not appear that Hesiod's instruction was really in the details which, once grasped, would enable the beginner better to perform the task. Hesiod dealt with farming in what he saw as its elementary core: it is the truth of human existence in which man's subjection to God is the central theme.

I am sure that no Boeotian farmer would have learned farming from a book anyway, and this book hardly comes close even to the practical instruction in Virgil's consciously literary work, the *Georgics*. West in his commentary ruefully notices the want of the specific and the detailed in Hesiod's plan of instruction. The differences from Cato and Varro in their agricultural teaching are truly astonishing. The works of Cato and Varro are recognizably technical within our sense of the term; that is, they see detail as the minor but telling illustration of the main theme that must first be grasped by the learner.

Hesiod gives lots of detail, but not the detail that we would regard as valuable in learning farming. Instead, his account of farming bears on the total *picture* of the farmer's work, a picture that clearly takes possession of Hesiod's mind when he ostensibly sets out upon the how-to-do-it part. This not only covers the picturesque details of the farming moment but also gives the farming substance. Hesiod tells his brother how to make a plough and a wagon. This indeed seems relevant detail. It involves knowing what kind of tree to use for both tools, and what kind of tree both carpenter and farmer must work with. It might be assumed that Perses would not know about this. Perhaps Perses does not know enough to select a team of nine-year-old bullocks as work animals—but why is he given the wonderful image of the bullocks struggling in the furrow and thereby testing the strength of the plough? I cannot think that Perses in such a time and place of elementary farming did not know how to scatter seeds behind the plough. Even if he didn't, did he also need instruction in hiring a small boy, as an additional helper, to cover the seeds with earth stirred by his foot, thereby causing "trouble for the birds"? Did he need instruction as to the exact dimension of the loaf that is to go for the forty-year-old ploughman's lunch?

This instruction in farming that Hesiod gives to Perses is a kind of celebration, not a lesson. Hesiod's approach to farming is rather like that of the Amish in modern rural America, placing farming in the main track of God's relation to man. Hesiod is the poet of this exemplary way, which by studying and pursuing one discovers the true nature of the world and its government. Hesiod does not feel that he has to include just the useful details of a farming scene to promote his pupil's more successful application of the lesson. He is inducting this pupil—or perhaps a hypothetical pupil as well as Perses—into farming as itself the imaginative clue to the universe. The detail fades into the whole as he illuminates the total scene, for it is in the total scene that the truth exists. In the same way the farming calendar and perhaps finally the lucky and unlucky days, in their arbitrary denial of so much of the rational planning of the farming program, complete the chart of the cosmos.

For Hesiod to understand farming he must place it in the cosmos and in mythological history. Rhetorically all this instruction can be harnessed to make a better man, and a somewhat better farmer, of even a minor scoundrel like Perses. The enthusiasm for the major objective—the recreation of the imaginative moment and the imaginative whole, which is Hesiod's vision—somewhat swamps the literal teaching of Perses with which the poem begins. Thus, in the later parts the emphasis on teaching Perses fades before the stronger purpose of revisiting the sequence of the farming year for its own sake.

The poem's first most important observation about the nature of the universe is one that seems to link the practice of farming with a later passage on ethics itself. It is Hesiod's expression of the deliberateness of the deity in making the conditions of life hard, both in farming and in the choice of right and wrong.

For the Gods have hidden his livelihood from man. You could easily work for a day's space and have enough to keep yourself in idleness for a year. You could hang your steering oar over the chimney smoke, and all the work of oxen and drudging mules would be finished. But Zeus was angry in his heart and hid this livelihood, because Prometheus had cheated him. (42)

The proof of the harsh design of the gods lies in Hesiod's awareness of the infinitely greater potentiality of the earth's fertility over what it achieves—because of the inhibition of weather, that is, Zeus. (Every farmer that has ever thought and felt knows this to be true.) Getting the right weather at the right time is where the trouble is. Consequently, in Hesiod's mythological history there has been some fundamental change about this since primeval time. In the Golden Age and in the Age of Heroes there was no difficulty about crops. The land yielded generously without working or with minimal and fairly pleasant work.

The links between topics in the *Works and Days* are often severely noted by the commentators. They speak as though the work were a haphazard jumble of subjects, but they rarely pay attention to the subtlety of the transitions made. Here the writer opens his subject with "The Gods have hidden this livelihood from man" (43). "Zeus *hid* it [the livelihood] because his heart was angry because Prometheus had cheated him, and therefore he devised against man sorrowful troubles" (47–49). "Yes, he *hid* fire, for the son of Iapetus [Prometheus] again stole it for men from Zeus the counsellor" (50–51). (Fire was apparently already in man's possession, however it was obtained, but then it was removed and only finally restored by Prometheus. This contrasts with Aeschylus's version, where the god made the first and original transfer of fire to man.) In the quoted passages, the repetition of the word "hid" and its dramatic placing in the final line not only joins the original punishment, the hiding of the livelihood, to the removal of fire from humanity, but stresses in both cases the depriving and covert nature of this punishment.

There is the same kind of emphasis on hardness, on the ethical side, that we have found in the farming.

> It is easy for even a crowd to choose wickedness. The road is a smooth one, and very near to us, but the immortal Gods have put sweat in the way of virtue. The path to it is long and steep and rough at first. When one comes to the top, thereafter, it is easy, though there is difficulty in it still. (287)

The hardness of the task in farming and the hardness of the choice in ethics are bound together. In both cases there was a primitive condition when such difficulty did not exist. The hardness is a modern thing, that is, a feature of life in mankind in its present form, and identifiable presumably with the Fifth or Iron Age, in which Hesiod lived. This change is traceable in the accounts of both Aeschylus and Hesiod to some radical break between the old order of existence, after which at different levels of degeneration new compulsions and new rewards are necessary for men. It is most remarkable that neither Hesiod nor Aeschylus reports this punishment of man in moral terms in which man is obviously the sinner. In both, the change in man is due to the arbitrary authority of Zeus and perhaps more doubtfully to some natural and destined process in which both Zeus and his predecessors have their appointed roles. The Golden Age men existed during the reign of Kronos (111) and went on to become daemons through the plans of great Zeus (122). The Second Age men (if one could call them men) refused to worship the gods, *as they should*, and so they were sent to their death, but under earth they are called gods by mortals, and "honor attends on *them* also" (142). Clearly this is a very different destiny from that of the fallen angels under Lucifer. After the destruction of the Bronze Age men through mutual slaughter, Zeus—for no apparent reason—created a better breed of men. There are therefore no compelling reasons why those that follow them, the Iron Age, should be so much worse. There is certainly in this some notion that the will of Zeus in bringing about such changes is not explicable in human terms, as the simpler story of Prometheus says: "Prometheus made Zeus angry and so he did this and that to man." Here in the Five Ages one has something moving in accordance with some immutable process, by the agency of a supreme God who, all the same, is neither omniscient (see Aeschylus) nor explicable (Hesiod), but part of some universal design originating one knows not where (Aeschylus). For when Hesiod has completed the Prometheus story as the first of his mythological explanations why man's lot on earth is what it is, he says with seeming casualness: "If you will, I will give you the substance of another story well and truly told—and you lay it up in your heart—of how both Gods and men came from the same stock" (106).

The first account, that of Prometheus and his quarrel with Zeus, is ostensibly given to show why mankind no longer lives easily with farming. It is because of Zeus's hiding of the possibility of such easy access to fertility; and the story drifts indirectly into the history of the theft of fire from Zeus to man. It ends with the full-scale account of something like our modern world, afflicted not only with hard work but with disease, with only hope to make the condition tolerable—that is, if we make an explanation out of coalescing both of the Hesiod cosmologies and Aeschylus's reference in the *Prometheus* to "blind hopes." The second story tells of the common origin of gods and men. These two stories must be in some sense complementary in Hesiod's mind. How are they complementary, and what sort of cosmology results if one looks at the two of them in conjunction?

In three of the Five Ages of the Declining Metals (the second story), the links between gods and men are so close that these latter become a *sort* of god. The Golden Age men after death become daemons and are Zeus's guardian spirits presiding over justice on earth. The Silver Age men, who are seemingly the rebel Titans of Aeschylus's story, are punished for refusing to worship the immortal gods, as they should (139), but are still called gods of the underworld by men. The Heroes of the Heroic Age (between those living in the Bronze and the last or Fifth or Iron Age) go to the Islands of the Blessed after death—some of them, anyway. Only the Bronze Age men end in mutual destruction, without renown, and "death seizes them for all their terribleness" (154). Unlike the other three, they have no mark of their divine origin after death. The Fifth Age, of Iron, is distinguished from the others in that it is not yet over, but bears all the marks of decay and destruction. The story of decline is nearly finished.

The specifically human condition is associated with death and work. In the case of the favored ages, where the divine stock exists in some element of man, death and work are modified to a shadowy likeness of the divine condition. The Golden Age men fall asleep in death, thereby contrasting markedly with those that die of diseases released on earth by Zeus's evil emissary Pandora. They ply their tasks only "at their ease and voluntarily" (118–19). This is as much mitigation as one can expect while remaining human. The Heroes (Fourth Age) go to the Islands of the Blessed after death and during their lives their fields bear three crops a year (173).

It does look as if the Story of the Ages is directed to just what Hesiod says he would tell—the nonseparability of human and divine. It is only in the Fifth Age (that of Iron and Hesiod) that we hear about the duties to family and hospitality, and then only when these are flouted and Aidos and Nemesis depart the earth. It appears certain that Justice (*dikē*), which is Zeus's particular contribution to man as distinct from the animals, Dike, Zeus's daughter, and the daemons who attend her in her opposition to Violence (*bia*), are elements of the Fifth Age. At least it is only in this last evil state of the world that we hear of the typical human deeds of injustice and perjury and the probable defeat of the human virtues that oppose them.

Both of Hesiod's stories bear on process and change in mankind's history, perhaps even in the history of the cosmos. The gods are inevitably the controlling element; yet it almost seems as though they cannot exist—or cannot exist comprehensibly to us—without reference to man. Man is at worst the victim or plaything of the gods; at its best, a shadow of them. But always man is some sort of *completing* of the universe in which the gods function. The Prometheus story shows man as the victim of the gods. The Ages story shows the grades of distinction that exist between god and man. It is a kind of inspired natural history—of the human and divine. It modifies the first personal story of the struggle between Zeus and Prometheus with man as at least part of the field of battle and finally as the main victim. I think, in fact, that in

Hesiod the second story is almost a temptation to supersede the first. ...
No, says Hesiod; perhaps you should see the two aspects of life, the human and the divine, so distinct in the first story with the proper roles allotted to each, as *not* so truly separable, but different as they have developed or failed to develop their potentiality. It is surely very tempting to connect this with Hesiod's work in the *Theogony*, where so many human passions and even human situations are daemons.

But the big question is whether we can understand, *at all*, mythological cause and mythological origin as Hesiod saw them. It is doubtful, but there is a personal directness very characteristic of Hesiod which appears to me to make it possible. The two stories look like a rather sophisticated provocation of the imagination, balanced against each other, with mutual impact: I can imagine a Hesiod speaking with a twentieth-century voice:

> You know the story of Prometheus and Pandora and the ruin of mankind? I wonder if that really is the truest way to see how the cosmos is and has been. There is another story perhaps more embracing. (Hence, "another story *if you like* ... I will give you the substance of it. ...). Man and the gods are essentially one; they grow different under different states of the world and develop or fail to develop what is in them, as one or the other, as we recognize when we call them daemons or underworld gods.

The Ages of the Metals in Hesiod are not exactly a parable. They are a study of visualized degradation in color and quality. One should not see the metals simply as metaphors for changes in man. This is not Bunyan with the Slough of Despond nor Evangelist nor Pliable. They are dominated by the form and substance of the metals in which the change is rooted. The story is equally surely not the book of Genesis. It is a vision of Gold, Silver, Bronze, Iron, and, paradoxically and audaciously, the Age of Heroes who fought at Thebes and Troy superimposed on a poet's dream of cosmological process.

The transitions in this poem are the clues to much of its meaning, especially when the dozen lines or so that constitute an episode or reflection appear abrupt or incoherent. After the stern closing glances at the destructive wickedness of the Iron Age (202), Hesiod claims the attention of the kings ("though they are wise themselves also") for a story. He tells of a tuneful nightingale seized by a hawk, complaining pitiably to her captor. The hawk tells her that her complaints are useless: "A far stronger One has you in his grasp, and I will carry you where I will, for all your singing. I will make a meal of you if I will, or let you go." There has been much dispute as to what this means, and no explanation seems entirely satisfactory. Most editors are so impressed with the identification of Hesiod with the tuneful nightingale that they choose to ignore the effective brutality of the hawk. If this story is specifically addressed to the kings and the point is their helplessness, Zeus has to be the hawk and the kings the victim. This indeed is the drift of the whole passage before and after: You kings do not realize that "you are in the grip of someone far stronger." There is surely no point in appealing to the kings to be compassionate to the songster. What is needed is a threat to themselves. Admittedly it is uncomfortable to have the kings in the role of the nightingale, but the emphasis is on the helplessness and stupidity of man before God.

We go straight from this to the adjuration to Perses to heed Hesiod's advice and follow justice. At the beginning of the poem Hesiod tells us that his exposition is for both Perses and the kings, both of them guilty in the offense against justice in the award of part of the farm's ownership. Hesiod keeps switching the particularity of his discourse from Perses to the kings and back again (203, 213, 248, 274). The climax is reached when Hesiod settles down to address the rest of his general ethical comment to Perses (274). When he starts with Perses (213), it is to caution his brother about the natural opposition of *dikē* (Justice, either in the abstract or concretely in legal decisions and judgments) and *hybris* (pride). *Hybris* is the *feeling* against Justice (and law) that results in Violence, of hand or tongue (320–22). Justice appears here in her mythological form, as dragged off where bribed men carry her, who render crooked justice (224).

Clearly the poet is looking at Justice both as it springs from the understanding and goodness of the individual and as it is reflected in the lawcourts. The latter part forces us to look at the agencies of Justice on earth. A very remarkable expression occurs where Hesiod, with Justice's voice, refers to the judges as "those who drive her out and have rendered *her* crookedly" (224). Justice is an ideal which can then be corrupted in the execution of her alleged agents. Horkos (Oath) attends her, and, if we switch to the further account of the same process in the part of the argument addressed to the kings, we learn that Justice, who is declared to be Zeus's daughter, is also backed by the thirty thousand immortals (these are the ex-Golden Age men after death), who watch over infractions of justice in ordinary mortal circumstances. This is all further amplified: "The eye of Zeus sees all and observes all and now looks on these matters *if he will* and well he notices what sort of Justice is that that city has within itself" (268).

The most apocalyptic account of Justice is given directly to Perses himself by Hesiod:

> Perses, lay these things up in your heart, and listen to Justice and forget Violence utterly. For this is the law that the son of Kronos laid upon the

fish and the wild things and winged birds, that they should eat one another, for there is no Justice among *them*. But to mankind he gave justice which is far the best. For if a man wills to speak what is just out of his knowledge, to him Zeus, whose voice is borne afar, gives prosperity. But whoever shall consciously swear a perjury with witnesses, and has committed the incurable sin in the injury to justice, the generation of that man is left the weaker for it, but the generation of the man strong in his oath remains better thereafter. (275–85)

As Zeus's daughter, Justice is certainly of immemorial antiquity. Moreover, if one is going to follow the chronology of the Metal Ages strictly, one must see the guardians, all thirty thousand of them, as stemming from a period just after the First Age. But it seems very much as though what Hesiod has to say about Justice belongs specifically to the Age of Iron and to a somewhat new condition existing between Zeus and man. It might not be too fanciful to say that this horrible Age of Iron is the first entirely human age, as we know it. The blamelessness of the Golden Age would demand no punishment and no lawcourts; the Titans (if that is what they are) of the Second Age would certainly have no use for such agencies; the Third Age is given over exclusively to Violence and mutual destruction, and the Age of the Heroes to heroic wars at Troy and Thebes. Only in the Fifth and Iron Age, when Aidos and Nemesis (Shame and Fear of Retribution) are leaving mankind, when family duties are abandoned, does the gift of Zeus's Justice stand in its implacable defense against Violence—for those who are willing to try to find it and live by it, citizen and judge. The eye of Zeus is unerring; his rewards and punishments demonstrable.

Yet there follows the discordant note—and such a significant one: "As things are (*nyn de*), I would not be a just man among men, nor would I have my son so; for it is a bad thing to be a just man if an unjuster shall have more of justice. But I do not expect that Zeus will yet bring this to pass" (267). The clue to this passage must be the progressive degeneration of the Iron Age with no respite till its ultimate destruction. Justice, as ordinary humans experience it, is what the courts deal out. It is a bad thing to be just if someone who is unjust manages to get more court justice than you do. There is, one may suppose, an arbitrariness and a mysteriousness about Zeus that make it impossible to be *sure* that he will not allow, in the last phase of the Iron Age, the just one to get a smaller share of what the courts give as justice, as the perjurer will be readier to perjure himself to his own advantage. It is this very scenario (285) that is dismissed as against Zeus's plan. We might remember Herodotus's third in the sequence of Egyptian kings, who is punished for not having realized that the gods wanted the complete toll of three unjust kings and had their designs interfered with by the pious resolves of this same third, Myerinus (*History* 2.129ff.).

There is a bridge between ethics, which is mainly devoted to justice in the first part of the poem, and farming in the latter. It is work. "Work, Perses, man of good stock, that hunger may hate you and fair-crowned revered Demeter love you, and fill your barn with substance. For hunger is the wholly untoward companion of the man who does not work" (298–303). Again: "If you work, soon the man of no work will envy you as you grow rich. For virtue and renown attend upon wealth" (313).

Perhaps the connections are something like this: Justice is a lifeline thrown to us by Zeus, especially in the bad days of the Iron Age. It is for us a matter of courts and decisions. Whatever good can come from this degenerate time, whatever escape humans can make from the violence that settles disputes among animals, depends on Justice and on those who formally, at least, deal it out.

In the Iron Age, work is what is blessed by both men and gods (309–10). In the best ages, that of Gold and of the Heroes, very little exertion was necessary to win a livelihood from the land. But now it is far otherwise. Man must make a virtue of his necessity. Man must win wealth, and virtue and glory will attend him who gets it, providing of course that it is not gotten by literal robbery or robbery of the tongue (321–22). All this sort of work involves the good Eris (spirit of competition), and the not-working man will envy you—this being the bad sort of Eris.

Even in farming the arbitrariness of Zeus is to be reckoned with, but here as a blessing rather than a curse:

> If you plough the good earth at the turning of the sun [the solstice, i.e., late in the season] you will do your harvesting sitting down; there will be little for your hand to bind and you will bind the sheaves against themselves, covered in dust and unrejoicing; you will carry home your harvest in a basket and few will gaze upon you. But the mind of Zeus is various at various times, and it is hard for mortal men to know it. If you should be late with your ploughing, there may be a cure for it. When the cuckoo first sings in the oak leaves and gladdens men's hearts over the boundless world, sometimes Zeus will rain on the third day unceasingly, just as much as will cover an ox's hoof and no more. Then the man who ploughed late and he who ploughed early will be on an equality. But, still, do not let the grey spring go unnoticed by you when it comes, nor the rain that falls at its due time (478ff.).

In farming there is a prescribed course that should bring successful results, and usually does. But one must always remember that the mind of Zeus is hard to know and sometimes all the care and virtuous conduct prove no better in results than heedlessness. There is a great deal of the doctrine of honest labor and its success in Hesiod, more than at times one enjoys, especially when one notices the cruelty that it warrants as when he recommends turning the hired help out of doors at the beginning of winter rather than feeding him (602). But at least Hesiod does not believe that the good invariably inherit the earth nor even win each individual trick in the game.

All of this account of Hesiod deals with the close relation of the writer's religion, his didacticism in farming, and his poetry. It is easy enough to see the special relation of farming to Hesiod's religion. Farming is that area in which God's purposes and how they bear on us become clearest, and the sanction of those purposes is most significant. The timeliness and transitoriness of each phase of farming are also of immediate concern and in them again there is the evidence of Zeus's harsh formulation of his government. Witness the great differences between humanity's relation to the cultivation of earth now and in the Age of Heroes.

What kind of farming, then, is rewarded in Hesiod's poem? And what kind of poem *is* the *Works and Days*?

In the light of M. I. Finley's studies of the economic and social side of the *Odyssey*, those who are interested in Hesiod have been inclined to speak of his farming as subsistence farming. Perhaps that is a fairly accurate title, but not entirely so. There should be no doubt that his farming was governed by much the same considerations as is modern farming in a country like India, where most farms are very small tracts of land and there is almost no mechanization but plenty of labor. I do not know what the true position of money was in Hesiod's agricultural world. But when he speaks of the good Eris (competition) that Zeus has placed in the roots of earth, and what is good for men and stimulates them to work, he concludes, "For one who is scanting in his work looks at another who is rich, and he hastens to plough and to sow and to establish his household securely. Yes, a neighbor will envy a neighbor that is hastening toward wealth" (23). One knows that feeling and that world, and it is the world of the small farmer at any time, then or now. "Plead for the graciousness of the gods with libations and sacrifice, both at your going to bed and when the sacred light comes, that they may have a gracious heart and mind towards you and so you may buy the farm of another man and he may not buy yours" (338). However the various transactions are accomplished, Hesiod's farmer lives in the hope of an affluence that comes *after* the bare subsistence of food and shelter. Failure in this matter of reserves (surely these reserves must be mostly money) means that someone has the right means, if not the right, to take away your chance of a livelihood altogether.

Of course, some of the implications of subsistence farming were very much part of Hesiod's time and only present in varying degrees for modern small farmers. For instance, Hesiod makes his own plough from his own trees; he makes his own fur cap from his own wool; it is his own heifer that is slaughtered for his summer picnic. Some of these things are, surely, not part of the modern small farming scene, at least in many places. But the *drive* in Hesiod is indeed toward the accumulation of something we can call wealth, and Hesiod has a clear distinction between the constant pursuit of this wealth (which is all right) and the acts that achieve wealth more quickly and more easily are wrong:

> Possessions (*chrēmata*) are not to be ravaged; they are far better when they come as the gift of God. For if a man gets great wealth (*olbos*) by violence, or if he makes his plunder of it by his tongue [e.g., Perses, Hesiod's brother] as often happens, when profit deceives the mind of mankind and shamelessness pours contempt on shame—lightly do the gods maim that man, and bring his house low and his wealth (*olbos*) lasts for a short time only. (320)

Perhaps most interesting of all for our picture of how Hesiod saw wealth as the pursuit of his farmer is his attitude toward boats and sailing. He begins the story of ships and sailing on an unmistakably grudging note: "If the desire for the rude sea possesses you" (618). West has also made clear that Hesiod is speaking of boats in the life of the small farmer in two categories. The first is a small boat (he can beach it in the winter and bring the plug for it and all the gear into his own house), but there is another side to the matter:

> If so be that you turn your sinful (*aesiphrona*) mind to commerce (*emporion*) because you would *flee debts and unlovely hunger*, I will tell you the measures of the surging sea, though I am no one with deep knowledge of sailing or ships, for I never sailed over the broad sea but once ... (647).

If you are set on commerce (leaving aside the doubtful implication of the sinfulness of the mind that does so), "praise a small boat, but put your cargo in a big one" (643). The first boat, it would seem, is to be actually a tool of the small farmer, presumably to convey produce of his own to a bigger and better market than Ascra in Boeotia; the second is indeed a capitalistic venture of some sort or another. I am constantly teased by the uncertainty of *what* kind of produce Hesiod was shipping from his farm. Oil? Wine? Conceivably goats or sheep as they are hauled among the islands on the Dalmatian coast still? Or what kind of material for commerce in the larger venture? And to where? The Gulf of Corinth somewhere, I suppose. But to what ultimate destination?

Hesiod writes mostly in Ionic, as Homer does, and this implies an adherence to a traditional form of epic speech that was certainly not his own, which must have been Doric. But instead of Homer's formal professional style, Hesiod relies on almost proverbial, folk versions of sentiment and description. The poetry lives often in the eyes and ears:

> Mark you when you hear the voice of the crane, high above in the clouds, when she has uttered her yearly cry. She it is who sets the sign for ploughing and shows forth the seasonableness of the rainy time. She bites the heart of the oxenless man. Then is the moment when you should fodder your cattle to sleekness, when they are still within doors. For it is easy to say the word, "Give me a team of oxen and a wagon." But the word of denial is easy, too: "*I have work for my oxen.*" (445–54).
>
> Invite to supper him that loves you, but leave alone your enemy. Most of all invite him that lives nearest to you. For if any untoward thing happen you, your neighbors come, their belts ungirt. But your kinsfolk will take the time to gird up theirs. (342–45)

Sometimes there is a queer streak of fantasy supporting the visual quality of the poetic passage: "On the winter day when the cuttlefish gnaws his foot in his fireless home and the miserable places of his habitation" (525). Or the power of the rhythm and the suggestiveness altogether: "When a man gives out of his whole will, though what he gives is a great gift, he is glad in the giving, and delight is in his own heart. But whosoever himself takes, persuaded by shamelessness, though the gift be but a little one, the frost is upon his heart" (356).

Brendan Kennelly, the Irish poet, eloquently states the relation between myth and poetry in a way which has a special significance applied to Hesiod: "Myth is a sustaining structure outside the poet that nourishes his inner life, and helps him to express it."[4] Homer and Hesiod are seen by the later Greeks as the originators of Greek religion through myths (*mythoi*) and poetry. Homer approached the subject of the Wrath as many of his ancestors and professional forebears did. It is the old bottle into which he pours new wine. He is transforming an old story by his personal feeling for Achilles, Patroclus, Hector, Helen. Who will not add, for Zeus and the Olympian Pantheon as well? The subject was well known. What is original and new is the individual vitality of the characters—the poet's gift—and the freshness of the impact of the episodes.

Hesiod knows his subject matter, farming, not through any literary medium, if we may be permitted such an anachronistic expression applied to Homer. Farming itself is for him the traditional configuration

---

4. *The Penguin Book of Irish Verse,* introduced and edited by Brendan Kennelly, 2nd ed. (Harmondsworth, Middlesex, and New York: Penguin Books, 1981) 42.

of man's life—that he may eat, clothe himself, and maintain his social position. This lies for him in the pattern of acts. Each act when performed links him with its past performance, and with the story attending the pattern, in the history of man in the world. Each time it is performed, its depth is reinforced. But now a time has come for *him*, Hesiod, in the *Works and Days*, when the pattern uniquely emerges into expression, when the acts in all their pastness and presentness acquire something new, an image, and not only a descriptive image of themselves but an image placed in the world to include gods, men, and the order of the universe. This has come about because of Hesiod's personal bitter experience of his brother's wickedness and the wickedness and folly of the corrupt judges. This is one way in which Hesiod and Homer are separated. The mythological is the source of the poetry in both, and it is also inseparable from religious feeling in both. But the myth is, for Homer, already literature (or what we call literature) and, for Hesiod, the experiencing of the mythological moment that moves the poet. The mythological moment exists when past and present are united, not as in the narrative of history but in already repeated acts—not, as Eliade has it, to control the outcome by repeating the original act, but to participate in an unknowable certainty. The landscape includes everything from the warning cry of the cranes, which signals the beginning of ploughing, to the watchfulness for the plough beams, which may be worm-eaten, to the struggle, naked, with the toil of harvest, to the picnic afterward. All this is in the context of Hesiod's warning about the value of justice, but also in the context of doubt about whether this justice will bring happiness, because any formulation that man makes of Zeus's true designs is lamentably unsure. Zeus could have made farming easy, he could have made life easy. He made both difficult. This feeling disowns the strength of doctrine and removes itself to a poetry of vision and hearing, in physical detail. Thus paradoxically the *dikē* of farming—that is, the *dikē* that expresses in farming the *dikē* of the world of man in general—is not a true doctrine or belief, as much as it is the myth of the conjunction of time and event.

Yet it is the vision that persists and captures us. The sweating flanks of the oxen under the goad descending on them as they struggle—these are the details that pertain to the completeness of the evolved presence, not necessarily to rhetorical effect. Hence it is the *poetry* that is essential to understanding what Hesiod is telling us about farming, and finally about the world of reality in it that he seeks to express.

PART THREE
PLURALISM AND THE HISTORY OF RELIGIONS

11
ANOTHER PATH TO TRUTH: FROM RITUAL TO THEOLOGY IN JUDAISM

Jacob Neusner

SINCE DAVID TRACY has placed in the center of public discourse the themes of radical pluralism in religious truth, we turn, in celebrating his first half century, to a hermeneutical problem pertinent to his contribution to hermeneutics. Specifically, I want to show how a mode of thought quite alien to our own philosophical one in the conduct of theology undertakes to address issues critical to theology. It is a mode of thought that comes to expression in debate on questions of ritual, specifically, the conduct of a Temple rite. But when we grasp what is at stake in the discussion, we realize that while at the surface issues of cult occupy the arena of discussion, these in fact concern issues of profound theological interest. Tracy's recognition that there are other approaches to truth and to the expression of truth besides those with which we are familiar then makes possible the argument that through ritual an authorship in fact pursues a program of theology. This recognition opens the way to a deeper appreciation, within the study of Judaism, of how people talk and what in speaking of one thing they propose to say about some other. I cannot think of a more apt illustration of Tracy's appreciation of the nuances of the question of truth—or a more real tribute to the man who has taught us to think in fresh ways about familiar matters. Now to the case at hand.

While some religions, Christianity and Islam for example, are rich not only in law but also in theological writings, and others in myth, still others make their systemic statements about the nature of being and the realm of the sacred primarily through law. Accordingly, we have to ask details of rite to teach us about the systemic myth, that is, move backward from way of life to world view. In the case of early rabbinic

Judaism we have a considerable corpus of laws that prescribe the way things are done but make no effort to interpret what is done. These constitute ritual entirely lacking in mythic, let alone theological, explanation. Accordingly, the processes and modes of thought of earlier rabbinic Judaism turn out to be encapsulated in descriptions of ritual. Yet much of the law contained in the Mishnah in fact was not practiced; indeed, the earlier rabbis scarcely claim that it was. Further, the laws about ritual cleanness or purity, so far as they had to be kept so that a person could enter the Temple, bore no more concrete relevance to everyday life than did the cultic laws, and only a small part of the Jewish population of Palestine was expected to keep those laws outside of the cult. Accordingly, we have before us the paradox presented by the most serious effort to create a corpus of laws to describe a ritual life that did not exist. The processes of making those laws themselves constituted the rabbis'—and their predecessors'—mode of thinking about the same issues investigated in other circumstances through rigorous theological thought, on the one side, or profound mythic speculation, on the other.

So far as the laws describe a ritual, the ritual itself is myth, in two senses. First, the ritual is myth or world view in the sense that it was not real, was not carried out. Second, while lacking mythic articulation, the ritual expresses important ideas and points of view on the structure of reality. What is lacking, specifically, is not myth but an explicit articulation of myth or world view. The law contains myth and so serves as an artifact of a world view in that it encompasses cognitive content. The law does not explicitly articulate the content in a particular form of abstract discourse, but leaves its content embedded in ritual. What people are supposed to do, without a stage of articulation of the meaning of what they do, itself expresses what they think. The explanation of the ritual, drawing from that explanation some sort of major cognitive statement, is skipped. The world therefore is mapped out through gesture. The boundaries of reality are laid forth through norms on how the boundaries of reality are laid forth. Accordingly, we deal with laws made by people who never saw or performed the ritual described by those laws. It is through thinking about the laws that they shape and express their ideas, their judgments upon transcendent issues of sacred and profane, clean and unclean. It follows that thinking about the details of the law turns out to constitute reflection on the nature of being and the meaning of the sacred. The form—the ritual—lacking myth or world view is wholly integrated to the content, the mythic substructure. The structure of the ritual is its myth and conveys the systemic way of life.

We turn to the particular ritual in hand, the burning of the red cow for the preparation of ashes, to be mixed with water and sprinkled on a person who has become unclean through contact with a corpse. Let us first consider once again the way in which the priestly author of Numbers 19:1–10 describes the rite, the things he considers important to say about it:

> Tell the people of Israel to bring you a red cow without defect, in which there is no blemish, and upon which a yoke has never come. And you shall give her to Eleazar the priest, and she shall be taken outside the camp and slaughtered before him. And Eleazar the priest shall take some of her blood with his finger and sprinkle some of her blood toward the front of the tent of meeting seven times. And the heifer shall be burned in his sight; her skin, her flesh, and her blood, with her dung, shall be burned; and the priest shall take cedarwood and hyssop and scarlet stuff and cast them into the midst of the burning of the heifer. Then the priest shall wash his clothes and bathe his body in water, and afterwards he shall come into the camp, and the priests shall be unclean until evening. And a man who is clean shall gather up the ashes of the heifer and deposit them outside the camp in a clean place; and they shall be kept for the congregation of the people of Israel for the water for impurity, and for the removal of sin. And he who gathers the ashes of the heifer shall wash his clothes and be unclean until evening. (Num 19:1–10a)

How is the ash used? Numbers 19:17 states:

> For the unclean they shall take some ashes of the burnt sin-offering and running water shall be added in a vessel; then a clean person shall take hyssop and dip it in the water and sprinkle it upon the tent... [in which someone has died, etc.].

Let us now ask, what to the biblical writer are the important traits of the rite of the burning of the cow and the mixing of its ashes into water? The priestly author stresses, first of all, that the rite takes place outside the camp, which is to say, in an unclean place. He repeatedly tells us that anyone involved in the rite is made unclean by his participation in the rite: 19:7, the priest shall wash his clothes; 19:8, the one who burns the heifer shall wash his clothes; 19:10, and he who gathers the ashes of the heifer shall wash his clothes and be unclean until evening. The priestly legislator therefore takes for granted that the rules of purity which govern rites in the Temple simply do not apply to the rite of burning the cow. Not only are the participants *not* in a state of cleanness, but they are in a state of uncleanness, being required to wash their clothes, remaining unclean until the evening and only then allowed back into the camp which is the Temple. Accordingly, the world outside the Temple is by definition not subject to the Temple's rules and is not going to be clean.

What is interesting, when we turn to Mishnah tractate *Parah*, which deals with the same topic, the burning of the red cow, is its distinctive agendum of issues and themes. The predominant concerns of Mishnah tractate *Parah*, deriving from the period before 70, are two: first, the degree of cleanness required of those who participate in the rite and how these people become unclean; second, how the water used for the rite is to be drawn and protected, with special attention directed to not working between the drawing of the water and the mixing of the ashes referred to in Numbers 19:17. The theoretical concerns of *Parah* thus focus on two important matters of no interest whatever to the priestly author of Numbers 19:1–10, because the priestly author assumes that the rite produces uncleanness, is conducted outside of the realm of cleanness, and therefore does not involve the keeping of the levitical rules of cleanness required for participation in the Temple cult.

By contrast, *Parah* is chiefly interested in that very matter. An important body of opinion in this tractate demands a degree of cleanness higher than that required for the Temple cult itself. Further, the whole matter of drawing water, protecting it, and mixing it with the ash, is virtually ignored by the priestly author, while it occupies much of this tractate and, even more than in quantity, the quality and theoretical sophistication of the laws on that topic form the apex of *Parah*. Accordingly, the biblical writer on the rite of burning the red cow wishes to tell us that the rite takes place outside the camp, understood in Temple times as outside the Temple. The rite is conducted in an unclean place, and it follows that people who are going to participate in the rite, slaughtering the cow, collecting its ashes, and the like, are not clean. The mishnaic authorities stress exactly the opposite conception, that people who will participate in the rite must be clean, not unclean, as if they were in the Temple. And they add a further important point, that the water to be used for mixing with the ashes of the cow must be mixed with the ashes without an intervening act of labor not connected with the rite.

The authorities of the Mishnah describe a ritual which, in fact, they have never seen and about which they claim to have few traditions. The ritual under description is a myth or world view in two senses. First, the ritual is something that is not part of observed reality. Second, the laws of the ritual themselves contain important expressions about the nature of the sacred and the clean. The articulation of the laws, through the standard legal disputes of the late first- and second-century authorities, contains within itself statements about the most fundamental issues of reality, statements which, in describing the form of the ritual, also express the content of the ritual, its myth. These statements, it goes without saying, further carry forward the conceptions of the period before 70.

For the purpose of the present discussion, we have now to review familiar materials. The first dispute concerns which hand one uses for sprinkling the blood toward the door of the Holy of Holies; the second asks about how we raise the cow up to the top of the pyre of wood on which it is going to be burned; and the third deals with whether intending to do the wrong thing spoils what one actually does. The first is in m. *Parah* 3:9:

> They bound it with a rope of bast and place it on the pile of wood, with its head southward and its face westward.
> The priest, standing at the east side, with his face turned toward the west, slaughtered it with his right (northern) hand and received the blood with his left (southern) hand.
> R. Judah says, "With his right hand did he receive the blood and he put it into his left hand, and he sprinkled with (the index finger of) his right hand."

Before analyzing the pericope, we call to mind the corresponding Toseftan supplement (*t. Parah* 3:9):

> They bound it with a rope of bast and put it onto the wood pile.
> And some say, "It went up with a mechanical contraption."
> R. Eliezer b. Jacob says, "They made a causeway on which it ascended."
> Its head was to the south and its face to the west.

In the present set, therefore, are which hand we use for sprinkling the blood and how we raise the cow to the top of the pyre of wood. Let us notice, first of all, the placing of the cow and the priest. The rite takes place on the Mount of Olives, that is, to the east and north of the Temple Mount in Jerusalem. Accordingly, we set up a north-south-east-west grid. The cow is placed with its head to the south, pointing in the direction of the Temple Mount, slightly to the south of the Mount of Olives, and its face is west — that is, toward the Temple. The priest then is set east of the cow, so that he too will face the Temple. He faces west — toward the Temple. When he raises his hand to slaughter the cow, he reaches over from north and east to south and west, again, toward the Temple. We have, therefore, a clear effort to relate the location and slaughter of the red cow, which takes place outside the Temple to the Temple itself. In fact, each gesture is meant to be a movement toward the Temple. Just as Scripture links the cow, outside the camp, to the camp, by having the blood sprinkled in the direction of the camp (a detail the Mishnah takes for granted), so that the sprinkling of the blood, which is the crucial and decisive action that effects the purpose of the rite — accomplishes atonement, or *kapparah*, in mishnaic language — so all other details of the rite here are focused on the Temple.

This brings us to Judah's opinion, which disagrees about slaughter with the left hand. We have set up a kind of mirror to the Temple, with the whole setting organized to face and correspond to the holy place. The priest in the Temple slaughtered with his right hand and received the blood in his left. Likewise, the anonymous rule holds, the priest now does the same. In other words, our rite in all respects replicates what is done in the Temple setting: What is done there is done here. Judah, by contrast, wants the blood received with the right hand and slaughtered with the left. Why? Because we are not *in* the Temple itself. We are facing it. Thus if we want to replicate the cultic gestures, we have to do each thing in exactly the opposite direction. Just as, in a mirror, one's left is at the right, and the right is at the left, so here, we set up a mirror. Accordingly, he says, if in the Temple the priest receives the blood in his left hand, on the Mount of Olives and facing the Temple, he receives the blood in his right hand. All parties to the dispute, therefore, agree on this fundamental proposition, that the effort is to replicate the Temple's cult in every possible regard. The issue is cultic, but the theological principle is different: can there be a realm of sanctification, represented by cultic cleanness, outside of the cult. And, if there can be, how shall we represent and acknowledge its presence?

This brings us to the dispute about how we get the beast up to the top of woodpile. The anonymous rule, shared by the Mishnah and Tosefta, is that we bind the sacrificial cow and somehow drag it up to the top. But in the Temple the sacrifices were not bound; they would be spoiled if they were bound. Accordingly, Eliezer b. Jacob, a contemporary of Judah, imposes the same rule. He says that there was a causeway constructed from the ground to the top of the wood pile on which the cow will be slaughtered and burned, and the cow walks up on its own. Self-evidently, both parties cannot be right, and the issue is not what really was done in "historical" times—let us say, seventy-five years earlier. As in the dispute between Judah and the anonymous narrator, the issue is precisely how we shall do the rite, on the Mount of Olives, so as to conform to the requirements of the rite on the Temple Mount itself.

To state matters in general terms, it is taken for granted by all parties to the present pericope that the rite of the cow is done in the profane world, outside the cult, *as if* it were done in the sacred world constituted by the Temple itself. How is the contrary viewpoint expressed? The simplest statement is in *m. Parah* 2:3B–D:

B. The harlot's hire and the price of a dog—it is unfit.

That is to say, if the red cow is purchased with funds deriving from money spent to purchase the services of a prostitute or to buy a dog, the cow is unfit for the rite. The pericope continues:

C. R. Eliezer declares fit,

D. since it is said, *You will not bring the harlots hire and the price of a dog to the house of the Lord your God* (Deut 23:18). But this (cow) does not come to the house (of the Lord, namely, the Temple).

The issue could not be drawn more clearly than does the glossator (D). Eliezer holds that since the burning of the cow takes place outside the Temple, the Temple's rules for the acquisition of the cow simply do not apply.

A more subtle question appears at m. *Parah* 4:1 and 4:3. The first item, 4:1, is as follows:

The cow of purification which one slaughtered not for its own name (meaning, not as a cow of purification, but for some other offering), or the blood of which one received and sprinkled not for its own name, etc., is unfit.
R. Eliezer (Eleazar) declares fit.

What is at issue? In the sanctuary, we have correctly to designate the purpose of a sacrifice. Eleazar holds that this is not a rite subject to the rule of the Temple cult. The rule continues,

And if this was done by a priest whose hands and feet were not washed, it is unfit.
R. Eliezer declares fit.

Priests in the Temple of course had to be properly washed. Since the rite is not in the Temple, Eliezer says that the priest need not even be washed. In this connection, Tosefta supplies:

If one whose hands and feet were not washed burned it, it is unsuitable.
And R. Eleazar b. R. Simeon declares fit,
as it is said, *When they come to the Tent of Meeting, they will wash in water and not die* (Exod 30:20)—lo, the washing of the hands applies only inside (the Temple, and not on the Mount of Olives).

The issue is fully articulated, and the glosses in both the matter of the harlot's hire and the matter of washing spell out the implications. The law which describes the ritual—the *structure* of the ritual itself—also expresses the *meaning* of the ritual. The form imposed on the ritual fully and completely states the content of the ritual. If now we ask, What is this content? we may readily answer: The ritual outside of the cult is done in a state of cleanness, as is the ritual done inside the cult. The laws of the cult, furthermore, apply not only to the conduct of the slaughtering of the cow (the cases given here) but also to the preservation of purity by those who will participate in the slaughtering.

The authorship of the Mishnah presupposes that what scripture takes for granted is not possible, namely, that the rules of purity apply outside the Temple, just as the rules of Temple slaughter apply outside the Temple. And the reason is, of course, that the Mishnah derives, in part, from the Pharisees, whose fundamental conviction is that the cleanness taboos of the Temple and its priesthood apply to the life of all Israel, outside of the Temple and not of priestly caste. When Israelites eat their meals in their homes, they must obey the cleanness taboos as if they were priests at the table of God in the Temple. This larger conception is expressed in the acute laws before us.

Let us now proceed to a matter which is by no means self-evident and which was not understood in the way I shall explain it even by the second-century authorities. It concerns the issue of drawing the water. The rule, as we know, is that if I draw water for mixing with the ashes of the red cow, and, before actually accomplishing the mixture, I do an act of labor not related to the rite of the mixing of the ashes, I spoil the water. This is stated very succinctly, "An act of extraneous labor spoils the water." This conception is likely to originate before the destruction of the Second Temple in 70, because taken for granted at m. *Parah* 7:6–7 is the principle, evidently deriving from Pharisaism before 70, that an act of extraneous labor done between the drawing of the water and the mixing of ashes and water spoils the drawn water. The rule lies far beyond the imagination of the priestly writer of Numbers, because he tells us virtually nothing about the water into which the ashes are to be mixed. But that is of no consequence. As we observed earlier, what is interesting is the language that is used—*unfit*, not *unclean*. So the matter of the cleanness of the water—its protection against sources of contamination—is not at issue. Some other consideration has to be involved. The drawing of the water is treated as intrinsic to the rite. That is: I burn the cow. I go after water for mixing with the ashes of the cow. That journey—outside of the place in which the cow is burned—is assumed to be part of the larger rite.

Now this matter of extraneous labor is exceedingly puzzling. We have to ask, to begin with, for some sort of relevant analogy. Do we know about other rites in which we distinguish between acts of labor that are intrinsic and those that are not? And on what occasion is such a distinction made? The answer to these questions is obvious. We do distinguish between acts of labor required for the conduct of the sacrificial cult and those that are not required for the conduct of the sacrificial cult; in particular, we make that distinction on the *Sabbath*. On the Sabbath day, labor is prohibited. But the cult is continued. How? Labor intrinsic to the sacrifices required on the Sabbath is to be done, and that which is not connected with the sacrifice is not to be done.

When we introduce the issue of extraneous labor (and the issue extends to the burning of the cow itself, but I think this is secondary), what do we say about the character of the sanctity of the rite? Clearly, we take this position: the rite is conducted by analogy with the sacrifices that take place in the Temple, so that the place of the rite and all its participants in the Temple sacrifices must be clean. So too with the matter of labor. When we impose the Temple's taboos, we state that the rite is to be conducted in *clean space.* When we introduce the issue of labor, we forthwith raise the question of *holy time,* the Sabbath. For it is solely to the Sabbath that the matter of labor or no labor, labor that is intrinsic or labor that is extrinsic, applies. When we impose the taboos applicable to the Temple on the Sabbath, we state that the rite is to be conducted in holy time—wherever it is done.

The cleanness laws in the present instance create in the world outside the cult a *place of cleanness* analogous to the cult. The Sabbath laws in the present instance create in the world outside the cult a *time of holiness* analogous to the locus of the cult. The ritual constructs a structure of clean cultic space and holy Sabbath time in the world to which, by the priestly definition, neither cleanness nor holiness (in the limited sense of the present discussion) apply. The laws, it is clear, do not contain explanations. The issues themselves are trivial, ritualistic; yet even the glossators at the outset introduced into the consideration of legal descriptions of ritual extralegal conceptions of fundamental importance. Accordingly, the processes of thought that produce the rabbis' legal dicta about ritual matters also embody the rabbis' judgments about profound issues.

The final stage is to consider other sorts of sayings in which the rabbis speak more openly and directly about matters we should regard as theological, not ritual, in character. These are general, not specific, theologic-mythic sayings which lack ritual altogether and treat questions of salvation, not the conduct of rite. They constitute a quite distinct mode of expression about the same questions answered by the Mishnah through law. These theological sayings contrast, therefore, to the ones about ritual law, showing a separate way in which the authorities of the same period form and express their ideas.

The issue at hand is the relationship between cleanness and holiness. We have already considered the matter in our interpretation of the ritual laws, showing that cleanness is distinct from holiness, and the two are related to and expressed by the laws about burning the red cow. Pinhas b. Yair gives us a statement (*m. Soṭa* 9:15, translated following MS Kaufman) that links the issues of cleanness and holiness to salvation:

> R. Pinhas b. Yair says, "Attentiveness leads to (hygienic) cleanliness, cleanliness to (ritual) cleanness, cleanness to holiness, holiness to humility, humility to fear of sin, fear of sin to piety, and piety to the holy spirit, the holy spirit to the resurrection of the dead, and the resurrection of the dead to Elijah of blessed memory."

Pinhas therefore sees cleanness as a step in the ladder leading to holiness, thence to salvation: the resurrection of the dead and the coming of the Messiah. Maimonides, much later, introduces into the messianic history the burning of the cow of purification. Referring to the saying that nine cows in all were burned from the time of Moses to the destruction of the Second Temple (*m. Parah* 3:5), he states (*Red Heifer* 3:4): "Now nine red heifers were prepared from the time this commandment was received until the Temple was destroyed the second time . . . and a tenth will King Messiah prepare—may he soon be revealed."

Maimonides thus wishes to link the matter of burning the red cow, which produces water for ritual purification, to the issue of the coming of the Messiah. Both sayings, those of Pinhas b. Yair and Maimonides, show that it is entirely possible to speak directly and immediately, not through the language of ritual law, about fundamental questions. And when we do find such statements, we no longer are faced with ritual laws at all, but have theology: *myth without ritual*. Yet it seems to be clear that Pinhas b. Yair and Maimonides saw in the issues of purity, in the very specific questions addressed by the rabbinic lawyers who provide the ritual law, matters of transcendent, even salvific, weight and meaning. Having seen the issues of the tractate in episodic form, let us now turn back to examine how these same matters are set out in context. To ease the burden on the reader, given the unfamiliarity of the materials, I provide only a brief sample of the way in which discourse actually is carried on. This will permit the reader to understand how intractable are the writings, how rich the detail, how rare the possibility for abstraction. And yet, the reader will readily see, principles, not merely details, are at stake. Here is one instance:

Mishnah tractate *Parah* 4:1

A. The cow of purification which one slaughtered not for its name [not as a cow of purification but for some other offering],
B. [the blood of which] one received and [or] sprinkled
C. not for its own name,
D. or [which one received] for its own name and [sprinkled] not for its own name,
E. or [which one received] not for its own name and [sprinkled] for its own name,
F. is unfit.
G. R. Eliezer (Pa., Katsh, Plate 106, PB, P, N, M, K, C: Leazar) declares fit. [Since it is done outside the sanctuary, it is distinguished from the sin-offering.]
H. And [if this was done by one] whose hands and feet were not washed, it is unfit.
I. R. Eliezer (Katsh, Plate 106, PB, P, N, M, K, C: Leazar) declares fit.
J. And [if it was done] not by the high priest, it is unfit.

K. R. Judah declares fit.
L. And by one not wearing proper garments—it is unfit.
M. And it was done in the white garments.

        Mishnah tractate *Parah* 4:1 (b. *Zeb.* 20a)

We have three disputes, A-F vs. G, H vs. I, J vs. K, and a law phrased as a simple declarative sentence, L, spelled out by Mishnah tractate *Parah m. Zeb.* 1:1 states that all animal offerings slaughtered under the name, that is, for the purpose of some other offering, are valid, except for a Passover offering and a sin offering, understood as the purification offering of the red cow. That is to say, in all the named cases one may nonetheless toss the blood against the altar base and burn the sacrificial portions on the altar. A repeats that law, adding the matter of the receiving and sprinkling of the blood, B, which is completed by C in the model of A, then spelled out in D-E with reference to the two separate acts of B. Eliezer's view, unlike Judah's in Mishnah tractate *Parah* 3:9, is that this is not a rite subject to the rule of the Temple cult, since it is performed outside the cult. He therefore rejects A-F as well as *m. Zeb.* 1:1, at which point he will delete the reference to the sin-offering. His view is carried forward at Mishnah tractate *Parah* 4:3. The same issue recurs at H-I. *m. Zeb.* 2:1 insists that the priest be properly washed. Eliezer says the rule differs for the rite of the cow, as against Mishnah tractate *Parah* 3:1-7 (!). J-K then reverse the matter. Sacrifices do not have to be done by the high priest. This one, J insists, does. Judah differs, consistent with his view that this is like all other sacrifices. M defines L. The point is that even a high priest carries out the rite in white garments, which are four, worn by any priest, and not in the eight of the high priest (*m. Yoma* 7:5). It follows from Judah's opinion in K, but, if L does not continue Judah's saying, the absence of a differing view tells us that the authority behind J (A-F, H) at this point concedes that the rite is comparable to any held in the Temple itself. We see in detail, therefore, that the issue is the relationship of a rite performed outside the Temple to one that is performed inside: alike, opposite, something in between. Now to a more fundamental statement.

Mishnah tractate *Parah* 4:4

A. All those who are engaged in the work of the cow from the beginning to the end [of the process]
   (1) render clothing [or other utensils which they touch] unclean,
   and (2) render it [the rite] unfit through [other] work.
B. If an invalidity happened to it in its slaughter, it does not render clothing unclean.
C. If it happened to it in its sprinkling [=of the blood toward the Holy of Holies],

all who participate in the work involving it before its unfitness—it renders clothing unclean.
D. And [those who do so] after its unfitness—it does not render clothing unclean.
E. It turns out that its strict rule is its lenient rule. [Danby: Thus wherein stringency applies leniency applies also.]
F. At all times—
   (1) do they commit sacrilege against it;
   (2) and do they add wood to it
G. (1) And its rites are done by day;
   (2) and by a priest.
H. (1) And [other] work [done by those involved in the rite] renders it unfit,
   (2) until it is made into ashes.
I. (1) And [other] work [done by those involved in the rite] renders the water unfit,
   (2) until they will put the ashes into it.
Mishnah tractate *Parah* 4:4 (b. Hul. 29b, b. Yoma 42b)

The present pericope contains the fundamental laws of our tractate (Maimonides, Mishnah commentary). First, a person involved in the rite renders utensils unclean (A1). But this depends on the proper completion of the rite. If the cow was not properly slaughtered, then those occupied in the rite are not going to make clothing unclean (B). C further qualifies. If the rite was properly carried out to the point of slaughter, then the uncleanness will apply to all matters affecting the cow before it was discovered to be unfit, but not afterward. A further basic principle, A2, is that a person who carries out the rite must pay close attention and not do any other work whatsoever, which is repeated at H-I, with appropriate qualifications. The point of H-I is that the act of preparing the ashes and mixing them with water ends the rite, and thereafter the participants may engage in other work. This applies to the making of the ashes, H, and the mixing of the water, I. The observation of E is that we are strict as to the invalidation of the rite, but thus also lenient when it comes to rendering utensils unclean.

The set F-I is formed of four rules, each divided into two parts. F's *all times* applies to F2 and 2. G is clear; T. will qualify this rule in the light of H-I, that is, the invalidation is a possibility until the act of mixing the rite is done by day and by a priest, at which point the period of vulnerability ends. Other actions may be done by night and by a layman. H-I are clear as stated. The whole is phrased in simple declarative sentences, but, self-evidently, these are of two sorts: fully spelled out sentences, A-E, a complete unit; and rather abbreviated, but completely clear ones, in the second unit. That we have two distinct units is clear, and the repetition of the issue of work (A2) in H-I confirms that the stylistic distinctiveness also is substantive.

Let us now return to the issues raised at the outset and summarize the entire argument. It is now clear that the mishnaic rabbis express their primary cognitive statements, their judgments on large matters, through ritual law, not through myth or world view or theology, neither of which is articulated at all. Indeed, we observe a curious disjuncture between ritual laws and theological sayings concerned with the *heilsgeschichtliche* meanings of the laws. Since the ritual was not carried out by the authorities of the law, the purpose and meaning of legislation in respect to the ritual of burning the cow are self-evidently not to describe something that has been done, but to create—if only in theory—something which, if done, will establish limits and set boundaries to sacred reality. The issue of the ritual is *cleanness* outside the Temple, and, if I am right about the taboo connected with drawing the water, *holiness* outside the Temple as well.

The lines of structure, converging on and emanating from the Temple, have now to be discerned in the world of the secular, the unclean, and the profane. Where better to discern, to lay out these lines of structure, than in connection with the ritual of sacrifice not done in the Temple but outside it, in that very world of the secular, unclean, and profane. As I have stressed, the priestly author of Numbers cannot imagine that cleanness is a perquisite of the ritual. He says the exact opposite. The ritual produces contamination for those who participate. The second-century rabbis who debated the details of the rite held that the rite is performed just as it would have been done in the Temple. The laws which describe the ritual therefore contain important judgments on its meaning. With remarkably little eisegesis of those laws—virtually none not coming to us from the glossators themselves—we are able to see that their statements about law deal with metaphysical reality, revealing their effort to discern and to define the limits of both space and time.

The structure of the ritual contains its meaning. Form and content are wholly integrated. Indeed, we are unable to dissociate form from content. It follows that what is done in the ritual, the sprinkling with one hand or the other, the binding of the cow or the use of a causeway to bring it to the pyre, the purchase of cows with the wrong sort of money, the employment of unwashed priests, the exclusion of the issue of the wrong intention—all of these matters of rite and form alone contain whatever the rabbis will tell us about the meaning of the rite and its forms. The reason, as I have stressed, is that the rabbis before us think about transcendent issues primarily through rite and form. When, as I showed at the end, they choose another means of discourse and a different mode of thought entirely, matters of rite and form fall away. Theological and mythic considerations to which ritual is irrelevant take their place. Judah, Eleazar b. R. Simeon, Eliezer b. Jacob, and the others, however, refer to no myth or world view, make use of neither mythic nor theological language, because they think about reality and speak about it through the norms of the law. Since, as I have stressed, the law concerns a ritual which these authorities have never seen and certainly would never perform, *the law itself constitutes its own myth:* (1) the fabulous myth of a ritual no one has ever done; and (2) the transcendent myth or world view of the realm of the clean and the sacred constructed through ritual and taboo in the world of the unclean and the secular. The ritual *is* the myth. What people are told to do is what they are supposed to think. The gestures and taboos of the rite themselves express the meaning of the rite, without the mediation of myth or world view.

The particular truth before us warrants further articulation. Through debate on the rite, the sages of Judaism have explored the issue of the relationship between the (spatial) realm of the sacred and the (actual) realm of human deed. Is the location of the sacred decisive? Then the Temple forms the locus of the sacred, and all things are to be positioned in relationship to the Temple. What is done in the Temple then must be done in one way; what is done elsewhere in the opposite way, so underlining the particularity of the Temple as the source of defining what is unique. Are the actor and the deed definitive? Then who does the action, and not where it is done, what the actor does, and not where he (now: or she) does the act—these form the operative considerations. In that case acting, wherever one is, as though one were located in the Temple, will convey the truth that it is the person that is holy, or the deed that is holy, and not the accidents of location or circumstance.

For Judaism these are not trivial or ritualistic questions. The great question facing Jewry in the first century, to which our texts refer, was whether the Temple contained and defined the sacred, or whether the people surviving the Temple formed the medium of the holy in this world. If location was decisive, then, as a matter of fact, all was lost with the destruction of the Temple in 70 C.E. If the people Israel formed the medium for God's consecration, in this world, of worldly things, then wherever the people Israel was located, holiness would derive from what that people did and how it conducted itself; its acts, its will bore the power of sanctification.

The theological interest proves more than narrowly historical, when we recall that, even today, the Jewish people, the people Israel, finds itself still in the process of debating precisely the same question. The Jewish state, located in the land we Jews call "the land of Israel," calls itself "Israel" without qualification. The implication, made explicit from the founding of the State, is that if you are "Israel," you are here, and if you are somewhere else, you are not "Israel," or you are less "Israel" than you would be if you were here. So, in terms we have considered, holiness is a function of location, along with descent from the holy people. The contrary position, implicit in the choices made by Jews throughout the world to make their lives elsewhere than in the State of Israel and in the holy Land of Israel, is that holiness—"being Israel"— derives from not where one is but who one is (descent) and how one lives (action). The issue is vivid today, because inherent in the theological structures of the Judaism of the written and oral Torah (scripture, the Mishnah, and related writings and commentaries) is the conflict between the holiness of place, whether Land or Jerusalem in particular, and the holiness of the people. People go from here to there, freely or under duress. Place and people contradict. Place is locative; people, utopian. Holiness then travels within them, their children being Israel by reason of their birth and the covenant encompassed within that birth as Israel.

So if the Land is holy—and Judaism insists that it is—and the people is holy, then when people wander, as they do, the theology of holiness (which scripture defines as Judaism, and as the Mishnah and the Talmuds and Midrash compilations explain in detail as the way of life of Judaism) will bear within itself a heavy burden of theological consequence. If the one, then how about the other? And which is primary? And wherein, in the end, does the power of consecration with which God has endowed Israel reside? So within the recondite and arcane details before us, a mighty debate unfolds, and one that, even today, fixes the attention of all authentic thought within Judaism. That then shows us the map of another path to truth, a different mode of exploring issues that we are able to understand, even within the odd idiom of the Torah.

12

PLURALISM IN CHRISTOLOGY

John Macquarrie

"WHAT IS BOTHERING me incessantly is the question what Christianity really is, or indeed who Christ really is, for us today."[1] These words, of course, are Dietrich Bonhoeffer's, and they occur in a letter he wrote to a friend while he was in prison just about a year before his execution. But the questions he asked are questions that have to be faced by all thinking Christians and, above all, by theologians, who have within the church a special responsibility to think about the meaning of Christian faith. It is the second part of the question that is most troubling. Who really is Christ for us today? For many centuries theologians thought that they had a satisfactory answer to the question. They believed that the New Testament gives us reliable historical information about the life and teachings of Jesus. They believed also that through theological reflection as expressed in the pronouncements of the great ecumenical councils the church had grasped the significance of Christ for the salvation of the human race. But for more than two hundred years the traditional answers have been put more and more in question. The New Testament records, considered as history, seem to have become more and more undermined. At the same time, the dogmatic pronouncements concerning incarnation and the presence in Jesus Christ of the two natures, human and divine, begin to seem very improbable, and we even ask whether we can make sense of them, let alone affirm them as true. Am I exaggerating? I do not think so. If we ask, Who really is Christ for us today? we can expect to hear a large number of different answers. Historians will give us a much-abridged account of his career, differing significantly from the Gospels. Many theologians will tell us that a "christology" or theological account of

---

1. D. Bonhoeffer, *Letters and Papers from Prison* (London: SCM, 1967) 139.

Jesus Christ must begin "from below," as it is expressed, that is to say, from the human Jesus, but then they are embarrassed to tell us that they know very little about the historical Jesus. There has in fact been a most unfortunate coincidence. Just as New Testament scholars have been telling us that the historical Jesus has slipped beyond our grasp, systematic theologians have become almost unanimous in their desire to begin christological reflection from the human Christ, considered as a historical person. But there are still some who insist on developing a christology "from above," as it is called. Perhaps they remember Kierkegaard's warning: "If one begins with the assumption that Jesus Christ was a man . . . one may conclude, with an ascendingly superlative scale, great, greater, greatest, exceedingly and astonishingly the greatest man that ever lived"—but you can carry on the series as long as you wish, and you will never arrive at God, for that, in Kierkegaard's view, would involve the fallacy of a *metabasis eis allo genos*.[2]

What a myriad of problems are opened up as soon as we begin to think about christology! And there seem to be as many proffered solutions as there are problems. Some of these solutions are frankly reductionist, others try to salvage the whole body of classical christology. Some of the solutions are so reductionist that the Christianity we have known in the past would on their terms be impossible in the future. For if Christ is attenuated beyond a certain point (difficult to determine, no doubt) it would become senseless to celebrate the Eucharist or to invite people to have faith in him as their "Saviour and Lord" in the phrase which, at its foundation in 1948, the World Council of Churches took as the minimal criterion for recognizing an ecclesial community. On the other hand, those who still advocate a complete traditional christology can with a good conscience continue the worship and preaching of the church, but they find that, at least in Western countries, it seems to be meaningful to fewer and fewer of their contemporaries. So the nagging question comes back. Who really is Jesus Christ for us today? We owe it to ourselves to find an answer, for only if we can give some answer can we with integrity remain Christians. And we owe it to society at large to give an answer, especially when people who have felt some attraction to Christianity or in what they have learned about the person of Jesus Christ come and want to learn more.

Christians today speak with many voices even on this most central question in their faith. Yet the sheer pluralism should not in itself worry us too much. Even in the New Testament itself, there are several ways of understanding the person of Christ. The different ways do not

---

2. S. Kierkegaard, *Training in Christianity* (Princeton: Princeton University Press, 1944) 30.

necessarily conflict with one another, but we are probably less aware than we should be of the differences. This is mainly because for centuries Christians had an almost superstitious veneration for the words of scripture. If anything stood there in the text, then it had authority; and if it seemed to conflict with something that stood elsewhere in the text, then something had to be done to harmonize the two accounts. Even a short generation ago, in the heyday of what was called "biblical theology," scholars who were far from being fundamentalists nevertheless insisted on the unity of the Bible. Even the great Karl Barth (who, one must suspect, never took biblical criticism quite seriously) said, "To understand the Bible would mean from beginning to end and from verse to verse to understand how everything in it is related to Jesus Christ as its visible/invisible centre."[3] Such a view seems to ascribe to the Bible a unity it never had. But when the era of biblical theology was drawing to an end, scholars seemed to go to the opposite extreme, emphasizing the differences between the biblical writers to the point at which the Bible was beginning to look like a mere collection of fragments. This suggested in turn that the commonly accepted teaching about the person of Christ is just a patchwork of different ideas from different sources on which believers have imposed a superficial unity. James Dunn, for instance, writes:

> What many Christians both past and present have regarded as orthodox christology may be regarded (not altogether unfairly) as a curious amalgam of different elements taken from different parts of first-century Christianity—personal pre-existence from John, virgin birth from Matthew, the miracle-worker from the so-called "divine man" christology prevalent among some Hellenistic Christians, his death as atonement from Paul, the character of his resurrection from Luke, his present role from Hebrews and the hope of his parousia from the earlier decades.[4]

I am not sure how seriously Dunn intends us to take this criticism, but it does indeed point to an often uncritical lumping together of disparate material. The human mind has a tendency to unify and harmonize the information that it picks up from various quarters, and to do so prematurely and superficially. But while that is certainly a danger, it can equally well be argued that our understanding is both broadened and deepened as we learn to see connections between items that at first seemed quite unrelated. In any case, the significance of Jesus Christ was not grasped all at once. The construction of a christology acceptable to the Christian community at large took place by stages over a long time.

3. Karl Barth, *Church Dogmatics* 1/1 (Edinburgh: T. & T. Clark, 1936) 131.
4. J. D. G. Dunn, *Unity and Diversity in the New Testament* (London: SCM, 1977) 226–27.

Pluralism in Christology

We can see development within the New Testament itself, and the development continued for three or four centuries after the last books of the New Testament had been written. To bring together material from different sources and to show that it can be related within some unitary framework is not necessarily a bad thing. We live in an age when there is great stress on analysis, but knowledge demands synthesis as well as analysis. We have to seek for coherence among the isolated facts and different points of view.

In the New Testament itself, there must be at least half a dozen fairly distinctive christologies, and some of them differ so much from each other that they seem to be in conflict. Let us just briefly remind ourselves of some of the diversity to be found here.

The oldest written testimony to Jesus Christ is, of course, that of Paul. Contrary to what many people believe, Paul's christology is beautifully simple. Its basis is a contrast between two men—the first Adam, of whom we read in Genesis, and the last Adam, Jesus Christ. The first Adam was created by God with a share in the image of God and with the potentiality for realizing that image, but he failed and fell into sin. The second Adam, Jesus Christ, is also a man—a Jew and a descendant of David, according to Romans 1:3, for Paul was no docetist—but this new Adam fulfilled God's purpose for the human race; he manifested the image of God (Col 1:15) and revealed the true human destiny as resurrection and life with God. This is a simple straightforward "christology from below" and may well have been current even before Paul, so that it has some claim to be the oldest christology of all. Taken by itself, it might be criticized as "adoptionist," but Paul was himself aware of this problem. "All this is from God," he declared (2 Cor 5:18), indicating that God had the initiative in all these events, so that there is no "christology from below," set over against a "christology from above," but the two movements are joined together at every stage. If it is objected that this simple statement of Pauline christology succeeds in being simple only by ignoring a great deal of Pauline teaching, I do not think this is the case: We have space to consider only one aspect of Pauline teaching which seems to go against it— the famous Christ hymn of Philippians 2, believed by many scholars to be pre-Pauline. Surely that hymn, especially as it was interpreted for us in the kenotic christologies of the nineteenth century, speaks of a preexistent supernatural Christ and therefore calls for a "christology from above," with its emphasis on incarnation such as we do not find in the two-Adams christology. It seems to me, however, that the recent studies of James Dunn have shown that we need not read a theory of preexistence into this hymn. It fits very naturally into the two-Adams christology. Adam thought that "equality with God" was something to be grasped; Jesus did not but chose the way of the servant. No doubt one could go on arguing about the correct exegesis of this passage, but from the theological point of view, Dunn has the great advantage of offering the most economic interpretation.

Let us now contrast Paul's christology with Mark's. The discovery in the nineteenth century that Mark's Gospel is in all probability the oldest of all made it a prime favorite for those who were in search of the historical Jesus, the human Galilean who, it was believed, underlay all the theological and mythological constructions which Christian faith had erected round him. Mark's Gospel too begins from below, with the human Jesus, without any stories of a virgin birth or a supernatural origin. At his baptism, the Spirit descends on him and his ministry begins, and this Spirit christology may again strike us as something simple and intelligible. But before long we find ourselves becoming puzzled. It was William Wrede who exposed the difficulties raised by this Gospel. "It would indeed be most highly desirable that such a gospel as Mark's should not be the oldest," he wrote,[5] but apparently it is the oldest and much of it passed into the two other Synoptics. Why did Wrede regret that it had been the first? No doubt there were several reasons, but the main one is that this first of the Gospels did not fulfill the hopes of those who hoped to encounter in its pages the unvarnished Jesus of history. In the early chapters, it is clearly a supernatural figure who is portrayed, a miracle worker, a *theios anēr* or divine man, to use the common expression. In Rudolf Bultmann's words, the Jesus of Mark's Gospel "is the very Son of God, walking the earth."[6] So although Paul and Mark both begin from below, with the human Jesus, there could hardly be a stronger contrast than that which is seen between the Pauline Christ, reckoned among the weak and foolish things of this world (1 Corinthians 1), renouncing any equality with God in order to take the part of a servant (Philippians 2), and the Marcan Christ who demonstrates his messianic status through miracles: except that one has to say here that a dramatic change takes place in Mark's account when he comes to the passion. If one is right in seeing something like a *theios anēr* christology in the earlier parts of Mark, we come much closer to the spirit of Paul's kenotic christology when we hear Jesus say (Mark 10:42–46): "You know that those who are supposed to rule over the Gentiles lord it over them, and their great men exercise authority over them. But it shall not be so among you; but whoever would be great among you must be your servant, and whoever would be first among you

---

5. W. Wrede, *The Messianic Secret* (Cambridge: James Clarke, 1971) 148.
6. R. Bultmann, *The History of the Synoptic Tradition* (New York: Harper & Row, 1963) 241.

must be the slave of all. For the Son of Man came also not to be served but to serve, and to give his life as a ransom for many."

In this all-too-brief reminder of the diversities in New Testament christology, we must hurry on to John's Gospel, which contrasts with both Paul and Mark. For now we definitely come to the so-called christology from above, to what appears to be a clear doctrine of incarnation. The Logos, which has been from the beginning, is made flesh in Jesus Christ. Yet, when I say "a clear doctrine," I am not doing justice to the subtlety of John's language. He is a master of paradox, saying things that appear to be contradictory, yet point to something that we cannot say directly. "The Word was with God, and the Word was God." If the Word was with God, then it must have been distinct from God; if the Word was God, then it must have been identical with God. John's meaning hovers between distinctness and identity.

I do not accept that John's Gospel is docetic, but because he begins from the opposite end, in comparison with Paul and Mark, his christology has a quite different feel from theirs. In his famous commentary, Bultmann portrays Jesus in the role of a gnostic teacher sent with a revelation from the God whom no one has ever seen. Whatever be the true explanation of John's Gospel, why it was written and exactly what it is saying, most Christians accept it as an important part of their heritage, even though, when they begin to think about it, it is hard indeed to know how John's teaching can be coherently related to Paul's or Mark's.

Here I have just drawn our attention to some of the problems occasioned by the different views of Jesus Christ that are found in the New Testament itself. Elsewhere I have tried to deal with some of these problems in much greater detail,[7] but here I have been concerned to show that our own position in the twentieth century when there seem to be so many conflicting views of Jesus Christ is, in one respect at least, not so very different from that of Christians living at the end of the first century. If we met Christians from that period who severally claimed "I am of Paul" or "I am of Mark" or "I am of John," we could not simply blame them as schismatics—we might well believe that they were genuinely perplexed. Pluralism is not a modern phenomenon in the church, but seems to have been there from the beginning. Of course, there have always been limits to what may be included within the bounds of Christian belief. From the very beginning, there has been not only pluralism but heresy—forms of belief so disruptive that they could not be recognized as Christian.

The centuries after the time when the books of the New Testament

---

7. J. Macquarrie, *Jesus Christ in Modern Thought* (London: SCM, 1990).

were written continued to be lively, but the centrifugal proliferation of views concerning Jesus was being balanced by the search for common formulas on which all could agree. In that great formative era of Christian theology, there were two moments of special importance for christology—Nicea and Chalcedon. At Nicea, Jesus Christ was confessed to be of the same substance as the Father (*homoousios*). At Chalcedon, he was acknowledged as one person in whom there concur two complete natures, a human nature and a divine nature. In spite of all the modern criticism of these ancient formulas, they helped to hold the church together for many centuries—indeed, even today the Nicene Creed must be the most ecumenical document that has ever been devised. A glance at the great histories of christology—Dorner, Harnack, Grillmeier, and others—shows that for more than a thousand years very little happened apart from adjustments to the standards that had been laid down by the great ecumenical councils. They survived even the stormy years of the Reformation and of the religious wars virtually unscathed. Bernard Lonergan gives a very favorable estimate of the achievement of the years up to Nicea, seeing them as a time when the confused teachings of the New Testament were universalized and unified. He wrote:

> The Nicene dogma marks a transition from a multiplicity of symbols, titles and predicates, to the ultimate ground of these, namely, the Son's consubstantiality with the Father. Equally, it marks a transition of things as related to us, to things as they are in themselves, from the relational concepts of God as supreme agent, creator, omnipotent Lord of all, to an ontological conception of the divine Substance itself. It marks no less a transition from the Word of God as accommodated to a particular people at a particular time under particular circumstances, to the Word of God as it is to be proclaimed to all people, of all times, under whatever circumstances—the transition from the prophetic oracles of Yahweh, the gospel as announced in Galilee, the apostolic preaching and the simple tradition of the Church, from all of these to Catholic dogma.[8]

Obviously, some of Lonergan's assertions are open to question, and people of different historical eras and different geographical cultures would have difficulty in accepting such far-reaching claims for Nicea. But at least the general direction can be applauded—the church in those days was reaching out for ways of thinking and speaking that would communicate as widely as possible, as well as embracing what seemed to be essential in its own heritage of belief. Just as the church sometimes thought of itself as a third nation, a new people embracing both Jew and gentile, so these early theologians could be said to be

---

8. B. Lonergan, *The Way to Nicea* (London: Darton, Longman & Todd, 1976) 136–37.

creating a third conceptuality, neither Hebrew nor Greek though drawing on the resources of both.

The doctrinal foundations laid there endured, as I have said, for many centuries. It was not until the eighteenth century, the time we call the Enlightenment, that they were seriously challenged. But from that time nothing has been left untouched. The New Testament history of Christ has been gradually eroded, until we wonder what can be asserted about him that is beyond question. The dogmas have been equally shaken—ideas of incarnation and atonement, of salvation and eternal life, even of a God to be trusted and adored. Nicea and Chalcedon, which seemed to bring a measure of unified belief to the church, can no longer be assumed as universal standards. The Enlightenment marks the beginning of the decline of Christian faith, at least in the Western world, and inevitably christology has been caught in that decline. That indeed is why we have to ask the question that stands at the beginning of this essay: Who really is Christ for us today?

Yet we have to notice that, although the Enlightenment shook Christian faith to its very foundations, it did not wipe it out. Even today, two or three centuries after the intellectual revolutions of the eighteenth century (as well as all the political and social revolutions), Christianity still stands and still has power to attract people of all races and classes, even though it seems to speak with an uncertain voice and can give no definitive answer to that all-important question, Who really is Christ for us today? Certainly we have not reached the point at which we could say he is nobody or has no further significance. Hans Küng has said in his important book *The Incarnation of God*, "The christological debate that has persisted since the dawn of the modern age has not yet been resolved."[9]

What has happened is that once the church recovered from the shock of the new intellectual climate of the Enlightenment, Christian theologians and philosophers set about rethinking the significance of Jesus Christ. Some of their attempts were very reductionist in tendency and others were unsatisfactory in one way or another, but there was an honest recognition that a new situation had arisen and that it would not do simply to go on appealing to the Bible and the creeds or parroting the ancient formulas as if nothing of importance had happened. Again let me cite a perceptive remark by Küng: "Whoever (as often still happens) sees in the development of the modern conception of Christ since the Enlightenment mere apostasy, not only undervalues the fertile new impulses that emerged here, but also fails to appreciate the many

---

9. H. Küng, *The Incarnation of God* (Edinburgh: T. & T. Clark, 1987) 19.

throwbacks that are made to the representations of Christ of earlier ages."[10]

Let me pass rapidly in review the main types of new christology that appeared in the nineteenth century, all of them with some promise, yet all of them, as I shall point out later, showing defects. There was Kant's *rationalist* christology, expounded in *Religion within the Limits of Reason Alone* (1793). For him, Jesus Christ is the historical exemplar of the archetype of an ideal human life "well pleasing to God" to which we are all directed by reason, functioning at the deepest level of conscience. Then Schleiermacher in *The Christian Faith* (1821) set forth Christ as "the completion of the creation of humanity," recalling that ancient christology of Paul based on the first Adam and the last Adam, and echoed in the great hymn of another nineteenth-century churchman, Cardinal Newman.

> O loving wisdom of our God!
>   When all was sin and shame,
> A second Adam to the fight
>   And to the rescue came.
>
> O wisest love! that flesh and blood
>   Which did in Adam fail,
> Should strive afresh against the foe,
>   Should strive and should prevail.

The great philosopher Hegel had a lifelong interest in religion, and in one way or another that interest shows itself in all his writings. He developed a more metaphysical type of christology. He believed that the Absolute Spirit has from all eternity been moving into the realm of the finite in an act of self-sacrifice and that the historical climax of that movement is seen in the cross of Christ. Christ's sufferings and death are the earthly counterpart of the suffering of God himself in his sympathy (or perhaps one should say "empathy") in and with the creation. This is what Hegel understood by the death of God, a phrase he quotes from a Lutheran hymn. Long before it was used in an atheistic sense by Nietzsche, God's death was understood by Hegel in a Christian sense as his self-emptying in Jesus Christ. In the last decades of the century, new ways of thinking about Christ appear in the works of such so-called liberal theologians as Ritschl and Harnack, who tried to bring us back from the high speculations of Hegel to the historical Jesus who in Galilee and Jerusalem made his lasting impression on the human race through his disciples.

10. Ibid., 97.

All of these christologies can be faulted in one way or another. Kant so stressed the power of reason and conscience in every one of us that the figure of Jesus began to appear superfluous. Schleiermacher's view of Jesus seemed to many too subjective and humanistic. Hegel's lofty thoughts are associated with a system of philosophy so vast and demanding that it might seem that only the most brilliant graduate students could ever come to an understanding of who Christ is. The liberals were discredited by the next generation of theologians under Karl Barth, who accused them of conforming the Christian gospel to the demands of secular culture and for several decades seemed to be putting back the clock to Nicea and Chalcedon. But by the late twentieth century, Barth and neo-orthodoxy were only an episode, and today we are plunged again into the pluralism of the post-Enlightenment christologies. There are many new names—Rahner, Schillebeeckx, Moltmann, Pannenberg, and on it goes—yet in most of them we recognize ideas that have already appeared in different forms and in different terminological dress. Perhaps there has never been such an upsurge of christological thinking since the first century, which produced the variety of christologies we find in the New Testament. What happened then, as we have seen, was that the church moved toward statements like those of Nicea and Chalcedon, which were broad enough to include the important insights of Paul, Mark, John, and others, and also broad enough to permit of new developments, so that, as Karl Rahner pointed out, Chalcedon was as much a beginning as an end.

But what happens in our case? A sheer pluralism certainly acts as a spur to new creative thinking, but it can also be very bewildering to Christians at large. They have not been able to escape that awkward question, Who really is Christ for us today? and the church has the responsibility of trying to give some answer, and not just of gesturing helplessly either toward a whole range of conflicting statements about Christ or toward the ancient formulas which can scarcely be understood today even by experts. The question about Christ, together with the question about God, which is inseparable from it, seems to me to constitute the great challenge to theologians today. We have to find a way of speaking that will reach the hearts and minds of modern men and women, yet we will not do this by reducing Christianity to something so inoffensive that no one will care very much whether it is accepted or rejected. We must say something that is not less than what the fathers of the church said at Nicea and Chalcedon, but we must say it in the language of today. The enormous intellectual energy expended on christology since the Enlightenment has set before us a great wealth of insights into who Jesus was and what his continuing significance is. It would be a mistake to think that these can all be synthesized or combined together, for Kierkegaard was not altogether wrong when he called the incarnation the "Absolute Paradox." If there is a sense in which God was in Christ, this is something so stupendous that we could only destroy it by trying to package it too neatly. But we do have a duty to come clean about what faith in Christ means today and to find a way of expressing it that is both adequate to the reality and honest toward those with whom we communicate.

13
LOVE AND JUSTICE
Paul Ricoeur

TALKING ABOUT LOVE may be too easy, or rather too difficult. How can we avoid simply praising it or falling into sentimental platitudes? One way of finding a way between these two extremes may be to take as our guide an attempt to think about the dialectic between love and justice. Here by dialectic I mean, on the one hand, the acknowledgment of the initial disproportionality between our two terms and, on the other hand, the search for practical mediations between them—mediations, let us quickly say, that are always fragile and provisory.

The insight promised by such a dialectical approach seems to me to have been overlooked by the method of conceptual analysis that seeks to extract from some selection of texts by ethicists or theologians who talk about love the most systematic recurrent themes. This, of course, is the approach used by many of our colleagues in philosophy and theology influenced by the discipline of analytic philosophy. To cite just one example of such a work, and it is a noteworthy one, in Gene Outka's *Agape* the subtitle *An Ethical Analysis* is indicative of the general orientation.[1] For this author it is a matter of isolating the "basic normative content" that Christian love or *agapē* "has been said to possess irrespective of circumstances."[2] By using what method? His answer is what my own approach would like to call into question: "Such an inquiry is formally similar to the one philosophers have pursued in discussing, e.g., utilitarianism as an ultimate normative standard, criterion, or principle for judgments of value and obligation."[3] The

---

1. Gene Outka, *Agape: An Ethical Analysis* (New Haven and London: Yale University Press, 1972).
2. Ibid., 7.
3. Ibid.

187

whole issue for me is contained in this response: Does love in our ethical discourse have a normative status comparable to that of utilitarianism or even of the Kantian categorical imperative?

I shall provisionally set aside the three fundamental features of *agapē* that Outka sees as being the most systematic and the most recurrent ones in the literature he considers. Far from neglecting them completely, however, we shall return to them below in some closing remarks devoted to the practical mediations between love and justice linked to the exercise of moral judgment in a particular situation. For the moment, though, I will limit myself to listing these features without commenting on them, in order to give some idea of the ultimate end of our own investigation: first, an equal "regard for the neighbor which in crucial respects is independent and unalterable"; then, self-sacrifice, "the inevitable historical manifestation of agape insofar as agape was not accommodated to self-interest"; and, finally, the mutuality characteristic of those actions "which establish or enhance some sort of exchange between the parties, developing a sense of community and perhaps friendship."[4]

We cannot reproach Outka for not having caught sight of the conceptual incoherencies that such a typology seeks to lay bare. In fact, each of his basic features is constructed at the expense of setting aside variations, disagreements, and confusions which he deplores more than once throughout his study. What is more, it is obvious that his third feature, the one that in fact seems most decisive to him, is highly discordant with the second one. Yet these deceptions encountered in the process of an ethical analysis devoted to isolating a "basic normative content" are, to me, an indication that such a direct method is, in fact, inappropriate to our making sense of the relationship between love and justice, and that we should instead start from what in the *topos* of love resists such treatment of love as "an ultimate normative standard, criterion, or principle for judgments of value and obligation."

I would like to put this first part of my own remarks on our topic, dedicated to the disproportionality between justice and love, under the emblem of a quotation from Pascal:

> All bodies together and all minds together and all their products are not worth the least impulse of charity. This is of an infinitely superior order. Out of all bodies together we could not succeed in creating one little thought. It is impossible, and of a different order. Out of all bodies and minds we could not extract one impulse of true charity. It is impossible, and of a different, supernatural order.[5]

---

4. Ibid., 9, 24, 36.
5. Pascal, *Pensées*, trans. A. J. Krailsheimer (Harmondsworth: Penguin, 1966) 125.

I will not conceal the fact that this harsh judgment of Pascal will make it more difficult subsequently to find the mediations required by moral judgment in a particular situation, provoked by the question, what ought I to do here and now? For the moment, however, my question is the following. If we begin by acknowledging disproportionality, how can we avoid falling into one or the other of the dangers mentioned above, exaltation or emotional platitudes? In other words, unthinking sentimentality?

It seems to me that one possible way presents itself which would consist in looking for those forms of discourse—which are sometimes quite complicated—that resist the kind of leveling down brought about by the kind of conceptual analysis carried out by analytic philosophy. For love does speak, but it does so in a kind of language other than that of justice, as I shall phrase it at the end of my remarks.

I would like to focus on three aspects of such language as it is shaped by the biblical tradition that are indicative of what I shall call the strangeness or oddness of the discourse of love.

The first of these aspects has to do with the link between love and praise. Indeed, we may say that the discourse of love is initially a discourse of praise, where in praising, one rejoices over the view of one object set above all the other objects of one's concern. In this abbreviated formula, the three elements—rejoicing, seeing, and setting above all else—are equally important. By saying this, do we fall once again into a kind of conceptual analysis or into sentimentality? Neither, I suggest, if we are attentive to those original features of praise for which such verbal forms as the hymn are particularly appropriate. For example, the glorification of love by Paul in 1 Corinthians 13 is akin to those "songs of praise" indicated by the Hebrew title of the book of Psalms: *mizmôrê těhillîm*. Beyond this, we should also bring together the hymn and the discourse of benediction: "Blessed is the man who walks not in the counsel of the wicked. . . . He is like a tree planted by streams of water" (Ps 1:1, 3). "O Lord of hosts, blessed is the man who trusts in thee!" (Ps 84:12). In this way we are brought to the literary form of the macarism, familiar to readers of the Beatitudes: "Blessed are the poor in spirit, for theirs is the kingdom of heaven" (Matt 5:3). Hymn, benediction, macarism—in these forms of discourse we find a complex interweaving of literary expressions which we can link together in terms of the central aspect of "praise."

In turn, such praise refers us back to the more general, broader domain of biblical poetry, which Robert Alter has shown functions discordantly in relation to the rules of a discourse that would seek univocity at the level of principles.[6] In such poetry the key words undergo

---

6. Robert Alter, *The Art of Biblical Poetry* (New York: Basic Books, 1985).

amplifications of meaning, unexpected assimilations, hitherto unseen interconnections, which cannot be reduced to a single meaning.

As an example, we may consider the rhetorical strategies at work in 1 Corinthians 13. The initial strophe exalts the greatness of love by a kind of negative hyperbole, announcing the annihilation of everything that is not love: "If I speak in the tongues of men and of angels, but have not love, I am a noisy gong or a clanging cymbal." The same formula recurs a number of times: "And if I have . . . but have not love . . . I am nothing." The second strophe then develops the vision of the eminence of love in the indicative mode, as though everything were already consummated: "Love is patient and kind; love is not jealous or boastful; it is not arrogant or rude. Love does not insist on its own way; it is not irritable or resentful; it does not rejoice at wrong, but rejoices in the right. Love bears all things, believes all things, hopes all things, endures all things." The reader will have noted the interplay of assertion and denial, as well as the playful use of synonyms that makes akin quite distinct virtues, all of which run counter to our legitimate concern to isolate individual meanings. Finally, in the third strophe, a movement of transcendence beyond all limits carries the day: "Love never ends; as for prophecy, it will pass away; as for tongues, they will cease; as for knowledge, it will pass away. . . ." And, as a final passing to the limit: "So faith, hope, love abide, these three; but the greatest of these is love."

This is the first kind of resistance that love opposes to "ethical analysis," in the strong sense of the term "analysis," that is, as conceptual clarification.

The second oddity of the discourse of love has to do with the disturbing imperative form in such well-known expressions as: "You shall love the Lord your God . . . and you shall love your neighbor as yourself." If we take the imperative in the usual sense of obligation, whose case is so powerfully stated by Kantian ethics, there seems to be something scandalous about commanding love, that is, about ordering a feeling. Kant diminishes this difficulty by distinguishing "practical" love, which is nothing but respect for persons as ends in themselves, from "pathological" love, which has no place in the sphere of ethics. Freud is more obviously indignant over what is at stake here. If so-called spiritual love is just a sublimated erotic love, the commandment to love can only be the expression of the tyranny of the superego over the affective sphere. At this point in our reflections, the difficulty, however, does not have to do with the status of love within the realm of feelings (to which I shall return below), but rather with the status of the commandment, particularly as a commandment to love. Does this commandment, on the plane of acts of discourse, have the same illocutionary force as, let us say, those ordinary commands that call for obedience, such as closing a door or opening a window? And, on the ethical plane, is this commandment comparable to moral principles, that is, to those first propositions that govern subordinate maxims, as do the utilitarian principle or the Kantian categorical imperative?

I found an unanticipated source of help in responding to this question in Franz Rosenzweig's *Star of Redemption*.[7] It may be recalled that this work, which itself is far from the commonplace, is divided into three sections, corresponding respectively to the idea of creation (or the eternal before), revelation (or the eternal present of encounter), and redemption (or the eternal not yet of messianic expectation). Coming to the second section, revelation, the reader may expect to be instructed concerning the Torah, and in a sense this is what happens, but the Torah, at this stage of Rosenzweig's meditation, is not yet a set of rules. Rather, it becomes so, because it is preceded by the solemn act that situates all human experience in terms of the paradigmatic language of scripture. And what is the most apt symbol for this imposing of a primordial language on the human sphere of communication? It is the commandment to love. Yet, contrary to our expectation, the formula for this commandment for Rosenzweig is not that of Exodus, nor that of Leviticus, nor that of Deuteronomy, but rather that of the Song of Solomon, which is read at every Passover celebration. Love, says the Song of Songs, "is as strong as death."[8] Why does Rosenzweig refer to the Song of Solomon at this place? And with what imperative connotation? At the beginning of his section on revelation, he considers just the intimate colloquy between God and an individual soul, before any "third" person comes on the scene, which is taken up in the section on redemption.[9] His insight is to show in this way how the commandment to love springs from the bond of love between God and the individual soul. The commandment that precedes every law is the word that the lover addresses to the beloved: Love me! This unexpected distinction between commandment and law makes sense only if we

---

7. Franz Rosenzweig, *The Star of Redemption*, trans. William W. Hallo (New York: Holt, Rinehart & Winston, 1971).

8. Ibid., 202.

9. If anyone is surprised to see all reference to the neighbor put off until the third category, redemption, it should be recalled that Rosenzweig's three categories are contemporaneous with one another even though the third also develops the second one. Thus the historical dimension unfolds beyond the solitary I–thou conversation. From here on there are laws and not just the commandment: Love me, at the same time as there are others. In other words, the second great commandment proceeds from the first, insofar as the always imminent future of a history of redemption, with all its historical and communal implications, proceeds from the Today of the commandment to love. In this sense, there is not just a lover and a beloved, but a self and an other than oneself—a neighbor.

admit that the commandment to love is love itself, commending itself, as though the genitive in the "commandment of love" were subjective and objective at the same time. Or, to put it another way, this is a commandment that contains the conditions for its being obeyed in the very tenderness of its objurgation: Love me!

If anyone should doubt the validity of this ever-so-subtle distinction Rosenzweig makes between commandment and law, I would reply by adding that we need to relate this deviant use of the imperative to the forms of discourse referred to earlier—praise, hymn, benediction, macarism—and thereby dare to speak of a poetic use of the imperative. This poetic use of the imperative has its own connotations within the broad range of expressions extending from the amorous invitation, through pressing supplication, to the summons, to the sharp command accompanied by the threat of punishment.[10] Thanks to this kinship between the command "Love me!" and the song of praise, the commandment of love is revealed as being irreducible, in its ethical overtones, to the moral imperative, so legitimately equated by Kant to obligation, or duty, with reference to the recalcitrance of human inclinations.

It is from this gap between what I have called the poetic use of the commandment and the commandment in the properly ethical sense of the term that I shall undertake my attempt below at a dialectic centered on the economy of the gift.

But before attempting this dialectic, I should like to add a third feature to our canvassing of the strange and odd expressions of love. This time, I should like to consider those expressions that have to do with love as a feeling. I have held off until this point any consideration of such expressions so as not to give in to the sirens of sentimentality. But now it is under the sign of the poetics of the hymn and the commandment that we can place this third feature, which I will sum up in terms of the power of metaphorization linked to the expressions of love. We may take up this theme beginning where we left off the preceding one: the pressing appeal—Love me!—which the lover addresses to the beloved, confers on love the dynamism thanks to which it becomes capable of mobilizing a wide variety of affects which we designate by their end states: pleasure versus pain, satisfaction versus discontent, rejoicing versus distress, beatitude versus melancholy, and so on. What is more, love is not limited just to deploying this wide variety of affects around itself like some vast field of gravitation. It also creates a kind of ascending and descending spiral out of them, which it traverses in both directions.

10. There is here a broad semantic field whose exploration calls for the insightfulness and subtleness of a second J. L. Austin!

And what I have just described in the psychological terms of affects and end states has its linguistic counterpart in the production of a vast field of analogies among all of the affective modes of love, thanks to which they mutually signify one another. Thus it is thanks to what I have called the process of metaphorization on this linguistic plane that erotic love is capable of signifying more than itself and of indirectly intending other qualities of love. But it is the underlying analogy between an affect and the linguistic process of metaphorization that we must emphasize. This is what Anders Nygren and all those who have followed him in setting up a dichotomy between *eros* and *agapē* have underestimated.[11] Analogy on the level of feelings and metaphorization on the linguistic plane refer to a single phenomenon, which implies that here metaphor is more than just a trope, or rhetorical ornament. To put it another way, in this instance the trope expresses what we might call the substantive tropology of love: that is, both the real analogy between feelings, and the power of *eros* to signify *agapē* and to put it into words.

I want to end these initial remarks by considering those features of the discourse of justice that most obviously are opposed to these aspects of the discourse of love. I shall consider justice first on the level of social practice (where it is identified with the judicial structure of a society and characterizes a state based on law), then on the level of those principles of justice that govern our use of the predicate "just" as applied to such institutions.

Beginning with justice as a kind of social practice, I would like rapidly to recall the circumstances or occasions where justice arises, how it is applied, and what arguments it makes use of. As regards the circumstances of justice, taken as judicial practices, they form one part of the activities of communication in a society. More specifically, justice is at issue when a higher court is asked to decide between the claims of parties with opposed interests or rights. How this is carried out depends on a judicial structure which itself includes a number of aspects: for example, a body of written laws; courts of justice, invested with the function of passing judgment; judges—that is, individuals like us, held to be independent, and charged with passing a just sentence for a particular situation. To this we must add that these structures are held to have the monopoly of power, that is, the power to impose their decision regarding what is just by using the public means of force.

As we can see, neither the circumstances nor the means of justice are those of love. Still less are the arguments of justice those of love. In fact,

---

11. Cf. Anders Nygren, *Agape and Eros*, trans. Philip S. Watson (Philadelphia: Westminster, 1953).

love does not argue, if we take the hymn from 1 Corinthians 13 as our model. Justice does argue. And it does so in a quite specific way, by confronting reasons for and against some position, which are taken as plausible, capable of being communicated, and worth discussing by all parties involved. Thus to say, as I suggested earlier, that justice is one part of the communicational activity of a society takes on its full meaning here. A confrontation between arguments before a tribunal is a noteworthy example of the dialogical use of language, and this kind of communication even has its own ethics: *audi alteram partem* (Listen to the other side).[12]

There is one aspect of this argumentative structure of justice that we must not overlook in our comparison between justice and love. The clash of arguments is in a sense infinite, inasmuch as there is always the possibility of a "but . . . ," for example, through recourse to a higher court of appeal. Yet it is also finite inasmuch as the conflict ends with the rendering of a decision. So the exercising of justice is not just a case of arguments, it also involves a decision, and this is the responsibility of the judge, as the last link in the chain of procedures, wherever this may occur. And when the judge's words are those of condemnation, we recall that statutes of justice carry a sword as well as a balance scale. Taken together, all these characteristics of judicial practice allow us for the first time to define the formalism of justice—not as a fault, but as a sign of force.

However, I do not want to take up the too-easy task of reducing justice to that judicial apparatus that makes it a part of social practice. We have also to take into consideration the idea or ideal of justice, whose borderline with love is less easy to trace. Nevertheless, taken even at the quasi-reflective level of social practice, justice can be opposed to love in terms of some well-marked features that will bring us to the threshold of our reflections devoted to the dialectic between love and justice.

These distinctive features result from the almost complete identification of justice with distributive justice. This has been the case from Aristotle's *Nicomachean Ethics* right up to John Rawls's *A Theory of Justice*, and it is the significance of this identification that we now have to consider.[13] It presupposes that we give the idea of distribution an amplitude that surpasses the realm of economics. It is society as a whole, seen from the angle of justice, that appears as an assigning of roles, tasks, rights, and duties, of advantages or disadvantages, of goods

---

12. In the case of a crime and the pronouncing of a guilty verdict that the accused does not accept, the passing of sentence is still a form of communication. As J. R. Lucas puts it, "Punishment is a language. It translates the disesteem of society into the value system of the recalcitrant individual" (*On Justice* [Oxford: Clarendon, 1980] 134).

13. John Rawls, *A Theory of Justice* (Cambridge, MA: Harvard University Press, 1971).

and costs. The strength of this representation of society as a system of distribution is that it avoids the double trap of wholism (which makes society an entity distinct from the members who compose it) and individualism (which makes society an additive sum of individuals and their interactions). In a distributive conception of society, society does not exist apart from the individuals among whom the "parts" are distributed and who thus "take part" in the whole. These individuals have no social existence apart from the distribution rule that confers on them a place within the whole. This is where justice comes in as the undergirding virtue of the institutions presiding over this division. To render each his or her due—*suum cuique tribuere*—is, in some particular situation of distribution, the most general formula of justice.

But in what way is there a virtue involved here? With this question, we raise the question of the status of the predicate "just" in our moral discourse. Since Aristotle, ethicists have sought an answer in the tie that binds justice and equality. On the judicial plane, this equation is easy to justify: treat similar cases in similar ways is the very principle of equality before the law. But how does this apply to those notoriously unequal distributions of wealth and property, of authority and responsibility, of honor and status that have characterized human society? Aristotle was the first who, when he found himself confronted with this difficulty, distinguished between proportional equality and mathematical equality. A division is just if it is proportional to the social importance of the parties involved. At the other end of history, we rediscover the same attempt to preserve the equation between justice and equality in the aforementioned work of John Rawls, when he argues that the increase in the advantages of the most favored is compensated for by a decrease in the disadvantages of the least favored. This is his second principle of justice, which completes the first principle of equality before the law. To maximize the smallest portion, this is the modern version of the concept of proportional justice stemming from Aristotle. With it, we have in a second manner characterized the legitimate formalism of justice, this time not just as judicial practice but as the ideal of an equitable division of rights and goods to the benefit of everyone.

What are the consequences for our reflections? Let us consider further the two concepts of distribution and equality which are the pillars of the idea of justice. The concept of distribution, taken in its broadest extension, confers a moral basis on the social practice of justice, in the sense we have given it, as the regulation of conflicts. Here society is seen, in effect, as the space of a confrontation between rivals. The idea of distributive justice covers all the operations of the judicial apparatus by giving them the end of upholding the claims of each person within the limit that the freedom of the one does not infringe on that of the other. As for equality, as the mathematical equality of rights and the proportional equality of advantages and responsibilities within an unequal division, this idea indicates both the strength and the limits of the very idea of the highest form of justice. The equality of rights, completed by that of chances, is certainly a source of social cohesion. Rawls even expects his principles of justice to reinforce social cooperation. But what kind of bond is thereby instituted between social partners? My own suggestion would be that the highest point the ideal of justice can envision is that of a society in which the feeling of mutual dependence—even of mutual indebtedness—remains subordinate to the idea of mutual disinterest.

We may in this regard recall Rawls's striking formula of a "disinterested interest," by means of which he characterizes the basic attitude of the parties in the hypothetical situation of the original social contract. The idea of mutuality is by no means absent from this formula, but the juxtaposition of interests prevents the idea of justice from attaining the level of a true recognition and a solidarity such that each person feels indebted to every other person. I shall attempt to show below that these ideas of recognition, of solidarity, of mutual indebtedness can be seen as the unstable equilibrium point on the horizon of the dialectic of love and justice.

In the next part of my essay I would like to build a bridge between the poetics of love and what we might now call the prose of justice, between the hymn and the formal rule. We cannot avoid this confrontation once one or the other of these terms makes some claim concerning individual or social practice. In our reflections on the hymn, this relation to praxis was not considered. As we saw, love was simply praised for itself, for its elevation and its moral beauty. And in the rule of justice, no explicit reference was made to love, this latter if anything being left to the realm of possible motives. Yet both love and justice are addressed to action, each in its own fashion, for each makes a claim on action. Our dialectic must therefore move beyond our separate examination of love and justice to consider their interaction.

Rather than just confusing them or setting up a pure and simple dichotomy between love and justice, I think a third, difficult way has to be explored, one in which the tension between two distinct and sometimes opposed claims may be maintained and may even be the occasion for the invention of responsible forms of behavior. Where might we find the paradigm of such a living tension? Perhaps we can find it in the fragment of the Sermon on the Mount in Matthew and the Sermon on the Plain in Luke or, in what is a single context, in the new commandment, where love of one's enemies and the golden rule are brought into juxtaposition. These two commandments are stated in the greatest proximity in Luke 6: "But I say to you that hear, Love your enemies, do good to those who hate you, bless those who curse you, pray for those who abuse you" (6:27–28). And just a bit further on: "And as you wish that men would do to you, do so to them" (6:31). Before trying to make sense of this strange contiguity, let us ask two preliminary questions: how, on the one hand, is the commandment to love one's enemies linked to the hymn of love? In what way, on the other hand, does the golden rule announce the rule of justice?

Our first question is equivalent to asking how the poetic quality of the hymn gets converted into an obligation. What was said above regarding Rosenzweig's discussion of the commandment "Love me!" points us in the direction of an answer. To put it briefly, the commandment to love one's enemies is not sufficient by itself; rather, it is the hyperethical expression of a broader economy of the gift, which has many other modes of expression besides this claim on us to act. This economy of the gift touches every part of ethics, and a whole range of significations confers a specific articulation on it. At one extreme, we find the symbolism, which itself is quite complex, of creation, in the most basic sense of an originary giving of existence. The first use of the predicate "good" applied to all created things in Genesis 1 belongs to this symbolism: "And God saw everything that he had made, and behold it was very good" (1:31). The hyperethical dimension of this predicate extended to all creatures is what we must emphasize, for the result is that it is as a creature that we find ourselves summoned. The sense of radical dependence that is at stake here, insofar as it is attached to the symbolism of creation, does not leave us face to face with God; rather, it situates us within nature considered not as something to exploit but as object of solicitude, of respect and admiration, as we hear in St. Francis's *Canto de Sole*. The love of neighbor, in its extreme form of love for one's enemies, thus finds its first link to the economy of the gift in this hyperethical feeling of the dependence of the human creature, and our relation to the law and to justification stems from this same economy. These two relations even constitute the core of the recital of this economy, for, on the one hand, the law is a gift inasmuch as it is bound to the history of liberation, as told, for example, in Exodus 20:2 — "I am the Lord, your God, who brought you out of the land of Egypt, out of the house of bondage." Justification, on the other hand, is also a gift inasmuch as it is a free pardon.

At the other end of the range of significations that articulate the economy of the gift we find the symbolism, symmetrical to creation and no less complex, of the final end, where God appears as the source of *unknown* possibilities. In this way, the God of hope and the God of creation are one and the same God at both extremes of the economy of the gift. At the same time, our relation both to the law and to salvation is shown to belong to this economy by being placed "between" creation and the eschaton.

Now it is from its reference to this economy of the gift that the "new" commandment draws the signification we have termed hyperethical. Why "hyperethical"? It is ethical owing to its imperative form, akin to what we considered above in discussing the commandment "Love me!" However the commandment here is more determinate inasmuch as it is linked to a structure of praxis, the distinction between friends and enemies, which this new commandment abolishes. It is ethical, therefore, but also hyperethical in that this new commandment constitutes in a way the most adequate ethical projection of what transcends ethics, the economy of the gift. In this sense, an ethical approximation of this economy is set forth which may be summed up in the expression "*since* it has been given you, give. . . ." According to this formula, and through the force of the "since," the gift turns out to be a source of obligation.

Yet this approximation is not without its paradoxes. By entering into the practical field, the economy of the gift develops a logic of superabundance that, at first glance at least, opposes itself to the logic of equivalence that governs everyday ethics.[14] If we consider the other pole of the opposition, it appears as though it is from the logic of equivalence, which we have just opposed to the logic of superabundance of the "new" commandment, that the golden rule stems, the rule that the Sermon on the Mount and, even more so, the Sermon on the Plain, juxtapose in great contextual proximity with the commandment to love one's enemies. That the golden rule does stem from a logic of equivalence of some kind is indicated by the reciprocity, or the reversibility, that this rule establishes between what one person does and what is done to another, between acting and being acted upon—hence by implication between the agent and the patient, which, although

---

14. This logic of superabundance finds a great variety of expression in the New Testament. It governs the extravagant twist of many of Jesus' parables, as is evident in those called parables of growth: one seed that produces thirty, sixty, a hundred grains; a tiny mustard seed that becomes a tree where birds may nest, etc. In a different context, Paul interprets the whole history of salvation following the same law of superabundance: "If because of one man's trespass, death reigned through that one man, much more will those who receive the abundance of grace and the free gift of righteousness reign in life through the one man Jesus Christ" (Rom 5:17). The extravagance of the parables, the hyperbole of the eschatological sayings, the logic of superabundance in ethics are all different expressions of what I am calling the logic of superabundance.

irreplaceable, are proclaimed as being able to substitute for each other.

A reconciliation between this logic of equivalence, illustrated by the golden rule, and the logic of superabundance, incarnated in the new commandment, is made almost impossible if, following certain exegetes such as Albrecht Dihle in *Die Goldene Regel,* we link the golden rule to the law of retribution, the *jus talionis,* which is the most rudimentary expression of the logic of equivalence and its corollary, the rule of reciprocity.[15] Yet this incompatibility between our two logics even seems to be sanctioned by the declaration of Jesus that, in Luke 6:32–34, somehow leads to the statement of the golden rule:

> If you love those who love you, what credit is that to you? For even sinners love those who love them. And if you do good to those who do good to you, what credit is that to you? For even sinners do the same. And if you lend to those from whom you hope to receive, what credit is that to you? Even sinners lend to sinners, to receive as much again. But love your enemies, and do good, and lend, expecting nothing in return.

Is not the golden rule retracted by these harsh words?

This apparent condemnation of the golden rule has to disturb us inasmuch as the rule of justice can be taken as a reformulation of the golden rule in formal terms.[16] This formalization is already visible in justice considered as a social practice, as the precept *audi alteram partem* bears witness, and as does the rule, treat similar cases in similar ways. It is given a more complete statement in the principles of justice referred to earlier with reference to the work of John Rawls. This does not, however, prevent our recognizing the spirit of the golden rule in even the quasi-algebraic form of Rawls's second principle: maximize the smallest portion. This formula is equivalent in effect to equalizing portions as much as permitted by the inequalities imposed by economic and social efficiency. Therefore it is legitimate for us to extend to the social practice of justice and to the principles of justice themselves the suspicion that strikes the golden rule through the logic of superabundance underlying the hyperethical commandment to love one's enemies. The rule of justice, the expression *par excellence* of the logic of equivalence and reciprocity, thus seems to suffer the same fate as the golden rule when put under the judgment of the new commandment.

But must we remain with this assertion of incompatibility? Let us return to our paradigm, the Sermon on the Mount (or the Plain). If the

---

15. Albrecht Dihle, *Die Goldene Regel* (Heidelberg: C. Winter, 1989).

16. In truth, a certain formalism already appears in the golden rule. We are not told what it is that we are to love or hate if it is done to us; however, this formalism is imperfect inasmuch as it still appeals to emotions, to love and hate, which Kant will put on the side of "pathological" desires.

difference between our two logics were merely as we have stated it, how are we to explain the presence in one and the same context of the commandment to love one's enemies and the golden rule? Another interpretation is possible, wherein the commandment of love does not abolish the golden rule but instead reinterprets it in terms of generosity, and thereby makes not just possible but necessary an application of the commandment whereby, owing to its hyperethical status, it does not accede to the ethical sphere except at the price of paradoxical and extreme forms of behavior, those forms which are in fact recommended in the wake of the new commandment:

> Love your enemies, do good to those who hate you, bless those who curse you, pray for those who abuse you. To him who strikes you on the cheek, offer the other also; and from him who takes away your cloak do not withhold your coat as well. Give to every one who begs from you; and of him who takes away your goods, do not ask them again. (Luke 6:27–30)

These are those unique and extreme forms of commitment taken up by St. Francis, Gandhi, and Martin Luther King, Jr. Yet from what penal law and, in general, from what rule of justice can we deduce a maxim of action that would set up nonequivalence as a general rule? What distribution of tasks, of roles, or advantages and obligations could be established, in the spirit of distributive justice, if the maxim of lending while expecting nothing in return were set up as a universal rule? If the hypermoral is not to turn into the nonmoral—not to say the immoral, for example, cowardice—it has to pass through the principle of morality, summed up in the golden rule and formalized by the rule of justice.

Yet the opposite is no less true. In this relation of living tension between the logic of superabundance and the logic of equivalence, the latter receives from its confrontation with the former the capacity of raising itself above its perverse interpretations. Without the corrective of the commandment to love, the golden rule would be constantly drawn in the direction of a utilitarian maxim whose formula is *do ut des*, I give *so that* you will give. The rule Give *because* it has been given you corrects the "in order that" of the utilitarian maxim and saves the golden rule from an always possible perverse interpretation. It is in this sense that we may interpret the harsh words of Luke 6:32–39, just after the reaffirmation of the golden rule in 6:31 and just before the reaffirmation of the new commandment in 6:35. In these intermediary verses the critical point of the logic of superabundance is directed not so much at the logic of equivalence of the golden rule as against its perverse interpretation. The same rule is capable of two readings, of two interpretations, one of which is based on interest, the other of which is disinterested. Only the commandment can decide the case in favor of the second against the first.

Having said this, can we not extend to the rule of justice the same test and the same critical interpretation? We have already referred to the dissimulated ambiguity of the rule of justice. We saw the rule of justice oscillate between the disinterested interest of parties concerned to increase their own advantage as far as the accepted rule will allow, and a true feeling of cooperation going as far as the confession of being mutual debtors to one another. In the same way that the golden rule, given over to itself, sinks to the rank of a utilitarian maxim, the rule of justice, given over to itself, tends to subordinate cooperation to competition, or rather to expect from the equilibrium of rival interests the simulacrum of cooperation.

If such is the spontaneous tendency of our sense of justice, must we not admit that if it were not touched and secretly guarded by the poetics of love, even up to its most abstract formulation, it would become merely a subtly sublimated variety of utilitarianism? After all, does not even the Rawlsian calculation of the maximum run the risk in the final analysis of appearing as the dissimulated form of a utilitarian calculation?[17] What saves Rawls's second principle of justice from falling into this subtle form of utilitarianism is finally its secret kinship with the commandment to love, inasmuch as this latter is directed against the process of victimization that utilitarianism sanctions when it proposes as its ideal the maximization of the average advantage of the greatest number at the price of the sacrifice of a small number, a sinister implication which utilitarianism tries to conceal. This kinship between Rawls's second principle of justice and the commandment to love is finally one of the unspoken presuppositions of the well-known reflective equilibrium which this theory warrants in the last resort between its abstract theory and our well-considered convictions.

The tension we have discerned in place of our initial antinomy is not equivalent to the suppression of the contrast between our two logics. Nevertheless, it does make justice the necessary medium of love; precisely because love is hypermoral, it enters the practical and ethical sphere only under the aegis of justice. As I have said elsewhere about the parables of Jesus, which reorient by disorienting, this effect is obtained on the ethical plane only through the conjugation of the new

---

17. This calculation would run as follows. If, once the veil of ignorance were lifted, the worst portion were to fall to me, would it not be better to choose behind the veil of ignorance the rule of distribution that, undoubtedly, would deprive me of the highest gains I might attain under a less equitable division, but which would also protect me from the greater possible disadvantages of another form of division?

commandment with the golden rule and, in a more general way, through the synergistic action of love and justice. To disorient without reorienting is, in Kierkegaardian terms, to suspend the ethical. In one sense, the commandment to love, as hyperethical, is a way of suspending the ethical, which is reoriented only at the price of a reprise and a rectification of the rule of justice that runs counter to its utilitarian tendency.

Allow me to say in conclusion that the formulas we find in reading analytical philosophers concerned, as is Outka, with disengaging the normative content of love are formulas that describe those figures of love that have already been mediated by justice, in a culture marked by our Jewish, Greek, and Christian heritages. In this sense, we come back once again to Outka's three definitions: equal regard, self-sacrifice, and mutuality.

It is the task of both philosophy and theology to discern, beneath the reflective equilibrium expressed in these compromise formulas, the secret discordance between the logic of superabundance and the logic of equivalence. It is also their task to say that it is only in the moral judgment made within some particular situation that this unstable equilibrium can be assured and protected. Thus we may affirm in good faith and with a good conscience that the enterprise of expressing this equilibrium in everyday life, on the individual, judicial, social, and political planes is perfectly practicable. I would even say that the tenacious incorporation, step by step, of a supplementary degree of compassion and generosity in all of our codes—including our penal codes and our codes of social justice—constitutes a perfectly reasonable task, however difficult and interminable it may be.

Translated by David Pellauer

14
THE "ONE WORLD": A CHALLENGE TO WESTERN CHRISTIANITY

Johann Baptist Metz

I

CHRISTIANITY DOES NOT encounter the experience of the "one world" only from the outside. Actually, it is itself already on the way toward a real World Christianity. For almost two thousand years Christianity was bound to a relatively united cultural sphere, namely, the European and Western sphere. It is today expanding toward a World Christianity that is rooted in a variety of cultures. It stands today at perhaps the most fundamental historical turning point since its very beginning. It is on the way from a culturally more or less unified, thus a culturally monocentric, European and North American Christianity toward a World Christianity rooted in many cultures, and in this sense culturally polycentric. For the Catholic Church the recent Vatican Council stands out as the institutionally tangible expression of this awakening.

At this point the theme of the "one world" becomes crucial for Christianity, both practically and in theological reflection. I begin with the problem that starts from the *empirical* situation of our present-day world and the processes toward uniformity emerging within it. The discussion of a World Christianity which is culturally polycentric presupposes that indeed such a living cultural variety in our modern world does exist. But this is in no way as obvious at it might seem at first glance. More and more the question imposes itself whether the macrocultural variety in our world is invisibly disappearing, whether this variety—slowly, but surely—is being broken down and leveled by that secular westernizing of the whole world that we call "science" and "technology," or even "technological civilization." This process with its information and culture industries rumbles like a bulldozer across the planet. It affects not simply the praxis but clearly also the mentalities of peoples. A woman from Bali who drives a car is already a half-secularized Westerner. A South American Indian who watches television and no longer listens to the tribe's storyteller is just as much so. This modernizing of minds in the Western fashion is at work everywhere. For a long time non-Western countries have been under siege from a "second colonization": through the invasion of the Western culture industry and its mass media, especially that of television, which holds people prisoner in an artificial world, a world of make-believe. It alienates them more and more from their own cultural images, from their original language and their own history. This colonization of the spirit is so much harder to resist because it appears as a sugar-coated poison, and because the gentle terror of this Western culture industry operates not as an alienation but as a narcotic drug. For a long time, the opium of the poor has no longer been religion but much more the culture of the mass media, which breaks down the power of resistance in these poor and exploited peoples, before they have a chance to become subjects, bearers of their own freedom. This mass media culture robs them of their own memory, scarcely before they have become aware of their own history of suffering. It threatens their languages, even before they have finally managed to express themselves, before they learn the "alphabet" of their own culture. It seems at least as if the non-Western peoples and cultures have fallen into a Western whirlpool. As the German writer Hans Magnus Enzensberger remarks: "What causes one's heart to sink is not the fact that the population of a poor country is compelled with a gentle but elementary force toward an improvement of their living conditions, but rather the path of the forced imitation that they thereby take. . . . The 'idée fixe' of progress for Europeans and North Americans has fallen more and more into doubt; it now reigns unchallenged only in the 'developing' countries of Asia, Africa and Latin America. The really Western oriented people—these are precisely the others."[1] Even if one thinks that this formulation is exaggerated, it cannot be disputed that the non-Western peoples and cultures in the meantime have fallen under a massive pressure to conform to the secular westernizing of the world.

Has not then the cultural polycentrism in our world already been undermined in its foundations? Is there still enough cultural identity and resistance to fight against such a mass-produced world civilization

---

1. Hans Magnus Enzensberger, *Politische Brosamen* (Frankfurt, 1982) 40–42.

so empty of substance? What does it mean then: the "one world," in other words, the *oikoumenē* in its literal sense of the "inhabited earth"? This question draws attention to a deep-seated conflict: the one world now being formed as a result of the secular westernizing wins its unity through the triumph of one-dimensionality. It wins it through the shrinkage and leveling of cultural differences and othernesses, by turning their special historical and ethnic characteristics into folklore, as it were. Opposed to this, Western Christianity as it transcends itself toward a polycentric World Christianity in the course of enculturation seeks the one world precisely in its ethnic and cultural diversity and dignity.

Yet exactly at this point when we assume that such a diversity in our one world of today still exists and that it must be preserved, there arises—as the second problem—the real *theological* question: How should Western Christianity form a bond with these non-Western cultures when it clearly cannot regard the project of the technological world civilization, and thus the secular westernizing of the world, as an innocent and neutral catalyst for World Christianity? This question, as you know, is treated in present-day theology under the catchword "enculturation." I am not able here to expound thoroughly the entire breadth of meaning of this concept in its use in theology and in the church. It is simply a question of excluding from the start a misunderstanding that very often occurs when people discuss Christianity's taking root in non-Western cultures. It seems to me essential to point out this misunderstanding if we do not want to misrepresent theoretically the challenge of the one world to Western Christianity, and if we want to understand the project of enculturation as a project for peace.

There are today many well-meaning attempts to protect Christianity from ethnocentric fallacies and, by taking into account foreign peoples and cultures, to prevent a second late takeover of World Christianity by the West. These attempts are often accompanied by proposals like this: Christianity must finally discard its Western clothing; it must finally strip off its Western shell, and so forth. Evidently, behind this approach is hidden the idea of a nonhistorical Christianity, of an ethnically innocent Christianity which is free from cultural limitations, whose identity one can conceive like one of Plato's ideas. I could also say: behind this is hidden the idea of a "pure" or "naked" Christianity whose substance at first only consists of itself and then later dresses itself in various cultural robes. But this idea is a fiction; it is nourished by the unproven, metaphorical talk of "bare facts" or of "pure truth." A Christianity that was preexistent to culture and history, or a culturally divested, culturally naked Christianity does not exist.

The culture that Christianity cannot simply take off as one takes off a piece of clothing is that European and Western culture that was formed from the Jewish and Hellenistic Greek traditions. With this arises the crucial question: If Christianity cannot simply strip off this historically contingent cloak in order to slip into this or that cultural mantle, how can there be a World Christianity that is rooted in truly diverse cultures? With this starting point, how can a real enculturation of the gospel take place that would be something more than simply an expansion of Western culture concealed for tactical reasons? Thus, is what we call cultural polycentrism in World Christianity ultimately anything more than the continuation of a monocultural colonization of the souls of foreign peoples and cultures, only now carried out with less drastic means than used previously in the history of the church?

II

The attempt to respond to these questions outlines the challenges that are posed to Western Christianity in the face of the one world. A culturally polycentric World Christianity that cannot and must not strip off its Western historical origins is possible under the presupposition that this Christianity remembers two fundamental characteristics of its biblical heritage. It must more and more realize these traits, realize them above all as a dangerous memory within the Western world itself in order to break the one-dimensionality which today overshadows the whole world. Western Christianity must, as its first characteristic, remember its biblical heritage and actualize it as the ferment of a *political* culture that seeks freedom and justice for all. It must, as the second, remember its biblical heritage and actualize it as the ferment of what might be called a *hermeneutical* culture, that is, a culture that recognizes the others in their otherness, as should be well known to us from the early history of Christianity. Both characteristics of the biblical heritage belong inseparably together. Actually, the suggested distinction between the two is relative, for the hermeneutical culture is also of vital political relevance — and not least in view of the contribution of Christianity toward the peaceful living together of the peoples of the world. Enculturation, when properly understood, is really also work for peace.

I would like to treat here very briefly the question in what way Western Christianity has to protect and to fulfill its biblical heritage as the ferment of a political culture of freedom and of universal justice. In the last few years there have been significant contributions made in the discussion about a new political theology and about liberation theology. I would thus like to limit myself here to treating the threats to this political culture within the Western world.

First of all, a word about the threats to the basic concept of *freedom*. Has not an economic sense been superimposed on the understanding of freedom that was painfully won and gradually developed in the history of the West? Has not the goods and exchange principle of our civilization in the meantime extended beyond the economic sphere, reaching into the spiritual foundation of our society and in its own way "colonizing" the relationships among people? Does not in principle everything appear marketable, even relationships among human beings in which freedom concretely lives and actualizes itself? And has not technology already superimposed itself on our freedom as well? The precipitous acceleration in which we live, the abrupt changes in consumption and in styles, extending even to cultural fashions, cannot be concretely comprehended. Our impressions become less and less concrete because we can at best only quickly glimpse back at the people and things around us. In this way individuals are trained more and more toward accommodating themselves to an abstract, ungraspable, and opaque world. Even the return to the images of childhood seems blocked, because in our automated world, we have smothered these images before they could develop. Everything becomes capable of being technically reproduced, even the productive human being himself or herself. It seems that the human person becomes less and less his or her own memory and his or her freedom rooted within that memory. Instead, the human person becomes only his or her own experiment. What will become of the human person? In the United States of America the official search for a successor to the human person has already begun. *Time* magazine portrayed it as "Man of the Year" on their cover a few years ago: the robot, a gentle machine that works without complaint, resistant to all crises, a computerized intelligence that is not capable of remembering because it also cannot forget. In other words, an intelligence without history, without the ability to suffer, without morality. It is true that this may sound like science fiction (still?), but it forces us to question the substance of our freedom and the consequences of a secular westernization of the world.

With a view toward a political culture that seeks *justice for all*, I would like to indicate a further potential danger. My concern is based on the impression that I have received in the last few years above all in my own country, but also throughout Europe, and which continues to grow within me. It refers to a change in our attitude toward the poorer countries of the world as they seek justice, and in this way toward commitment to universal justice. Is there not in our countries of the West a new mood, new "habits of the heart" (to use Robert Bellah's expression), which push the misery and need of the poor peoples of the so-called Third World further back into a greater existential distance? Does there not spread among us a new provincialism, a new form of privatization in our lives, a rather voyeuristic approach to the great situations of crisis and suffering in the world? Are there not in our enlightened Western world more and more signs of a regression back to a second immaturity, so to speak, which is fed from the conviction that, indeed, today we are better informed about everything than ever before, above all even about what threatens us? We know about all the crises and all the fears in the world; yet the step from knowledge to action has never seemed so great and never so futile as today. Does not such an impression lead us toward resignation? Or toward flight into myth and its dreams of innocence (removed from the world of action)? Is there not growing among us more and more an attitude of getting accustomed to crises and to the human misery in the world? We become numb before the crises of poverty which continually seem to reoccur. In response, we shrug our shoulders and delegate the problem to an impersonal social evolution: Does the Third World really exist? Is it not finally merely a projection? Does it exist, perhaps, only rhetorically?

For the church, however, the sorrow-filled reality of these poor countries has become a vital question and a test case for proving itself as a World Church. Finally, the church no longer "has" a Third World church, but in the meantime it "is" to a great degree a Third World church—with an unrenounceable European and Western history as part of its roots. The Western church must not therefore—almost in postmodern fashion—allow itself to be talked out of its standards or allow them to be discarded under the pressure of circumstances. It cannot withdraw from the tension between mysticism and politics into a mythical thinking removed from history. With its creed—"suffered under Pontius Pilate"—it is and remains bound to concrete history, to that history in which people have cried and loved, but also hated, tortured, crucified, and massacred. No myth can give back to the church the innocence that it has lost in such history. Of course, the church is not primarily a moral institution, but rather the bearer and transmitter of hope. Its theology is not primarily an ethics but an eschatology. And it is here that its strength is grounded: that even in a situation where it is powerless, it does not surrender its standards of responsibility and solidarity and does not simply abandon the "preferential option for the poor" to the poorer churches themselves. This is what I mean when I say that our Western Christianity should remember and realize its biblical heritage as the ferment of a political culture in which freedom and justice are sought for all. In this way it will mature into a culturally polycentric

World Christianity which accepts the challenges of the one world in the spirit of the gospel.

I would like now to treat the other challenge which the one world implies for Western Christianity. If Western Christianity is to mature into a culturally polycentric World Christianity, then it must remember and realize its biblical heritage as the ferment of what can be called a *hermeneutical culture*, that is, a culture of the acknowledgment of others in their otherness, a culture of togetherness, of the earthly *oikoumenē* which in its heart is *freed*, as Nietzsche says, *from "the will to power."*

This question not only involves the living together of the various cultures and the one world. It has to do first with what we today call the "ecological crisis" and what is described in Christian terms as the mission of the "stewardship of creation." From all sides we are called upon today to practice ecological wisdom. Here, nonetheless, we must guard against a theoretical naïveté. In order to exercise this ecological wisdom, we cannot simply in feigned innocence begin with nature itself. Nature itself cannot become the principle of a new way of acting without social and anthropological mediation. We must rather concentrate on the cultural history of nature, that is, the history of human beings interacting with nature. This history, however, is a history of domination, or of subjugation: a history of the will to power.

At the beginning of what we call "the Modern Age," the limits of which we are now reaching with ever-increasing clarity, there unfolds— embryonically and overlaid with many religious and cultural symbols— this anthropology of domination. In it (and here I consciously employ the exclusive term) man understands himself as a dominating, subjugating individual over against nature; his knowledge becomes, above all, knowledge via domination, and his praxis is one of exerting power over nature. In this dominating subjugation, in this activity of exploitation and reification, in this seizing power over nature, man's identity is formed. Man *is* by subjugating. All nondominating human virtues such as gratitude and friendliness, the capacity for suffering and sympathy, grief and tenderness, recede into the background. They are deprived of social and cultural power or, at best, in a treacherous "division of labor" they are entrusted to women, who are deprived of power anyway in this dominating male culture. These nondominating attitudes become undervalued also as unique kinds of knowledge. What dominates is knowledge as subjugation: knowing as "grasping," as "appropriating," as a kind of taking possession. Other forms of sensitive-intuitive access to reality, such as through the eyes and their gaze, are forced aside into the realm of the private and the irrational.

In the meantime, this principle of subjugation has long since permeated the psychic foundations of our total sociocultural life. It has become the secret regulating principle of all interpersonal relationships; the psychosocial pathologies of our times provide a surfeit of illustrative material on this. In this sense, we could and should speak, not only—and not even primarily—of a poisoning through unrestricted technical exploitation of the outer nature surrounding man but also of a poisoning of the inner nature of man himself. An identity thus formed through the principles of domination and subjugation makes the individual profoundly disconnected and, in the strict sense of the term, egoistic. It makes the human being incapable of seeing himself and judging himself through the eyes of his victims.

These marks of a dominating anthropology may have long since escaped us, since the drive to subjugation which belongs to this form of anthropological identity shifted its focus very early on outward— against foreign minorities, foreign races, and foreign cultures. The European history of colonization has its roots therein, and the fact that the history of Christian missions accompanied this all too closely, arching, as it were, over this history of subjugation, may serve as an illustration of the pervasive way the mechanism of subjugation has also penetrated our church life and religious life.

For me the ecological question, whether there will be a new cultural history of nature, is closely tied to the question whether there can exist at all in our Western world a new hermeneutical culture that is divested of the will to power. Its touchstone is not primarily our relationship with "nature" but rather our behavior toward the multicultural diversity in a world which over our heads has long since grown into the one world. Here again I repeat the challenge to our Western Christianity, which wants to become a culturally polycentric Christianity: it must develop itself into this hermeneutical culture based on the acknowledgment of the others in their otherness by taking up this early Christian impulse.

From the beginning Christianity has wrestled with this culture of acknowledgment. The argument between Peter and Paul (see Gal 2:11ff.) and the struggles at what is called the Council of Jerusalem (Acts 15) whether the circumcision of the Gentiles should be observed may serve as examples. The refusal of the Jewish Christian Paul to submit the gentile Christians to circumcision is an expression of this acknowledgment of the others in their otherness. This calls to mind that the compassionate acceptance of the stranger is a genuine biblical quality which is also continuously commented on in the accounts of Jesus' ministry. Moreover, many parables of Jesus point toward the character of promise that lies in the acknowledgment of the stranger, of the others in their otherness. Thus, the impulses toward a hermeneutical culture of acknowledgment lie at the roots of the Jewish-Christian tradition, even if in the course of European history it was later overshadowed and pushed into the background. This hermeneutical culture did not gain at all the significance in church history that one would have expected from these biblical sources. *Exempla docent.*

In his book *Die Eroberung Amerikas: Das Problem des Anderen* (The Conquest of America: The Problem of the Other), Tzvetan Todorov, a researcher living in Paris, shows that the conquest of America in the sixteenth century succeeded above all because the Europeans were hermeneutically superior to the natives.[2] For example, the Aztecs could recognize and evaluate the small troop of Spanish soldiers led by Cortés only within their own world view (in this case, falsely). In contrast, the Europeans had the capability of perceiving these strange others in their otherness, of grasping them within the Aztecs' own "system," so to speak. Yet, as we know, this grasping of the others in their otherness did not serve for their true acknowledgment: it was a perception of the others in the interest of sizing them up and outwitting them. It was the expression of a hermeneutics of domination, and not that of a hermeneutics of acknowledgment to which all acts of violence, any "will to power" in the acknowledgment of the others in their otherness is foreign. The year 1992 will be the five hundredth anniversary of America's "discovery." With which eyes was this continent "discovered"? Did the early Christian hermeneutics of the acknowledgment of the others in their otherness play the predominant role? Or was the process of christianizing America rather much more—and all too much—directed by a questionable hermeneutics of assimilation which could not see the trace of God in the otherness of the others and which therefore turned the uncomprehended others more and more into victims?

Allow me in this context to make two suggestions very briefly about how this almost epochal concealment of the culture of acknowledgment could occur, theologically and ecclesially. If I am not mistaken, the development of the hermeneutics of acknowledgment *in theology* has been obstinately prevented because of the acceptance early on within Christian theology of an epistemological principle that arose from the Greek philosophy of identity (since Parmenides). This principle became effective religiously in Mediterranean Gnosticism. It finally flowed through Plotinus into Christian theology and then left a substantial imprint on the form of Christian thought and Christian philosophy of religion from Neo-Platonism up through German idealism. I mean that principle of epistemology according to which "like can

---

2. (Frankfurt: Suhrkamp, 1985).

only be known from like." If, however, one does not follow the Greek ontological thinking, but rather the covenant thinking of the biblical traditions, if one follows Paul (e.g., in his conflict with Peter), then one should really formulate another theological principle of knowing: precisely that the unlike recognize—in acknowledging—one another. Only with this hermeneutical axiom can, in my opinion, the problem of "unity and plurality" as it is given to us today in the face of the one world be approached hopefully.

What led *ecclesially* to the suspension of the biblical hermeneutics of acknowledgment? Now, clearly, the church fell again and again into the temptation of confusing the universality of the mission entrusted to it with the universality of the kingdom of God, and thereby neglected or ignored the eschatological difference between the church and the kingdom of God. That is why its mission was not guided by a hermeneutics of acknowledgment, but by a hermeneutics of assimilation, even of subjugation. The tragedy of the Jewish people in the history of Christianity has here one of its roots.

It is true that there are signs of a new consciousness and new orientation in present-day Christianity. Looking at the Catholic Church, I recall the recent Vatican Council where clearly the beginnings of a culture that acknowledges the others in their otherness, a culture sought by the church itself, are to be found. Thus in the "Declaration on the Relation of the Church to Non-Christian Religions" there is recommended for the first time a positive evaluation of these religions and their cultures in contrast to the previously purely apologetic and defensive attitude. Clearly, one would have wanted to hear more: whether and to what degree the church itself needs to listen to the external prophecy from these non-Christian religions. Above all, one would have wished—especially in the face of the catastrophe of Auschwitz—a more detailed appreciation of the unsurpassable relationship to Israel and to the Jewish religion itself as the root religion of Christianity and Islam. And yet! In the "Decree on Religious Freedom," the church of the Council expresses itself as an institution of a religion of freedom, which in the preaching and sharing of its convictions renounces any use of coercion which would counteract this freedom, because the church does not want (any longer) to be guided by an abstract right of truth, but rather by the right of the (alien) person in her truth. We have good reasons to promote precisely these principles in an offensive faithfulness to the council.

The biblically rooted culture of the acknowledgment of the others in their otherness does not aim at a romantic elevation of the alien others. But it makes possible that the tendency toward universality interiorized in the Western spirit itself be joined with the wisdom and the memories of suffering of other cultures in a promising way. In these cultures there is resistance to an abstract logic of evolution in which finally history is replaced by economical laws of nature, and memory is replaced by the computer. To me, this attitude seems to be capable of becoming allied with that Western spirit which today itself is genuinely searching—and indeed searching not for the dismantlement of our scientific technological world and its achievements, but rather for new ways of working with it. This search takes place against the cultural background of our Western rationality and its increasingly self-running, increasingly subjectless processes of modernization in which the human person—as mentioned—is less and less his or her own memory and more and more only his or her own experiment. Here the death of the human person, as we historically know it, already seems to be taken into the planning. Probably such a creative exchange between the worlds of culture would be what today most deserves the name "progress." At any rate, this suggested hermeneutical culture seems to me to be the indispensable precondition for the continuously threatened peace in the world. Could a Western Christianity which matures into cultural polycentrism even become a productive model for the shaping of world peace? This question is directed to all of us, to us who are part of Western Christianity.

III

It is true that the isolated individual stands powerless and helpless before such a question. She can really hear it only as pure rhetoric, as an empty appeal. But Christianity is neither individualism nor existentialism. No one is a Christian for herself alone. Christianity lives, when it lives, in its communities of memory. It is committed to the one undivided discipleship of Jesus, which does not permit a dualism between mysticism and politics, between spirituality and responsibility for the world. The liturgical celebration of the *memoria passionis, mortis et resurrectionis Jesu Christi* thus becomes the expression of a dangerous memory that continually intervenes in our daily lives. These communities of memory resist a life that is dictated by the will to power. They resist a life that is more and more incapable of discovering a trace of God in the countenance of the alien and uncomprehended other. And they resist a life in which the substance of our freedom is threatened when this life becomes more and more apathetic and without bonds to other human beings, when the happiness of this life ultimately becomes nothing more than an unhappiness free of longing and suffering, nothing more than the apocalypse of banality. These communities finally allow themselves—continually failing, continually trying again—to be committed to a great solidarity: to the solidarity in memory with the dead whose past sufferings have not been erased; to the solidarity of presence with those who are today suffering unjustly; to a solidarity of anticipation toward the coming generations. And so they become, persistently and not without reverses, bearers and witnesses of a vision without which there will be no peace, no justice, and no saving of the earth.

Will this vision prevail? Will there be enough time? Time enough for a political culture of freedom and of universal justice and a hermeneutical culture of acknowledgment to arise among us? We Christians are not optimists of progress. Our hope is not based on a gentle, evolutionary-flavored eschatology. We are not ashamed of our apocalyptic traditions. Time for us is not an empty and surprise-free endless continuum in which we project our progressive advance, and which, nevertheless, continuously swallows us up. For us, time is and remains in the hands of God.

Translated by Peter P. Kenny

15
PLURALISM AND INTOLERANCE IN HINDUISM

Wendy Doniger

Introduction

IT IS USEFUL to distinguish between two significantly different sorts of pluralism—sociological and intellectual. Contemporary pluralism is a sociological phenomenon that can itself be approached on two levels, both the fact of the existence of many religions in our world today and our reaction to that fact. Our preferred mode of response to pluralism is to attempt to harmonize different religious beliefs in a spirit of tolerance and mutual appreciation, in the hope of reducing the kinds of fanaticism that lead to everything from bigotry to holy wars. This is a way in which people come to terms with Otherness and come to treat Others.[1] It is the way to which David Tracy has devoted so much of his life and his work.

The ancient Hindu pluralisms that I intend to discuss in this essay are of a different sort. They tackle the problem of ontology from several (plural) different angles, branching off from an ancient and still ongoing argument about the way the world *is*, about whether it is basically uniform or basically multiform. This is an intellectual phenomenon, a pluralism of ideas within a single social group that regards all of these ideas, some of which might seem contradictory to us, as valid—though not necessarily equally valid.

---

1. For a discussion of mythological attitudes to this otherness, see Wendy Doniger O'Flaherty, *Other Peoples' Myths: The Cave of Echoes* (New York: Macmillan, 1988) esp. 15–21.

We might subsume under intellectual pluralism the category of internal or individual pluralism, the problem of personal dissonance. More emotional than purely intellectual pluralism, internal pluralism might be regarded as a kind of mediating category, between the mental constructs of intellectual pluralism and the physical reality of sociological pluralism incarnate in real people. As we shall see, Hindu ontological categories postulate speech as mediating between the mental and the physical in a similar way.

The two basic sorts of pluralism, sociological and intellectual, are interconnected in any number of (plural) ways. We might ask if the intellectual pluralism of India has led to the sociological pluralism that David Tracy has striven for. I will argue, in my conclusion, that ancient Hindu intellectual pluralism does not lead to ancient Hindu sociological tolerance. But we may still learn something from ancient Indian intellectual pluralism that might help us to achieve the sociological pluralism to which we aspire in the world today.

The Vedic Background

The world of traditional, Vedic, worldly Hinduism was pluralistic in several senses. Sociologically, it maintained the pluralistic caste system, with separate, different *dharmas* for each social group and individual *dharmas* for each person (*svadharmas*). Intellectually, it advocated a pantheon of many gods. Pluralism, like everything else in India, begins with the *Rig Veda,* at the start of the first millennium B.C.E., and it begins with polytheism, but polytheism of a peculiarly monistic hue. One hymn will praise a god as the supreme god (though not the only god), but another hymn will use exactly the same words to praise another god. F. Max Müller aptly named this phenomenon "henotheism" or "kathenotheism," the worship of one (supreme) god at a time. Bearing in mind the way in which the metaphor of adultery has traditionally been used by monotheistic religions to stigmatize polytheism[2] (and used by Hinduism itself to characterize the love of god), we might regard this attitude as a kind of theological serial monogamy: "I love you, Indra/baby, and have never loved any other god/woman." "I love you, Vishnu/baby, and have never loved any other god/woman."

Even this uneasy polytheism was challenged from the start by a more blatant monistic tendency. The most enigmatic cosmogonic hymn of

---

2. See Avishai Margalit and Moshe Halbertal, *Idolatry: A Conceptual Analysis* (Cambridge, MA: Harvard University Press, forthcoming).

the *Rig Veda* (10.129)[3] ends with a question about the very nature, perhaps the very existence, of god: "Whence this creation has arisen—perhaps it formed itself, or perhaps it did not—the one who looks down on it, in the highest heaven, only he knows—or perhaps he does not know." This question pops up in another cosmogonic hymn (10.121) of the *Rig Veda*, in which each stanza ends with the questioning refrain, "Who is the god whom we should worship with the oblation?" Later Indian tradition was troubled by this open-ended refrain and invented a god whose name was the interrogative pronoun *ka* (cognate with the Latin *quis*), Who. This resulted in an affirmative statement ("Indeed, Who *is* the god whom we should honor with the oblation") somewhat reminiscent of the famous Abbott and Costello routine about the baseball team with players named "Who" and "What" ("Who's on first?" "No, Who's on second. What's on first").

But, if the gods existed, how many gods were there? The gods were often called "The Thirty-Three" (rather like The Three Hundred, the closed canon of blue-blooded families in New York), but one of the earliest Upanishads mocked this number with a dialogue in which, in response to the pupil's repeated question, "But how many gods *are* there, really?" the increasingly impatient teacher replies, first, "Three hundred and three, and three thousand and three," then, "Thirty-three," then, "Six," then, "Three," then, "Two," then, "One and a half," and, finally, "One" (*Brihadaranyaka Upanishad* 3.9.1). Significantly, all of these numbers are variants of "three" except for "two" and "one." And three remained the basis of further pluralistic constructions, though it continued to be challenged by the dualism and monism of the Upanishads.

Triads and Quartets: Squaring the Circle

The history of triads and quartets in Hindu intellectual history provides an armature for the ways in which Hindus attempted to coordinate two different realms, the singular and the plural (or, if you prefer, the transcendent and the immanent). The pluralists in this sense were usually plural in threes: three became a kind of shorthand for "lots and lots." These threes represented the multivalent, multifaceted, multiform, multi-whatever-you-like nature of the real phenomenal world.

The Indo-Europeans, in Georges Dumézil's formulation, saw the

---

3. See the full translation in *The Rig Veda: An Anthology*, translated and annotated by Wendy Doniger O'Flaherty (Harmondsworth: Penguin, 1981) 25–26.

world in threes, all of which were worldly, earthy, and nontranscendent. They divided that world into three social classes: kings/priests, warriors, and producers of fertility. In the Vedic period in India, one of the first recorded political coups took place: the kings were pushed down into the second class of what were thenceforth warriors-kings, leaving the priests (Brahmins) alone to rule the roost of the first class, with the commoners/workers still below both of them. To this basic triad other triads were soon assimilated, some of which were later to become quartets.

First, and perhaps most basic, is the triad of the three strands of matter, already paired with their transcendent fourth, spirit. The three strands or qualities of matter (the *gunas*) are lucidity or goodness (*sattva*), energy (*rajas*), and darkness or entropy (*tamas*). Together they are contrasted with spirit (*purusha*). This triad, which underlies many of the other triads that we will soon encounter, is fully expounded in Sankhya philosophy.[4] Indeed, as Gerald Larson has demonstrated, Sankhya abounds not only in triads, but in dyads and pentads.[5] The dyads include consciousness/materiality, unmanifest/manifest, cause/ effect, generative/generated, subtle/gross, merit/demerit, knowledge/ ignorance, power/impotence, and liberation/bondage. The triads include intelligibility/activity/inertia (Larson's translation of *sattva/rajas/ tamas*), intellect/egoity (*ahamkara*, "the sense of 'I'")/subtle elements, divine/human/animal-plant, satisfaction/frustration/confusion, and perception/inference/authority. And the pentads include the subtle elements (sound/touch/form/taste/smell), the gross elements (space/ wind/fire/water/earth), the action capacities (speaking/grasping/walking/ generating/excreting), and the sense capacities (hearing/feeling/seeing/ tasting/smelling).

The three qualities (*gunas*) may be contrasted or combined with the three humors of the body (*dosha*s: phlegm, bile, and wind); it is probably also significant that *guna* and *dosha* in combination mean "virtues and faults." Then one might mention the three Vedas (canonical scriptures); the three stages of life: chaste student, householder, and forest-dweller; the three goals of life (*purushartha*s, also called the triple path or *trivarga*): pleasure, profit, and religion (*dharma*); and the three

---

4. See Gerald J. Larson, *Classical Samkhya: An Interpretation of Its History and Meaning* (Santa Barbara, CA: Ross/Erikson, 1979).

5. Gerald James Larson and Ram Shankar Bhattacharya, eds. *Samkhya: A Dualist Tradition in Indian Philosophy*, volume 4 of *Encyclopedia of Indian Philosophies*, ed. Karl Potter (Delhi: Motilal Banarsidass, 1988) 86–95. See also Gerald James Larson, "*India through Hindu categories:* A Samkhya response," a review of the edition of *Contributions to Indian Sociology* of that title (23.1, 1989), in *Contributions to Indian Sociology* 24.1 (1990) 237–39.

emotions: desire, anger, and fear (or, in the Buddhist formulation, greed).

Other triads were never squared, such as the three debts that every man owed: study to the sages, funeral offerings to the ancestors, and sacrifice to the gods; the three worlds; mind, body, and speech; the unholy trinity of Brahma, Vishnu, and Shiva (a false construction, since Brahma was not worshiped as were the other two); the three times (past, present, and future); and so forth. And each of these triadic systems of classification may be applied on three major levels: the cosmos (divided into three worlds), the chain of being on earth (divided into various classes), and the human body (divided into various members). Thus the final book of *The Laws of Manu*, the most influential book of social law, composed in the first centuries of the Common Era, correlates the three qualities of matter with the three goals of life, with three kinds of bodily action (good, bad, and neutral), three bases of action (the mind, speech, and the body), the three times (past, present, and future), the three classes of gods, humans, animals, and so forth.[6]

McKim Marriott has reformulated these interrelated triads in terms of his own scheme of equivalences, which might be translated in gross terms (for his system is very subtle indeed) thus:
(1) Non-reflexive: fire (*tejas*) / bile (*pitta*) / energy (*rajas*) / pleasure (*kama*) / mixing and unmixing / dividuality
(2) Non-symmetrical: water (*ap*) / phlegm (*kapha*) / lucidity (*sattva*) / profit (*artha*) / unmarking and marking / hierarchy
(3) Non-transitive: wind (*vayu*) / wind (*vata*) / darkness (*tamas*) / irreligion (*adharma*) / unmatching and matching / disorder.[7]

Against these triads, or against the whole pluralistic vision regarded as a single system and assigned one pole of the new dichotomy, was set monism. For the Vedic world view was challenged by the renunciatory philosophies of the Upanishads and later Vedantic texts (as well as of Buddhism and Jainism), which were both sociologically and intellectually monistic. Sociologically, the renunciatory movements proposed a single, universal dharma (*sanatana* dharma), involving general moral precepts such as honesty, generosity, and nonviolence.[8] This was an overararching, unitary, nonhierarchical category of religion for everyone, a universal goal. (Later, this final goal was sometimes compared

---

6. Wendy Doniger, *The Laws of Manu* (Harmondsworth: Penguin Classics, 1991).

7. McKim Marriott, "Constructing an Indian ethnosociology," *Contributions to Indian Sociology* 23.1 (1989) 1–39.

8. Cf. the story of the two demons, Harikesha and Sukeshin, in Wendy Doniger O'Flaherty, *The Origins of Evil in Hindu Mythology* (Berkeley: University of California Press, 1976) 94–97, 128–31.

with that other universal goal, freedom.) Intellectually, they envisioned a single godhead. These ideas, which might have challenged the Vedic pluralisms of caste and pantheon, came instead to supplement them, by adding a transcendent fourth to the preexisting triads. Hinduism validated the plurality (and the hierarchy) of *dharma* by calling itself "the religion of the four classes and the four stages of life" (*varnashrama dharma*). But at the same time, it validated the unity of *dharma* by endorsing *sanatana dharma*.

Here I should make it clear that I am using the word "Vedic" not in its narrower sense, designating the *Rig Veda* and the texts dependent on it (which include the Brahmanas and the Upanishads and constitute what the Hindus call *shruti*), but in its broader sense, designating the subsequent Hindu tradition that defines itself (as Louis Renou and, later, Brian K. Smith have argued) by its allegiance to the Vedas (the tradition that Hindus call *smriti*).[9] In this broader sense, "Vedic" Hinduism (which developed into "Puranic" Hinduism when the encyclopedic texts called the Puranas were composed in the medieval period) may be contrasted with "Vedantic" Hinduism, which defines itself primarily by reference to the Upanishads (which are technically part of *shruti* but are called "Vedanta," literally, "the end of the Veda"). Though this side of Hinduism has its seeds in the Upanishads, it is fully developed only in the great commentaries on the Upanishads, particularly those of the Vedantic philosophers Shankara and Ramanuja, at the end of the first millennium of the Common Era.[10] So basic to these two systems is the principle of hierarchy versus nonhierarchy that they might best be characterized as cardinal and ordinal.[11]

Many, though not all, of the Vedic triads became quartets when later Hinduism added a fourth term, usually a transcendent Vedantic fourth. Even as early as the *Rig Veda*, the *Hymn of Man* (*purusha sukta*, 10.90) adds to the three Indo-European classes a fourth class, servants (Shudras), the outside class within society that defines the others (just as, later, Untouchables, entirely outside society, define Brahmins). The hierarchical distinction is clear: "Three parts rose above, and one remained below." Indeed, this distinction makes it possible to view the final combination not as a quartet but as a dualism: all of us (who are

---

9. Louis Renou, *The Destiny of the Veda in India*, ed. and trans. Dev Raj Chababa (Delhi, 1965); Brian K. Smith, *Reflections on Resemblances, Ritual, and Religion* (New York: Oxford University Press, 1989).

10. I owe this corrective to Gerald Larson. Indeed, the doctrines in question here owe so much to the philosophy of Sankhya that this school might better be called Sankhyan rather than Vedantic. I persist, however, in using the better-known term.

11. This is Gerald Larson's wise suggestion.

already given several names, such as Aryans or twice-born) versus all of them (the non-us, the Others).

Soon, too, there was a fourth Veda, the *Atharva Veda,* the book of magic. The Vedas continue to be regarded as a triad, and many Hindus to this day are named Trivedi, "Knower of Three Vedas." But they are also regarded as a quartet, and many Hindus to this day are named Chaturvedi, "Knower of Four Vedas."[12] And, caught up in the train of the Veda, other triads became fourths, often involving the concept of silence: to the three priests of the sacrifice was added a fourth priest who was merely the silent witness; to the three syllables of "Om" (a-u-m) was added the sound which is not heard; to the three Vedic modes of experience (waking, dreaming, and deep sleeping), was added the "fourth" (*turiya*) state, of merging into ultimate reality.[13]

The Vedantic shift away from sacrifice and worldliness is at the heart of all the additional fourths. To the three stages of life was added the fourth stage of the renouncer (Sannyasin), roughly corresponding to the Shudra, both inside and outside the system. To the three goals of life was added freedom, the goal for the renouncer. Again, we may regard this as more of a duet than a quartet, for freedom (*moksha* or *mukti*) comes to be contrasted with the rest of the group, the original immanent triad, called "enjoyment" or "consumption" (*bhoksha* or *bhukti*),[14] as asceticism is contrasted with enjoyment (*yoga* vs. *bhoga*).

The three paths to salvation (*marga*s)—*karma* (works, rituals), *jnana* (knowledge, meditation), and *bhakti* (worship, love, devotion)—at first remain a triad. But when we look more closely at it, we see that the group was originally constituted as a dualism mediated by a third term. The first term, *karma,* contains within it the worldly Vedic triad, equivalent to the three human goals and the three stages of life. In this sense it may be contrasted with the second term, *jnana,* that represents the transcendent Vedantic fourth. In order to round off the square, more precisely to paper over the conflicting claims of the original binary

---

12. In one sense, the Vedas as a class are intrinsically and definitively transcendent, and so this additional fourth, the inversion of the inversion, is *not* transcendent (it gives useful information on ways to make your wife's lover impotent, and so forth). But, on the other hand, when we realize that the Vedas are the basis of the sacrificial tradition that is *non*transcendent, the basis of the later worldly Hindu tradition of *dharma* texts and temple worship, we can see that as a group, including the *Atharva Veda,* they form one part of a new dualism, of which the second half, the nonworldly, transcendent, Vedantic half, is supplied by the later Aranyakas and eventually by the Upanishads.

13. See Troy Organ, "Three Into Four in Hinduism," *Ohio Journal of Religious Studies* 1 (1973) 7–13.

14. The verb *bhuj* designates the enjoyment or consumption of food, sex, experience, *karma,* or fuel (by fire).

opposition, a new term, *bhakti*, was introduced (by the *Bhagavad Gita* and other texts). In this way, a brand *new* triad was created, on the archaic model of the old triads, to solve, dialectically, the problem posed by a set of polar oppositions. But that very dualism (of *karma* vs. *jnana*, action vs. meditation) was originally composed of a triad (the three goals or stages of life) plus a fourth (the goal of freedom, *moksha*, and the stage of renunciation, *sannyasa*). Moreover, each member of the triad was regarded by its adherents as the best, if not the only, path to salvation. Finally, eventually *yoga* was added to the list as a fourth *marga*.

There are also some new quartets that never seem to have been triads, such as the four ages of time, or Yugas, which formed a quartet in ancient Greece, too,[15] and were apparently invented in Hinduism when four had already become the number of choice and had provided many quartets to which paradigm the four ages were easily assimilated. But the fourth age was always, from the start, entirely different from the first three: unlike the other ages, it is now, it is real. Thus the first three form one group (Eden, the Golden Age, the way it was *in illo tempore*) and the last item (the Kali Yuga) forms the other group (now, reality).

But then the square is circled again. Instead of remaining linear, as in Greece, time becomes both linear (fourfold) *and* cyclical (threefold), a Möbius strip: it declines and is reborn over and over again, as each successive doomsday undergoes its sea-change into each successive cosmogony. The four ages (from the Golden Age to the Kali Yuga) become three cosmogonic stages (creation, maintenance, and doomsday); the linear and worldly ages are combined into one whole polar element (an aeon, or *kalpa*) that is then set in opposition to another polar element: cyclical time, which is transcendent. *Pace* Mircea Eliade, in India it appears that history came first, to be later modified by the cyclicity of the eternal return. When keeping time in music, too, Indians count three "heavy" beats and a fourth "empty" beat.[16]

The idea of the cyclicity of time leads to the circle of *karma* and rebirth, which carries with it from the start the idea of escaping from that very circularity. First came the fear of re-death (the early version of the theory of *karma*), which led to the desire for freedom (including freedom from the values of Vedic Hinduism); then the ideal of freedom was reabsorbed into Vedic Hinduism, and inverted into the desire to be reborn, but reborn better in worldly terms (richer, fatter,[17] with more

---

15. Actually, Hesiod really has five ages, but that is another story.
16. See Joan Erdman, "The Empty Beat: Khali as a sign of Time," in *American Journal of Semiotics* 1.4 (1982) 21–45.
17. For worldly Hindus wisely believe that, *pace* the contemporary vogue, you can't be too rich or too fat.

sons, and so forth). This is the India of fabled elephants encrusted with jewels and temples covered with copulating couples, the world of sensuality from which the omphalosceptic yogis fled.

Indian tradition came up with, appropriately, four principle solutions to these conflicts between the one and the many, between a unitary *dharma* and a pluralistic *dharma*, between renunciation and the other three stages of life. Troy Organ suggests four rationalizations of his own and argues that "These four theories to account for movement from three into four in Hinduism—expanding, transcending, integrating, and polarizing—are related to each other in that strangely amorphous Hindu relationship which is often called 'tolerance' but which deserves a more descriptive label—perhaps 'harmonious opposition.'"[18] His four theories make sense of the theory from our point of view. I would like to suggest four, somewhat similar to his, that are expressed within the Hindu tradition itself.

First (roughly equivalent to "expanding"), it was said that the stages (or goals) were to be followed not simultaneously but seriatim. Freedom was made a fourth stage, often indefinitely postponed while theoretically extolled. Many Hindus prayed, with Saint Augustine, "Make me chaste, O lord, but not yet." But this trivialized the original claims of the renunciant philosophy, which were opposed to the other three stages altogether.

Second ("transcending") was the argument from symbiosis or plenitude: the two groups, worldly and transcendent, impure and pure, need each other to compose society as a whole. There are two forms of immortality, one through one's own children and one achieved through renunciation.[19] Thus Louis Dumont speaks of the renouncer whose holiness and knowledge are fed back into the society that supports him, and Jan Heesterman speaks of the paradox of the Brahmin, who must remain outside society in order to be useful inside.[20] But this is a self-contradictory situation.

The third solution was compromise (rather the inverse of "polarizing"), the stage of life of the forest-dweller or married ascetic, which proved unsatisfactory for a number of reasons, but basically because compromise is not a Hindu way of solving problems.[21]

18. Organ, "Three Into Four," 13.
19. Wendy Doniger O'Flaherty, *Shiva: The Erotic Ascetic* (New York: Oxford University Press, 1971) 76–77.
20. Louis Dumont, *Homo Hierarchicus* (Paris, 1967); *Homo Hierarchicus: The Caste System and its Implications*, trans. Mark Saisbury, Louis Dumont, and Basia Gulati (Chicago: University of Chicago Press, 1980); J. C. Heesterman, *The Inner Conflict of Society: Essays in Indian Ritual, Kingship, and Society* (Chicago: University of Chicago Press, 1985).
21. See O'Flaherty, *Shiva*, for a discussion of myths of forest-dwellers.

The fourth and most successful solution was identification ("integrating"), which came to replace hierarchy as Vedanta largely superseded Vedic thinking.[22] Thus it was said that the householder *was* a renouncer, if he played his role correctly, that *dharma* was freedom (as the god Krishna tells prince Arjuna in the *Bhagavad Gita:* do your work [of killing your cousins] well and you win the merit of renunciation). And now it was also said that one must have sons to achieve freedom. Tantrism (and Zen) took this line of argument to the extreme: thus, just as freedom=enjoyment (*moksha*=*bhoksha*), so, in the formulation of the Buddhist philosopher Nagarjuna, the world of rebirth (*samsara*)= the place or condition of freedom from rebirth (*nirvana*).

Categorizing the One and the Many

What do we learn from these texts? First, I think we learn that we have asked the wrong question when we ask why they combine categories that should be kept separate, such as the worldly and the renunciant. When the categories "don't fit" we are tempted either to dismiss them (calling them "inscrutable" or "illogical") or to romanticize them as conceptually incoherent.[23] But the recurrence of combined entities that *we* must categorize as contradictory should set off an alarm or a red light in our heads: if too many of *their* integral items do not fit into *our* categories, the categories, not the items, are wrongly conceived.

If they do not seem to regard the "dichotomies" between worldly and nonworldly as significant, what *do* they care to distinguish? The first answer that comes to mind is, "Not much." There is an astonishingly free flow of everything into everything. Yet the authors of these texts are the people who categorize *everything,* who anticipate and outdo the most obsessional structuralists in their need to impose arbitrary order on every conceivable aspect of human existence (positions in sexual intercourse, places where twists of hair may appear on the body of a horse, times of day when it is and is not advisable to eat yogurt). Why did they not impose similarly elaborate categories on the order of the universe?

In fact, they did, but we must look for *their* categories, not for ours, and then we will discover that they have other ways of drawing boundary lines. For example, where we have a tendency to distinguish mind and body or to regard mental qualities as mediating between

---

22. See Smith, *Reflections.*
23. See Wendy Doniger, "The Coherence of Manu," in the introduction to *The Laws of Manu.*

abstract and physical entities, Hindus tend to mediate these two polarized oppositions with the liminal category of speech: the acts that one can commit are mental, verbal, or physical (*manas-vach-sharira*), a distinction that is made also, for instance, in the Catholic formula of confession. A further complication is introduced when we realize that *manas* includes both the intellectual and the emotional functions and is therefore best translated not as "mind" but as "mind-and-heart." The plot further thickens when we recall that, on the other hand, *manas* is still part of the material world, *prakrti*, in contrast with spirit, *purusha*. For, ontologically speaking, mental qualities are, in the Hindu view, all physical, since they partake of the nature of the three material qualities (or *gunas*).

Yet it is significant that it is not only *our* categories that require the stipulation of liminal entities that do not quite fit the scheme; theirs do too. For example, faced with the problem of correlating the three qualities of matter with the four classes of society, one text, predictably, assigns lucidity to the priests, energy to the warriors, and darkness to the servants, but is forced to assign a combination of energy and darkness to the workers (Vaishyas).[24] For whatever their ways of distinguishing categories may be, the repetitions, the contradictions, the inconsistent and multiple attempts at enumeration, and the recurrence of liminal entities in their ontological schemes demonstrate that neither our categories nor theirs succeed in systematizing the permeable boundaries of the universe.

In Indian cosmologies, too, pluralism failed, and necessarily must fail: it is not possible to explain our experienced multiplicity in terms of an ideal *Ur*-unity.[25] The multiple layers in the cosmogonic accounts may have been designed to obfuscate the basic insoluble paradox of all cosmogonies: how to get from the postulated original state of nothing (nonmaterial and nonsexual), the one, to the presently experienced state of something (material and sexual), the many. Rather than simply confess, as in the old joke about the Irishman giving directions, that "You can't get there from here," the myth generates excessively complex directions, which amount, in the final analysis, to the instructions proposed in another joke: "How do you catch a lion?" "Catch two and let one go." To obscure the fact that one cannot explain the transition from the first condition to the second, the second is expanded with baroque

---

24. *Vishnu Purana, with the commentary of Shridhara* (Calcutta, 1972) 1.6.1–6.
25. Wendy Doniger O'Flaherty, "Ethical and non-ethical implications of the separation of heaven and earth in Indian mythology." In *Cosmogony and Ethical Order: New Studies in Comparative Ethics*, ed. Frank Reynolds and Robin Lovin (Chicago: University of Chicago Press, 1985) 177–98.

detail in order to make it seem that the transition from *illud tempus* to now has been explained, when in fact it has not been explained, and can never be explained.

Finally, we must recognize that various groups are already set out in a particular hierarchical order: like the pigs in Orwell's *Animal Farm*, all ontological categories are equal, but some are more equal than others. Thus, although the three goals of life (*purusharthas*) are often said to be separate but equal, there is a tendency for the textbooks of erotic love to give pride of place to pleasure, for political handbooks to privilege profit, and for *dharma* texts to rank *dharma* above the other two goals.[26] For the rococo lists were ultimately made hierarchical: not only are the four categories different, but one is definitely better than another. We can see the ways in which Hinduism deals with these hierarchies in the multilevel triads and quartets based on the social paradigm; hierarchy also explains the importance of the priest in cosmogonies, and the essential role played by the social classes in defining nature. The social or, more precisely, socioreligious element — the priest, the sacrificer, the human being in a particular class or stage of life — recurs in Hindu cosmogonies as a defining factor in the basic framework of the cosmos. The implications of this presence seriously restrict the apparently fluid pluralism that seems to pervade Hindu cosmogonies, and these intellectual formulations have social repercussions: those at the top often enforce their positions in dramatically intolerant ways.[27] Moreover, even Vedantic monism is elitist and hierarchical, rather than egalitarian; the Vedantic vision transcends the political world and leaves it intact.

Monism, Hierarchy, and Intolerance

Thus intellectual pluralism was supplanted by two different sorts of nonpluralism that determined the course of subsequent Hindu thinking: the monism of the Vedanta and the hierarchy of Vedic Hinduism. The two sorts of pluralism, sociological and intellectual, are *not* connected in the way that might seem most obvious and has indeed seemed obvious to many Orientalists and Western theologians. That is, ancient

---

26. See Friedrich Wilhelm, "The Concept of Dharma in Artha and Kama Literature," in *The Concept of Duty in South Asia*, ed. Wendy Doniger O'Flaherty and J. Duncan M. Derrett (London: Vikas Publishing House, for the School of Oriental and African Studies, 1978) 66–79.

27. See Brian K. Smith, *Classifying the Universe* (New York: Oxford University Press, forthcoming), for texts and arguments substantiating the social basis of Indian classificatory systems.

Hindu intellectual pluralism does not lead to ancient Hindu sociological tolerance.[28] One reason for this may simply be that Hindu intellectual pluralism did not ultimately carry the field. As we have seen, it was successfully challenged and overlaid by ancient Hindu monism, though both pluralism and monism continued (and continue) to exist cheek by jowl in uneasy symbiosis.

The pluralistic world, the world of Vedic ritual, was primarily orthoprax, not orthodox.[29] That is, it did not insist on doctrine (doxis) as long as ritual and social behavior (praxis) satisfied the standards of the particular group (usually a small caste group). It was intellectually pluralistic in that, in a manner still reminiscent of the *Rig Veda*'s kathenotheism, each sect acknowledged the existence of gods other than their god(s), suitable for others to worship, but did not care to worship them themselves. On the other hand, when it came to sociological pluralism, there was a further split: the orthoprax world saw all social roles as equally valid (from the God's eye view), and the world of action as cumulatively pluralistic, exemplifying a desirable plenitude.[30] Still, orthopraxy gave the *individual* no choice at all in his social role, no pluralism of action, though the hierarchy of values assigned to different roles might well have inspired the wish to make such choices.

The monistic world, by contrast, the world of philosophy, was primarily orthodox. That is, renunciant sects (including Buddhism and Jainism), monistic both sociologically and intellectually, were far less doctrinaire about the behavior of the layperson (though certainly not about the behavior of the monk, which was in many ways far more important) than orthoprax Hinduism was; but they believed that there was only one correct belief. Thus, unlike orthoprax Hindus, these sects proselytized—that is, they went around telling people that they were right and everyone else was wrong.

Later, the monistic view turned itself inside out to generate yet another sort of tolerance: it argued not only that all physical and immaterial things were one, but that all *religions* were also one, that Muslims and Christians really worshiped the same god that Hindus worshiped, but just called him Allah or Christ. This led to interesting misunderstandings when Christian missionaries fired their canons across the bows of South Asians. The Mughal emperor Akbar, for instance, was a true pluralist; born a Muslim but with a Hindu wife, he

---

28. See Frits Staal, "Über die Idee der Toleranz in Hinduism," in *Kairos: Zeitschrift für Religionswissenschaft und Theologie* 1 (1959) 215–18.
29. Ibid.
30. A plenitude that extends, ultimately, to a proposed solution to the problem of evil, or theodicy: cancer and moral evil must exist, to make the universe complete.

entertained a veritable circus of holy men at his multireligious salons. He flirted with Christianity to such a degree that the missionaries congratulated themselves that he was on the brink of converting—until they realized that he still continued to worship at mosques (and, indeed, Hindu temples).

Logically, this sort of universalism should have led Hindus to the belief that there was no point in trying to convert a Muslim to Hinduism, yet this was not always the case. Vedic, orthoprax Hindus certainly made no efforts to convert anyone to Hinduism, arguing that you had to be born a Hindu to be a Hindu. But Vedantic Hindus lapsed back into the shadows of orthodoxy and argued that *their* particular brand of monism was more monistic than thou. Such Vedantins went about proselytizing like mad. (Similarly, Krishna in the *Gita* allows that all other gods are aspects of himself, but still suggests that the *best*— quickest, most secure—way to God is directly through him.) It might well be argued that this sort of conversion is a form of intellectual violence commensurate with the physical violence of enforced behavior.

Medieval, Puranic Hinduism is a strange mixture of these two currents, which join but never merge, like streams of oil and water. Ritually, Puranic Hindus are Vedic, orthoprax. The fanatics among them kill people (such as Muslims) who do not respect the bounds of the caste system. Philosophically, some remain orthoprax/heterodox and view with disdainful tolerance the divergent views of other religions. Others, however, are philosophically Vedantic, orthodox, and correspondingly intolerant of deviant doctrines. This gives them yet another reason, exacerbating their orthoprax reasons, to try to convert (if not to kill) people like Muslims.

The Vedantic emphasis on nonviolence, *ahimsa*, that Gandhi made so famous in the West, is far from typical of Hindu thinking, let alone Hindu action. Of course, Gandhi did not invent *ahimsa*; Hindus—Vedic, pluralistic Hindus, as well as Vedantic Hindus—have sworn allegiance to the concept of nonviolence at least from the time of *The Laws of Manu*. But it may well be that such Hindus doth protest too much. Nonviolence became a cultural ideal for India precisely because it holds out the last hope of a cure, all the more desirable since unattainable, for a civilization that has always suffered from chronic and terminal violence. Nonviolence was an ideal propped up against the cultural reality of violence. Classical India was violent in its politics (war being the *raison d'être* of every king), in its religious practices (animal sacrifice, ascetic self-torture, fire-walking, swinging from hooks in the flesh of the back, and so forth), in its criminal law (impaling on stakes and the amputation of limbs being prescribed punishments for relatively minor offenses), in its hells (cunningly and sadistically contrived to make the punishment fit the crime), in its color schemes, and, perhaps at the very heart of it all, in its climate, with its unendurable heat and unpredictable monsoons.[31]

It is against this background that we must view the doctrine of nonviolence. Indian sages dreamed of nonviolence as people who live all their lives in the desert dream of oases. In *The Laws of Manu*, the two views, violent and nonviolent, are juxtaposed in an uneasy tension: there is a chain of food and eaters (dog eat dog, or, in the Indian metaphor, fish eat fish), which both justifies itself and demands that we break out of it: it happens, but it must not happen.[32] Wrestling with this same problem, five of the earlier Vedic sacrifices (animal sacrifices in which violence is assumed) become assimilated to the three debts and then are further transformed into (five) Hindu sacrifices (vegetarian sacrifices that avoid violence).[33] In this ambivalence, the Hindus are no different from the rest of us.

It was the neo-Vedantin idealists who gladly embraced the Gandhian hope that the Hindus might set an example for the human race in passive resistance. Their naïve self-image was encouraged by the liberal American transcendentalists (Thoreau was a great one for nonviolence and the *Gita*) and by their own desire to prove to the disdainful British that the Hindus were not the lascivious, blood-thirsty savages depicted in the colonial caricature. We can therefore see a kind of pizza-effect (a rather complex, Chicago deep-dish pizza-effect) in the contemporary Hindu investment in nonviolence: an ancient Indian idea was given new power by Indians (such as Gandhi) who had been influenced by Western thinkers (such as Tolstoi) who were acquainted with the neo-Vedantins, making these ideas more attractive both to Westerners and to Indians still living under the shadow of Western domination. But Gandhi was whistling in the dark.

Hindus were happy enough to boast about their own tolerance, and continue to do so. Recently a member of the Fundamentalist and anti-Muslim Hindu association, the RSS, remarked that, since Hindus are, as is well known, the most tolerant people in the world, they deserve to have the land of India to themselves, and therefore the (less tolerant) Muslims should be disenfranchised:

---

31. See, e.g., Nirad C. Chaudhuri, *The Continent of Circe: An Essay on the Peoples of India* (London: Chatto & Windus, 1965).

32. See the introduction by Wendy Doniger and Brian K. Smith, to *The Laws of Manu*. See also the conflict between sacrifice and nonviolence in Wendy Doniger O'Flaherty, *Other Peoples' Myths*, chap. 4.

33. *The Laws of Manu* 3.70, 73-74. See the analysis of this process in Smith, *Reflections*, 198-99.

The spirit of broad catholicism, generosity, toleration, truth, sacrifice and love for all life, which characterizes the average Hindu mind not wholly vitiated by Western influence, bears eloquent testimony to the greatness of Hindu culture.... The non-Hindu peoples in Hindustan ... must not only give up their attitude of intolerance and ungratefulness towards this land ... but must ... stay in the country wholly subordinated to the Hindu Nation, claiming nothing, deserving no privileges, far less any preferential treatment—not even citizen's rights.[34]

Here it is perhaps appropriate to recall that it was an RSS man who killed Gandhi.

The sort of pluralism that has prevailed in India was thus more of a multiplicity, often a belligerent multiplicity, than the mellow universalism that it has often claimed to be. Thus, for example, Hindus and Indologists often cite the story of Vishnu's incarnation as the Buddha as an example of Hindu tolerance. But a closer look at this myth reveals its true purpose: Vishnu became the Buddha in order to teach the wrongheaded doctrine of Buddhism to a group of dangerously pious demons in order to lead them from the Vedas, disarm them of their sacrificial merit, and kill them.[35] Certainly this particular brand of pluralism has not led to tolerance or nonviolence, nor was it able to diffuse the political and economic factors that, in India as everywhere else in the world, erupt in communal violence—in India, in the bloodbath of Partition. These same political and economic factors, enflamed and perhaps manipulated by the rhetoric of religious intolerance, have resurfaced in the incidents recorded in daily news reports: the killing of Hindus by Sikhs, Sikhs by Hindus, Hindus by Muslims, Muslims by Hindus, Tamil Hindus by Buddhists, Buddhists by Tamil Hindus, Untouchables by Brahmins, Brahmins by Untouchables, and on and on.

Conclusion: What's in It for Us?

Returning from this grim scene to the pluralistic optimism of David Tracy, we may ask again what a Western theologian stands to gain from an encounter with Indian pluralism. I'm sorry, David: if you had hoped to find in India the model for your gentle world of mutual understanding and tolerance, you had better look somewhere else. The world that the open-ended cosmogonies envision never existed except in the minds of people already shackled by the realities of social oppression

---

34. M. S. Golwalkar, *We or Our Nationhood Defined* (Nagpur, India: Bharat Prakashan, 1947) 48–49, 55–56.
35. See O'Flaherty, *Origins of Evil*, chap. 4.

and mutual hatreds. But perhaps we can learn from India's long and complex history of pluralism some of the pitfalls to avoid, some of the mistakes that we need not repeat. On the other hand, perhaps we can emulate some of India's successes, some of the ways in which individuals like Akbar or Gandhi transcended the cultural agendas that had bred as much violence as nonviolence.

We learn from the history of Hinduism that would-be pluralists must realize and avoid two dangers, that they walk a razor's edge between denying diversity and hierarchizing it. As for the first danger, the Hindu example suggests that, for those who hope to "enhance diversity" and celebrate plenitude, to create a world where difference is a value, the hypothesis of an original unity from which all religions derive may not be as useful as the hypothesis of an original and essential pluralism. The Hindu example shows us the perils of universalism and warns us that monism is the kiss of death. Granted, the universalistic hypothesis makes dialogue possible, for us as well as for ancient Hindus: it shows that all religions share some of the same problems. But there is then a danger of lapsing into the pablum world of Joseph Campbell, the Carl Sagan of religion, who cooks up the TV dinner of mythology so that it all tastes the same. We must take the harder but ultimately more rewarding path of cooking up our pluralism "from scratch," and go on to acknowledge that various religions offer rather different solutions to basic human problems and, indeed, that they also recognize different problems.

On the other hand, when we consider the second danger, it is evident that, although the rigid social system of ancient India does make possible a kind of pluralism in which various religions are acceptably different, as are men and women, blacks and whites, with complementary talents and weaknesses, it renders the other separate but unequal. This essential hierarchical modification of the democratic paradigm renders that social system unacceptable to us.

We need to be clear about what kind of pluralism we want. We need to ask where our definition of Otherness lies. And the Hindu experience may prove useful for this. We might, for instance, look at four steps that are sometimes postulated in the pluralist agenda and compare them with the parallels in Indian history—parallels that, being both shockingly extreme and shockingly foreign, might help us to see our own versions of those stages more clearly.[36]

Others exist.
This assertion may seem obvious to readers of this essay, but it is no

---

36. See O'Flaherty, *Other Peoples' Myths,* chap. six.

more obvious to many contemporary American Christians and Jews confronting Muslims (or Afro-Americans or gays or women) than it was to Brahmins confronting Untouchables. They may have heard that others exist, but they don't really believe it, for they have not experienced it.

We can live in a world where others exist without being harmed or threatened or changed.

This theorem has two corollaries: (a) We are safe from them and (b) they are safe from us. The first corollary in India led to the compartmentalization of the hierarchical caste system, with the injustices discussed above. The second corollary, with its implication of moral relativity, is easier to state than to act upon; it is challenged when the Other seems to be harming or threatening the rights of other Others (including, perhaps, ourselves).

The forced conversion of Hindus by Muslims during the Mughal period and the preferential treatment of Muslims by the British in later centuries were major sources of the Hindu intolerance of Muslims. People tend to fight when they fear they will lose something—a job, or a faith (hence the general observation that people who are secure in their own faith are usually more generous to people of other religions). This is a lesson well worth learning.

When we live in a world where others exist, we become better. We can reflect on what is other and use the other as a catalyst to our own creativity.

Hindus and Buddhists in the early period shared ideas so freely that it is impossible to say whether some of the central tenets of each faith came from one or the other (just as Picasso and Braque worked so closely together that they sometimes signed one another's paintings). So, too, the great poet and saint Kabir is a self-conscious conflation of Hinduism and Islam, as are many of the great Sufis saints. This is, I think, the ideal paradigm of pluralism.

We can be the other.

This can be taken passively, as a variety of monism: we can do nothing, and merely come to understand that all people are one, all religions are one. Or, taken actively, we can convert. Each of these options is, as we see from India, fraught with dangers. Monism, however passive, often conceals a submerged form of intellectual imperialism. Conversion can lead to new forms of fanaticism, often fueled by self-revulsion projected against the abandoned religion, the rejected self. To the extent that conversion argues, again, that one religion is better than the other, it is just the flip side of bigotry. We have seen this in Indian history, where the uneasy monism of the Veda gave way to Vedic and Puranic polytheism but then rebounded back into Vedantic monism.

Yet, finally, there is a positive lesson to be learned from India, too. For the ancient Indian pluralistic world represents an ideal—a myth—that was once available to Hindus and is still, perhaps, available to us. Indeed, it may now be truly available, potentially realizable, in the world for the first time. Perhaps ancient Indian religion is an idea whose time has now come. Teilhard de Chardin has taught us that the golden age is a myth not of the past but of the future. Perhaps now is the moment for theologians to create for the first time a world of religious tolerance *in illo tempore*, before the Fall, before the squaring of the circle.

PART FOUR
INTERRELIGIOUS DIALOGUE

16

DIALOGABILITY AND STEADFASTNESS: ON TWO COMPLEMENTARY VIRTUES

Hans Küng

IN VIEW OF the ever more urgent issues of interconfessional and interreligious ecumenism, I would like to reflect here on two basic virtues which appear to me central for the work of an ecumenical theologian, namely, dialogability and steadfastness. The theological work and the personal attitude of David Tracy in particular invite such reflection. To my mind, David Tracy has always been a man who combines dialogability with steadfastness in a very personal and exemplary manner. But it may still be worthwhile to ask how these virtues differ and how they are essential for ecumenical work, both intraecclesiastical and interreligious. At this point in time such a connection is by no means a matter of course. Actually, it is not even a matter of course that both dialogability and steadfastness can be declared "virtues" at all. First a word on the origin of the virtue "dialogability," which will be followed by a reflection on the meaning of "steadfastness" as a possible complementary "counter-virtue," supported by concrete examples from the interreligous dialogue.

Dialogability—A New Virtue

It is the nature of virtues that they change. Even the word "virtue" sounds odd these days. Thoughts of narrow-minded piety or bourgeois

---

This article is based on my reflections in *Theology for the Third Millennium* (New York, 1988) and in *Concilium* No. 183 (1986): *Christianity Among World Religions*, ed. Hans Küng and Jürgen Moltmann.

mediocrity spring to mind; at any rate, it has nothing in common anymore with the original Latin *virtus* and even less with the full-blooded Renaissance *virtù*. As everyone knows, there were some attempts made in history to find something like obligatory virtues: among them the cardinal virtues of temperance, fortitude, prudence, and justice; the three "divine" virtues of faith, hope, and love; or civic virtues such as diligence, obedience, discipline, and humility. However, systems of virtues have come and gone. (No one wrote better about *Wesen und Wandel der Tugenden* than the Tübingen philosopher Otto Friedrich Bollnow, as early as 1958.) None of these systems of virtues did true justice to the complexity of human life and human reality. Individual virtues likewise came and went. Who today would propagate humility, obedience, and diligence so uncritically and undialectically as great virtues? Who has not seen through the course of history the extent to which such virtues frequently turned to vices?

The reverse happened as well: new virtues emerged, old ones returned in a new guise. Thus, "humility" in the guise of self-criticism and realism, "obedience" in the guise of nonopportunistic loyalty to one's own convictions, "diligence" as untiring social commitment. Yet this means at the same time that much of what is being actually practiced by countless people as attitudes toward life and intellect has not yet been recognized as a "virtue." New generations are already living basic moral attitudes that have taken the place of former virtues in an anonymous fashion.

Dialogability is such a *misunderstood, anonymous virtue*. Relatively young historically, it could only emerge and succeed on ground that was socially and intellectually prepared. True, there was "dialogue" and people able to dialogue in former centuries too, and yet dialogability as a modern basic virtue presupposes, from a political point of view, a modern democratic society and thus the basic inner attitude of striving for a fair balance of interests with the corresponding opponent, an attitude oriented toward standard procedures and rules. Consequently, dialogability presupposes the realization of modern, enlightened ideals such as freedom, autonomy, and tolerance and hence the inner readiness to accept the other as someone whose opinion will be respected down to the last dissent (thus also protecting "dissenters") and to correct one's own standpoint where necessary.

Dialogability is therefore a deeply *democratic virtue* which can only survive under the umbrella of a positive intellectual, cultural, and religious pluralism, under the reign of liberty, equality, and fraternity. With this programmatic slogan of the French Revolution we have the same situation as with dialogability as a modern basic virtue. There was liberty, equality, and fraternity in former years too, but as a basic demand encompassing all spheres of life, the demand for liberty, equality, and fraternity is typically modern. The same applies to the virtue of dialogability.

The political *effects* of this virtue have an impact similar to the slogans of the French Revolution. Any regime, be it ecclesiastical or political, which is based on the absolute power of an individual or an oligarchy, a party or hierarchy, any regime that monopolizes truth with the help of juridicism, centralism, or triumphalism is essentially incapable of dialogue. The tactics of survival may necessitate dialogue for a while, but it will never reach the roots of self-understanding; if it did, these systems of power would collapse like a house of cards. Therefore, dialogability is intrinsically a virtue *critical of power and dominion* and is actually feared by all spiritual and secular potentates just as holy water is feared by the devil. Why? Despots and potentates cannot tolerate their opposites as partners, only as subjects. Dialogue for them is equivalent to weakness; willingness to communicate means self-degradation. The price of such a relationship, which is built on command and obedience, is speechlessness. Those leading a dialogue do not want to impose their will on others; they do not perceive others any longer as a threat, but as an enrichment to life, not as competitors but rather as partners. Actually, how many crises, catastrophes, and human miseries could have been avoided, had this virtue of dialogability not been continuously kicked about?

The reality in our Christian churches and also among the world religions is still far away from the ideal of a "religiousness open to dialogue," of an "ideal communication community." Nevertheless, much has been achieved in our "age of dialogue," which measured in historical terms should not be diminished. But it only happened because all these men and women held doggedly to their objective of communication and always gave dialogue a chance. Let us not forget one thing: dialogability between Christian denominations in the twentieth century sprang from a terrible *common history of suffering*; it took its strength from the experience of a bloody period of mutual laceration and from a brutal history of suppression by fascist rulers. Dialogability will stay alive as a virtue only so long as the history of suffering of peoples and nations is not repressed from memory.

Since the Second Vatican Council, which met under the keyword *aggiornamento*, the Catholic Church has irrevocably taken the path of dialogue: dialogue with its Protestant and Orthodox sister churches; dialogue with the "world," with science, art, and ideologies; dialogue with Judaism and other world religions; dialogue with "society" with a view to its commitment to the underprivileged, suppressed, and outlawed. In doing so, the church has shown its willingness to learn and to adjust itself. It has started to cope with its own history of injustice, to overcome ecclesiocentrism and to relativize Eurocentrism. It had to take a stance for liberation, human rights, and social justice; above all, it had to learn that it is not the sole possessor of Christian truth but, together with others, is on the way to it. Therefore, the virtue of dialogability requires insight into the *historicity of truth* and the relativity of *one's own standpoint*. Claims of infallibility, no matter who raises them, are hardly compatible with such a virtue.

Steadfastness—An Almost Forgotten Virtue

Historicism or even the relativity of truth? One can sense that the demand for dialogability will lead to an issue of principles, which has not yet been sufficiently considered. Those engaging in interreligious dialogue must sooner or later face this issue. Dialogability as a virtue? Might it not be misused as an alibi for a cosy indifference, for a surrender of firm convictions, a sellout of commitments at give-away prices? Is the capacity for dialogue in itself sufficient to be credible? Does it suffice to want to have a dialogue "about everything" and "with everybody," without showing any commitment, any standpoint, any steadfastness in the dialogue oneself? Does not the capacity for having a dialogue presuppose that I and my partner have a standpoint worthy of dialoging about? Could it possibly be that the person who has abandoned everything is not really capable of dialogue, but only the one who still holds up the truth of his own standpoint?

What is meant by "steadfastness"? Surely no moralizing perseverance, no stubbornness of the this-way-and-no-other sort; surely no rigid adherence to antiquated positions, no narcissistic love of dear old habits. What then? A search in popular theological or philological dictionaries is disappointing: There are satisfactory explanations on dialogue and dialogability, but nothing or only a few lines on "steadfastness." Even more up-to-date psychological, pedagogical, or sociological dictionaries do not find it necessary to waste any further thoughts on this term. Yet the "turnabout" of a politician, the "yielding" of a boss, the "weakening" of a judge is considered anything but a virtue. In politics and public life a "standing firm," "standing up," "standing fast" is asked for, desired, requested: firmness as against turning or weakening, quite simply and generally "steadfastness" as a basic attitude and virtue, which will enable one to stand fast in any given situation against temptations or pressures.

As distinct from dialogability, it is quite easy to recognize an old classic virtue in steadfastness. In the classical teaching of virtues it would have been found alongside the cardinal virtue of *fortitude*.

Indeed, already the Greeks (*andreia* in Plato or Aristotle, also *karteria* in the Stoa) and the Latins (*fortitudo* in Cicero and Macrobius) covered a whole range of words with the term "fortitude": from a quite passive form of acceptance and endurance, via resistance and perseverance, to rather more active forms of decisive tackling and altercation. The New Testament does not know concepts like *andreia* or *karteria* directly, but there are definitely corresponding concepts: hope (*elpis*), constancy (*hypomonē*), patience (*makrothymia*), founded in trusting faith (*pistis*). Thomas Aquinas then emphasized fortitude as a specifically moral virtue and called it steadfastness for the sake of the good, as proving oneself in the difficult tasks, dangers, and miseries of life: "firmness of mind (*firmitas animi*) in enduring or repulsing whatever makes steadfastness outstandingly difficult; that is, particularly serious dangers" (*Summa theologica* II-II, q. 123, a.2.)." Therefore, steadfastness is another name for fortitude, just as civic courage would be another name for it today. But whereas civic courage relates more to individual acts in the political and social sphere, steadfastness as a fundamental spiritual attitude determines the whole life of a person.

Even more closely related to modern steadfastness is *constantia*, the classic virtue of the Romans, which, however, is mentioned only once in the Latin New Testament: in Acts 4:13 for the *parrhesia*, the "constancy," of Peter and John. *Con-stare* means to stand fast, to preserve a firm attitude, to remain steadfast, constant, faithful to oneself, consequent. *Con-stantia* means a firm attitude, direction, constancy, steadfastness and, implicitly, also stability, perseverance, consequence, persistency, intrepidity, courage. Thomas Aquinas, who transforms ancient Roman virtues to the Christian model, sees in *constantia* (and in the related *perseverantia*) a subvirtue of fortitude: "To continue firm in the good," "persistendo firmiter in bono" (*Summa theologica* q. 137, a. 3), against inner weariness and temptation and also against external difficulties and obstacles. This virtue enjoys a central place not only in Calderon's *The Constant Prince* and the classic dramas of Corneille but even in the "Be constant!" of Mozart's *Magic Flute*.

Therefore, in this context steadfastness is related to *resistance* to external powers and the powerful: to self-assertion, not giving in, persevering with courage, decision, power of performance—all this with the objective of the individual's freedom and responsibility. Seen from the classical tradition, steadfastness is not a rigid or static but dynamic reality which proves its worth in the processes of life. Not in vain was courage always linked for the ancients with high-spiritedness, generosity, and broad-mindedness. All this is based for Christians upon their belief in God and in him whom God has risen from the dead, who being weak and powerless has been appointed *Kyrios* and *Christos* by God himself.

But does not precisely such a faith conviction render a dialogue with other persuasions of faith impossible a priori? Does not such steadfastness in faith block serious dialogue between religions? More concretely put: If one believes in Christ as the way, the truth, and the life, can one also accept that there are other ways, other truths, another life that emerge out of transcendence? Can one, therefore, combine openness and truth, plurality and identity, dialogability and steadfastness in the interreligious dialogue? The main issue in any interreligious undertaking is precisely this: Is there a theologically justified way that allows Christians to accept the truth of other religions without relinquishing the truth of their own religion and thus their own identity? Some further reflections on this, although concise, may help us to perceive the problems more clearly and envisage a constructive solution.

Four Unsatisfactory Standpoints

1. The *atheist position* must always be considered in any interreligious dialogue. It holds that no religion is true or that all religions are equally untrue! Who would contest that this is the conviction of millions of people on earth, and therefore a view that must be taken seriously? Yet one argument should be considered here: our pure, theoretical reason, which is bound to this world, does not reach far enough to definitively reject the question whether in reality religion corresponds to a nothing or to an absolute. Saying yes to an original motive, support, and reason for the world and human beings, as assumed by the great religions, is not a matter of strict proof but of rational trust, for which there are many good reasons.

2. The *absolutist position* has been the official Catholic one for a long time and is still adhered to today with vehemence in Protestant fundamentalist circles. In this instance dialogue is actually superfluous, since it holds that only one religion is true and therefore that all other religions are untrue! Yet one should consider the following: Since the Second Vatican Council even the Catholic Church no longer adheres to the dogma of the Fourth Lateran Council (1215) and the Council of Florence (1442) that "outside the Church there is no Salvation," although this has never been openly corrected. On the Protestant side, it is still a moot point even with the World Council of Churches whether non-Christians can achieve salvation, although this would correspond to God's general will of salvation and the positive statements on the heathen world which can be found in many passages of the Bible. Even

the great Karl Barth felt compelled in the last volumes of his *Church Dogmatics* to accept "other lights" (which do not belong to the Christian revelational world) beside the "one light" (Jesus Christ).

3. The *relativistic position* also makes dialogue superfluous in its own way. It holds that every religion is true and therefore that all religions are equally true! Here again, let us stay sober: People who really know religions will hardly contest the fact that they are all equal, especially when considering the different basic types of religion, namely, mystical, prophetic, or wisdom religions. Recourse to a religious (mystical) fundamental experience, alleged to be the same everywhere, does not solve the question of truth either, since every religious experience is, a priori, an interpreted experience and therefore determined by the corresponding religious tradition and its various forms of expression.

4. The *inclusivistic position* seems to solve all problems. It holds that one religion is the true one but that all religions share in their own way in the truth of the one religion! But here again one must pose a further question, both with regard to the Indian variant (all religions represent merely different levels of a universal truth) and also with regard to the Christian variant (all willing and well-meaning religious people are "anonymous Christians"): Does this not in actual fact debase the other religions to a lower or partial cognition of truth? Does this not elevate one's own religion from the start to a super system which is slipped over all other religions, thus raking them into the net? Actually, what looks like tolerance proves in practice to be a sort of conquest by hugging, an integration by relativization and loss of identity. What would be an alternative?

The Critical Ecumenical Standpoint

Catchwords like "indifferentism," "relativism," and "syncretism" are frequently brandished against interconfessional and interreligious dialogue. I, too, reject the indifferentism, relativism, and syncretism that are void of any clear standpoint. But if one wishes to link steadfastness and dialogability, one might be able to paraphrase the ecumenical position as follows: Instead of indifferentism, where everything is indifferent, what is demanded nowadays is more *indifference* to alleged orthodoxy, which makes itself the measure of the salvation or calamity of people and tries to push its claim to truth by means of power and force. Instead of relativism, which does not know an absolute, what is demanded is a greater sense of *relativity* vis-à-vis all human enunciations of the absolute, which prevent a productive coexistence of the various religions, and also a greater sense of *relationality*, which views every religion in an interrelated network. Instead of syncretism, where all sorts of things are "mixed together," amalgamated, what is demanded is a greater will toward *synthesis* of all confessional and religious opposites, antagonisms which still cost blood and tears daily, so that there may be *peace* among the religions instead of war and strife.

Put differently: in view of all religiously motivated intolerance, not enough tolerance and religious *freedom* can be demanded. No betrayal of freedom for the sake of truth! But also the reverse applies: No betrayal of *truth* for the sake of freedom! The issue of truth must be neither minimized nor sacrificed for the utopia of a future world unity and a uniform world religion. Such a stance would rightly be regarded by the Third World, where the colonial past and the related missionary past are by no means forgotten, as a threat to their own cultural religious identity.

In my view, we as Christians are challenged to reflect afresh on the question of *truth* within the spirit of a Christian based *freedom*. For contrary to arbitrariness, freedom does not simply mean freedom from all commitments and obligations, as in a purely negative sense, but it also means positive freedom *for* new *responsibility*: toward our fellow human beings, ourselves, the absolute. True freedom is therefore a freedom for truth. However, that means in a self-critical fashion. A Christian does not own a *monopoly of truth* either, nor the right to renounce the *confession of truth* in the form of an arbitrary pluralism. Dialogue and witness are not mutually exclusive. The confession of truth includes the courage to recognize an untruth and to broach the subject. Today we know better than ever that the boundary between truth and untruth runs straight through our respective religions. Criticism of other positions can only be tolerated therefore on the basis of strict self-criticism. Only by doing so can an eventual integration of the values of other traditions be justified. That means: *not everything is equally true and good in the various religions*. There are things that are neither true nor good in the doctrines of faith and morals, in religious rites and customs, institutions and authorities. This applies naturally to Christianity as well.

From the necessity of differentiating between true (good) and false (bad) religion in all religions results the urgency of an *interreligious criteriology*, which can only be briefly considered here. According to a general ethical criterion a religion is true and good if and insofar as it is humane, does not suppress and destroy, but rather protects and promotes, humanity. According to a general religious criterion a religion is true and good if and insofar as it remains truthful to its own origin or canon, hence truthful to its authentic "essence," the decisive scripture or form to which it continuously refers. According to a specifically Christian criterion a religion is true and good if and insofar as it reveals in its theory and practice the spirit of Jesus Christ. This criterion can be applied *directly* only to Christianity, on the basis of the self-critical question whether and to what extent the Christian religion is Christian at all. The same criterion can certainly and without presumption also be applied *indirectly* to other religions: for the critical clarification of the question whether and to what extent we can find some of the spirit we call Christian also in other religions (Judaism and Islam, specifically).

The Specifically Christian Criterion

What is preached today as a "brand new" doctrine often proves to be an old teaching in the spirit of Protestant liberalism, which truly heard God speak "also" through Jesus Christ and his message, but which had abandoned the normativity and "finality" of Jesus Christ, going so far as to level him to the rank of a prophet "together with others" (Christ together with other religious figures or other revealers, saviors, Christs), thus losing all criteria for a discernment of spirits in the process. The protest of Karl Barth and "dialectical theology" (including Rudolf Bultmann and Paul Tillich) turned rightly against such liberalism. Going back is not progress.

The theologian who does not wish to give up the normativity and finality of Jesus Christ does not do so primarily for the reason that only with Christ as critical catalyst can the other religions adapt to our "modern technological world," but for the reason that otherwise the central statement of all those scriptures that constitute the New Testament would be abandoned. Whether it is convenient or not, Jesus Christ is *normative* and *definitive* for the whole New Testament. He alone is the Christ of God (the oldest and shortest creed of the New Testament: *Iēsous Kyrios*); He alone is "the way, the truth, and the life."

If one sticks to this two-thousand-year-old conviction of faith, without fear or apologetic interests, but for good reasons—just as Jews, Muslims, Hindus, and Buddhists stick to theirs—it is not at all the same as a theological "imperialism" and "neocolonialism," which denies the other religions their truth and rejects other prophets and revealers. We must distinguish between viewing religions from the outside and viewing them from the inside (or whatever this may be called), if we wish to avoid the basic pitfalls of absolutistic-exclusivist or relativistic-inclusivist positions. Only in this way does a differentiated answer to the question of the truth of the religions become possible.

Viewed from the outside, from a science-of-religions point of view, there are, of course, several true religions, which, however ambivalently, correspond in principle at least to certain general criteria (both ethical and religious); several ways to salvation (with several saviors) toward one goal, which overlap if only partially and which at any rate can fertilize each other. Viewed from the inside, from the standpoint of a believing Christian oriented by the New Testament—which means for me, as a concerned, challenged human—there is only one true religion, Christianity, insofar as it testifies to the one true God as he revealed himself in Jesus Christ. The one true religion by no means precludes truth in other religions, but it is able to acknowledge other religions as true with reservations or *conditionally true*. As far as these do not directly contradict the Christian message, they may actually supplement, correct, or deepen the Christian religion. Therefore we must ask:

Where Does Dialogability Lead Without Steadfastness?

What consequences would a dialogue have without normative feedback to one's own tradition? Formulated like a thesis, the answer can only be thus: (1) Those who would renounce the normativity of their own tradition, basing their considerations on the indifference of the various "Christs" (Jesus, Moses, Muhammad, Gautama), presuppose as a result something that would not necessarily be desirable even after a long process of agreement. Such a method appears to be aprioristic. (2) They expect of the non-Christian partners in dialogue what most of them reject: to give up a priori their belief in the normativity of their own message and savior and to adopt the typically Western, secular-modern standpoint of the basic indifference of all paths. Such a path seems unrealistic, because it would be literally naïve to demand that a Buddhist give up the normativity of Buddha (his way and his doctrine), that a Jew give up the normativity of the Torah, or that a Muslim that of the Koran. (3) They then expect Christians to reduce Jesus Christ to a temporary Messiah and to give up the conviction of faith, based on and required by the New Testament, that the normative and definitive Word of God is given through Christ—they would do this in favor of ranking Jesus Christ among the other revealers and saviors (*Kyrios Iēsous* on a par with *Kyrios Kaisar* or *Kyrios Gautama*). On the basis of the New Testament, such a standpoint would have to be called non-Christian—even if no one should be accused of heresy. (4) They classify the various leader figures paratactically side by side, as if they were not historically interdependent in part (such as Moses and Jesus, or Jesus and Muhammad) and as if they did not have a completely different value within their own religion (how different is the position of Moses in Judaism, of Jesus in Christianity, of Muhammad in Islam, and of Gautama in Buddhism). Such a viewpoint seems unhistorical.

In practice, all this means that those adopting such a standpoint as Christians or non-Christians run the danger of willy-nilly distancing themselves from their own religious community, even giving up something essential for their own religion. However, for the dialogue between the religions it is of little help if some Western and Eastern intellectuals agree on an "interreligious" plane. What I already hinted at at the beginning of these reflections now becomes finally clear: Actually, no dialogue would be needed if there was nothing normative or definitive anymore in anyone's religion. Put differently: the virtue of dialogability needs the virtue of steadfastness (not statically but dynamically understood). Both virtues belong together.

Where Does a Dialogue Based on Steadfastness Lead?

Those who adhere to their own tradition, but at the same time are open to other traditions, start with what there is and leave totally to the course of the conversation and understanding what will finally emerge as a result and—to quote here just the Christian–Muslim dialogue as an example—what will be said in the final analysis about the relationship between Jesus Christ and the prophet Muhammad, a clearly a posteriori approach. They allow their conversation partners from the beginning their own religious standpoint and expect from them initially just the unconditional readiness to listen and to learn, an unrestricted openness which entails a transformation of both partners during the course of the communication process, a patient, realistic approach. They profess from the beginning their own religious conviction that Jesus is the Christ for them, normative and definitive, but that they recognize the function of, say, Muhammad as a genuine (post-Christian) prophet and that they will take his "warning" regarding the deviation in christology from belief in one God very seriously, a self-critical Christian standpoint. They view the various traditions, their original messages, and their saviors within their context and in their proper place (for example, the position that Jesus Christ holds in Christianity is not that held by Muhammad in Islam, but rather by the Koran), so that a differentiated vision of interlinking traditions becomes possible: despite its religious anchorage, a strictly historical approach.

In practice this means that Christians or non-Christians adopting such a basic attitude will be able to combine religious commitment and willingness to communicate, religious loyalty and intellectual integrity, plurality and identity, dialogability and steadfastness. They will preserve a critically reflective contact with their community and at the same time try not only to interpret things freshly within their own and other religious communities but to bring about changes with a view to a growing ecumenical community. The fundamental attitude of true ecumenicity knows neither an aggressive attitude toward those of a different opinion nor an escape from decisions; it knows neither a dogmatic fight nor the neutralization of all standpoints. The fundamental attitude of true ecumenicity is that of "steadfastness": holding fast in faith to the Christian issue, unbribable and without fear of reprisals. Guided by a similar basic attitude, a few Catholics and Protestants, settled in their own faith, rooted in their traditions and yet self-critical, started to communicate with each other over half a century ago and thus by the very fact of remaining faithful to their own religious communities, they changed themselves and others, and in time also the two church communities. It is hoped that a similar evolution will take place among the world religions, albeit over longer periods of time.

Dialogue in Steadfastness

Have I worked out the differences between the two methods too crassly? Perhaps. In practicing dialogue many things should be simpler, and I am sure that many Christians will agree to the following: (1) We should no longer want to pursue our own Christian way, stolidly dogmatic and uninformed about other ways, without understanding, tolerance, and love for others. (2) Neither should we, in disappointment at our own way and fascinated by the novelty of another, change over to other ways. (3) Finally, neither should we externally add what we have learned from other religions to the old belief. (4) Instead, out of a truly Christian commitment and in continuous eagerness to learn, we should transform ourselves ever new on our own way; we should let ourselves be transformed by the newly learned, so that the old belief will not be destroyed but enriched. This is "the way of creative transformation" (John Cobb), the way of the Christian faith as challenged by the ecumenical commitment. Are we thus faced with a completely new task? By no means.

Did not our predecessors in the old church do the same, the apologists and the Alexandrians Clement and Origen, when they came across the Neoplatonic Stoic ways and had to work out a theology in the ecumenical paradigm of the ancient church? Did not Augustine and Thomas, when confronted with a new Roman-Germanic world, have to undergo a process of transformation when they had to reconsider theologically the way in and through the Middle Ages for a Western Latin paradigm? Did not Luther and the Reformers have to change when during the great crisis of medieval theology and church a reconsideration of the old evangel had become necessary?

The Christian churches have lost a lot of credibility when faced intensively with the world religions for the first time in the modern paradigm, during the age of belief in science and technology, colonialism, and imperialism. The time has come in our postmodern, postcolonial, polycentric age to start afresh with the dialogue between Christianity and world religions.

Let us now summarize: How about dialogability and steadfastness? Already the ancients knew that virtues always indicate the middle of two extremes, of what is too much and what is too little. "Dialogability" indicates this mean, between a monopoly of truth on the one hand and an arbitrary pluralism on the other. Therefore, "steadfastness" as a complementary "counter-virtue" is always included. Put differently: Only those are truly able to dialogue who are able to bring in a standpoint and know how to defend it until convinced of the contrary. Only when keeping up the strife for truth will dialogue not decay into a mere discussion technique. But the reverse is true, too: Those who think they have definitively solved the question of truth or wish to push it on to others through an aggressive attitude are incapable of dialogue.

In the final analysis dialogability becomes a virtue of capability for peace. In this it is deeply human, because it knows its history of failure. Whenever dialogues were cut off, wars would break out in the private and the public domain. Where conversation failed, reprisals would start and the club-rule of the more powerful, superior, or crafty would reign. Those leading a dialogue will not shoot, which means (when translated into religious-ecclesiastical language) those committed to dialogue will not have recourse to disciplinary measures in their own church or religion—and all religions, Christianity in particular, have a history of intolerance, persecution, and war on heretics. Those committed to dialogue have the inner strength to put up with the dialogue and to respect the standpoint of the others, where necessary. One thing is certain. The intolerance to dissent which again and again breaks out in all religions everywhere in the world has understood nothing about a virtue of dialogability. And yet, the spiritual, perhaps even physical, survival of all of us will literally depend on this virtue. We must not only be capable of dialogue, dialogue in steadfastness; we must also be ready for it.

Translated by Marianne Klein

17

TOWARD A HERMENEUTICS OF INTERRELIGIOUS DIALOGUE

Claude Geffré

PLURALISM IS NOT ONLY an intrinsic dimension of our historical experience; it has become one of the major features of our religious experience. Indeed, it can be readily seen that, throughout the centuries, every religion was able to accommodate a number of diverse attitudes and interpretations. This applies not only to the phenomenon of religion itself but also to the investigation of ultimate reality and ways of human salvation. David Tracy, whose work has been largely concerned with plurality and ambiguity as features of our modern historical consciousness, insists that religions are even more pluralistic than art, ethics, philosophy, or politics.[1] One could refer to the different interpretations of ultimate reality offered by the various religions: for some it has to do with a personal God, whereas for others it is a matter of the impersonal Absolute or, indeed, of the Void. At the same time, one can view religion as the salvific way through which one is brought beyond the prison of the Self into harmony or union with the mystery of Reality.

Nonetheless, if we are to talk of pluralism as a peculiar feature of contemporary religious experience it certainly cannot be in terms of whatever plurality there exists within each religious tradition, nor of the plurality of presuppositions and interpretations of each individual religion. It is more a matter of actual coexistence in the absolute commitment to, respect for, and understanding of these religious traditions as diverse ways to the Absolute. It is still not clear, however, whether

---

1. D. Tracy, *Plurality and Ambiguity: Hermeneutics, Religion, Hope* (San Francisco: Harper & Row, 1987) 86.

we can reconcile total engagement or the authentic faith of each religious tradition with the notion of dialogue and openness to the truth of the other religions. Pluralism has become a challenge to all the world religions, and this challenge is crucial for any religion that regards itself as absolute and universal by virtue of its appeal to divine revelation.

In what follows I would like to consider the question of interreligious dialogue from the point of view of Christian faith. First, it will be necessary to explain a number of theological principles which are able to clarify the relationship between Christianity and the other religions. Later I will show why interreligious dialogue *in general* does not exist: the relationship between the faith of Christianity and the faith of each of the other religions remains the appropriate criterion for judging either convergence or divergence. Finally, it remains for us to ask ourselves what is *peculiar* to Christianity as one religion among a plethora of world religions. For the first time in centuries, the post-Vatican II church has come to respect and esteem the great religious traditions of humankind. Immediately, however, a number of questions arise: What is it that is unique in Christ's mediation between God and humankind? Why is it that we still speak of Christianity as the one true religion? Should we not admit that all religions see themselves as divinely revelatory and salvific? And the question put to Christianity is also that of every great religious tradition: How can we sustain a non–a priori concept of dialogue while at the same time being deeply entrenched in our own identity?

Theological Foundations for Interreligious Dialogue

Christian Tradition and Christian Experience

It is necessary to remind ourselves of the golden rule of all theological hermeneutics. Interpretation can hardly be called Christian if it does not involve a mutually critical correlation between the foundational Christian experience, witnessed to in the writings of the New Testament and transmitted through the tradition, and contemporary historical experience.[2] To speak of critical correlation means that it is impossible to reread the Christian tradition in abstraction from our contemporary historical experience. On the other hand, how can we

---

2. On the method of Christian hermeneutics, in addition to the well-known works of E. Schillebeeckx and D. Tracy, see my *Le christianisme au risque de l'interprétation* (Paris: Cerf, 1983). Eng. trans. *The Risk of Interpretation* (New York: Paulist, 1987).

understand our present historical experience if we ignore the whole of the Christian tradition, which itself forms the basis of our language and culture? Far from being its master, we belong to language, and it is only through language that we can understand the effects of history, whether consciously or unconsciously, which condition our ways of thinking and imagination. This is particularly important when it is a question of the relationship between Christianity and the other religions, for we are always tempted to project our own foundational categories onto other religious systems. This is especially true of the word "religion," whose meaning has been fatally restricted to its Western Christian usage.

Twentieth-century Christian theology has been deeply affected by the atheistic Enlightenment critique of religion. It is, moreover, becoming increasingly clear that we must tackle the challenge of religious pluralism—itself an indication that we have already entered postmodernity. This corresponds to a development in Western culture that cannot be viewed solely in terms of either atheism or religious indifference but must also be viewed in terms of what one could call the "fullness" of religion—a return to the sacred, an increasing interest in philosophies other than those of the Mediterranean basin, especially those of the Far East. In regard to this new dimension of interreligious dialogue, one could well speak of a "planetary ecumenism." This expression is not out of place inasmuch as interreligious dialogue coincides with a heightened awareness of the unity of the human family, together with a sharpened awareness of religion's communal responsibility for the future of the human being and her/his environment. It would be absurd to think that this new version of ecumenism, which has been spreading worldwide, renders secondary or out of date that other version of ecumenism to which we are more accustomed—that is, inter-Christian dialogue.

It would be nearer the truth to say that it was the ecumenical dialogue that began more than fifty years ago which shattered that particularly Roman Catholic absolutist model, and which gradually encouraged dialogue between the Roman Catholic Church and the other two monotheistic religions, as well as with the major religions of the East. The Council document on the relations between the church and the non-Christian religions (*Nostra Aetate*) enshrined this new beginning, and the meeting of world religious leaders gathered in Assisi for a World Day of Prayer for Peace, on 27 October 1986, was a kind of consecration of this new revolutionary openness. In a sense we are still only on the verge of ecumenical dialogue; we need time to change our old ways of thinking and begin to understand that frank and open dialogue does not necessarily lead to a false ecumenism—that is, religious indifference. And just as ecumenism cannot any longer be considered to be merely a matter of ecclesiology, but is rather a necessary dimension to all theological reflection, so also must religious pluralism become more and more the horizon of all Christian theology. Moreover, from the point of view of interreligious dialogue we can identify a number of features of classical theology that have been thoroughly revised. I am thinking especially of the theology of *salvation* together with the theology of *mission*. To what extent can one reconcile believing in Jesus Christ as the only mediator between God and humankind with the conviction that the other religions may also be "ways of salvation" for those who follow them? On the other hand, the goal of mission is no longer a matter of the salvation of men and women from eternal damnation by virtue of their entry into the visible church, but of witnessing to the kingdom already accomplished in Jesus Christ, which itself can happen only in history and in the hearts of men and women, while at the same time respecting the great religious traditions of humankind.

The Bible and Religious Pluralism

It is in the light of our actual experience of interreligious dialogue that it is necessary for us to reread our foundational scriptures. It is well to note here that the Bible as such is of little use in helping us to discover the significance of religious pluralism in the divine plan. Like religious traditions themselves, cultural diversity is essentially ambiguous (think of the myth of Babel) in regard to the unique divine plan for humanity. Religious diversity may well be a manifestation of the limits, the development, and the fallenness of the human spirit tempted by the evil spirit in history (Vatican II, *Lumen Gentium*, 16). But it may also very well be the expression of the spiritual "riches" which have been distributed by God among the nations (Vatican II, *Ad Gentes*, 11). Finally, the Bible does not reveal to us God's judgment on religious pluralism. This is why Karl Barth considered all theology of the non-Christian religions to be illusory and even blasphemous. Religious pluralism is for us a historic destiny, allowed by God, the meaning of which is beyond us. Yet as John Paul II suggested in his speech on the spirit of Assisi on 22 December 1986 the program for interreligious dialogue which had been recommended and promoted by the Second Vatican Council can be justified only if it does not interfere with the plan of God. Other religions can be considered to be less important than this unique plan.[3]

3. See *Documentation catholique*, no. 1933 (1 February 1987).

In the New Testament itself, one can find some statements that at first sight seem difficult to reconcile. On the one hand, there is the basic affirmation of the universal salvific will of God, which extends to all men and women since creation. On the other hand, all the New Testament texts insist that there is no salvation apart from an explicit knowledge of Jesus Christ. The universal salvific will of God and the uniqueness of Christ's mediation must be the two incontrovertible principles for any hermeneutics of interreligious dialogue. This is precisely why Paul affirms in the same text that "God desires all to be saved and come to the knowledge of the truth" and that "There is one God, and there is one mediator between God and humans, Jesus Christ, who gave himself as a ransom for all" (1 Tim 2:4–6). And in Acts 4:12 it says: "There is no other name given . . . by which we must be saved."

Our interpretation of texts must take into account our experience of an ineluctable pluralism. This is also the case if we are to take seriously the testimony of the ecclesial tradition. This is why it is useless to invoke, for example, the extremely harsh verdict of the church fathers in regard to the many religions and cults of their time, which they tended to consider to be inspired by the devil, while they were ready at the same time to recognize the "seeds of the Word" in the philosophical wisdom of the pagans. This particular theme, very rich theologically speaking, allowed Justin, Clement of Alexandria, and Origen to think in terms of the veritable presence of God in the universe of "nations," while they continued to treat pagan practices and beliefs as incompatible with the true religion. Our historical experience is radically different, and it is hard for us to imagine what would be the attitude of the early church fathers to such religions as Islam or to the great religions of the East, which they hardly knew. Rather, we must ask whether the theology of the "seeds of the Word" does not remain one specific way of thinking of the positive value of the non-Christian religions without, at the same time, impinging on the normativity of Christian revelation. In any case, this is the main orientation of what has become known as inclusivism within Catholic theology in the years 1950–1960, and which was sanctioned in the Vatican II document *Nostra Aetate*. The Roman Catholic Church "rejects nothing that is true and holy" in the non-Christian religions:

> She has a high regard for the manner and conduct, the precepts and doctrines which, although differing in many ways from her own teaching, nevertheless often reflect a ray of that truth which enlightens all men. Yet she proclaims and is in duty bound to proclaim without fail Christ who is the way, the truth and the life (John 14:6), in whom God reconciles all things to himself and in whom men find the fullness of their religious life. (*Nostra Aetate*, 2)

The Council did not go so far as some contemporary theologians do in considering other religions as genuine ways of salvation, but it did recognize that they, despite their errors and shortcomings, and subject to purification and proper discernment, could nevertheless be considered as *pierres d'attente* or as a *praeparatio evangelica* in the total mystery of Christ.

The Meaning of Religious Pluralism

A Christian hermeneutics of interreligious dialogue is not really a question of the salvation of those huge numbers of men and women who, through no fault of their own, have been born and died outside of the Christian way of salvation. Rather, it inquires into the *meaning* of religious pluralism within the divine plan and seeks for a reconciliation between Christianity's particular claim to truth and the other religious traditions—all of which are considered ways to the Absolute. The really pressing question is whether, given our greater awareness of the relativity of the Chrisitan religion and our increased knowledge of the world religions, we can overcome several stereotypical judgments and prejudices.

The difficult and hazardous task for a hermeneutics of interreligious dialogue, therefore, consists in our being able to hold together an awareness of the ineluctable plurality of the different ways toward God without at the same time compromising Christian identity. Because they remain concerned solely with the question of salvation, some Catholic and Protestant theologians view the new theologies of religions as unnecessary on the grounds that classical theology had always accounted for the possibility of salvation for all right-minded persons.[4] This is precisely to confuse the *theology of salvation of the heathen* with the *theology of religion*. It is not enough to appeal to the principle of good conscience according to which someone, even in a state of genuine ignorance, can be saved; nor is it advisable to compare members of the other religions with unbelievers in general. One must consider the other religions in terms of their own history, independently of the subjective intentions of their members, and ask whether they possess "salutary value." It would indeed be a rash theologian who would consider the non-Christian religions to be the *means of salvation* as such. Nonetheless, we can at least see them as "means of grace" or even "sacraments of salvation."

This insistence on the historical specificity of the religions assures us

---

4. J. Moingt, "La recontre des religions," *Études* (January 1987) 97–110.

that, from the perspective of interreligious dialogue, we cannot speak of religions in an abstract manner by putting them all in the same boat. One must deploy a *typology* of religion in an effort to respect the originality of each. In order to avoid a hasty apologetics, which consists of viewing the other religions either as corruptions or as prefigurements of the only true and absolute religion, hermeneutics needs the objectivity of a science of religion. Thus, for example, the Christian theologian makes a distinction between the great religions such as Hinduism and Buddhism, and then between the great monotheistic religions such as Judaism and Islam. Judaism will always enjoy a privileged position insofar as it inaugurated the salvation history which Christ completed. The status of Islam offers difficult questions for Christian thought. Just as one cannot compare it with the Eastern religions of immanence, neither can one graft it onto the pure olive tree of Israel. Personally speaking, I have become more and more convinced that despite its astonishing ignorance of Christianity Islam has a special relationship with salvation history insofar as it can legitimately claim to be descended from Abraham. As a *wild* branch, it has at the same time been living off the roots of both Judaism and Christianity; and some people are ready to concede that according to the providential will of God it will adopt a prophetic mission in regard to Judaism and Christianity—namely, by confirming the primitive faith of Israel in the uniqueness of God against all forms of idolatry. But at the same time I remain convinced that the confession of belief in the One God by all the sons and daughters of Abraham does not authorize us to speak of a unique monotheism. In fact, we have three specifically different forms of monotheism. For this very reason it is hard for us to understand the words of John Paul II in his speech delivered at Casablanca on 21 August 1985: "We [Christians and Muslims] believe in the same God." The declaration of *Nostra Aetate* (no. 3) is more nuanced and more cautious: "The Church regards with esteem Islam which worships the One God, living...."

The Dialectic of Faith and Religion

A hermeneutics of interreligious dialogue must distance itself from the dialectic of faith and religion which has dominated twentieth-century theology (Protestant and Catholic) since Karl Barth. The overly disjunctive separation between faith and religion leads to those a priori negative judgments concerning even the most valuable aspects of the non-Christian religions. It must not be forgotten that Christian faith is always incarnate in "religion"—a phenomenon that must be explained in terms of a sociology of knowledge. It is dangerous to underestimate a whole aspect of the Christian tradition already referred to above—namely, the course of the patristic tradition, which emphasizes that, besides the history of salvation beginning with Abraham and culminating in Jesus Christ, we must recognize the presence of the Word and the Spirit of God in human consciousness. The Lutheran theologian G. Siegwalt writes:

> We challenge that distinction introduced by Karl Barth between faith and religion insofar as he identified the latter with idolatry and who characterised true religion as faith and not as religion. It is clear that according to our definition of religion, faith is always religious and that religion is always faith.[5]

Accordingly, Karl Barth advocates the case for the exclusiveness of Christianity for the reason that Christianity is the only revealed religion of grace, whereas the other religions are "attempts by man to justify and sanctify himself before God."[6] Yet the Pauline distinction between grace and works is not a satisfactory hermeneutical key when comparing one religion with another. In fact, every religion, including Christianity, may be at once a religion both of *grace* and of *works*. One could go so far as to say that a religion is true only insofar as it is a religion of grace, and that religion is somehow distorted and false if it is considered to be only a religion of works. It is therefore not possible to exclude in an a priori manner non-Christian religions as not being religions of grace. In any case, a comparison between Christianity and other religions can be made only by treating them as religions of works—that is, at the level of ritual, institution, and doctrine. If, in order to know the relationship between humanity and the mystery of God, one takes into consideration that which is most authentic in religion, one cannot then establish so easily a hierarchy or even a comparison between the religions. The domain of grace is, by definition, totally unobjectifiable.

Moreover, it could be said that the negative attitude to the non-Christian religions held by some Protestant theologians has been conditioned by the New Testament understanding of the religion of Israel as a religion of the law and of works only—a view no longer tenable today. Jesus' condemnation was primarily directed at a party within Judaism and could in a sense be considered a caricature of Judaism. It is only

---

5. G. Siegwalt, *Dogmatique pour la catholicité évangélique* (Paris: Cerf; Geneva: Labor et Fides, 1987) 151.
6. K. Barth, *Church Dogmatics* (French trans.; Geneva: Labor et Fides, 1954) vol. I, II, chap. 2, s. 3, ss. 17, p. 71.

when Judaism absolutizes the law and becomes legalistic that it becomes subject to the judgment of the gospel. In reality, the law was always subject to the gospel and one cannot deny that Judaism, as a religion of covenant and election, was a religion of grace.[7] It is erroneous to compare the non-Christian religions with the religion of Israel—if the latter is considered a religion of works as distinct from the new covenant notion of religion as grace.

Roman Catholic theology of religions has been searching for ways by which such exclusivism could be overcome. It has dispensed with a narrow ecclesiocentrism (remember the famous expression "Outside the Church there is no salvation") in favor of a christocentrism. More exactly, we do not refer to Christianity in superior or exclusivist terms in relation to the other religions, and thus we recognize an inclusive uniqueness in it. Instead we should speak of an *inclusivism* in relation to what is called the theology of *l'accomplissement* developed before and during the Council by such theologians as Y. Congar, H. de Lubac, and K. Rahner. It is not merely a matter of affirming that persons of goodwill can achieve salvation in the other religions; one must also concede that the world religions can assume the role of *praeparatio evangelica* for those men and women who have not yet met Jesus Christ.[8]

This view is being challenged by a number of theologians who view this inclusivist position as a form of Christian imperialism insofar as it sees everything that is true, good, and holy as implicitly Christian. (This is the criticism leveled at Karl Rahner's notion of the "anonymous Christian.") We should attempt a reconciliation between a christocentrism and an even more radical theocentrism in accordance with which the world religions will appear as differing human responses to the one divine reality. We need not question the unique mediation of Christ as the source of grace to recognize the other religions as "distinct ways of salvation" (cf. H. Küng). The permanent vocation of the church is to reveal and to promote the kingdom of God, begun at creation, which will continue in the future in the religious history of humankind beyond the visible structures of the people of God.

For some theologians, especially those deeply rooted in the religious traditions of the East, this position is too conservative. The exigencies of interreligious dialogue require nothing less than a Copernican revolution in the theology of religions. Beyond exclusivism and inclusivism

---

7. Siegwalt, *Dogmatique*, 114–15.
8. See C. Geffré, "La théologie des religions non chrétiennes vingt ans après Vatican II," *Islamo-christiana* 11 (1985) 115–33.

it is largely a matter of adopting a pluralistic theology of religions.[9] Clearly, this means that we must abandon the Ptolemaic, traditional view that all religions move around Christ and Christianity as their center and accept that all religions, including Christianity, are centered on the Light which is the mystery of God as ultimate reality. Practically speaking, this requires that we move beyond a "theocentric model" while at the same time holding on to the normativity of the event of Jesus Christ in interreligious dialogue.

I do not think this is possible without compromising the very identity of Christianity, which through the centuries has always insisted on the uniqueness of Christ's mediation as the definitive and normative revelation of the face of God. The first necessity of interreligious dialogue—as indeed in every dialogue—is a faithfulness on the part of each participant to his or her deepest being. Why then will only a radical theocentrism be able to deal with the exigencies of interreligious dialogue? It seems, then, that only a more thorough examination of christology will provide more fruitful means of holding together the dialectic of genuine religious pluralism and Christian identity. In accordance with the patristic tradition, one could consider the economy of the incarnate Word as the sacrament of a much larger economy—that of the eternal Word of God which has resonances within the religious history of humanity. This idea need not necessarily lead to a disastrous separation between the eternal Word and the created Word. I would not go so far as to say, as R. Panikkar does, that the historical Jesus does not exhaust the Christ-Logos, but I think it would be appropriate to say that the humanity of Jesus of Nazareth does not exhaust the mystery of Christ in his eternal preexistence as God and as human. Nonetheless, one of the basic prerequisites of any meeting between Christianity and the other religions is learning not to confuse the universality of Christ as Word become flesh with the universality of Christianity as a historical religion. We must avoid making Christianity an absolute religion which could absorb everything that is valuable in the other religions. This is precisely to fall victim to the type of relativism and liberalism which states that Christ is but one mediator among others between the Absolute and humankind.

Finally, the task of a hermeneutics of interreligious dialogue consists in learning how to think of the absolute as a relational absolute and not

---

9. This particular theological position is associated with the Anglican J. Hick and the Roman Catholic P. Knitter: see J. Hick, *God and the Universe of Faiths* (New York: Macmillan, 1973); idem, *Problems of Religious Pluralism* (New York: Macmillan, 1985); P. Knitter, *No Other Name?: A Critical Survey of Christian Attitudes toward the World Religions* (Maryknoll, NY: Orbis Books, 1985).

as an absolute of either exclusion or inclusion. We must try to conceive of Christianity as a *relative* reality, not in the sense that *relative* is the opposite of the absolute, but rather in the sense of relation in which we can have mutual understanding between the religions. The truth witnessed to by Christianity is neither exclusive nor inclusive of every other truth; it is relative to whatever truth there is in other religions. Referring to the uniqueness of Christianity as a relative uniqueness rather than that of superiority or integration does not involve a compromise between the absolute identity of Christianity and the other religions. A limiting principle exists which is inherent in faith itself and which leads to a "pratique cordiale de l'altérité" in the dialogue between the religious traditions.10

The Criteria and Concrete Forms of Interreligious Dialogue

As in every dialogue, interreligious dialogue allows for the consciousness of personal identity and the recognition of the otherness of the conversation partner. In the case of Christianity and the other religions, respect for those who believe differently is not based solely on the dignity of the other, but rather on theological principles which we can summarize briefly. On the one hand, the Christian is aware that all persons are under the aegis of the creative and redemptive Word (John 1:1–4). On the other hand, one also knows that the different religious traditions are a part of God's mysterious plan (*Ad Gentes*, 3, which refers to the religious events through which in various ways one looks for God; or *Lumen Gentium*, 16, which states that "the religions reflect a ray of this truth which enlightens all men"). And in his speech to the Roman Curia following the meeting at Assisi, Pope John Paul II was not slow to affirm that "every genuine prayer is inspired by the Holy Spirit who is mysteriously present in the hearts of every person."11

Having explored the complex theological questions involved in the dialogue between Christianity and the other religions, it is fitting to inquire more precisely into the criteria for assessing the convergence between the religions as well as the different levels of interreligious dialogue.

---

10. S. Breton, *Unicité et monothéisme* (Paris: Cerf, 1981) 157.
11. *Documentation catholique*, no. 1933 (1 February 1987) 136.

An Analogical Imagination

Just as it would be absurd to declare—under the pretext of openness—that all religions are essentially equal, so also would it be contrary to the rules of dialogue to lay down a hierarchy among religions with Christianity as the absolute. We must demonstrate an "analogical imagination," as referred to by David Tracy: that is, while recognizing distinctions, we must discern similarities or at least convergences.[12] This is why the theologian, in order to be more critical of his or her own presuppositions, needs the objectivity of a science of religion. If not, he or she risks succumbing to the temptations either of syncretism or a cryptoimperialism. With regard to syncretism, one might be tempted to consider everything that is noble and true in the other religions as preparatory for Christianity; in regard to imperialism, one is equally tempted to regard the unfamiliar or unusual aspects of the other religions as distortions of true religion, namely, Christianity. In his book *Le génie du paganisme*, Marc Augé emphasizes the extent to which the spirit of paganism is radically different from Christianity: "The ideological imperialism of the missionary . . . largely consists in viewing local beliefs either as an aberration or a prefiguration of true religion."[13]

The main feature of Christian ecumenism is the search for unity in diversity, which can be extended to a fraternal dialogue between the world religions. But this principle can be verified only in an analogical way; and, as has already been pointed out, it is important not to confuse interdenominational ecumenism with interreligious ecumenism. In the former, every church must question its pretensions to being the absolute church nothwithstanding its belief in the absoluteness of Christ. Essentially, the Christian churches proclaim the same faith in Christ and in the triune God, and unity can be restored only if each of them renounces its claim to be the true church to the exclusion of the others. In the case of interreligious ecumenism, the other religions not only question the claims about the absoluteness of Christianity but even of Christ. This is why, at the level of doctrine, dialogue between Christianity and the world religions is so difficult.

In identifying and respecting divergence, the real question is about finding ecumenical criteria for convergence. This can happen only by attending to each religion in turn. We must begin by distinguishing the kind of dialogue between the three monotheistic religions from the

---

12. See D. Tracy, *The Analogical Imagination: Christian Theology and the Culture of Pluralism* (New York: Crossroad, 1981).
13. M. Augé, *Le génie du paganisme* (Paris: Gallimard, 1982) 64.

more extended dialogue between the main world religions—the kind of dialogue symbolized so well by the meeting at Assisi. Although Christianity is a trinitarian monotheism and is radically different from the two others, it does share a common heritage with both Jews and Muslims insofar as all three believe in "One God, living and subsisting, merciful and all-powerful, creator of heaven and earth, and who has spoken to man." We must remind ourselves, however, that in the past the monotheistic religions were more intolerant of each other and of other religions than the great pagan religions were. Even if they share belief in a creator God, they still appeal to an absolute truth as the spoken Word of God recorded in a book.

Accordingly, belief in a personal God is not a criterion that automatically favors interreligious dialogue. One can go deeper into the matter by appealing to the anthropological criterion of *homo religiosus* (Mircea Eliade) as testimony to the reality of all genuine religion. Each religion is concerned with the quest for ultimate Reality, whether that Reality is conceived of in terms of a personal God or not. In any religion, we can identify a fundamental faith (consider Paul Tillich's ultimate concern or "that which concerns us unconditionally," which at the same time serves to designate faith as fundamental reality and God as ultimate reality) and then a collection of beliefs which have to do with specific truths and rules for life. Ultimate reality can, as in the biblical tradition, be about a personal God; the transcendent absolute of Hinduism; the hidden source of things (Brahman), which coincides with the secret force in the Self (Atman); or indeed the Void, as in Buddhism. Religions resemble one another insofar as they share a fundamental faith; they are distinct from one another by virtue of fundamental disagreements in matters of belief.

Finally, while it may be true that each religion has its own criteria of truth, which are not necessarily shared by the other religious traditions (revelation, sacred books, myths, etc.), it may still be possible to find a criterion of consensus at the ethical level which might well correspond to a universal human consciousness. Whatever the plurality of ethical systems, the human community shares a number of "basic convictions" which have been subject to systematic codification such as the "rights of human beings." At this stage in the twentieth century, more than forty years after the Declaration of the Rights of Man in 1948, I do not think I am exaggerating in saying that the more *inhuman* aspects of religion must be either condemned to die or be transformed. We can at least get rid of the negative criteria in our investigation of whether, according to either its rituals, institutions, dogmas, or ethics a religion violates the dignity of the human person and contradicts the more legitimate aspirations of human conscience.[14]

Degrees of Dialogue

Interreligious dialogue never exists in the abstract. It must adhere to the different criteria of the religion concerned. Our own historical experience has shown us that there are at least three types of encounter or three degrees of dialogue between the different religions. First, there is that silent dialogue in prayer, in which each religious tradition calls on its own spiritual experiences. In this regard, the Meeting at Assisi was the supreme expression of what could be called a "planetary ecumenism" between the world religions. One could say that it is not so much a question of communal prayer as of a meeting where the representatives of the main world religions gather together to ask for the peace that exceeds human capacity. Prayer is more universal than belief in a personal God. Some religions are reluctant to refer to ultimate reality as transcending the universe. Yet in and through prayer all religions witness to a supreme reality transcending the finitude of men and women and the limitations of their history. And genuine prayer does not exist without some kind of conversion of the heart—a commitment to nonviolence which by degrees has become the seed of peace for the international community. Throughout the centuries the various religions—and particularly the monotheistic religions—have often been associated with violence, fanaticism, intolerance, and human conflict. Yet if Jews, Christians, Muslims, Hindus, Buddhists, and others gather together to pray for peace, we can truly speak of a revolution, a revolution attesting to the fact that the Spirit of God has not abandoned the main world religions.

Second, the interreligious dialogue which garners the insights of each religion contributes to the making of a better world as well as to the

---

14. In relation to this basic consensus one could refer, for example, to the statement of the *Conférence Mondiale des Religions pour la Paix* held in Kyoto in 1970: ". . . we have realized that the things which unite us are more important than the things that separate us. We discovered that we have in common: the certainty of the fundamental unity of the human family; the equality and dignity of all human beings; the respect for the individual and his/her conscience; the awareness of the worth of every human community, that power is not in itself a right; that human power is not in itself sufficient and is not absolute; the faith in the fact that love, compassion, self-denial and sincerity are ultimately more important than hate, enmity, and selfishness; the commitment to siding with the poor and the oppressed in their struggle against the rich and the oppressor; the great hope that good will finally triumph.

promotion of world peace. Despite a number of encouraging signals—for example, the *détente* between East and West—the situation within the world continues to challenge the historical consciousness of every religion. The crisis of confidence of contemporary humanity in regard to the future arises from both its enormous power and its egotism. This crisis is only too clearly to be seen in the realms of justice, peace, and nature. It is the injustice of the structures of the international economic situation that give rise to the poverty of millions of men and women, the increasing indebtedness of the Third World countries, together with the dramatic phenomena of emigration and unemployment. Such political, racial, and religious conflicts may account for the millions of refugees especially from Africa and Asia. It is also the exorbitant power of modern technology that accounts for our anxiety about the biological future of humanity and its environment.

On the eve of the third millennium, this situation of our consciousness of ourselves as "planetary" beings offers a challenge to the various religions. We can seriously question whether any religion can call itself a "world religion" if it does not espouse universal human aspirations, namely, the struggle for justice and the promotion of peace. It is precisely the aim of interreligious dialogue to promote the conversion of each religion to its own inner being. In each of the great religions, there is an awareness of the need to go beyond its own particular ritualistic, institutional, and dogmatic limits. Are the various religions in fact prepared to renounce their own particular interests, their will to power, their obsessive traditional cult in order to serve humanity in its totality? The prophetic words of Jesus are still a permanent guide for every religion: "man was not made for the sabbath, the sabbath was made for man."

The World Conference of Religions for Peace, which has been in existence since 1970, is just one of those privileged places where this interreligious dialogue is taking place. In taking part in and encouraging this dialogue, as was the case in the last general assembly at Melbourne in January 1989, the Roman Catholic Church, in accordance with the teachings of Paul VI and John Paul II (both of whom have been tireless in their struggle for justice as integral to the Christian mission) was aware of its obligations toward this particular dimension of its mission. To recall an idea close to the heart of John Paul II one could say that the future of the great religious traditions follows the path of humanity.

There is, finally, a third type of dialogue—a more ecumenical one wherein each religion is confronted with the particular beliefs and deepest spiritual experiences of the other. Clearly, this is the most difficult type of dialogue since it concerns those religious systems which are most difficult to reconcile. Yet only such a dialogue will enable us to overcome the centuries-old ignorance and prejudice concerning the other religious traditions. At the same time, it invites us to understand better the originality of the message to which we witness, and it encourages us to look for the God beyond God—that is, to go beyond those inadequate conceptualizations through which we attempt to grasp God. Thus, this dialogue concerned with discerning the truth leads us into a mutual conversion. In the experience of dialogue, we discover that we cannot establish either intellectually or existentially the truth which we claim. Conversely, my partner in dialogue may arrive at a different understanding of his or her religious truth. This means that there can be no genuine dialogue without human community or a communal celebration of the truth which transcends it. John B. Cobb has clearly shown us how a non–a priori dialogue between Christians and Buddhists would lead to a *mutual transformation* of both religions.

> The Christianity which will be transformed by incorporating the Buddhist understanding of reality will be very different from any form of Christianity with which we are already familiar. Buddhism which incorporates Jesus Christ will be very different from the Buddhism that we know. This will not erase the difference between the two religions; rather, it will offer a new basis for a renewed dialogue and an unprecedented transformation. All those entrenched positions will gradually begin to disappear.[15]

The dialogue between the three monotheistic religions is well under way, and we are not in a position to prejudge its efficacy in finding a new understanding which every religion has of its specific traditions. Ought we to speak of a mysterious complementarity between the three prophetic religions as we await the kingdom of God? We are well aware of the extent to which the historical association between Israel and the Christian churches is an important theme in both Christian and Jewish theology. On the other hand, we can see how much the critical challenge of an intransigently monotheistic Islam urges us to clarify our fundamental doctrines of the incarnation and the Trinity. Conversely, the Christian understanding of the Bible as the Word of God never ceases to put important questions to Muslim fundamentalism.

Within this dialogue between Christianity and the great religions of the East we must accept that we must proceed slowly and experience that diversity and even that strangeness before we begin any hasty engagement in the search for possible convergences. With regard to

---

15. J. B. Cobb, *Bouddhisme, christianisme: Au-delà du dialogue?* (French trans.; Geneva: Labor et Fides, 1988) 78–79. English: *Beyond Dialogue: Toward a Mutual Transformation of Christianity and Buddhism* (Fontana Press, 1982).

those religions that could be considered religions of the One, which do not distinguish ultimate Reality and the reality of the self and world, it is undoubtedly the case that biblical revelation introduced something radically different to the understanding of God, to the relation between God and humanity, and to the privileged relationship between God and history. We must never forget, however, that at the core of the monotheistic religions, and especially Christianity, there has always been both a mystical and a theological element (consider negative theology), which has attempted to overcome an excessive anthropomorphism in the dialogical relation between the created "I" and the divine "Thou." In its widest theological sense, prayer attests to an original unity which is more radical than the outward relations between the Creator God and the created self. Meister Eckhart has testified in a profound and bold manner to this ultimate quest by human interiority. He even claims that "If I did not exist, God would not exist anymore." As indicated by the title of his famous sermon, it is a question of humanity's becoming free of everything including God: "Why we must be freed even of God himself."

"The freedom from God himself," about which Eckhart speaks, introduces a more radical theme and brings the question of gratuitousness to its logical conclusion. It is that of *death* as an expression of overflowing love. This theme is entirely in keeping with the notion of Christianity as a religion of the paschal mystery. But it also has universal implications: only through death does humanity encounter in prayer the ultimate reality of the universe. In speaking of the paschal dimension of prayer as a more radical expression of the gratuitousness of love, we are reminded of a basic human phenomenon underlying every spiritual experience—notwithstanding the infinite diversity within the religions. Prayer affirms that one does not define oneself only by needs and the satisfaction of these needs; one is also defined in terms of desire and the overcoming of desire: the quest for the Ultimate.

The Distinctiveness of Christianity

Whether we are dealing with the question of solidarity in the creation of a more just world or with fraternal discussion of this particular ideal, the new interreligious dialogue does not necessarily lead to apathy or a lazy syncretism. All of the world religions have gained a better understanding of their historical responsibilities toward the human condition and society. Yet even in the effort to make this dialogue more fruitful they cannot ignore the paradox of their own religious message. In attempting to be relevant to the world, the world religions risk becoming no more than ideologies in the service of human liberation and the transformation of the world. It is rather by being faithful to their own origins—that is, by witnessing to a *fundamental faith* in a supreme Reality beyond human experience—that they better serve the future of humanity.

Nonetheless, by contrasting their own particular customs and practices with those of historical humanity, the religions are invited to examine themselves seriously and to ask themselves whether their beliefs, rituals, and customs contradict that basic trust in the worthwhileness of existence by contemporary men and women, together with the real yearning for happiness and freedom. Thus, it is clear that we cannot interpret the texts of a tradition without constant reference to the practices inspired by such texts. Whether it is a question of a reciprocal emulation of each religion or a direct confrontation between one tradition and another, interreligious dialogue does not necessarily involve questioning Christian identity. To conclude our discussion of these ideas, we shall deal briefly with this last point.

The option for a pluralistic theology of religion, going beyond exclusivism and inclusivism, consists neither of a sacrifice of the distinctiveness of Christianity nor of a compromise of its own truth. On the contrary, greater attentiveness to the ineluctable aspirations of human consciousness urges us to emphasize the distinctiveness of Christianity in the midst of the world religions. Without being too complacent one cannot deny that, according to its own origins, Christianity is not comparable to any other religion, even though, according to historians and sociologists, it comprises all the identifying features of every world religion. Christianity is defined essentially in reference to the gospel—that is, the good news of salvation not only in regard to the Mosaic law, but also in relation to every religious code, every morality or ritual which claims to be pleasing to God.

It is true that the new covenant instituted by Christ did not immediately bring about the birth of a new religion in the usual sense of the word. The disciples who followed Jesus intended to remain thoroughly Jewish. The church, as a community born of the gospel, was not immediately instituted as a new cult, a new temple, or a new priesthood. In terms of ethics, Christ's teaching was a radicalization of what was written in the Torah as the law of the love of God and of neighbor, a filial attitude toward God and fraternity among human beings.

In the difficult discussion concerning religious pluralism, it is always helpful to compare the relationship that nascent Christianity had with Judaism with the relationship that present-day Christianity maintains with the other religions. In regard to Judaism, the religious tradition could be seen as "pedagogues" in relation both to the discovery of the true image of God and to the concept of religion which received normative expression in the event of "Jesus Christ." Yet both Judaism and these traditions were overtaken by the newness of the gospel. Historically speaking, while the other religions were exclusive of one another by virtue of the fact that they were deeply rooted in their own particular cultural traditions and ethical systems, the gospel could be considered representative of all human persons, over and above the culture, the language, and even the religious tradition to which they belong. It does not bind the concept of salvation either to a law, a religious tradition, a race, or a country.

The gospel has universal significance inasmuch as it enjoins the human aspiration for liberation from a religious code that would still be dependent on "the things of this world" of which Paul spoke. This is not to imply that it would destroy genuine religious truth as a yearning for the Absolute. It is because Christianity is more than a religion that it can absorb and transform the spiritual, moral, ascetic, ritualistic, and symbolic resources of the other religious traditions without becoming syncretistic. It is only if it is faithful to the absoluteness of the gospel that it can pass judgment on the outdated character of the other religions.

At this final stage in the second millennium, interreligious dialogue also impacts on several cultures. Christianity is still very much a Western religion, while the non-Western religions belong to a great religious tradition. Thus, the church will be faithful to its catholic, universal vocation not by a destruction of the religions but rather by witnessing to the gospel through respect for the authentic values contained in the various religions. This idea of inculturation might well be the beginning of such new developments as an African, an Indian, a Japanese or an Arabian Christianity.... Historically, the relationship between Christianity and the other religions was largely exclusivist; yet this situation is not necessarily normative for the future. As we know, there have been a number of men and women who have been converted to the spirit of the gospel without belonging to the visible church of Christ. Would it be too much to ask whether there is a Christian way of being a Hindu, a Buddhist, a Taoist, or a Confucian?

In drawing attention to this problematic of dual religious adherence, I merely seek to underline both a structural homology between the relationship between primitive Christianity and Judaism and the relationship which contemporary Christianity has with the non-Christian religions. The divine plan includes not only a linear or diachronic point of view but also a synchronic one. All the non-Christian religions, not least Judaism, have been superseded by the newness of the gospel.

Nevertheless, one of the tasks of theological thinking which we have hardly mentioned involves a reinterpretation of the uniqueness of Christianity without sacrificing the absoluteness of the gospel. The future of interreligious dialogue depends on making Christianity more relevant than ever to this absolute. Certainly, Christianity is still prone to the dangers inherent in every religion—namely, exclusivism, sectarianism, cultural particularism, legalism, and intolerance. Yet faithful to its own origin and spirit, it is characterized by the tension between the *letter* and the *spirit*. Even if one can find a similar tension in every world religion, Christianity remains the only religion that sees itself as basically a religion of grace and not of law. Thus, it is faithful to its vocation only by continually reforming itself without transforming into a human work that which is God's free gift. As a religion of the gospel, Christianity, therefore, is a "leaven" for all the other religious traditions of humanity.

Translated by Joseph O'Kane

18

PROBLEMS IN THE CASE FOR A PLURALISTIC THEOLOGY OF RELIGIONS

Schubert M. Ogden

THE CASE FOR a pluralistic theology of religions has increasingly gained support from a number of Christian theologians, some of whom have recently contributed essays to a volume devoted to making this case.[1] Because the discussion documented by this volume is close to the heart of contemporary Christian theology, the arguments advanced in it deserve careful criticism. With this in mind, I propose to consider the case for pluralism that is presented by three of its contributors: Gordon D. Kaufman, Rosemary Radford Ruether, and John Hick. If I am right, each of their essays confirms that there are more or less serious problems in making such a case.

Of course, to develop this criticism is to say nothing whatever about other logically independent lines of argument by which the case for pluralism might be made; and, more important, one can develop the criticism without being in the least unsympathetic with the theological intentions of those who seek to make the case. But the point of theological criticism is to see to it that the arguments for claims are sufficient to support them; and we will all be more likely to realize our theological intentions if we are aware of the full range of alternatives from which reasoned choice can be made in our attempts to do so.

---

1. *The Myth of Christian Uniqueness: Toward a Pluralistic Theology of Religions*, ed. John Hick and Paul F. Knitter (Maryknoll, NY: Orbis, 1987). All parenthetical references in the text are to this book.

"Religious Diversity, Historical Consciousness, and Christian Theology"

The problem discussed in Gordon D. Kaufman's essay, as I understand it, is how "Christians are to take other faiths, other life-orientations, with full seriousness" (p. 4). This problem, as he views it, is of a piece with the general problem of how human beings can now learn to cope sufficiently with their religious and cultural diversity to be able "to live together fruitfully, productively and in peace in today's complexly interconnected world" (p. 3). This general human problem raises special issues for Christians because of "the absolutistic claims about divine revelation and ultimate truth that have often been regarded as central to faith" (p. 3). Kaufman contends that these claims demand "careful theological scrutiny" and that serious attention to the issues they raise "suggests that we must today become self-conscious about Christian faith in new ways—ways that will enable us to move toward some fundamental revisions of the tasks and methods of Christian theology" (p. 3). "If we are to approach sympathetically, and enter into dialogue with, others of quite different commitments and convictions, we must find ways of relativizing and opening up our basic symbol system" (p. 5). Specifically, Kaufman holds, "the complex of attitudes and consciousness that underlies modern attempts to engage in historical and comparative studies of human religiousness can provide a way to break through the tendencies toward absoluteness and self-idolatry that often obstruct interaction between Christians and others" (p. 5). The purpose of his essay, then, is to explain these contentions and to justify them theologically.

I want to begin my criticism by saying that there is much in Kaufman's argument that I have no difficulty appropriating, both in its understanding of the problem and in its basic proposal for resolving the issues that Christians and theologians have to face in dealing with this problem. I particularly appreciate the way he situates the special Christian problem in the context of the larger human problem of learning to live in peace rather than in conflict, given religious and cultural diversity. In fact, he does a better job than most theologians have done in remembering that not only religious but also secular communities and traditions have resources for interpreting and orienting human existence and must, therefore, always be reckoned with in any of our attempts to come to terms with "the other ways of being human" (p. 4). But with all of my appreciation for his argument and agreement with it, I also see some basic problems that need to be brought out for discussion.

One such problem is indicated by the kind of reasoning Kaufman offers for developing a Christian theology informed by "modern historical consciousness" (p. 11). Such a development is needed, he argues, because "only as we find ways of stepping back from, and thus not remaining confined within, those features of our traditions (both religious and secular) that wall us off from others, can we hope to come into genuine understanding of and community with them. Building such community with others," he adds, "is the most profound religious necessity of our time. Promoting it, therefore, is the most important task to which Christian theology today can attend" (p. 14). Unless I am mistaken, this is the only kind of case that Kaufman ever makes for his proposal; for while he does contend, as I noted earlier, that such a development is needed because of "the tendencies toward absoluteness and exclusivity in traditional Christian faith," such tendencies evidently demand to be counteracted only because of the same religious necessity that we should come to genuine understanding and community with others despite our particular traditions (p. 5). But if I am right about this, Kaufman's reasoning is in principle defective as theological reasoning. So one must judge it, at any rate, if one believes as I do that any theological proposal must be justified not only by the religious needs of the contemporary situation but also by the normative witness of the Christian community.

A classic example of such justification is Rudolf Bultmann's case for demythologizing. Had Bultmann reasoned as Kaufman does, he would have concluded simply from the modern religious need for a demythologized formulation of the Christian witness to theology's having the task of providing it. But the fact, of course, is that Bultmann reasoned very differently, insisting that, however necessary demythologizing may be if modern men and women are to be able to respond to the Christian claim, it cannot be undertaken "on the basis of a postulate that the New Testament proclamation must under all circumstances be made viable in the present. On the contrary, we simply have to ask whether it really is nothing but mythology or whether the very attempt to understand it in terms of its real intention does not lead to the elimination of myth."[2] The defect in Kaufman's reasoning is that it omits entirely to ask the same kind of question about the absolutistic claims that have often been regarded as central to Christian faith. If the Christian witness really is nothing but such claims, then I for one should concur that it simply cannot meet a profound religious need of our time. But if we are to contend, on the contrary, that Christian theology has the task of

---

2. Rudolf Bultmann, *New Testament and Mythology and Other Basic Writings*, ed. and trans. Schubert M. Ogden (Philadelphia: Fortress, 1984) 9.

addressing this need, I submit that this can only be because a serious attempt to understand the Christian witness in terms of its own real intention leads to the elimination of all absolutism, and so justifies the development that Kaufman proposes we undertake.

The problem indicated by his methodological reasoning, however, is evidently basic to his whole approach. Not only does he take theology's task to be set simply by the needs of its apologetic situation, but he also proceeds as though the only question theology has to ask is about the credibility of Christian claims. This becomes evident from his discussion of the conclusion to which one may be brought in criticizing Christian claims with "the sort of historical self-consciousness" that he advocates (p. 11). It is always possible, he allows, that one may conclude that "the basic Christian categorial scheme" itself "orders and interprets human life in a way no longer viable or helpful. Perhaps one or more of the principal categories requires drastic revision, drawing on ideas suggested by other religious or secular traditions. The theologian may even feel forced to conclude (as some have in recent years) that such central Christian symbols as 'God' or 'Christ' must be given up entirely, other images or concepts being given categorial status in their stead" (pp. 10, 12). But if this might seem to mean the end of Christian theology, Kaufman maintains otherwise. "There is," he argues, "an almost unlimited range of theological possibilities and permutations," including, one infers, the eventuality just considered. Even so,

> for a theology that wishes to remain "Christian" ... the fundamental task is quite straightforward: to work carefully and critically through the proposals for understanding human life and the world presented by the Christian tradition (and by theological reflection on that tradition); to try to grasp our contemporary experience and life in terms of these categories, images, and concepts; and to reconstruct them in whatever respects are required to enable them to serve as the framework for a worldview that can provide adequate orientation for life today. (p. 12)

Here, too, I can only judge that Kaufman's approach is defective. However unlimited the range of theological possibilities and permutations, it is certainly limited by the demand that any theology that wishes to remain Christian, like the witness on which it reflects, must not only be credible in terms of our contemporary experience and life but also appropriate in terms of normative Christian witness. But this means that Christian theology also has the task, no less fundamental than that which Kaufman rightly assigns it, of determining whether the proposals it judges to provide adequate orientation for life today are also adequate expressions of specifically Christian faith and life.

The other basic problem that needs to be brought out is closely related and is raised by his specific proposal that Christian faith and theology be relativized and opened up by the very different perspective of "modern historical consciousness," and thus by what he refers to as "a historical conception of human existence," or "an understanding of human existence as historical" (p. 8). Unlike other theologians who seek a solution to the problem of our traditional parochialism by moving to what they claim is a "universal position," Kaufman argues that "every position to which we might turn is itself historically specific" and that, therefore, "a universal frame of orientation for human understanding and life is no more available to us than is a universal language" (p. 5). Accordingly, he acknowledges that the perspective of "modern historical understanding," which grows out of "modern Western historical thinking," is "like all other perspectives—particular, relative, and limited" (pp. 9, 14). Nevertheless, he insists that it is by precisely this perspective that Christian faith and theology now need to be informed because it "enables us to break the grip of the absolutistic commitments that have characterized much traditional Christian faith and theology, thus enabling us to encounter other significant religious and secular traditions *in their own terms* instead of as defined by our categories" (p. 14).

I have already commented on the defective theological methodology revealed by this reasoning. But no less striking is the arbitrariness of Kaufman's assumption that all other religious and secular perspectives, including the Christian, must submit to be judged by his understanding of human existence as historical. If the constitutive claim of Christian witness is valid, the truth it asserts cannot fail both to confirm and to be confirmed by any other religious or secular truth of the same logical type, including that of a historical conception of human existence. Therefore, even if one agrees, as I do, that Christian claims can be validated as credible only on the basis of our common experience simply as human beings, one has no reason to suppose that this requires submitting these claims to the judgment of some other religious or secular perspective, whose own claims to validity are merely that, unless and until they, too, are critically validated. On the contrary, pending the inquiry required to validate all claims to credibility, one has every reason to assume that traditional Christian views may be as much the source of critical judgment as they are its object, while any other perspective, like Kaufman's historicism, may be as much in need of criticism as it is the basis for making critical judgments.

And this assumption will seem all the more reasonable when one considers the implications of Kaufman's perspective. If we understand "human historicity" as it enables us to do, he argues, Christian faith, like every other faith, is seen to be one among the many perspectives or worldviews that human beings have imaginatively constructed in "their search for orientation in life" (pp. 9, 7). Thus "we now see the great theologians of Christian history ... not simply as setting out the truth that is ultimately salvific for all humanity (as they have often been understood in the past), but rather as essentially engaged in discerning and articulating one particular perspective on life among others" (p. 9). In fact, so far from being in a position to claim that our assertions are "directly and uniquely authorized or warranted by divine revelation," we theologians can now acknowledge "forthrightly and regularly that our theological statements and claims are simply *ours*—that they are the product of our own human study and reflection, and of the spontaneity and creativity of our own human powers imaginatively to envision a world and our human place within the world" (p. 12). If these and other formulations clearly seem to express the same subjective reductionism often associated with historical understandings of human religiousness, Kaufman is quick to reassure us—in a parenthetical sentence—that he does not mean that theological assertions "are not in some significant sense grounded in God, as 'ultimate point of reference'" or that there "are no ways at all in which the concept of revelation might be used to articulate that grounding" (p. 12). But one hardly knows what to make of such reassurance when in the sentence immediately following one learns that all "religious activity and reflection," including Christian theology, are to be understood as "human imaginative response to the necessity to find orientation for life in a particular historical situation" (p. 12).

In any case, the theological implications of Kaufman's perspective seem plainly inconsistent with the claim to universal salvific truth that is evidently constitutive of the Christian witness. For they not only require that this claim be critically validated, they preclude the possibility of its ever being responsibly made.

To this extent, then, there are good reasons for resisting Kaufman's proposal. And one can be even more assured in doing so because a solution to the problem he discusses does not require theology to submit to some other particular perspective, whether his own or another. It requires only but ineluctably that theology acknowledge its claims for what they are: claims that can be validated as credible only in terms of our common human experience and critical reflection. To this extent, certainly, Christians can encounter other ways of being human, whether religious or secular, only, as Kaufman says, "on equal terms," although I maintain that if Christian faith means anything at all, it means the confidence that the promise of truth issued by the Christian witness cannot fail to be redeemed by all such encounters and that, therefore, our theological statements and claims cannot be "*simply* ours" (pp. 4, 12; emphasis changed).

But whether this confidence is well placed ever remains the question, and Kaufman is surely right that, in theology's attempts to answer it, the critical reflection provided by other perspectives, including the historicist, plays a necessary role.

"Feminism and Jewish-Christian Dialogue"

As I understand the argument of her essay, Rosemary Radford Ruether is concerned to counter "Christian claims to universalism," or, more generally, any claims, Christian or Jewish, that there is "a single universal biblical faith" (pp. 137–38). In her view, "the idea that Christianity, or even the biblical faiths, have a monopoly on religious truth is an outrageous and absurd religious chauvinism" (p. 141). This is particularly evident, she believes, in the light of two contemporary challenges: on the one hand, the challenge coming from Jewish-Christian dialogue, which by its very nature exposes "the hidden particularism" behind both Christian and Jewish claims to universalism; and, on the other hand, the challenge coming from feminism, which "looks back at the history of all religions as expressions of male-dominated cultures," again exposing the particularism behind the universalistic claims of Judaism and Christianity (pp. 138, 142). Ruether's purpose in her essay is to discuss the question that these two challenges sharply raise—namely, the question of "particularism and universalism in the search for religious truth"—although she is clear right from the outset that she will speak to this question "from the Christian side," rather than pretending to some kind of impartiality (p. 137).

In turning to criticism of her discussion, I want to say, first of all, that I too feel the force of these two challenges and am therefore grateful for her attempt to address the question that they raise for Christian theology. Moreover, there is much in her essay with which I can easily agree, especially in the second part, where she seems to me to explain persuasively why "the feminist challenge to Christianity cannot find sufficient response in the recovery of neglected texts in the Bible or in inclusive translation" and why, as a consequence, "women must be able to speak out of their own experiences . . . and, out of these revelatory experiences, write new stories" (p. 147). But if I thus find myself sharing many of Ruether's theological intentions, I nevertheless have problems with her argument.

The first and, for me, the most serious of these problems is that I see nothing that makes her argument properly theological. By "theological" here, I mean, of course, "Christian theological" since Ruether herself makes clear that it is "from the Christian side" that she wants to discuss the question of particularism and universalism in the search for religious truth. Aside from her one statement to this effect, however, I see nothing either in the form or in the content of her argument that would lead anyone to suppose that it is from the Christian side that she develops it. For all she says to the contrary, the position from and for which she argues is simply the religious or philosophical position of a feminist theist, or a theistic feminist, for whom "true revelation and true relationship to the divine is [sic] to be found in all religions," even though all patriarchal religions and ideologies are intrinsically biased and one-sided in their exclusion of women from shaping their traditions and handling their sacred objects (p. 141). My point is not that Christians or Christian theologians could not responsibly hold such a position, since it seems to me at least arguable that they both could and should do so. My point, rather, is that they certainly would not be alone in holding it, and that if they were to hold it responsibly as Christians or as theologians, they would need to find warrant for doing so in what Christians rightly acknowledge as normative for the appropriateness of their positions.

If I insist on this point, however, it is not only because Ruether's essay completely fails to take account of it. It is also because, in other contexts, she herself has insisted on the same point. Thus in arguing for a principle or norm for judging the sexist distortions of the Christian tradition, including the scriptures, she nevertheless allows:

> one can stand within this tradition and claim to be renewing it only if this principle is, at the deepest level, the true principle of the Scriptures and tradition as well, in spite of all distortion by the sin of sexism. If this is not the true principle of the biblical and Christian tradition, then this tradition itself must be evaluated to be irredeemable and must be transcended by a new vision that would include woman fully.[3]

I believe that Ruether is absolutely right about this and that her point is of the utmost importance for the many-sided dialogue between feminists for which she calls at the end of her essay. Not only post-Christian feminists like Mary Daly but also other Christian feminist theologians like Elisabeth Schüssler Fiorenza argue for a very different understanding of the norm or canon of theological judgment—and do so, in Schüssler Fiorenza's case, at least, by expressly arguing against Ruether and other feminist theologians who still insist on finding their critical

---

3. Rosemary Radford Ruether, "Theology as Critique of and Emancipation from Sexism," in *The Vocation of the Theologian*, ed. Theodore W. Jennings, Jr. (Philadelphia: Fortress, 1985) 28.

principle in Christian tradition itself.[4] But if Ruether is right in still insisting on this, I submit that she has the best of reasons for arguing in an exactly parallel way in discussing the question of particularism and universalism in the search for religious truth. If her argument for what she calls "true universality" is to meet her own standards for a valid theological argument, it demands to be developed beyond anything she provides in this essay—enough beyond, at any rate, to make clear that she would not argue for such a position at all unless there were warrant for doing so in what, at the deepest level, is the true principle of normative Christian witness.

A second problem I have with Ruether's argument is that the inference she draws concerning the equal integrity or adequacy of religions does not appear to follow from, or even to be consistent with, the basic assumption she takes to imply it. She explains:

> True universality lies in accepting one's own finiteness, one's own particularity and, in so doing, not making that particularity the only true faith, but allowing other particularities to stand side by side with yours as having equal integrity. Each is limited and particular, and yet each is, in its own way, an adequate way of experiencing the whole for a particular people at a particular time. (p. 142)

Part of what Ruether has in mind in saying this, presumably, is that each religion is like every other in being "a unique configuration of symbolic expressions," which incarnates some "way of symbolizing life and its relationship to the higher powers," or some one among "a broad spectrum of possible ways of experiencing the divine" (pp. 141–42). But more important for understanding her claim that all religions have equal integrity or adequacy is that "there is true relationship to the divine, authentic spirituality, and viable morality in all religious systems" (p. 141). This is the meaning, Ruether holds, of her counter-assumption to "Christian claims of universalism," to the effect, namely, that "the Divine Being that generates, upholds, and renews the world is truly universal, and is the father and mother of all peoples without discrimination" (pp. 141–42).

But does the assumption that "the Divine Being" is "truly universal" and the source of all peoples "without discrimination" really mean that "true revelation and true relationship to the divine is to be found in all religions"? I do not see how it could mean this—any more than I see how the universal presence of the world about which all judgments of fact are made could mean that there are true disclosure of the world and true

---

4. Elisabeth Schüssler Fiorenza, *Bread Not Stone: The Challenge of Feminist Biblical Interpretation* (Boston: Beacon, 1984) 12–13, 86, 167 n. 50.

relationship to it in all factual judgments. If we are justified in believing as we do that judgments about the world can be false as well as true, notwithstanding that the world is universally present in human experience, I fail to see why we would not be justified in believing the same thing about the symbolic judgments of religion concerning the truly universal reality of the divine. Had Ruether inferred from her assumption not that there *is* truth in all religions but simply that there *can be* truth in all of them, I, at least, would have had no difficulty with her inference. But it is clear enough from the formulations already quoted that she says "is," and I see nothing to suggest that she does not mean what she says, except, perhaps, one reference to "the possibilities of truth in all religions" (p. 142). That even this reference does not have to be taken as suggesting any other meaning, however, is clear from the reflection that if there actually is truth in all religions, then, of course, there are also possibilities of truth in them.

One may further ask, I think, whether Ruether's inference does not in fact contradict the assumption that she takes to mean it. If this assumption is properly construed, as I have construed it, as being in a broad sense theistic, then, clearly, any religion or ideology that denied or failed to affirm theism in the same broad sense could not possibly be equal in integrity or adequacy with any religion or ideology that affirmed it. Therefore, unless Ruether is prepared to claim that all religions and ideologies affirm her own theistic assumption, she can infer that they have equal integrity or adequacy only by implicitly contradicting this very assumption. I take it that her inference similarly contradicts her evident assumption of feminism, from which it follows that no patriarchal religion or ideology can be equal in integrity or adequacy with a religion in which women fully participate in shaping its symbols and controlling its sacred objects.

Considering the seriousness of this second problem, I can only wonder whether Ruether may really want to make a different point. She observes quite rightly that Christianity's judgment of other religions tends toward an unjust comparison of their practices with its own ideals. Against this she demands that "ideals must be compared with ideals, and practice with practice" (p. 141). But what is the implication of this demand for fair comparison if not that all judgments about the truth or validity of religions must be a posteriori, not a priori? And does this not mean, in turn, that there is a sense in which all religions are indeed to be treated equally, pending the inquiry by which their respective claims to validity can alone be validated?

Certainly, if Ruether's point is the one indicated by these questions, I have no reason to take issue with her. Religious claims to validity are exactly that—claims; and they are equally in need of validation once they have become problematic. But, clearly, this point can be made without arguing as Ruether argues. In fact, if the real wrong is apriorism, the mistake of judging a priori that one's own religion is the only true faith cannot be corrected by the no less a priori and, I should think, mistaken judgment that all religions have equal integrity or adequacy.

This leads directly to a third and, for the purposes of this criticism, final problem in Ruether's argument. Although the term she chooses to describe her answer to the question of particularism and universalism is "true universality," her right to use this term is far from clear, given no more than she says in developing her answer. "*True* universality," one assumes, is to be contrasted with "*false* universality"; and in context this could hardly be anything other than the claim that Ruether is concerned to counter, to the effect that one's own particularity as a Christian is the only true faith. But what does she set over against this claim, which she regards as not merely false but "outrageous and absurd" (p. 141)? Her only alternative is to call for allowing other particularities to stand side by side with one's own Christian particularity "as having equal integrity" (p. 142). But where is there any universality in this, as distinct from simply a relativistic acquiescence in the pluralism of particularities that it certainly appears to be?

Assuming, as I would like to do, that Ruether really does mean to affirm a true universality, I can only urge her to develop her argument more fully so as to remove any doubt about her intentions. One way of doing this, for which I am prepared to argue, would be to clarify the difference between claiming that one's own religion is the only true faith and claiming, instead, that any other religion must also be true just insofar as it both confirms and is confirmed by the truth in one's own. Of course, even this second claim is only that and, therefore, is as much in need of validation as the corresponding claim for any other particular religion. But I submit that it is different enough from the claim that Ruether and I are both concerned to counter to justify describing it precisely as "true universality."

"The Non-Absoluteness of Christianity"

By his own account, John Hick's essay is a theological treatment of "the question of the place of Christianity within the wider religious life of humanity" (p. 34). As he sees it, there has been a marked development in ways of answering this question since, roughly, the First World War. Prior to that time, the usual answers, whether Catholic or Protestant, were based on "the medieval assumption . . . of a Christian monopoly of salvific truth and life" (p. 16). During the last seventy years, however, this traditional Christian exclusivism has tended to erode, whether because of "more accurate knowledge and more sympathetic understanding" of the other great religious traditions, or because of a "new awareness of the pernicious side of Christian absolutism in history" (pp. 17, 20). Thus many, if not most, thinking Christians have been gradually moving from "an intolerant exclusivism" to a "benevolent inclusivism," according to which not only Christians but all human beings are somehow included within the salvation of which "the Christ-event is the sole and exclusive source" (p. 22). In Hick's view, however, such inclusivism still involves an a priori assumption of the superiority of Christianity as Christ's continuing agency in the world. Therefore, he sees us as having reached a critical point in the whole development, at which it may either halt with Christian inclusivism or else proceed to its "logical conclusion" in "a pluralist understanding of the place of Christianity in the total life of the world" (pp. 16, 32). The purpose of his essay, then, is to argue us across "this theological Rubicon" so as to complete the movement from exclusivism to pluralism (pp. 16, 22–23). This he attempts, in part, by undermining even an a posteriori case for Christian superiority and, in part, by pointing to resources already provided by the Christian tradition for those who would now assert "the non-absoluteness of Christianity."

If this is an accurate understanding of Hick's argument, certainly there is much in it with which I thoroughly agree. I too believe that the question of "Christianity's place within the total religious life of the world" now demands theological treatment and that any answer to it that is likely to prove adequate will have to be found somewhere on the other side of the old exclusivism as well as of any inclusivism involving the same a priori assumption of the superiority of Christianity (p. 16). But beyond thus agreeing with what I take to be some of Hick's main contentions, I especially appreciate his approach to the question. He seems to me to be exactly right in thinking of the development for which he argues as but one of three parallel developments that are now called for in Christian theology—the other two being carried forward by liberation theology, on the one hand, and feminist theology, on the other. I take him to be no less right, however, in looking to the Christian tradition itself for the warrants as well as the resources for carrying out these necessary developments. Even so, I want to raise the question whether there may not be yet another way of crossing over from Christian absolutism than the one for which he argues.

The first and basic problem here is whether pluralism in the sense in which he understands it is, as he claims, the "logical" (or "natural") conclusion of the trajectory whose path can be traced "from an exclusivist to an inclusivist view of other religions" (pp. 16, 22). By "pluralism," I take it, he means the kind of theological position from which "the Christian tradition is . . . seen as one of a plurality of contexts of salvation—contexts, that is to say, within which the transformation of human existence from self-centeredness to God- or Reality-centeredness is occurring" (p. 23). Thus for the pluralist, "Christianity is not the one and only way of salvation but one among several"—"*one* of the great world faiths, *one* of the streams of religious life through which human beings can be savingly related to that ultimate Reality Christians know as the heavenly Father" (pp. 33, 22). In Hick's understanding, then, pluralism entails asserting not only that there *can be* several ways of salvation, of which Christianity is but one, but also that there actually *are* these several ways.

But how, if at all, is this assertion the logical conclusion of the movement away from exclusivism? Granted that there is indeed a difference between the exclusivist claim that there is no salvation outside the church or Christianity and the inclusivist claim that all human beings are somehow included within the salvation accomplished solely by Jesus Christ, still what both positions assert in common is, as Hick puts it, that "the Christ-event is the sole and exclusive source of human salvation" (p. 22). In other words, they agree in asserting that there *cannot be* several ways of salvation of which Christianity is but one, since, unlike all other religions, it alone is established by the one and only event of salvation. But, then, it is this assertion that one must contradict in order to go beyond inclusivism by drawing the logical conclusion of the movement away from exclusivism. To contradict it, however, clearly does not require one to assert that there actually *are* several ways of salvation of which Christianity is only one. All that one needs to assert is that there *can be* these several ways, even if, as a matter of fact, Christianity should prove to be the only way of salvation there is. But this assertion can be made by any christology for which the significance of Jesus Christ is not that he *constitutes* salvation but that he *represents* it—namely, by somehow making explicit the gift and demand of God's love, which is the sole and sufficient source of human salvation. Because the meaning of God's love for us is always implicitly presented in human existence as such, it can always become more or less fully explicit in any human religion, whether or not there is any religion in which it in fact does so.

I submit, therefore, that pluralism in Hick's sense is not the logical conclusion of the movement away from Christian absolutism that he claims it to be, but an independent assertion to be considered on its merits. The real theological Rubicon does not run between exclusivism and inclusivism, on the one side, and what he means by pluralism, on the other; it runs, rather, between two fundamentally different kinds of christologies: those which claim a constitutive significance for Jesus Christ and those which understand his significance to be representative only, however decisive.

As for the question of pluralism, suffice it to say that in my view, even as, presumably, in Hick's, any answer to it must be a posteriori and at least in part empirically justified. So far as my own experience in such matters goes, I am not yet at the point at which I can assert that there are in fact several ways of salvation of which the Christian way is but one. Of course, I do not dispute the claim that human beings generally evidence a deep desire for some kind of ultimate transformation and that not only Christianity but each of the great religious traditions offers itself as the means for just such a transformation, as Hick says, "from self-centeredness to Reality-centeredness" (p. 23). But this claim I take to be purely formal in that it allows for a wide range of material differences between one religion and another in understanding transformation. And my own experience of the actual differences between religions, as subtle as they have sometimes proved to be, fully confirms Clifford Geertz's observation that "what all sacred symbols assert is that the good for man is to live realistically; where they differ is in the vision of reality they construct."[5] But, be this as it may, the possibility of pluralism in Hick's sense I understand to be securely grounded in the completely universal reality of God's love, which is savingly present throughout all human existence; and so I have every reason to look for more evidence of the actuality of pluralism than I have so far been able to find.

This is not to say, however, that I would think to look to what Hick takes to be the appropriate kind of evidence, namely, "the fruits of religious faith in human life," and thus the extent of individual and social transformation effected by particular religions (pp. 23–24). In my opinion, to expect this kind of evidence to settle the issue of the relative superiority or inferiority of particular religions is no less mistaken than to expect to settle the issue of the relative truth or falsity of empirical beliefs by considering the number of persons who sincerely hold them. It seems to me that in dealing with this issue Hick slips into the not uncommon confusion of the *validity* of particular religions with their *effectiveness*. This distinction, of course, is ordinarily made in discussions of the sacraments and, perhaps, means of salvation more generally. But if one holds, as I do, that the different religions themselves can

---

5. Clifford Geertz, *The Interpretation of Cultures: Selected Essays* (New York: Basic Books, 1973) 130.

be viewed at least analogically as different means of ultimate transformation, one can reasonably claim that all questions about their relative superiority or inferiority are questions about their relative validity or invalidity as sacraments of ultimate reality in its meaning for us—keeping in mind that the relative effectiveness or ineffectiveness of each of them depends on its being appropriated by the existential self-understanding of individual persons in accordance with an appropriately generalized form of the rule *nullum sacramentum sine fide*. In this case, the evidence appropriate to judging their relative superiority or inferiority is not only such empirical-historical evidence as is required to determine what are, in fact, their normative forms, but also such metaphysical and moral evidence as is required to determine the truth and the justice of their necessary implications for belief and action respectively. Thus if I am to assert not only the possibility of religious pluralism but also its actuality, I must have evidence for concluding that there are, in fact, one or more other religious traditions whose normative understandings of authentic existence are equally valid with that of normative Christianity when they are fairly compared with respect to their necessary implications both for metaphysical belief and for moral action.

This leads directly to the third and last problem I wish to raise with Hick's argument—namely, whether the "inspiration christology" to which he appeals as pointing the direction for theology today is the most adequate, if not the only, kind of representative christology open to those who would make the crossing away from Christian absolutism (p. 32). It seems clear that what he claims for this kind of christology is not that it is required by the religious pluralism for which he argues but only that it is "compatible" with such pluralism (p. 32). But since he does not consider any other possibilities, he evidently thinks that this is the most adequate answer that can be given to the christological question by those who are prepared to follow the movement away from exclusivism to its logical conclusion.

By his own admission, however, any such "inspiration christology" is open to the most serious objections. Aside from the fact that, as he himself long since showed elsewhere,[6] it can continue to talk of God's becoming incarnate in Jesus Christ only by radically redefining the meaning of "incarnation," it involves anyone who tries to defend it in the following dilemma: either one construes it in such a way that it is at least a plausible interpretation of the inspiration christology expressed

---

6. See John Hick, "The Christology of D. M. Baillie," *Scottish Journal of Theology* 11 (1958) 1–12; idem, "Christology at the Crossroads," in *Prospect for Theology: Essays in Honour of H. H. Farmer*, ed. F. G. Healy (London: James Nisbet, 1966) 137–66, 233–34.

in the New Testament itself, in which case one can assert the uniqueness of Jesus that is undoubtedly intended by that christology only a priori and not on the basis of historical evidence; or else one persists in justifying one's christological assertion by historical evidence, in which case the unavailability of the requisite evidence forces one to give an altogether implausible interpretation of the New Testament's own christology of inspiration, according to which Jesus is simply one more human being, more or less instrumental in the transformation of other individuals and societies (cf. pp. 31–32). Of course, the full force of this dilemma is obscured by Hick's proceeding as though the point of his inspiration christology and that of the New Testament's were the same—despite the fact that, if anything is clear from the historical study of New Testament christology, it is that the two ways of thinking make radically different kinds of claims.

But I have no intention of restating a case that I have presented elsewhere and that Hick has already had an opportunity to come to terms with.[7] I simply want to make the point that one can very well join him in crossing over from a constitutive to a representative kind of christology without having to shoulder the burdens of his particular way of doing this. In addition to a representative christology that can be historically responsible only by allowing that Jesus Christ is nothing more than one example of Christian faith among others, there can be a representative christology equally responsible to critical history for which Jesus Christ is nothing less than the primal Christian sacrament.

I conclude, therefore, by pressing my question: Is Hick's the only or the most adequate way for theology now to assert "the non-absoluteness of Christianity"?

---

7. See Schubert M. Ogden, *The Point of Christology* (San Francisco: Harper & Row, 1982); and John Hick, "The Foundation of Christianity: Jesus or the Apostolic Message?" *Journal of Religion* 64 (1984) 363–69.

BIBLIOGRAPHY OF DAVID TRACY

Stephen H. Webb

Books

Dialogue with the Other: The Inter-Religious Dialogue. Louvain: Eerdmans/ Peeters Press 1990.
Plurality and Ambiguity. San Francisco: Harper & Row, 1987.
A Catholic Vision. With Stephen Happel. Philadelphia: Fortress, 1984.
A Short History of the Interpretation of the Bible. With Robert Grant. 2d ed. Philadelphia: Fortress, 1984.
Talking About God: Doing Theology in the Context of Modern Pluralism. With John Cobb. New York: Seabury, 1983.
The Analogical Imagination: Christian Theology and the Culture of Pluralism. New York: Crossroad, 1981.
Blessed Rage for Order: The New Pluralism in Theology. New York: Seabury, 1975.
The Achievement of Bernard Lonergan. New York: Herder & Herder, 1970.

Articles

1991

"Hermeneutical Reflections in the New Paradigm" and "Some Concluding Reflections on the Conference: Unity Amidst Diversity and Conflict?" in *Paradigm Change in Theology,* edited by Hans Küng and David Tracy. Edinburgh: T. & T. Clark; New York: Crossroad, 1991. Translation of *Theologie—Wohin? Das Neue Paradigma von Theologie* (Zurich: Benziger, 1986).

1990

"God, Dialogue and Solidarity: A Theologian's Refrain." Christian Century 107 (Oct. 10, 1990): 900–904.
"God and Emptiness: Response to Abe Masao." In *God and Emptiness,* edited by Christopher Ives. Maryknoll, NY: Orbis, 1990.

"Charity, Obscurity, Clarity: Augustine's Search for True Rhetoric." In *Morphologies of Faith*, edited by Mary Gerhart and Anthony C. Yu. Atlanta: Scholars Press, 1990.

"Response to Robert Sokolowski." In *God and Creation: An Ecumenical Symposium*, edited by David Burrell and Bernard McGinn. Notre Dame: University of Notre Dame Press, 1990.

"On Naming the Present." *On the Threshold of the Third Millennium*," *Concilium* 1990 (1), 66–85. London: SCM; Philadelphia: Trinity Press International.

1989

"World Church or World Catechism: The Problem of Eurocentrism." *Concilium* 204: *World Catechism or Indoctrination?* Edinburgh: T. & T. Clark, 1989.

"The Uneasy Alliance Reconceived: Catholic Theological Method, Modernity, and Postmodernity." *Theological Studies* 50 (1989): 548-70.

"Recent Catholic Spirituality: Unity and Diversity." In *Christian Spirituality: Post-Reformation and Modern*, edited by Louis Dupré and Donald E. Saliers. World Spirituality 18. New York: Crossroad, 1989.

"Argument, Dialogue and the Soul in Plato." In *Witness and Existence: Essays in Honor of Schubert M. Ogden*, edited by Philip E. Devenish and George L. Goodwin. Chicago: University of Chicago Press, 1989.

"Hermeneutics." In *International Encyclopedia of Communication*. New York: Oxford University Press, 1989.

"Afterword: Theology, Public Discourse, and the American Tradition." In *Religion and Twentieth-Century American Intellectual Life*. Cambridge: Cambridge University Press, 1989.

1988

"Mystics, Prophets, Rhetorics: Religion and Psychoanalysis." In *The Trial(s) of Psychoanalysis*, edited by Francoise Meltzer. Chicago: University of Chicago Press, 1988.

"Can Virtue be Taught? Education, Character and the Soul." *Theological Education* 24, Supplement 1 (1988): 33–52.

"The Christian Understanding of Salvation-Liberation." In *Face to Face: An Interreligious Bulletin*, Anti-Defamation League of B'nai B'rith, 19 (Spring 1988): 35-40.

"Theology and the Symbolic Imagination: A Tribute to Andrew Greeley." In *The Incarnate Imagination: Essays in Honor of Andrew Greeley*, edited by Ingrid H. Shafer. Bowling Green, OH: Bowling Green State University Popular Press, 1988.

"*Models of God:* Three Observations (reply to Sallie McFague)." In *Religion and Intellectual Life* 5, no. 3 (Spring 1988): 24–28.

"The Problem of Comparative Religion." In *Metaphysik nach Kant?* edited by Dieter Henrich and Rolf-Peter Horstmann. Publication of the 1987 Stuttgart Hegel Conference. Stuttgart: Klett-Cotta, 1988.

"The Question of Criteria for Inter-Religious Dialogue: A Tribute to Langdon Gilkey." In *The Whirlwind in Culture*, edited by Donald W. Musser and Joseph L. Price. Bloomington, IN: Meyer-Stone, 1988.

"Author's Response." In "Review Symposium on *Plurality and Ambiguity.*" *Theology Today* 44 (January 1988): 513–19.

1987

"Comparative Theology." In *The Encyclopedia of Religion*, edited by Mircea Eliade, 14:446–55. New York: Macmillan, 1987.

"Christianity in the Wider Context: Demands and Transformations." In *Worldviews and Warrants: Plurality and Authority in Theology*, edited by William Schweiker and Per M. Anderson. Lanham, MD: University Press of America, 1987. Also published in *Religion and Intellectual Life* 4 (Summer 1987): 7–20.

"Practical Theology in the Situation of Global Pluralism." In *Formation and Reflection: The Promise of Practical Theology*, edited by Lewis S. Mudge and James N. Poling. Philadelphia: Fortress, 1987.

"The Christian Understanding of Salvation-Liberation." *Journal of Buddhist-Christian Studies* 7 (1987): 129–38.

"Exodus: Theological Reflection." *Exodus: A Lasting Paradigm, Concilium* 189, edited by Bas Van Iersel and Anton Weiler. Edinburgh: T. & T. Clark, 1987.

"On Hope as a Theological Virtue in American Catholic Theology." In *The Church in Anguish: Has the Vatican Betrayed Vatican II?* edited by Hans Küng and Leonard Swidler. San Francisco: Harper & Row, 1987.

1986

"Particular Classics, Public Religion, and the American Tradition." In *Religion and American Public Life*, edited by Robin Lovin. New York: Paulist Press, 1986.

Das neue Paradigma von Theologie. Edited by Hans Küng and David Tracy. Zurich: Benziger, 1986. Tracy's contribution, "Abschliessende Gedanken zur Konferenz: Einigkeit mitten in Verschiedenheit und Konflikt," is a reprint of "Project X..." below under 1983. English translation of this volume published by Crossroad in 1991.

"The Dialogue of Jews and Christians: A Necessary Hope." *Christian Theological Seminary Register* 76 (Winter 1986): 20–28.

"Religious Studies and its Community of Inquiry." *Criterion* 25 (Autumn 1986): 21–24.

"Hermeneutics as Discourse Analysis: Sociality, History, Religion." *Archivo Di Filosofia* 54 (1986): 261–84.

1985

"Lindbeck's New Program for Theology: A Reflection." *The Thomist* 49 (July 1985): 460–72.

"Tillich and Contemporary Theology." In *The Thought of Paul Tillich*, edited by J. Adams, W. Pauck, and R. Shinn. San Francisco: Harper & Row, 1985.

"Correlation between Theology and Catholic Charities." *Social Thought* 11 (Winter 1985): 24–31.

"Analogy, Metaphor and God-language: Charles Hartshorne." *Modern Schoolman* 62 (May 1985): 249–64.

1984

"Hermeneutische Überlegungen im neuen Paradigma." In *Theologie—Wohin? Auf dem Weg zu einem neuen Paradigma*, edited by Hans Küng and David Tracy, with a foreword by Küng and Tracy. Zurich: Benziger, 1984. English translation published by Crossroad in 1991.

"Is a Hermeneutics of Religion Possible?" In *Religious Pluralism*, edited by L. Rouner, 116–29. Notre Dame: University of Notre Dame Press, 1984.

"Levels of Liberal Consensus." *Commonweal* 111 (August 10, 1984): 426–31.

"Existential Trust." *Commonweal* 111 (August 10, 1984): 429.

"To Trust or Suspect." *Commonweal* 111 (October 5, 1984): 532–34.

"Karl Rahner, S.J.: All is Grace." *Commonweal* 111 (April 20, 1984): 230.

"The Role of Theology in Public Life: Some Reflections." *Word & World: Theology for Christian Ministry* 4 (Summer, 1984): 230–39.

"The Holocaust as Interruption and the Christian Return to History." With Elisabeth Schüssler Fiorenza. *The Holocaust as Interruption*, Concilium 175, edited with Elisabeth Schüssler Fiorenza. Edinburgh: T. & T. Clark, 1984.

"A Thoughtful Life (review of Arthur A. Cohen's *An Admirable Woman*)." *Commonweal* 111 (Feb. 10, 1984): 92–93.

"Creativity in the Interpretation of Religion: The Question of Radical Pluralism." *New Literary History* 15 (1983–1984): 289–309.

1983

"On Thinking with the Classics (389th Convocation address at the University of Chicago)." *Criterion* 22 (Autumn 1983): 9–10; Also published in *The University of Chicago Record* 18, (April 20, 1984): 40–41.

"Religion and Human Rights in the Public Realm." *Daedalus* 112 (1983): 237–54.

"The Questions of Pluralism: The Context of the United States." *Mid-Stream: An Ecumenical Journal* 22 (1983): 273–85.

"Project X: Retrospect and Prospect." *Twenty Years of Concilium*, Concilium 170, edited by P. Brand, E. Schillebeeckx, and A. Weiler. New York: Seabury, 1983.

"Schubert M. Ogden: Doctor of Humane Letters." *Criterion* 22 (Autumn 1983): 3–4.

"Editorial." *Cosmology and Theology*, Concilium 166. With Nicolas Lash. New York: Seabury, 1983.

"The Foundations of Practical Theology." In *Practical Theology*, edited by Don Browning. San Francisco: Harper & Row, 1983.

"Foreword." In *Edward Schillebeeckx: In Search of the Kingdom of God*. By John S. Bowden. New York: Crossroad, 1983.

1982

"The Necessity and Insufficiency of Fundamental Theology." In *Problems and Perspectives of Fundamental Theology*, edited by R. Latourelle and Gerald O'Collins. New York: Paulist Press, 1982.

"Religious Values after the Holocaust: A Catholic View." In *Jews and Christians After the Holocaust*, edited by Abraham J. Peck. Philadelphia: Fortress, 1982.

"Editorial." *The Challenge of Psychology to Faith, Concilium* 156, edited with Steven Kepnes. New York: Seabury, 1982.
"Some Reflections on Christianity in China." *Criterion* 21 (Spring 1982): 19–20.
"The Enigma of Pope John Paul II." *The Christian Century* 99 (January 27, 1982): 96–101.

1981
"Theoria and Praxis: A Partial Response [to E. Farley and R. W. Lynn]." *Theological Education* 17 (Spring 1981): 167–74.
"Defending the Public Character of Theology: How My Mind Has Changed." *The Christian Century* 98 (April 1, 1981): 350–56. Also published in *Theologians in Transition*, edited by James Wall. New York: Crossroad, 1981.
"Author's Response." In "Review Symposium of David Tracy's *The Analogical Imagination*." *Horizons* 8 (1981): 329–39.
"Theology of Praxis." In *Creativity and Method: Essays in Honor of Bernard Lonergan*, edited by Matthew Lamb. Milwaukee: Marquette University Press, 1981.
"Theological Models: An Exercise in Dialectics." In *Lonergan Workshop*, edited by Fred Lawrence, vol. 2. Chico, CA: Scholars Press, 1981.
"The Question of Pluralism in Contemporary Theology." *The Chicago Theological Seminary Register* 71 (Spring 1981): 29–38.
"Introduction." in *The Challenge of Liberation Theology: A First World Response*, edited by Brian Mahan and L. Dale Richesin. Maryknoll, NY: Orbis, 1981.
"Foreword." In *The Tremendum: A Theological Interpretation of the Holocaust*. By Arthur A. Cohen. New York: Crossroad, 1981.

1980
"Particular Questions within General Consensus [reply to H. Küng and E. Schillebeeckx]." *Journal of Ecumenical Studies* 17 (Winter 1980): 33–39. Also published in *Consensus in Theology? A Dialogue with Hans Küng and Edward Schillebeeckx*, edited by L. Swidler. Philadelphia: Westminster, 1980.
"Reflections on John Dominic Crossan's *Cliffs of Fall: Paradox and Polyvalence in the Parables of Jesus*." *Society of Biblical Literature 1980 Seminar Papers*, edited by P. J. Achtemeier, 69–74. Chico, CA: Scholars Press, 1980.
"Narrative and Symbol: Key to New Testament Spiritualities." In *Scripture Today*, edited by Durstan R. McDonald. Eleventh National Conference of the Trinity Institution, 1980.
"Books: Critics' Christmas Choices." *Commonweal* 107 (Dec. 5, 1980): 703.
Parish, Priest and People: New Leadership for the Local Church. By David Tracy, Andrew Greeley, Mary Durkin, John Shea, and William McCready. Chicago: Thomas More, 1981. Tracy made major contributions to chapter 4, "Systematic Theology of the Local Community"; chapter 8, "Theological Reflection on Local Religious Leadership"; and chapter 11, "Local Religious Leadership and Social Justice."
"Editorial." *What is Religion? An Inquiry for Theology, Concilium* 136, edited with Mircea Eliade. New York: Seabury, 1980.

"Grace and the Search for the Human: The Sense of the Uncanny." *Catholic Theological Society of America Proceedings* 34 (1980): 64–77.
"The Catholic Model of Caritas: Self-Transcendence and Transformation." *The Family in Crisis or Transition*, Concilium 121, edited by A. Greeley. New York: Seabury, 1979.
"Theological Pluralism and Analogy." *Thought* 54 (1979): 24–37.
"Metaphor and Religion." In *On Metaphor*, edited by Sheldon Sacks, 89–104. Chicago: University of Chicago Press, 1979. Publication of *Critical Inquiry* 5 (1978).
"The Particularity and Universality of Christian Revelation." *Revelation and Experience*, Concilium 113, edited by E. Schillebeeckx and Bas van Iersel. New York: Seabury, 1979.

1978

"A Catholic Answer." *Why Did God Make Me?*, Concilium 108, edited by Hans Küng and Jürgen Moltmann. New York: Seabury, 1978.
"Theological Response to 'Kingdom and Community' [J. G. Gager]." *Zygon* 13 (June 1978): 131–35.
"Responses to Peter Berger (with Langdon Gilkey and Schubert Ogden)." *Theological Studies* 39 (September 1978): 486–507.
"Introductory Essay and Preface." In *Toward Vatican III: The Work that Needs To Be Done*. New York: Seabury, 1978.
"Christian Faith and Radical Equality." *Theology Today* 34 (January 1978): 370–77.
"The Public Character of Systematic Theology." *Theological Digest* 26 (Winter 1978): 400–11.
"Introduction." In *Celebrating the Medieval Heritage*, edited by David Tracy. Chicago: University of Chicago Press, 1978. Originally published as *Journal of Religion* 58 (Supplement, 1978).

1977

"The Catholic Theological Imagination [Presidential Address]." *Catholic Theological Society of America Proceedings* 32 (1977): 234–44.
"Modes of Theological Argument." *Theology Today* 33 (January 1977): 387–95.
"Reflections on the Challenge of Marxism." *New Catholic World* 220 (May 1977): 116–17.
"Ethnic Pluralism and Systematic Theology: Reflections." *Ethnicity*, Concilium 101, edited by A. Greeley and Gregory Baum. New York: Seabury, 1977.
"John Cobb's Theological Method: Interpretation and Reflections." In *John Cobb's Theology in Process*, edited by David Ray Griffin and Thomas J. J. Altizer. Philadelphia: Westminster, 1977.
"Sin Against God, Man: Moral Choices in Contemporary Society." *National Catholic Reporter* 13 (May 6, 1977): 14.
"Theological Classics in Contemporary Theology." *Theological Digest* 25 (Winter 1977): 347–55.
"On Galatians 3:28." *Criterion* 16 (Autumn 1977): 10-12.
"Revisionist Practical Theology and the Meaning of Public Discourse." *Pastoral Psychology* 26 (Winter 1977): 83–94.

"We Still Have Some Unresolved Theological Differences." Symposium with Martin Marty, David Burrell, and Avery Dulles. *National Catholic Reporter* 14 (November 4, 1977): 9–10.

1976

"A Theological Brief." *American Academy of Religion, Philosophy of Religion and Theology Proceedings*, 197–200. Missoula, MT: Scholars Press, 1976.

"Analogical Vision: Some Reflections on the American Roman Catholic Bicentennial Social Justice Program." *Criterion* 15 (Autumn 1976): 10–16.

1975

"Editors Bookshelf: Contemporary Theology and Philosophy of Religion." *Journal of Religion* 55 (October 1975): 489–92.

"Theology as Public Discourse." *The Christian Century* 92 (March 19, 1975): 280–84.

"Whatever Happened to Theology? (symposium)." *Christianity and Crisis* 35 (May 12, 1975): 119–20.

"Tradition and Innovation: The Medieval Religious Heritage Lectures." *Criterion* 14 (Winter 1975): 20–22.

"Eschatological Perspectives on Aging." *Pastoral Psychology* 24 (Winter 1975): 119–34.

"A Response and Commentary on Heidegger and Theology." *Listening* 10 (Winter 1975): 73–77.

1974

"Task of Fundamental Theology." *Journal of Religion* 54 (January 1974): 13–34.

"Two Cheers for Thomas Aquinas." *Christian Century* 91 (March 6, 1974): 260–62.

"St. Thomas Aquinas and the Religious Dimension of Experience: The Doctrine of Sin." *Proceedings of the American Catholic Philosophical Association* 48 (1974): 166–76.

"Bernard Lonergan as Interpreter of St. Thomas Aquinas." *Listening* 9 (Winter-Spring 1974): 173–77.

"Religious Language as Limit Language." *Theological Digest* 22 (Winter 1974): 291–307.

1973

"The Religious Dimension of Science." *The Persistence of Religion*, Concilium 81, edited by Andrew Greeley and Gregory Baum. New York: Herder & Herder, 1973.

1972

"Catholic Presence in the Divinity School." *Criterion* 11 (Winter 1972): 29–31.

"God's Reality: The Most Important Issue." *National Catholic Reporter* 8 (June 23, 1972): 10–11. Also published in *Anglican Theological Review* 55 (April 1973): 218–24.

"Response to Dr. Ogden." *Thesis Theological Cassettes* 3 no. 9 (October 1972).

"Foundational Theology as Contemporary Possibility." *The Dunwoodie Review* 12 (1972): 3–20.

1971
"Lonergan's Foundational Theology: An Interpretation and a Critique." In *Foundations of Theology: Papers from the International Lonergan Conference, 1970*, edited by Philip McShane. Dublin: Gill & MacMillan, 1971.

1970
"Method as Foundation for Theology: Bernard Lonergan's Option." *The Journal of Religion* 50 (July 1970): 292-318.
"Why Orthodoxy in a Personalist Age." *Catholic Theological Society of America Proceedings* 25 (1970): 78-110.

1969
"Lonergan's Interpretation of St. Thomas Aquinas: The Intellectualist Nature of Speculative Theology," dissertation excerpt for the Theological Faculty of the Gregorian University, Rome, 1969.
"Prolegomena to a Foundation for Theology." *Criterion* 9 (Autumn 1969): 12-14.
"Review: *Jesus, God and Man*, and *Revelation as History*, both by Wolfhardt Pannenberg." *Catholic Biblical Quarterly* 31 (April 1969): 285-88.

1968
"Horizon Analysis and Eschatology." *Continuum* 6 (Summer 1968): 166-79.
"Holy Spirit as Philosophical Problem." *Commonweal* 89 (Nov. 8, 1968): 205-13. Reprinted in *God, Jesus and Spirit*, edited by D. Callahan. New York: Herder, 1969.
The Oneness of God. Edited by Jerome F. Filteau et al. Prepared by Theological College Class of 1971 at Catholic University of America School of Theology. Based on notes from the lectures of David Tracy during Spring, 1968. Published privately by Theological College Publications.

Selected Interviews

Kendig Brubaker Cully. "Interview with David Tracy." *The Review of Books and Religion* 10 (Mid-January 1982): 6.
Eugene Kennedy. "A Dissenting Voice, Catholic Theologian David Tracy." *The New York Times Magazine* (Nov. 9, 1986).
Cullen Murphy. "Who Do Men Say that I Am?" *The Atlantic Monthly* 258 (Dec. 1986). Includes an interview with Tracy.
Kenneth L. Woodward. "David Tracy, Theologian." *Newsweek* (August 24, 1981): 73.

CONTRIBUTORS

Gregory Baum is Professor of Religious Studies at McGill University, Montreal. He is a Roman Catholic theologian and sociologist of religion. For twenty years he served on the board of directors of *Concilium*. His recent publications include *The Priority of Labor* (1982), *Theology and Society* (1988), and *The Church in Quebec* (1991).

Wayne C. Booth is George M. Pullman Distinguished Service Professor of English at the University of Chicago and is widely known for his extensive work in literary criticism and rhetoric. His more recent publications include *Critical Understanding: The Powers and Limits of Pluralism* (1982), *The Company We Keep: An Ethics of Fiction* (1988), and *The Vocation of a Teacher* (1988).

Wendy Doniger is Mircea Eliade Professor of the History of Religions at the Divinity School of the University of Chicago. Her main areas of expertise are Hinduism and comparative mythology. She has published (under the name of O'Flaherty) *Other People's Myths: The Cave of Echos* (1988), and *Dreams, Illusion and Other Realities* (1984), and translated three Penguin Classics, *Rig Veda, Hindu Myths*, and (under Doniger) *The Laws of Manu*.

Seán Freyne is Professor of Theology at the University of Dublin, Trinity College. His main field of teaching and research is New Testament studies. His recent publications include *Galilee, Jesus and the Gospels: Literary Approaches and Historical Investigations* (1988).

Claude Geffré is Professor of Theology at the Institut Catholique in Paris. He was written on theological hermeneutics and contemporary trends in theology. Among his recent works is *The Risk of Interpretation: On Being Faithful to a Christian Tradition in a Non-Christian Age* (1987).

Mary Gerhart is Professor of Religion at Hobart & William Smith Colleges and served for many years on the editorial board of *Religious Studies Review*. She published *Metaphoric Process: The Creation of Scientific and Religious Understanding* with Allan M. Russell, and is author of *Genre: Choices, Gender Questions* (forthcoming).

Contributors

David Grene is Professor Emeritus in the Committee on Social Thought at the University of Chicago. His main field of teaching and research is classical studies. He is particularly known for his masterly translations of Greek tragedy. His latest works include a translation of Herodotus's *History* (1987) and *The Actor in History: A Study of Shakespearian Dramatic Verse* (1988).

Werner G. Jeanrond teaches systematic theology at the University of Dublin, Trinity College. His main research interests are in the field of theological method and hermeneutics. His recent publications include *Theological Hermeneutics: Development and Significance* (1991).

Hans Küng is Professor for Ecumenical Research and Director of the Institute for Ecumenical Research at the University of Tübingen. He has published widely in all areas of systematic theology. His latest book is *Global Responsibility: In Search of a New World Ethic* (1991).

Dermot A. Lane is Director of Studies at the Mater Dei Institute of Education in Dublin. He is internationally known for his work on christology and the social dimension of Christian faith. Among his recent publications are *Foundations for a Social Theology; Praxis, Process and Salvation* (1984), and *Christ at the Centre: Selected Issues in Christology* (1990).

Nicholas Lash is Norris Hulse Professor of Divinity in the University of Cambridge. He is well known for his work on the relationship between theological and philosophical reflection. His recent publications include *Theology on the Way to Emmaus* (1986) and *Easter in Ordinary: Reflections on Human Experience and the Knowledge of God* (1988).

John Macquarrie is Lady Margaret Professor Emeritus of Divinity at the University of Oxford. He was written on all central aspects of Christian faith. His most recent book is *Jesus Christ in Modern Thought* (1990).

Johann B. Metz is Professor of Fundamental Theology at the University of Münster. He is well known for his work on questions of contemporary Christian theology. Among his publications are *Faith in History and Society: Towards a Practical Fundamental Theology* (1981) and *The Emergent Church: The Future of Christianity in a Postbourgeois World* (1981).

Jacob Neusner is Graduate Research Professor of Religious Studies at the University of South Florida. He has published, edited, and translated prolifically on all branches of Judaism. Some of his more recent works are *The Ecology of Religion: From Writing to Religion in the Study of Judaism* (1989) and *The Economics of Mishnah: Chicago Studies in the History of Judaism* (1990).

Schubert M. Ogden is University Distinguished Professor of Theology at Southern Methodist University and has published widely in systematic and philosophical theology. His publications include *Christ Without*

Myth: A Study Based on the Theology of Rudolf Bultmann (1979), *The Point of Christology* (1982), and *On Theology* (1986).

Paul Ricoeur is John Nuveen Professor Emeritus in the Divinity School, Professor of Philosophy, and a member of the Committee on Social Thought at the University of Chicago. He was for many years Dean of the Faculty of Letters and Human Sciences at the University of Paris X (Nanterre). Among his most recent publications are *Time and Narrative*, 3 vols. (1984–88) and *Soi-même comme un autre* (1990).

Jennifer L. Rike is Assistant Professor of Theology at Boston University where she teaches contemporary Protestant and Roman Catholic theology. She has published in the *Tijdschrift voor Filosofie, Religious Studies Review*, and *Encounter*, and is working on a book about "Karl Rahner's Integrative Theology of Mystery."

Rosemary Radford Ruether is Georgia Harkness Professor of Applied Theology at Garrett-Evangelical Theological Seminary in Evanston, Illinois. Her areas of research interest and publication are the history of women in Christianity and feminist theology. Her many publications include *Liberation Theology: Human Hope Confronts Christian History and American Power* (1972), *Sexism and God-Talk: Toward a Feminist Theology* (1984), and *Woman-Church* (1986).

Nathan A. Scott, Jr., is William R. Kenan, Jr., Professor of Religious Studies at the University of Virginia. Professor Scott is known internationally for his work in literary criticism and hermeneutics. His publications include *The Poetics of Belief: Studies in Coleridge, Arnold, Pater, Santayana, Stevens and Heidegger* (1985) and *The Poetry of Civic Virtue: Eliot, Malraux, Auden* (1976).

Stephen Webb is Assistant Professor of Religion and Philosophy at Wabash College, Crawfordsville, Indiana. He has published *Re-Figuring Theology: The Rhetoric of Karl Barth* (1971); *Religion and the Hyperbolic Imagination* is forthcoming.

Book Shelves
BL87 .R24 1991
Radical pluralism and truth
: David Tracy and the
hermeneutics of religion